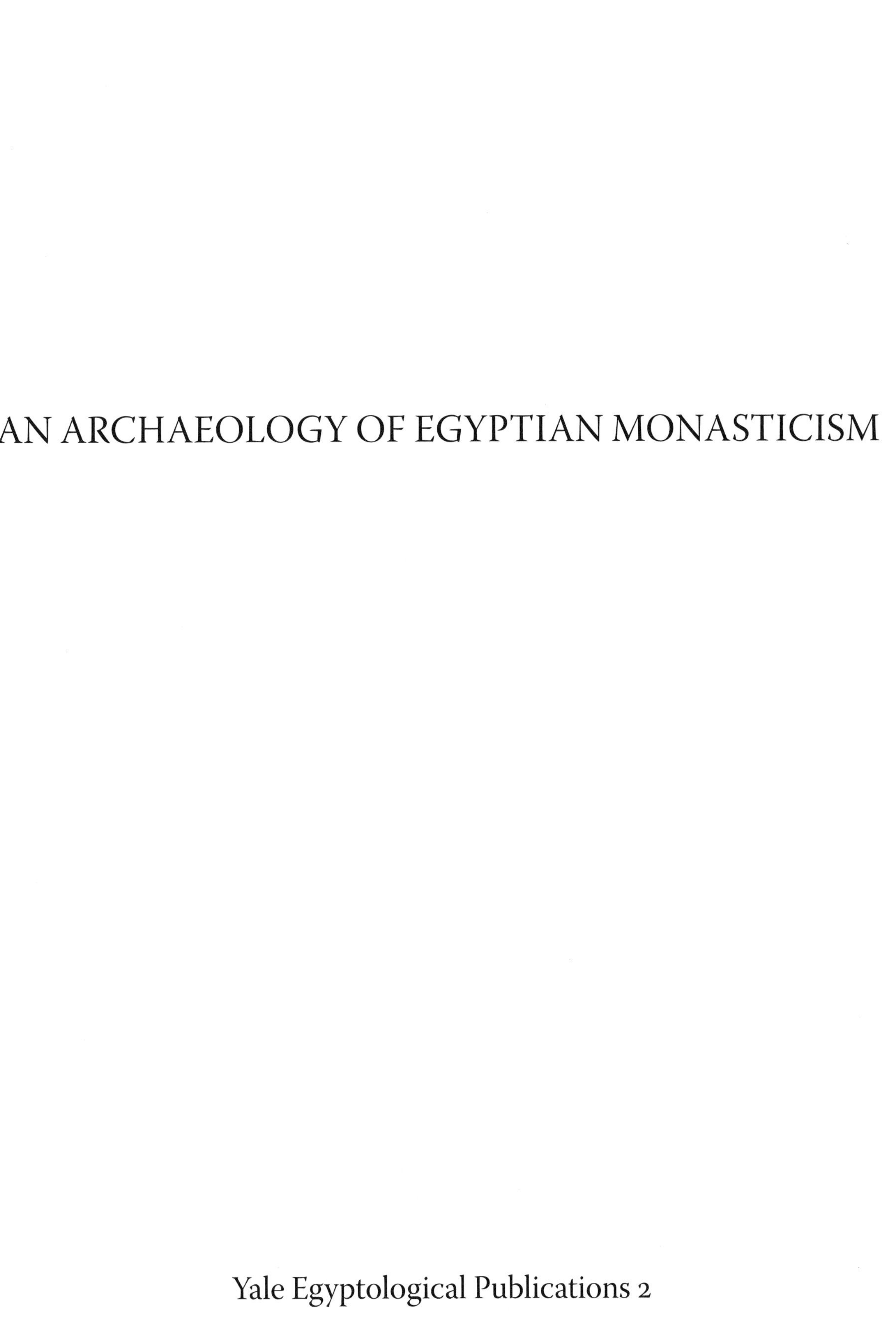

AN ARCHAEOLOGY OF EGYPTIAN MONASTICISM

Yale Egyptological Publications 2

Yale Egyptological Publications

Yale Egyptological Publications 2

An Archaeology of Egyptian Monasticism

Settlement, Economy and Daily Life at the White Monastery Federation

Louise Blanke

Yale Egyptology New Haven, CT

Yale Egyptological Publications 2

ISBN 978-1-950343-00-3

Library of Congress Cataloging-in-Publication Data

Names: Blanke, Louise, author.
Title: An archaeology of Egyptian monasticism : settlement, economy and daily life at the White Monastery Federation / Louise Blanke.
Other titles: Yale Egyptological publications ; 2.
Description: New Haven, CT : Yale Egyptology, 2019. | Series: Yale Egyptological publications ; 2 | Includes bibliographical references and index.
Identifiers: LCCN 2019004460 | ISBN 9781950343003 (hardcover : alk. paper)
Subjects: LCSH: Dayr al-Abyaḍ (Sūhāj, Egypt) | Sūhāj (Egypt)--Antiquities. | Christian antiquities--Egypt--Sūhāj. | Excavations (Archaeology)--Egypt--Sūhāj.
Classification: LCC DT73.D425 B53 2019 | DDC 932.323--dc23
LC record available at https://lccn.loc.gov/2019004460

Cover image: Shallcross FitzHerbert Jacson Widdrington (1827–1917), Dara el Abead, the Coptic Monastery, 1868, watercolour. Courtesy of W. V. Davies.

Typeset in Minion Pro and Warnock Pro.

Printed in the United States of America on acid-free paper.

For Luke and Casper

Contents

List of Illustrations ix
List of Tables xiii
Acknowledgements xv
Abbreviations xvi

INTRODUCTION 1
Background 2
Methodology 4
Structure of the Book 6
Practical Notes 7

CHAPTER 1 — APPROACHING EGYPTIAN MONASTICISM 9
1.1 Egyptian Monasticism—A Brief Survey 9
1.2 A Local Monastic Geography 17
1.3 The Architecture of Monasticism 21

CHAPTER 2 — FRAMING THE WHITE MONASTERY: HISTORY, HISTORIOGRAPHY, AND ARCHAEOLOGY 31
2.1 The White Monastery before the Monks 31
2.2 The Foundation of the White Monastery and its First Five Abbots (Fourth to Sixth Centuries) 33
2.3 The White Monastery from the Sixth to the Sixteenth Century 38
2.4 The White Monastery 'Discovered': European Travellers on the Nile 44
2.5 The Continued Legacy: Modern Exploration and Re-establishment 48
2.6 The Archaeological Exploration of the White Monastery 51
2.7 Summary 57

CHAPTER 3 — AN ARCHAEOLOGY OF THE WHITE MONASTERY 59
3.1 Background to the Study of the White Monastery 59
3.2 WM.1 — The Northernmost Part of the Ancient Monastery 63
3.3 WM.2 — The Funerary Chapel 66
3.4 WM.3 — North of the White Monastery Church 70
3.5 WM.4 — West of the White Monastery Church 71
3.6 WM.5 — South of the White Monastery Church 94
3.7 WM.6 — The Southeast Corner of the Monastery 102
3.8 WM.7 — The Southwest Corner of the Monastery 104
3.9 A Chronology of the White Monastery 109
Appendix — Areas, zones, and sections at the White Monastery 113

CHAPTER 4 — SETTLEMENT, ECONOMY, AND DAILY LIFE AT THE WHITE MONASTERY 117
4.1 Settlement 117
4.2 Economy: Production and Consumption at the White Monastery 130
4.3 Visitors to the White Monastery 143
4.4 Summary 149

CHAPTER 5 — THE RED MONASTERY AND ATRIPE 151
5.1 The Red Monastery 152
5.2 A Monastery in the Village of Atripe 169
5.3 Summary 177

CONCLUSION 179
Archaeology and Text 179
The White Monastery after Shenoute 181
The Economy of the White Monastery Federation 183
Future Perspectives 184

Bibliography 187
Webpages 208
Unpublished Archaeological Reports 208
Index 211
Plates 217

List of Illustrations

Fig. 1. The fifth century church of the White Monastery overlooking the cultivated Nile Valley. View towards northeast (photograph by the author; © YALE). 2
Fig. 2. Map of monasteries, towns and cities referenced in the book (map by the author). 5
Fig. 3. Seventh-century keep at the Monastery of St Antony. Note drawbridge (photograph by the author). 24
Fig. 4. Deir Anba Hadra, Aswan. Emphasis on refectory (modified from Monneret de Villard, *Les Couvents*, fig. 87). 25
Fig. 5. Seventh century refectory in the Monastery of St Antony (photograph by the author). 26
Fig. 6. Plan of the White Monastery church with an emphasis on the north conch and the adjacent room (modified from Clarke, *Christian Antiquities*, pl. XLV). 40
Fig. 7. *Ciborium*. View towards northwest (De Bock, *Matériaux*, pl. XIX). 43
Fig. 8. Denon's drawing of the White Monastery (Denon, *Travels*, pl. XVII, fig. 2). 46
Fig. 9. Domestic houses in nave of the White Monastery church c. 1900. View towards east (De Bock, *Matériaux*, pl. XX). 49
Fig. 10. Petrie and Ward's plan of the excavation at the White Monastery. 1. Enclosure wall and entrances; 2. Limestone slag heap; 3. Area of brick buildings (modified from Petrie, *Athribis*, pl. XLIII). 52
Fig. 11. Plan of excavation to the west of the White Monastery church (WM.4), showing approximate location of coin hoards A and B (map by Dawn McCormack and the author; © YMAP). 56
Fig. 12. Map of WM.1 identifying structures discussed in text (map by Dawn McCormack and the author; © YMAP). 62
Fig. 13. WM.1.2. Pottery kiln. View towards north (photograph by the author; © YMAP). 65
Fig. 14. Map of WM.2 showing main features discussed in text with emphasis on areas excavated by WMP (map by Dawn McCormack and the author; © YMAP). 66
Fig. 15. WM.2.1. Overview of funerary chapel showing entrance to tomb centrally placed in the nave. View towards east (photograph by Peter Sheehan; © YMAP). 67
Fig. 16. WM.2.1. Isometric view of funerary chapel (drawing by Nicholas Warner; © YMAP). 67
Fig. 17. WM.2.1. Figural representation of Shenoute in the *orans* pose (photograph by Gillian Pyke; © YMAP). 68
Fig. 18. WM.3 (map by Dawn McCormack and the author; © YMAP). 70
Fig. 19. WM.4.1.17. Overview of thoroughfare. View towards south (photograph by the author; © YMAP). 72
Fig. 20. WM.1.16. Overview of building identified as refectory. View towards southeast (photograph by the author; © YMAP). 73
Fig. 21. WM.4.1.18. Overview of building. Note central hallway with catchment pits at north and south ends. View towards east (photograph by the author; © YMAP). 74

Fig. 22. WM.4.1.19. Overview of building identified as cold store. Note entrance in bottom right side and mud brick lining along walls. View towards west (photograph by the author; © YMAP). 75
Fig. 23. WM.4.1.20. Note possible doorway and catchment pit in foreground. View towards south (photograph by the author; © YMAP). 75
Fig. 24. Map showing access routes in olive pressing area. Full lines go through preserved doorways or passages, dotted lines indicate where doorways could have been located (map by Dawn McCormack and the author; © YMAP). 76
Fig. 25. WM.4.2.4. Overview of hallway. View towards east (photograph by the author; © YMAP). 76
Fig. 26. WM.4.2.4. View of hallway. Note change of direction of limestone pavers to mark location of doorways. View towards north (photograph by the author; © YMAP). 77
Fig. 27. WM.4.2.3. Ceramic storage vessel built into north wall. Note vessel rim, possibly intended for lid. View towards north (photograph by the author; © YMAP). 78
Fig. 28. WM.4.2.3. Remains of storage bins built against north wall. View towards north (photograph by the author; © YMAP). 79
Fig. 29. WM.4.2.3. Example of oven/boiler installation. Note lime scale in ceramic vessel. View towards southwest (photograph by the author; © YMAP). 79
Fig. 30. WM.4.2.1. Overview of rooms identified as kitchen. Note cistern at the back of the photo. View towards south (photograph by the author; © YMAP). 80
Fig. 31. WM.4.3.6. Overview of four-pillared hall. View towards east (photograph by the author; © YMAP). 81
Fig. 32. WM.4.3.9. Overview of room with installations for oil production. Note foundation for crushing basin in foreground. View towards west-southwest (photograph by the author; © YMAP). 83
Fig. 33. WM.4.3.14. Overview of room with crushing basin and cistern. View towards north-northeast (photograph by the author; © YMAP). 83
Fig. 34. WM.4.3.14. Crushing basin. Note incised image resembling two pillars spanned by a double arch. View towards west (photograph by the author; © YMAP). 84
Fig. 35. WM.4.3.13. Overview of room. Note veneer of fired bricks inserted into the mud brick wall along the right edge of the photo. View towards north (photograph by the author; © YMAP). 85
Fig. 36. WM.4.3.15. Overview of rooms. View towards south (photograph by the author; © YMAP). 86
Fig. 37. WM.4.3.11. Type one vat. Note six limestone blocks and central slot. View towards north-northwest (photograph by the author; © YMAP). 86
Fig. 38. WM.4.3.11. Type two vat. View towards northwest (photograph by the author; © YMAP). 88
Fig. 39. WM.4.4.22. Steps giving access to large building. Note catchment pit. View towards west (photograph by the author; © YMAP). 90
Fig. 40. WM.4.5.31. View of well from bottom of staircase (photograph by the author). 92
Fig. 41. WM.5 with zones (map by the author; © YMAP). 94
Fig. 42. Overview of WM.5. View towards southwest (photograph by the author; © YMAP). 95
Fig. 43. Mounds of debris and discarded building material on the south side of the White Monastery church (photograph by Father Michel Jullien, reproduced with permission from College de la Sainte-Famillie, Faggalah, Cairo (nr. 521[1]). Courtesy of Cédric Meurice). 95
Fig. 44. WM.5.1. Overview of street. View towards south (photograph by the author; © YMAP). 96
Fig. 45. WM.5.1. Limestone and shafts in fired brick wall defining the east side of the street and interpreted by Grossmann as latrines. View towards west (photograph by the author; © YMAP). 97

Fig. 46. WM.5.2. Overview of building. View towards north (photograph by Gillian Pyke; © YMAP). 97
Fig. 47. WM.5.3. Overview of vats located south of the building. View towards north (photograph by the author; © YMAP). 99
Fig. 48. WM.6 (map by Dawn McCormack and the author; © YMAP). 102
Fig. 49. Map of southern part of the White Monastery archaeological site. Petrie's plan with overlay of the WMP survey map (© YMAP). 103
Fig. 50. WM.7 with zones (map by Dawn McCormack and the author; © YMAP). 104
Fig. 51. WM.7.1. Overview of single-room structure. View towards south-southwest (photograph by the author; © YMAP). 105
Fig. 52. WM.7.4. Overview of sunken storeroom. Note vaulting in far-left corner. View towards south (photograph by the author; © YMAP). 106
Fig. 53. WM.7.6. Overview of zone. View towards southwest (photograph by the author; © YMAP). 106
Fig. 54. Location of thoroughfares in WM.5 (diagonal lines) (map by Dawn McCormack and the author; © YMAP). 120
Fig. 55. Map showing thoroughfares, access routes and open courtyards in WM.4 (diagonal lines) (map by Dawn McCormack and the author; © YMAP). 121
Fig. 56. Western end of well in WM.4.5.31. Showing transverse arch for *saqiya* fitting. View towards south (photograph by the author; © YMAP). 122
Fig. 57. Section view of *saqiya* gear drive with installation for pot garland or bucket chain (Ménassa and Laferrière, *La Saqia*, fig. 25; © IFAO). 123
Fig. 58. View from above of ox driven *saqiya* gear drive with pot garland (Ménassa and Laferrière, *La Saqia*, fig. 24; © IFAO). 123
Fig. 59. Two distribution boxes in WM.4.7.30. View towards south-southeast (photograph by the author; © YMAP). 125
Fig. 60. Sluice gate in channel in WM.5.4. View towards south (photograph by the author; © YMAP). 127
Fig. 61. Crushing basins in WM.4.3.9 and WM.4.3.14. View towards southeast (photograph by the author; © YMAP). 135
Fig. 62. Plan of church. 1. Dedicated to St George. 2. Dedicated to St Shenoute. 3. Dedicated to the Virgin Mary. 4. Baptistery. Route showing possible movement into and through baptistery and adjacent room (modified from De Bock, *Matériaux*, fig. 60). 147
Fig. 63. Site plan of the Red Monastery showing location of church in relation to the archaeological remains and the modern monastery. Key: 1. Church; 2. Keep; 3. Well; 4. Structures related to the ancient monastery; 5. Modern church (drawing by Nicholas Warner; Warner, "Architectural Survey," fig. 6.2; © ARCE).[1] 153
Fig. 64. Overview of Red Monastery archaeological church. View towards east (photograph by the author). 155
Fig. 65. RM.1.1–3 (map by the author). 156
Fig. 66. RM.2.1–3 (map by the author). 156
Fig. 67. RM.3.1–2 (map by the author). 156
Fig. 68. RM.1.3. Overview of structure. View towards south-southeast (photograph by the author). 157
Fig. 69. RM.1.1. Note two crushing basins. View towards southwest (photograph by the author). 157

1 Full credit line for figures 63, 74 and plate 1: Reproduced by permission of the American Research Center in Egypt. This project was funded by the United States Agency for International Development (USAID). The Red Monastery Conservation Project (2003–2014) was directed by Elizabeth S. Bolman.

Fig. 70. RM.2.2. Overview of structure. Note paving in front of photo. View towards east-northeast (photograph by Gillian Pyke). 158
Fig. 71. RM.3.1. Suggested location of boundary wall indicated by dotted line. View towards south (photograph by the author). 159
Fig. 72. Storage vessel found in eastern part of excavated area (precise location unknown) (photograph by Gillian Pyke). 160
Fig. 73. Overview of Red Monastery church. View towards southeast (photograph by the author). 161
Fig. 74. Reconstructed plan of Red Monastery church with suggested dating (drawing by Nicholas Warner; Warner, "Architectural Survey," fig. 6.1; © ARCE). 161
Fig. 75. Suggested size of Red Monastery (map by the author). 163
Fig. 76. RM.1.1. Red Monastery well. Note internal niche and remains of transverse arches. View towards west (photograph by the author). 165
Fig. 77. RM.1.1. Sluice gate separating two tanks immediately east of the well. Note impression of pipeline feeding the tank in foreground. View towards east (photograph by the author). 165
Fig. 78. Overview of Red Monastery archaeological site, emphasis on suggested oldest buildings on site (map by the author). 167
Fig. 79. Map detail of convent with eight area divisions (AT.1-8) (modified from El-Sayed and El-Masry, Athribis, plate IV. Reproduced with permission by Christian Leitz and Universität Tübingen). 171
Fig. 80. AT.5. Preserved circular benches in refectory. View towards north (photograph by Gillian Pyke; © YMAP). 173
Fig. 81. Overview of the Monastery of St Moses, Abydos. View towards west (reproduced with permission by Ayman Mohammed Damarany). 175

Pl. 1. Map showing the location of the White Monastery federation in relation to Sohag and Akmim. Drawing by Nicholas Warner. Bolman, "Introduction," fig. 13. © ARCE. 217
Pl. 2. Overview of the seven excavated areas within the White Monastery. Map by Dawn McCormack and the author. © YMAP. 218
Pl. 3. WM.4 showing zones. Map by Dawn McCormack and the author. © YMAP. 219
Pl. 4. WM.4 showing sections. Map by Dawn McCormack and the author. © YMAP. 220
Pl. 5. Map details from the geophysical survey of the White Monastery. Map by Tomasz Herbich. Brooks Hedstrom & Bolman, "White Monastery," fig. 2. Image used with permission from Darlene L. Brooks Hedstrom and Elizabeth S. Bolman. 221
Pl. 6. Map showing changing locations of garbage dumps and cemeteries as the monastery decrease in size over time. Map by Dawn McCormack and the author. © YMAP. 222
Pl. 7. Map of archaeological remains at White Monastery, showing location of wells (blue circle with red core); cisterns and sedimentation tanks (blue circle with green core); distribution boxes (black circle with yellow core); inspection boxes (orange); and soak-aways (yellow). Map by Dawn McCormack and the author. © YMAP. 223
Pl. 8. Map showing distribution of pipelines in WM.4. Note concentration of east-west running pipes east of well in WM.4.6.32. Map by Dawn McCormack and the author. © YMAP. 224
Pl. 9. Red Monastery archaeological site with area division. Map by the author. 225
Pl. 10. Map detail of RM.3. showing extension of walls with dotted lines. Letters suggest location of rooms. Map by the author. 226
Pl. 11. Map of Atripe archaeological site. El-Sayed and EL-Masry, Athribis, plate IV. Reproduced with permission from Christian Leitz and Universität Tübingen. 227

List of Tables

Table 1. Chronological framework. 3
Table 2. Monasteries in Akhmim. 18
Table 3. Overview of the history of the White Monastery. 32
Table 4. Phasing of the White Monastery archaeological site. 109
Table 5. Coins found by the SCA at the White Monastery. 141
Table 6. Areas and zones at the Red Monastery. 155
Table 7. Areas at Atripe. 172

Appendix to Chapter 3. Areas, zones and section at the White Monastery 113

Acknowledgements

The seed for this book was planted in 2005 when I joined the White Monastery Project by invitation of then director Elizabeth S. Bolman, which in time led to the PhD that became the precursor for this volume. My work was further developed while I was a postdoctoral research fellow at Aarhus University, Denmark, as a part of the project, *The Emergence of Sacred Travel: Experience, Economy and Connectivity in Ancient Mediterranean Pilgrimage*. I completed this volume while holding a postdoctoral fellowship at University of Oxford, awarded by the Danish Carlsberg Foundation (2016–2019).

I am most grateful to Stephen J. Davis and the Yale Monastic Archaeology Project (South) for generously allowing me to publish the archaeological material from the White Monastery, with thanks to the William K. and Marilyn M. Simpson Endowment for Egyptology in the Department of Near Eastern Languages & Civilizations, Yale University. I am also grateful to Elizabeth S. Bolman, Darlene L. Brooks Hedstrom and Peter D. Sheehan for inviting me to join the Project in 2005, and to Elizabeth S. Bolman for her encouragement of my survey of the Red Monastery, which was carried out under the auspices of ARCE's Red Monastery Conservation Project with funding from the Danish Institute in Damascus.

Several other funding bodies have supported my research. Most importantly, the Faculty of Humanities at the University of Copenhagen, who generously funded my PhD research. Ingeniør Svend G. Fiedler og Hustrus Legat twice funded conference participation, while Augustinus Fonden, Knud Højgaards Fond, Elizabeth Munksgaard Fonden and the Danish Institute in Damascus supported my prolonged research stay at University of Oxford (2013–14), which commenced with logistical support from Bryan Ward-Perkins, Jacob Dahl and Wolfson College. During my Carlsberg postdoctoral fellowship, I enjoyed the hospitality of Wolfson College (as a Junior Research Fellow) and the Khalili Research Centre (as a Research Associate). I am most grateful to these institutions for supporting my research in Oxford.

My PhD was supervised by Alan G. Walmsley and examined by Bryan Ward-Perkins, Stephen J. Davis and Rachael J. Dann and it is partly owing to their encouragement that my book has seen a fairly swift turnaround from thesis to book manuscript.

I have benefitted from discussions, bibliographical assistance and information otherwise unobtainable from numerous friends and colleagues in Denmark, Egypt and UK as well as at various conferences and seminars. These include Ayman Abdelhameed Ahmed, Aiysha Abu-Laban, Ignacio Arce, Jere Bacharach, Mogens Blanke, Elizabeth Bolman, Darlene Brooks Hedstrom, Ines Castellano, Anna Collar, Jennifer Cromwell, Nicola Daumann, Stephen Davis, Jacob Engberg, Corisande Fenwick, Stefanie Hoss, Anders-Christian Jacobsen, Jeremy Johns, Hugh Kennedy, Marie Legendre, Judith McKenzie, Troels Myrup Kristensen, Arthur Obluski, Arietta Papaconstantinou, Birte Poulsen, Gillian Pyke, Stephen Quirke, Daniel Reynolds, Georgia Rogers, Alice Stevenson, Maher Taboush, Luke Treadwell, Nicolas Warner, Andrew Wilson and Ewa Wipszycka.

Images in this book have been reproduced with permission from the American Research Center in Egypt, Elizabeth S. Bolman, Darlene L. Brooks Hedstrom, Ayman Mohammed Damarany, Institut Français d'Archéologie Orientale, Michael Jones,

Christian Leitz, Cedric Meurice, Gillian Pyke, Universität Tübingen, Nicholas Warner and, most importantly, Stephen J. Davis and Yale Monastic Archaeology Project (South).

I am thankful to Stephen J. Davis, who invited me to publish with Yale Egyptology and the three official readers, Bentley Layton, Gillian Pyke and Bryan Ward-Perkins for their constructive comments and astute observations. Also, heartfelt thanks to Paul John Frandsen, Ine Jacobs and Paul Wordsworth who read drafts of chapters or the entire book at various stages of its completion, and especially Stephen J. Davis, Gillian Pyke and Luke Treadwell, who have been instumental in the completion of this work. I am also grateful to my research assistant, Alice Poletto, who briefly joined my project towards the end of its completion.

On a more personal level, my deepest thanks to all my friends, family and colleagues, and above all to my wonderful husband Luke, who has offered invaluable support and unfailing encouragement at all stages of my work.

Finally, but perhaps most importantly, my heartfelt thanks to the monks of the White Monastery and to the Sohag department of the Supreme Council of Antiquities for their continuous hospitality and support.

Abbreviations

ARCE	American Research Center in Egypt
AT	Atripe
IFAO	Institut Français d'Archéologie Orientale
RM	Red Monastery
SCA	Supreme Council of Antiquities
USAID	United States Agency for International Development
WM	White Monastery
WMP	White Monastery Project
YMAP	Yale Monastic Archaeology Project; Stephen J. Davis, Excecutive director

INTRODUCTION

In 1971, Nazeer Gayed Roufail—an Egyptian monk and bishop—was elected Pope of Alexandria and Patriarch of the Coptic Orthodox Church. He became the 117th Coptic Patriarch and the third to bear the name Shenoute. His saintly namesake—a monk from Upper Egypt—was the fifth-century leader of a monastic federation, an industrious writer of Coptic literature, a zealous anti-pagan, and an instrumental figure in the flourishing of the monastic movement. Shenoute's monastery—the White Monastery—was the leading partner of three federated foundations that also included a male congregation known as the Red Monastery and a convent of female monastics in the village of Atripe (pl. 1). Shenoute was the federation's third leader and through his rule, the White Monastery was transformed into one of the most prosperous and influential monastic foundations in Egypt. This situation persisted throughout Late Antiquity (c. 300–700) and into the Early Medieval period (c. 700–1100) (see also table 1), but in the fifteenth century, the historian al-Maqrizi described the monastery in ruins. During the reign of Pope Shenoute III, the monastery of St Shenoute was reclaimed from its derelict state; transformed from a small community of Christian families into, once again, a thriving community populated by monks.

Towering on a plateau above the cultivated Nile Valley, the church of St Shenoute stands, today as it did in Late Antiquity, against the backdrop of the low mountains of Egypt's Western desert as an imposing reminder of Christianity and its influence on the lives of the local community (fig. 1). Children are baptised in the church, the deceased are buried in the monastic graveyard and blessings, prayers and sage advice are sought from the monks on a daily basis. The success of the monastery derives from the patronage of Shenoute himself, who in time became one of Egypt's most famous saints, lending his name to three Coptic patriarchs.[2] During his annual festival, the monastery expands its reach far beyond the limits of the local community and draws in pilgrims from throughout Egypt, who come seeking the blessings of the patron saint.[3]

As an institution in society, the monastery has always been more than a locus of Christian spirituality. It is currently home to more than fifty monks and novices as well as numerous workers who maintain the running of the community and it is an economic unit sustained through a complex system of production and exchange. Material and agricultural goods are produced at the monastery's landholdings on the desert fringe and in the Nile Valley. Here, olives, wine,

2 Shenoute I, r. 859–880; Shenoute II, r. 1032–1046; Shenoute III, r. 1971–2012.

3 Gérard Viaud, *Les Pèlerinages Coptes en Égypte* (Cairo: Institut Français d'Archéologie Orientale, 1979); Otto F. A. Meinardus, *Two Thousand Years of Coptic Christianity* (Cairo: American University in Cairo Press, 2002).

Fig. 1. The fifth century church of the White Monastery overlooking the cultivated Nile Valley. View towards northeast (photograph by the author; © YALE).

honey and other agricultural products are made, while chickens and cows are raised inside the walls of the monastery. These products are consumed by the monks or blessed and sold or given as *eulogia* to visiting pilgrims, or distributed among the community's poor. Tile and carpentry workshops provide furnishings for the interior of the built environment as well as funerary equipment used for burials in the monastery by the local Coptic community.

The monastery's prosperity depends not only on the material goods that it produces. It also depends on a less easily quantified spiritual economy in which the Christian community provides monetary or material offerings in return for the monks' provision of services at the critical stages of life, such as birth (baptism), death (burial) as well as in the daily mediation between God and the earthly world. The successful continuation of this system of exchange hinges on the monastery's local reputation and its perceived importance in the eyes of contemporary Christians. As such, only a small part of the monastic economy is based today on a one-to-one exchange of material goods. The larger part depends on donations from Coptic benefactors made in response to the spiritual assistance provided by the monks.

This book is an attempt to write the biography of the White Monastery, to reconstruct its *longue durée* from its foundation in the fourth century until today and to assess its place within the Late Antique world. My main dataset derives from a detailed archaeological investigation of the site. This new archaeological material is used to review, complement and contextualise the textual sources (especially the rich corpus of early writings by Shenoute) that have hitherto informed our understanding of the monastery and its achievements.

BACKGROUND

The scholarly approach to Egyptian monasticism as a whole has long been dominated by the study of textual sources in the form of manuscripts, books, papyri and ostraca. These sources are preserved in abundance in Egypt's arid climate and have been obtained from monastic libraries through excavation or via the antiquities market. The textual sources are most commonly found in the form of monastic rules, letters, hagiographies, liturgical texts and documentary sources.

Throughout Egypt, the scholarly focus on these plentiful textual sources has in the past been accompanied by a lesser emphasis on the archaeological record, which has focused mainly on church architecture and on identifying individual buildings that

Neolithic period	6000–3200 BCE
Pharaonic period	3100–332 BCE
Hellenistic period	332–30 BCE
Ptolemaic period	332–30 BCE
Roman period	30 BCE–641 CE
Late Antiquity	300–700 CE
Islamic period	641 CE–today
Early Medieval period	700–1100 CE
Medieval period	700–1517 CE
Umayyad period	661–750 CE
Abbasid period	750–868 CE
Tulunid period	868–905 CE
Ikhshidid period	935–969 CE
Fatimid period	969–1171 CE
Ayyubid period	1171–1250 CE
Mamluk period	1250–1517 CE
Ottoman period	1517–1867 CE

Table 1. Chronological framework.

were thought to be characteristic of monastic communities.[4] Many archaeological studies have been concerned with the external modalities of monasticism rather than with its functional mechanisms and have been used quite loosely to endorse textual interpretations, rather than to provide an independent source of evidence by means of which the textual evidence may be measured and critiqued.

In the case of the White Monastery (and its federation), its fame in modern scholarship derives from the contents of its library – which began to reach the antiquities market in the eighteenth century – and from the extensive corpus of writings by Shenoute that were transmitted through nine volumes of canons (letters) and eight volumes of discourses (sermons). Shenoute's writings were continuously copied through the centuries at the White Monastery.[5] The several thousand pages that have survived until today (estimated at 10–15% of the original corpus) allow us to glimpse what life was like at the White Monastery in the fifth century. The texts portray the ideal practice for the monastics, but also deal with problems that were encountered within the community. We learn of the relationship between the monasteries in Shenoute's federation and of interactions with members of contemporary society. Altogether, these texts provide an extraordinarily detailed picture of Christian monastic life in the fourth and fifth centuries.[6] By comparison, the textual sources from the centuries that followed Shenoute's death are surprisingly scarce and provide little information until European travellers began to make their way to Egypt in the seventeenth century. For this reason, scholarly attention has focused on Shenoute's writings and the early history of the monastic complex.

The archaeological remains of the White Monastery federation offer a different and hitherto largely unexploited dataset, which allows us to substantially extend the range of our enquiry into the history of the sites. The archaeological record of the sites dates mainly to the post-Shenoute era and consists of a complex palimpsest formed by prolonged and continuous usage through the centuries. The White

4 For example, Clifford C. Walters, *Monastic Archaeology in Egypt* (Warminster: Aris & Phillips, 1974) and to some extent Peter Grossmann, *Christliche Architektur in Ägypten* (Leiden, Boston & Köln: Brill, 2002).

5 Stephen Emmel, *Shenoute's Literary Corpus*, 2 vols (Louvanii: In Aedibus Peeters, 2004), 4.

6 Bentley Layton, "Social Structure and Food Consumption at an Early Christian Monastery," *Le Muséon* 115 (2002): 25–55; Bentley Layton, "Rules, patterns, and the exercise of power in Shenoute's monastery: The problem of world replacement and identity maintenance," *Journal of Early Christian Studies* 15.1 (2007): 45–73; Bentley Layton, "The Ancient Rules of Shenoute's Monastic Federation," in *Christianity and Monasticism in Upper Egypt*, ed. Gawdat Gabra and Hany N. Takla, 73–82 (Cairo & New York: The American University in Cairo Press, 2008); Bentley Layton, "The Monastic Rules of Shenoute," in *Monastic Estates in Late Antique and Early Islamic Egypt. Ostraca, Papyri, and Essays in Memory of Sarah Clackson*, ed. Anne Boud'hors, James Clackson, Catherine Louis, and Petra M. Sijpesteijn, 170–177 (Cincinnati, Ohio: The American Society of Papyrologists, 2009); Bentley Layton, *The Canons of Our Fathers. Monastic Rules of Shenoute* (Oxford: Oxford University Press, 2014).

Monastery was extensively excavated by William Matthew Flinders Petrie (1907) and by the Supreme Council of Antiquities (1985–2011), but the few available publications are preliminary in nature.[7] Similarly, the Red Monastery archaeological site was excavated by the Supreme Council of Antiquities (1996–2009), while the focus of the work at the site of Atripe has been the Ptolemaic and Roman temple that was later reorganised for the use of the monastic congregation.[8] The limited research into the physical remains of the three communities means that the archaeological data has remained secondary to the textual evidence in the study of the White Monastery federation.[9] Only since 2005 have the monastic archaeological remains been systematically examined and recorded, firstly by the *Consortium for Research and Conservation at the Monasteries of the Sohag Region* (2005–2008) and subsequently by the Yale Monastic Archaeological Project (South) (2008–present). It is the results from these two projects that forms the basis of the research on which this book is based.

Formed on the premise that the archaeological remains can provide a fresh perspective on the study of monasticism, this book examines the organisation of settlement, economy and daily life of Egyptian monasteries, drawing on the evidence of the White Monastery and associated sites, concentrating in particular on the transition from the Late Antique to the Early Medieval periods. It argues that the built environment provides valuable information about the life that was led within the monasteries, and offers a supplementary perspective to the textual sources. Three recurring themes that are addressed throughout the book concern the relationship between the archaeological and textual sources; the development of the monastery after Shenoute's death; and the economic interdependency within the three communities belonging to the federation, as well as the federation's economic relationship with the extra-mural world.

METHODOLOGY

The data examined here derives from first-hand archaeological investigations of monasteries in Egypt, specifically those of the White Monastery federation, combined with published and unpublished archaeological reports, as well as textual sources that have been read in translation.

My participation in the archaeological exploration of the White Monastery began long before I had considered monasticism as a topic for the doctoral dissertation that is the precursor for this book. I joined the White Monastery Project in 2005 and participated in annual campaigns recording the archaeological remains until 2012. When the prospect of writing on the subject of Egyptian monasticism became a reality, I focused my investigations on those areas that were particularly important for understanding the layout of the settlement, its development over time and features that were associated with economic production.

In 2011, I received funding from the Danish Institute in Damascus to map and record the archaeo-

7 Grossmann et al., "The Excavation in the Monastery of Apa Shenute (Dayr Anba Shinuda) at Suhag, with an Appendix on Documentary Photography at the Monasteries of Anba Shinuda and Anba Bishoi," *Dumbarton Oaks Papers* 58 (2004): 371–382; Grossmann et al., "Second Report of the Excavation in the Monastery of Apa Shenute (Dayr Anba Shinuda) at Suhag," *Dumbarton Oaks Papers* 63 (2009): 167–219; William M. F. Petrie, *Athribis* (London: School of Archaeology in Egypt, 1908).

8 Rifaat El-Farag, Ursula Kaplony-Heckel and Klaus P. Kuhlmann, "Recent Archaeological Explorations at Athribis," *Mitteilungen des Deutschen Archäologischen Instituts Abteilung Kairo* 41 (1986): 1–8; Yahia El-Masry, "More Recent Excavations at Athribis in Upper Egypt," *Mitteilungen des Deutschen Archäologischen Instituts Abteilung Kairo* 57 (2001): 205–218; Petrie, *Athribis*; Rafed El-Sayed, Yahia El-Masry and Victoria Altmann, *Athribis. I, General Site Survey, 2003–2007 Archaeological and Conservation Studies: The Gate of Ptolemy IX: Architecture and Inscriptions* (Cairo: Institut Francais d'Archéologie Orientale, 2012).

9 For scholarly exploration of the relationship between archaeology and text see for example Anders Andrén, *Between Artifacts and Texts: Historical Archaeology in Global Perspective* (New York: Plenum Press, 1998); John Moreland, *Archaeology and Text* (London: Duckworth, 2001). See also Daniella Talmon-Heller and Katia Cytryn-Silverman, *Material Evidence and Narative Sources. Interdisciplinary Studies of the History of the Muslim Middle East* (Leiden & Boston: Brill, 2015).

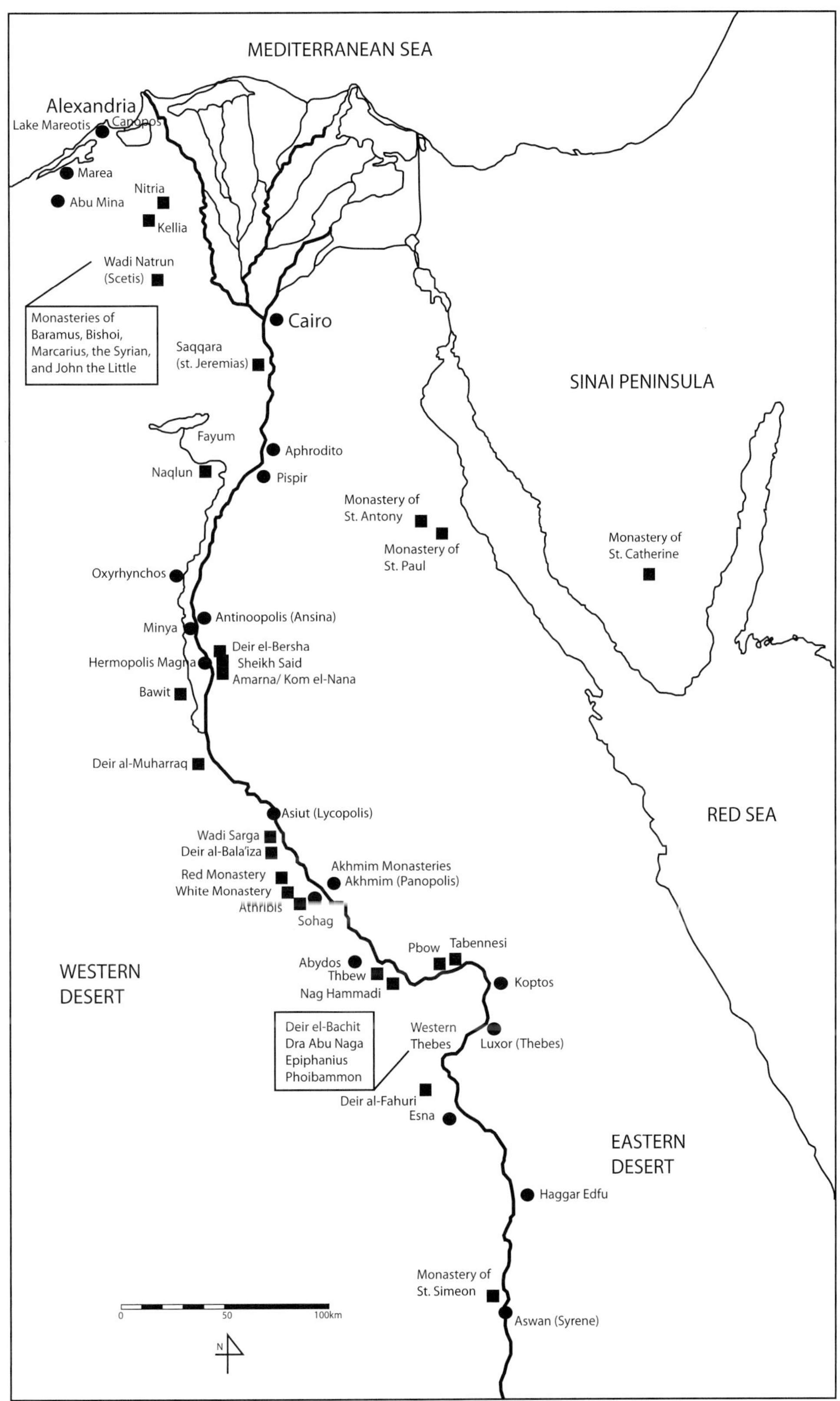

Fig. 2. Map of monasteries, towns and cities referenced in the book (map by the author).

logical remains of the Red Monastery to include this important site in my work on the White Monastery federation.[10] This project took place over a two-week season, during which time the archaeological remains were mapped with a total station and all architectural features were recorded in detail.

As an extension of my archaeological work, I visited monasteries and archaeological sites in several other regions in Egypt. Where relevant, I refer to observations made during these visits and use photographic material as comparanda (fig. 2). The archaeological methodologies applied to the examination of the White and Red Monasteries are described in detail in Chapters 3 and 5.

The aims of this book are achieved through a detailed analysis of the archaeological remains of firstly the White Monastery and secondly the White Monastery federation (the Red Monastery and the convent in Atripe). I examine the monasteries within the analytical categories of settlement, economy and daily life (where the material supports such analysis). Settlement refers to the organisation of the built environment and its infrastructure—in particular the supply, distribution and drainage of water. Economy refers to the production and consumption of food and material goods as well as the spiritual economy that pervaded all aspects of monastic life, even though it was less visible than the physical economy and not easily quantified. Daily life refers to the quotidian activities conducted within the built environment. When relevant textual material is available, it is presented in tandem with the archaeological remains.

The book does not aim to present an exhaustive survey of Egyptian monasticism.[11] On the contrary, only well-documented monasteries that can offer a significant contribution to the discussions of the White Monastery federation are included. Other monastic communities are mentioned in passing for comparative purposes. Urban monasteries and anchoritic settlements at important sites such as Kellia have not been integrated into this discussion. Additionally, church architecture and liturgical practices, cemeteries and burial practices are not dealt with unless relevant to other parts of the discussion, as these subjects have been studied elsewhere and fall beyond the scope of this book.[12] The pilgrimage industry is briefly explored in relation to the White Monastery (Chapter 4) and referred to in my discussion of the White Monastery federation (Chapters 3 and 5), however, the scope of this book does not permit a full exploration of this otherwise important theme.

STRUCTURE OF THE BOOK

This book consists of five chapters. Chapter 1 (Approaching Egyptian Monasticism) identifies the main branches of Egyptian monasticism. These branches are examined in order to position the White Monastery federation within the broader context of Egyptian monasticism, including the Pachomian federation and the neighbouring monastic geography in and near Akhmim (ancient Panopolis). In the final part of the chapter (1.3), individual structures that are commonly found in the monasteries are discussed thematically, drawing on examples from the archaeological record.

Chapters 2 to 5 narrow the focus to the White Monastery federation, of which Chapters 2–4 are mainly concerned with the White Monastery with reference to developments at the two other monastic foundations. Chapter 2 combines textual sources with historiography and archaeology in order to examine past scholarly exploration of the White Monastery, as well as to reconstruct a history of the site. Here I demonstrate how a continuous use of the site can be traced from its foundation in the fourth cen-

10 The survey of the archaeological remains of the Red Monastery were carried out as a subproject under the ARCE-USAID funded Red Monastery Project, directed by Elizabeth Bolman.

11 See Lukas A. Schachner, *Economic Production in the Monasteries of Egypt and Oriens, AD 320–800* (Unpublished PhD, University of Oxford, 2005), catalogue, for an attempt of an exhaustive list of Egyptian monasteries. Schachner, however, overlooked several important sites, such as the Red Monastery and the convent in Atripe. Both sites are dealt with in detail in Chapter 5.

12 See for example Grossmann, *Christliche Architektur*; Walters, *Monastic Archaeology*.

tury until today, although the size of the monastery and its use changed markedly over time. The final part of Chapter 2 provides an overview of the excavations carried out by Petrie in 1907 and by the Supreme Council of Antiquities from 1985 with a focus on their most significant discoveries.

Chapter 3 accounts for the archaeological work that I have carried out firstly as a participant in the White Monastery Federation Project (2005–2008) and subsequently as a member of Yale's Monastic Archaeology Project (South) (2008–2012)—these two projects are referred to collectively as the White Monastery Project. This chapter presents an overview of the archaeological remains of the White Monastery and reconstructs a chronology of the site based on its architectural stratigraphy. In the final part of the chapter (3.9), the process of the monastery's abandonment is discussed in relation to some major historical events, such as the Persian (619–629) and Islamic (641) conquests and the long-term consequences of these events, as well as the changes brought to Egypt by the Black Death (fourteenth century).

Chapter 4 interprets the remains of the White Monastery within the categories of settlement, economy and daily life. Here the textual and archaeological remains are combined to examine the layout of the site and its use. The chapter discusses the size of the monastery, its infrastructure and how many monastics the system could support. The second half of the chapter discusses production and consumption of material culture based on the architectural remains and ceramic material. Here the focus is on food production and on revenue-creating industries.

Following the detailed analysis of the better-preserved White Monastery, Chapter 5 investigates the White Monastery federation, by examining the archaeological remains of the Red Monastery and Atripe and discussing the relationship between the three monastic sites. Both the archaeological and the textual sources suggest an economic interdependency in which the monasteries were specialised in different types of production.

Finally, the conclusion is framed as broadly conceived responses to my three main themes, which concern the relationship between the archaeological and textual sources pertinent to the White Monastery; the development of the federation after Shenoute's death; and economic interdependency within the federation, as well as the federation's economic relationship with the extra-mural world. The chapter also explores future trajectories for the archaeological study of Egyptian monasticism in light of the findings presented within this book.

PRACTICAL NOTES
PLACE NAMES, DATES, ORIENTATION AND TRANSLITERATION

Several settlements and archaeological sites discussed within this book are commonly referred to by more than one name. This is particularly relevant for sites with long histories that span multiple periods and languages, during which their names gradually or purposefully were changed. An example of such is the city of Akhmim, which was known to ancient Egyptians as Ipu or Khent-min, to Greeks and Romans as Panopolis, to Copts as Chemmis and today it is known as Akhmim. To avoid confusion, I generally use one name only for each site and will in most cases use the English version of the modern name. When relevant, the Greek, Coptic or Arabic name is given in brackets. Exceptions are the monasteries that are commonly known by their Arabic name or those for which an adequate English translation does not exist. The female congregation in the White Monastery federation was located in the village of Atripe, often referred to as Athribis and today as Sheikh Hamad.[13] The name Athribis is easily confused with a Pharaonic-period site in the Delta by the same name, Sheikh Hamad is unknown to most non-locals, while Atripe is the name commonly used by scholars of Shenoute's federation.[14] Therefore, I will use Atripe to denote the location of the female congregation to the south of the White Monastery.

13 The site was known to ancient Egyptians as Hat-Repyt and to the Greeks and Romans as Tripheion, neither of which are used to identify the site today (Petrie, *Athribis*, 1).

14 Petrie, *Athribis*, 1.

I use the term monastery for both male and female congregations, while convent is used only for the female communities. I only rarely use the gender-specific monk and nun, but instead apply the gender-neutral monastic. Coptic denominates both language and the Egyptian branch of the Christian faith, while the term Copt describes followers of the Coptic orthodox faith.

All years are in CE unless otherwise stated, but it is not always possible to refer to a specific date or century. Depending on the source, I use a variety of chronological references. Some are dynastic, for example the Umayyad period, while other are more general, for example the Early Medieval period. An overview of all chronological references is found in table 1.

In my description of the archaeological remains, a nominal north is used rather than the magnetic north. This results from a local geography in which the Nile is generally used as one cardinal point and the mountain ranges that mark the beginning of the high desert on both the east and west sides of the Nile signify other cardinal points. This local orientation has been employed in the construction of, for example, churches and the buildings in their surroundings. The nominal north is applied to avoid lengthy descriptions of the exact location of archaeological remains. On maps and plans, the north-arrow indicates the magnetic north.

The production of some chapters (particularly Chapter 3) required the consultation of many unpublished archaeological reports from the White Monastery. These reports are referenced in footnotes and marked with the symbol * and listed towards the end of the bibliography under the separate heading Unpublished Archaeological Reports.

Finally, I have chosen not to use diacritical marks in the transliteration of names from Arabic. This decision was made based on the fact that the use of Arabic in this book is so limited that readers familiar with Arabic would not require the marks to recognise the word or name in question.

Chapter 1

APPROACHING EGYPTIAN MONASTICISM

This chapter aims to outline Egyptian monasticism, summarise its early history and account for its physical expressions. Through complementary approaches, it sets a framework in which the history and archaeology of the White Monastery federation can be studied. Chapter 1.1 investigates traditional as well as more recent approaches to the origin of Egyptian monasticism and its dominant forms represented in the literary, documentary and archaeological records. Of particular interest for the contextualisation of the White Monastery federation is the development of the Pachomian foundations on the east bank of the Nile in Upper Egypt. These foundations are almost exclusively known from written sources, but the formative role of the Pachomian monasteries in Egyptian monasticism is key to understand the mechanisms that resulted in the formation and development of the White Monastery and its associated monasteries. Chapter 1.2 explores the White Monastery's neighbouring monastic geography in and near Akhmim on the east bank of the Nile. These monasteries are not well-preserved and have been subjected to only few archaeological examinations. They will not be dealt with in detail, but their development is important for the context within which the White Monastery federation existed. In Chapter 1.3, I explore the Egyptian monasteries' physical layout. Here, the identification of individual structures and their organisation into architectural types—the focus of much past archaeological work—is used to explore what constitutes the monastic built environment.

1.1 EGYPTIAN MONASTICISM—A BRIEF SURVEY

The origin of Egyptian monasticism is a contested topic that, so far, has not brought forth any definitive conclusions.[15] Late Antique authors such as John Cassian (c. 360–435) believed that monasticism had been around as long as Christianity, while modern scholars suggest inspiration from the Jewish ascetic Therapeutae, a mystical order in the vicinity of Alexandria, or the Manicheans, whose presence is well-documented in Late Antique Egypt.[16] Oth-

15 See for example Derwas J. Chitty, *The Desert a City* (London & Oxford: Mowbrays, 1966); Marylin Dunn, *The Emergence of Monasticism. From the Desert Fathers to the Early Middle Ages* (Oxford: Blackwell Publishers Ltd, 2001); James E. Goehring, *Ascetics, Society and the Desert: Studies in Egyptian Monasticism* (Harrisburg: PA Trinity Press International, 1999); William S.J. Harmless, *Desert Christians. An Introduction to the Literature of Early Monasticism* (Oxford: Oxford University Press, 2004), 417-447; Birger A. Pearson and James E. Goehring, *The Roots of Egyptian Christianity* (Philadelphia: Fortress Press, 1986); Ewa Wipszycka, "A Look at the Origins of Monasticism in Egypt from a Geographical Point of View," *Przegląd Humanistyczny* 2 (2013): 109–126.

16 Harmless, *Desert Christians*, 417–447; Sigfried G. Richter, "The Coptic Manichaean Library from Madinat Madi in the Fayoum," in *Christianity and Monasticism in the Fayoum Oasis*, ed. Gawdat Gabra, 71–78 (Cairo & New York: The American University in Cairo Press, 2005).

ers have suggested that monasticism began among groups of ascetic Christians such as Jerome's (c. 347–420) fictional tale of Paul the hermit, who lived in the desert to escape persecution.[17]

At the core of the monastic lifestyle was an ideal of asceticism, often defined as a rejection of bodily needs, especially in the form of food and sexual relations.[18] For some, asceticism also came to mean a withdrawal from society and a rejection of family ties.[19] Within the Egyptian Christian tradition, two individuals are universally reckoned to be fundamental to the origins of Egyptian monasticism. The individuals, Anthony and Pachomius, and the movements that they inspired, are dealt with below.

Recent examinations of the archaeological remains of monastic settlements combined with studies of documentary papyri have revealed that the organisation of Egyptian monastic communities varied to a degree that, in the words of Ewa Wipszycka 'is unparalleled in the world of Late Antiquity.'[20] These variations included but were not limited to ascetics living in cities, towns or villages in groups or on their own; ascetics who retreated from the world to live in isolated dwellings on their own or with a servant, disciples or companions; ascetics who joined their hermitages to form a monastic settlement that maintained the solitary lifestyle, but was led by an abbot, shared a common economic foundation and weekly communal meals and prayers; ascetics who lived in communal monasteries. These groups were never fixed, and monastic settlements could include several different types of lifestyles. In the words of James E. Goehring, we should perceive Late Antique Egyptian monasticism as a 'complex continuum from the fully solitary monk to the fully communal monk.'[21]

Below follows an outline of some of the manifestations of Egyptian monasticism. Monasteries in cities and deserts are described in brief followed by a more in-depth treatment of the Pachomian monastic federations.

1.1.1 Urban and Desert Monasteries

The earliest form of organised Christian ascetic life in Egypt appears to have been groups of virgins or widows, who gathered in communities in towns, villages and cities.[22] According to Edwin A. Judge, the long tradition of Christian male asceticism adopted a social form only around the late third or early fourth

17 Dunn, *Monasticism*, 1; Roy J. Deferrari, *Early Christian Biographies; Lives of: St. Cyprian, by Pontius; St. Ambrose, by Paulinus; St. Augustine, by Possidius; St. Anthony, by St. Athanasius; St. Paul the first hermit, St. Hilarion, and Malchus, by St. Jerome; St. Epiphanius, by Ennodius* (Washington: Catholic University of America, 1964). See also Stephen J. Davis, "Jerome's 'Life of Saint Paul' and the Promotion of Egyptian Monasticism in the West," in *The Cave Church at the Monastery of St. Paul*, ed. William Lyster, 25–41 (New Haven: Yale University Press/American Research Centre in Egypt, 2008).

18 Dunn, *Monasticism*, 6. See also Vincent L. Wimbush and Richard Valantasis, *Asceticism* (Oxford: Oxford University Press, 1998).

19 See for example Niall Finneran, *The Archaeology of Christianity in Africa* (Stroud, Glouscestershire: Tempus Publishing ltd, 2002), 74–91 for a more traditional history of the origin of Coptic monasticism.

20 Ewa Wipszycka, "Resources and Economic Activities of the Egyptian Monastic Communities (4th–8th century)," *The Journal of Juristic Papyrology* XLI (2011): 162. See also Darlene L. Brooks Hedstrom, "Divine architects: Designing the monastic dwelling place," in *Egypt in the Byzantine World 300–700*, ed. Roger S. Bagnall, 368–389 (Cambridge: Cambridge University Press, 2007); Jean Gascou, "Monasteries, Economic Activities of," in *The Coptic Encyclopedia*, ed. Aziz S. Atiya (New York: Macmillan Publishing Company, 1991), 1639; James E. Goehring, "New Frontiers in Pachomian Studies," in *The Roots of Egyptian Christianity*, ed. Birger A. Pearson and James E. Goehring (Philadelphia: Fortress Press, 1986), 245–250; James E. Goehring, "Monasticism in Byzantine Egypt: Continuity and Memory," in *Egypt in the Byzantine World 300–700*, ed. Roger S. Bagnall (Cambridge: Cambridge University Press, 2007), 392 for variations in monastic settlements.

21 James E. Goehring, "Through a Glass Darkly: Diverse Images of the Apotaktikoi(ai) of Early Egyptian Monasticism," *Semeia* 58 (1992): 53.

22 Dunn, *Monasticism*, 42–58; Susanna Elm, *Virgins of God: the Making of Asceticism in Late Antiquity* (Oxford: Clarendon Press, 1994), 228; Harmless, *Desert Christians*, 440–445. See also Stephen J. Davis, *The Cult of Saint Thecla: A Tradition of Women's Piety in Late Antiquity* (Oxford: Oxford University Press, 2001), 81–194.

century.[23] These early monasteries most likely consisted of small independently-run communities of ascetics who lived in urban environments. The earliest known attestation of the use of the word *monachos* (monk) as a 'recognised figure in society' dates to 324, where a legal petition mentions the monk Isaac, who lived in a village in the Fayoum.[24] Such town-based monasticism, sometimes referred to as the *apotactic* movement, appears to have been common at least from the fourth century and was found in cities such as Antinoopolis, Oxyrhynchus, Hermopolis Magna, Lycopolis and Aphrodito. Fourth-century authors such as Palladius (c. 363–425) and the unknown author of the *History of the Monks in Egypt* described how monks could be found anywhere in Egypt—up and down the Nile and in the Delta.[25] When Rufinus (345–410) visited Oxyrhynchus towards the end of the fourth century, he claimed that the town contained more monasteries than houses and monks occupied public buildings as well as abandoned temples. The story goes that the local bishop reported that 10,000 monks and 20,000 virgins lived in the town.[26] These numbers should be perceived as highly idealized with only rhetorical significance and not as a reflection of the actual situation in the city. References to urban monasteries are found in documentary papyri, but their location in areas that were in continuous use through the centuries means that they are not found in the archaeological record.[27]

Although the town-based ascetic was more common and also more visible in the daily lives of the residents of Late Antique Egypt, this type of monastic lifestyle has been totally overshadowed in literary sources by the ideal of the desert and the monks who chose to reside in this harsh environment.[28] This literary bias resulted in part from the writings of Athanasius, the twentieth patriarch of Alexandria (r. 328–373), who through the authorship of the hagiographic work known as the *Life of St Antony* advocated for a proper ascetic practice—one that was not found in the cities.[29]

Many aspects of the *Life of St Antony* are questionable, but the value of the hagiography lies in Athanasius' fourth-century portrait of the exemplary Christian life.[30] The *Life* reports how Antony's spiritual journey reached its culmination through his further withdrawal from humanity into the desert.[31] Drawing in part on ancient Egyptian and Greek dichotomies of the desert and the city and in part on biblical precedence for theophany (Moses and Elijah) and for encountering and defeating true evil (Jesus' temptation by the devil), the desert was framed as the ideal topos for ascetics to combat the devil and his demons.[32] Through these means, Athanasius constructed the desert as the assumed location of ascetic perfection.[33]

23 Edwin A. Judge, "The Earliest Use of Monachos for Monk (P. Coll. Youtie 77) and the Origins of Monasticism," *Jahrbuch für Antike und Christentum* 20 (1977): 72–89.
24 Judge, "Monachos," 72–75.
25 Harmless, *Desert Christians*, 419.
26 Judge, "Monachos," 80. See also Colin H. Roberts, *Manuscripts, Society and Belief in Early Christian Egypt* (London: Oxford University Press, 1979), 70–71.
27 See for example James E. Goehring, "Withdrawing from the Desert: Pachomius and the Development of Village Monasticism in Upper Egypt," *The Harvard Theological Review* 89.3 (1996): 267–285; Ewa Wipszycka, "Le Monachisme Égyptien et les Villes," *Travaux et Mémoires* 12 (1994): 1–44.
28 Goehring, "Through a Glass Darkly;" Judge, "Monachos," 88. This situation has been enforced in modern scholarship by the pattern of archaeological preservation in which desert monasticism by far overshadows the urban equivalent.
29 Athanasius of Alexandria, *The Life of Antony: The Coptic Life and the Greek Life*, trans. Tim Vivian (Kalamazoo, Michigan: Cistercian Publications, 2003). See also Judge, "Monachos," 77.
30 Goehring, Monasticism, 13.
31 James E. Goehring, "The Encroaching Desert: Literary Production and Ascetic Space in Early Christian Egypt," *Journal of Early Christian Studies* 5 (1993): 82; James E. Goehring, "The dark side of Landscape: Ideology and Power in the Christian myth of the desert," *Journal of Medieval and Early Modern Studies* 33.3 (2003): 440.
32 Douglas Burton-Christie, *The Word in the Desert: Scripture and the Quest for Holiness in Early Christian Monasticism* (New York: Oxford University Press, 1993), 192–208; Goehring, "The Encroaching Desert," 83; Claudia Rapp, "Desert, City and Countryside in the Early Christian Imagination," in *The Encroaching Desert: Egyptian Hagiography and the Medieval West*, ed. Jitse Dijkstra and Mathilde van Dijck, 93–112 (Leiden: Brill, 2006).
33 Goehring, "The dark side," 445. See also Dag Ø. Endsjø, *Primordial Landscapes, Incorruptible Bodies. Desert As-*

The myth of the desert gave birth to the idea of the solitary hermit and the success of Athanasius' portrayal of Antony led to a literary *imitatio patrum*, where ascetic power was measured against the distance from urban society.[34] Literary works of fiction such as Jerome's *Life of St Paul* and the tale of Paphnutius' encounter with the hermit Onnophrius were based on this ideal.[35] The latter work reports on Paphnutius who travelled two weeks through the desert before he came across Onnophrius—a man so holy that he had 'become an angel on earth, and his withdrawn landscape a reflection of heaven.'[36] The literary ideal of the hermit who lived in total isolation on the edge of the world had no basis in any actual ascetic practice.[37]

In the Coptic Christian community, Anthony is credited with creating a model for monasticism, which constituted a society of ascetics who maintained a solitary lifestyle, but was led by an abbot, shared a common economic foundation and met on a weekly basis for a communal meal and prayers. This type of settlement is sometimes referred to as a *laura*. Three of the most famous Egyptian *laura*, Nitria, Sketis (Wadi Natrun) and Kellia, were founded in the first half of the fourth century.[38] These communities were located within a stretch of 50 km on the southwestern edge of the Delta. The location of Nitria has been proposed to be near the modern village of al-Barnuji, but it has not been conclusively identified. Sketis and especially Kellia have been subjected to extensive archaeological work.[39] The archaeological remains at Kellia contain more than one thousand scattered individual residences as well as several churches.[40]

The archaeological record contains extensive evidence for desert-based *laura*. Throughout Egypt, the Pharaonic mortuary landscape was made home by Christian ascetics.[41] Rock-cut tombs were remodelled into cells and temples were transformed into monasteries. Such conversions took place at, for instance, Amarna, Sheikh Said and Qubbat al-Hawa in Aswan.[42] The best example is perhaps from Western

ceticism and the Christian appropriation of Greek Ideas on Geography, Bodies and Immortality (New York: Peter Lang, 2008) for the myth of the Egyptian desert.

34 Goehring, "Landscape," 443. See also Darlene L. Brooks Hedstrom, *The Monastic Landscape of Late Antique Egypt: An Archaeological Reconstruction* (Cambridge: Cambridge University Press, 2017), 289–290.

35 Tim Vivian, *Histories of the Monks of Upper Egypt and the Life of Onnophrius* (Kalamazoo, Michigan: Cistercian Publications, 1993); Deferrari, *Biographies*. See also Stephen J. Davis, "Curriculum Vitae et Memoriae: The life of saint Onophrius and local practices of monastic commemoration," in *From Gnostics to Monastics: Studies in Coptic and Early Christianity*, ed. David Brakke, Stephen J. Davis and Stephen Emmel, 383–391 (Leuven: Peeters, 2018).

36 Goehring, "Landscape," 443–444.

37 Harmless, *Desert Christians*, 421.

38 Grossmann, *Christliche Architektur*, 246–247; Wipszycka, "Origins," 118.

39 For Nitria, see for example, Hugh G. Evelyn-White and Walter Hauser, *The Monasteries of the Wadi 'N Natrun* (New York: The Metropolitan Museum of Art Egyptian Expedition, 1926–1933), especially 17–43; for Kellia, see Philippe Bridel, *Le Site Monastique Copte des Kellia: Sources Historiques et Explorations Archéologiques: Actes du Colloque de Genève, 13 au 15 août 1984* (Genève: Mission Suisse d'Archéologie Copte de l'Université de Genève, 1986); Rodolphe Kasser, *Survey Archéologique des Kellia (Basse-Egypte): Rapport de la Campagne 1981* (Louvain: Peeters Publishers, 1983); Rodolphe Kasser, *Le Site Monastique des Kellia (Basse-Egypte): Recherches des Annèes 1981–1983* (Louvain: Peeters Publishers, 1984); for Scetis, see Brooks Hedstrom et al., "New Archaeology at Ancient Scetis: Surveys and Initial Excavations at the Monastery of St. John the Little in Wadi al-Natrun. Yale Monastic Archaeology Project," *Dumbarton Oaks Papers* 64 (2010): 217–227; Evelyn-White & Hauser, *Monasteries*; Maged S.A. Mikhail and Mark Moussa, *Christianity and Monasticism in Wadi al-Natrun: Essays from the 2002 International Symposium of the Saint Mark Foundation and the Saint Shenouda the Archimandrite Coptic Society* (Cairo: American University in Cairo Press, 2009).

40 Svetlana Popovic, "The Byzantine Monastery: Its Spatial Iconography and the Question of Sacredness," in *Hierotopy. Creation of Sacred Spaces in Byzantium and Medieval Russia*, ed. Alexei Lidov (Moscow: Progress-tradition, 2006), 163.

41 See for example Brooks Hedstrom, "Divine architects."

42 For Amarna, see Gillian Pyke, "Survey of the Christian church and later remains in the tomb of Panehsy (no. 6)," in "Tell el-Amarna, 2006–7," ed. Barry Kemp, Journal of Egyptian Archaeology 93 (2007): 35–49; Gillian Pyke, "A Christian Conversion: the Tomb of Panehsy at Amarna," *Egyptian Archaeology* 32 (2008): 8–10; Gillian Pyke, "Panehsy Church Project 2009: Settlement Survey," in "Tell el-Amarna, 2008–9," ed. Barry Kemp, *Journal of Egyptian Archaeology* 95 (2009): 27–30; Gillian Pyke, Louise Blan-

Thebes, where the entire mortuary landscape was transformed into a Coptic congregation of hermitages (e.g., the hermitage of Frange in TT29), *laura* (e.g., the Monastery of Epiphanius) and walled monastic communities (e.g., the Monastery of Phoibammon).[43]

1.1.2 Pachomius and the Monastic Federation

In the first half of the fourth century, two federations of *coenobitic* monastic communities also emerged in Upper Egypt. Pachomius was the leader of the first, which is commonly referred to as the Pachomian federation, while the other was the White Monastery federation—the focus of this book. *Coenobiticism* has been defined as a communal form of monasticism with 'an all-powerful abbot, communal worship, shared meals, a rigid schedule for work, an elaborate walled physical installation, and written rules.'[44] The *coenobitic* branch of monasticism is traditionally ascribed to Pachomius (292–348).[45] His contribution is considered as consisting partly in the organisation of several congregations under one leader—the *koinonia*—and partly in defining the internal organisation of the individual monasteries—the *koinobion*.[46]

Only a few letters and two hand-written instructions of Pachomius have survived to the present day.[47] The main sources for his life and teachings are a hagiographical text, found in multiple versions (in Greek, Sahidic, Bohairic and Arabic), and a set of monastic rules. The origins and development of these texts are still a matter of debate.[48]

According to the *Life of Pachomius*, Pachomius came from a village in Upper Egypt. He was twenty years old when he was recruited into the Roman army. During his time in the army, he experienced Christian compassion, which encouraged him to convert to Christianity upon his dismissal from the army. He became a disciple of an old ascetic, but after a couple of years he settled in the abandoned village of Tabennese. In 323 he constructed his first monastery at this site.[49]

In Pachomius' federation (*koinonia*), each monastery (*koinobion*) was divided into houses, with

ke and Mary Ownby, "Panehsy Church Project 2009–10: Settlement Survey," in "Tell el-Amarna, 2010," ed. Barry Kemp, *Journal of Egyptian Archaeology* 96 (2010): 1–30; Gillian Pyke, Anna Stevens and Johanna Sigl, "Panehsy Church Project 2008: Settlement Survey," in "Tell el-Amarna, 2007–8," ed. Barry Kemp, *Journal of Egyptian Archaeology* 94 (2008): 44–54; Michael Jones, "The Early Christian Sites at Tell El-Amarna and Sheikh Said," *Journal of Egyptian Archaeology* 77 (1991): 129–144 (Sheikh Said); Renate Dekker, "An Updated Plan of the Church at Dayr Qubbat al-Hawa," in *Christianity and Monasticism in Aswan and Nubia*, ed. Gawdat Gabra and Hany N. Takla, 117–136 (Cairo & New York: The American University in Cairo Press, 2013); Gawdat Gabra, *Coptic Monasteries: Egypt's Monastic Art and Architecture* (Cairo: American University in Cairo Press, 2002), 105–107; Karel C. Innemée, "The Word and the Flesh," in *Christianity and Monasticism in Aswan and Nubia*, ed. Gabra and Takla, 198; Mary Kupelian, "The Ascension Scene in the Apse of the Church at Dayr Qubbat al-Hawa. A Comparative Study," in *Christianity and Monasticism in Aswan and Nubia*, ed. Gabra and Takla, 201–21; Howard Middleton-Jones, "The Digital 3D Virtual Reconstruction of the Monastic Church, Qubbat al-Hawa," in *Christianity and Monasticism in Aswan and Nubia*, ed. Gabra and Takla, 221–229 (Qubbat al-Hawa).

43 Włodzimierz Godlewski, *Le Monastère de St. Phoibammon* (Warszawa: PWN, 1986); Elisabeth R. O'Connell, "Transforming Monumental Landscapes in Late Antique Egypt," *Journal of Early Christian Studies* 15 (2007): 239–274; Herbert E. Winlock, Walter E. Crum and Hugh G. Evelyn-White, *The Monastery of Epiphanius at Thebes* (New York: Metropolitan Museum of Art, Egyptian Expedition, 1926); Ewa Wipszycka, "Resources and Economic Activities of the Egyptian Monastic Communities (4th–8th century)," *The Journal of Juristic Papyrology* XLI (2011): 236.

44 Stephen Emmel and Bentley Layton, "Pshoi and the Early History of the Red Monastery," in *The Red Monastery Church: Beauty and Asceticism in Upper Egypt*, ed. Elizabeth S. Bolman, 11–15 (New Haven: Yale University Press, 2016).

45 Recent research has questioned Pachomius' formative role. See for example James E. Goehring, "Melitian Monastic Organization: A Challenge to Pachomian Originality," *Studia Patristica* 25 (1993): 388–395; Harmless, *Desert Christians*, 423–425.

46 Philip Rousseau, *Pachomius. The Making of a Community in Fourth-Century Egypt* (Berkeley, Los Angeles & London: University of California Press, 1985); Schachner, *Monasteries*, 5.

47 Dunn, *Monasticism*, 25.

48 Dunn, *Monasticism*, 31. For an overview of sources pertaining to Pachomius and his federation, see Goehring, "Pachomian Studies," 236; Rousseau, *Pachomius*, 37–56.

49 Wipszycka, "Origins," 116.

each house containing some twenty monastics, who were led by a housemaster, assisted by a second. Each house would exercise the same craft and three to four houses formed a group. Ideally, a monastery was comprised of ten groups, which meant that it would contain some 600 monastics. Each monastery was led by an abbot and one or two stewards, and all monasteries in the *koinonia* were ruled by the abbot general.[50] To join a *koinobion*, the novices were required to prove that they were not escaped slaves or criminals and were obliged to renounce their family as well as all possessions.[51] Once accepted into the community, all monastics were expected to learn how to read.

At the time of Pachomius' death in 347, his *koinonia* comprised eleven congregations, two of which were for nuns (at Pbow and Tse). The monasteries spread over 175 km along the course of the Nile between Akhmim (Panopolis) in the north to Esna (Latopolis) in the south.[52] Towards the end of the fourth century, the Pachomian *koinonia* was further expanded and extended throughout Egypt, as it now included a monastery in Canopos near Alexandria.[53] The federation was led from Pbow (modern Faw Qibli) some 85 km to the south of Akhmim and the White Monastery.

Individuals who practiced the *coenobitic* lifestyle had everything in common, whether it was work, material wealth, prayer or meals. The monastic rules were to be followed by all members of the communities. These rules regulated all aspects of communal life: when, how and what to eat, how to dress, when and how to wash, how to sit, stand, walk and talk. However, the most important rules for the Pachomian monasteries were:

- all monastics would share the same circumstances of life—they had everything in common (prayer, work and meals);
- voluntary poverty;
- work for the community;
- obedience to the superior;
- celibacy.[54]

In terms of the physical environment of the Pachomian monasteries, the communal lifestyle required a kitchen and a refectory, warehouses, workshops, stables, a church and an enclosure wall with only one entrance, where a guard controlled all visits to the monastery.[55] The wall served not only to protect the monastery from intruders, but also to set the lives of the monks apart from the surrounding world, construct a group identity and symbolically mark the monastics' withdrawal from the world.[56]

Attempts to locate the physical remains of the Pachomian *koinonia* have so far been mostly fruitless and only the second Pachomian foundation, located in Pbow, has been subject to some archaeological work.[57] Here, the location of the congregation's main church was visible from columns found on the surface. Excavations at Pbow uncovered two basilica churches—one replacing the other—built with fired brick walls and with red granite columns.[58] The later version measured 72 m EW by 36 m NS, contained five aisles and served as a gathering place for the *koinonia* on two annual occasions.[59] Ruins of several

50 Goehring, *Monasticism*, 27. See also Dunn, *Monasticism*, 29–32.
51 Armand Veilleux, *Pachomian Koinonia* (Kalamazoo: Cistercian Studies, 1980–1982), 152–153. See also Dunn, *Monasticism*, 30.
52 Goehring, *Monasticism*, 28
53 Dunn, *Monasticism*, 33; Emmel & Layton, "Pshoi," 12
54 Goehring, *Monasticism*, 26.
55 Wipszycka, "Origins," 116.
56 Hendrik Dey, "Building Worlds Apart. Walls and the Construction of Communal Monasticism from Augustine through Benedict," *Antiquité Tardive* 11 (2004): 357–371.
57 Louis T. Lefort, "Les Premiers Monastères Pachômiens: Exploration Topographique," *Le Muséon* 52 (1939): 379–407.
58 Bastiaan van Elderen, "The Second Season of the Nag Hammadi Excavation," *American Research Center in Egypt Newsletter* 99/100 (1977): 36–54, Bastiaan van Elderen, "The Nag Hammadi Excavation," *Biblical Archaeologist* 42 (1979): 299–331; Peter Grossmann, "The Basilica of Pachomius," *Biblical Archaeologist* 42 (1979): 232–236; Peter Grossmann, "Faw Qibli — 1986 Excavation Report," *Annales du Service des Antiquités de l'Égypte* 76 (2000): 143–148.
59 Goehring, "Pachomian Studies," 255.

fired brick structures and features associated with the water supply were excavated near the basilica, but were not published in any detail.[60]

The second known *coenobitic* federation in Upper Egypt—the White Monastery federation—was founded by Pcol (a Pachomian monk, according to Stephen Emmel and Bentley Layton) near Akhmim on the west side of the Nile, around the middle of the fourth century.[61] At the time of its foundation, four Pachomian monasteries already existed on the east side of the Nile, where Tsemine was the seat for a local leader of the Akhmim *koinonia*.[62]

During the rule of the federation's third leader, Shenoute (r. 385–465), the White Monastery became a leading monastic centre in Upper Egypt.[63] Compared to the Pachomian federation on the east side of the Nile, much more is known about the White Monastery federation, in part because of an extensive corpus of textual sources ascribed to Shenoute and in part resulting from the better preservation and study of the archaeological remains. References concerning the relationship between the White Monastery and the Pachomian Akhmim *koinonia*, however, remain surprisingly scarce.

Goehring describes Shenoute's federation and the Pachomian *koinonia* as 'parallel powerhouses of Upper Egyptian *coenobitism*' but does not take into consideration the complex narrative relating to the foundation of the White Monastery by a monk from a Pachomian monastery and how this would impact the further development and interaction of the two monastic federations.[64] The fairly equal wealth and spiritual importance of the two monastic organisations was expressed in the construction of their main churches at Pbow and the White Monastery. Both are basilicas constructed around the middle of the fifth century, measuring about 75 m in length and 37 m in width, and both were clearly designed to house large congregations.[65] According to the *Life of Shenoute*, Victor, the supreme leader (*archimandrite*) of the Pachomian *koinonia*, and Shenoute accompanied Cyril of Alexandria to the Council of Ephesus in 431.[66] If this information is correct, it offers significant insights into the importance of the two monastic federations in the fifth century.

The fate of Pbow and the Pachomian federation is to some extent revealed in the story of Abraham of Farshut, who was the last Coptic orthodox *archimandrite* of the Pachomian *koinonia*. According to three different *panegyrics* to Abraham—all found in the library of the White Monastery—he was removed as head of the federation by Emperor Justinian I (r. 527–565) and replaced by a pro-Chalcedonian leader, who was in line with the empire's official religion.[67] Abraham left Pbow with a group of orthodox monks and travelled to the White Monastery, where he copied the monastic rules before he founded a new monastery in Farshut, some 40 km to the south of the White Monastery. This purge of anti-Chalcedonians in Upper Egypt appears to have been limited to the Pachomian monasteries and did not affect the White Monastery.

60 Fernand Debono, "La Basilique et le Monastère de St. Pacôme (Fouilles de l'Institut Pontifical d'Archéologie Chretienne, à Faou-el-qibli, Haute-Egypte – Janvier 1968)," *Le Bulletin de l'Institut Français d'Archéologie Orientale* 70 (1971): 191–220. See also Goehring, "Monasticism in Byzantine Egypt."

61 Emmel & Layton, "Pshoi," 11–12.

62 James E. Goehring, "Pachomius and the White Monastery," in *Christianity and Monasticism in Upper Egypt*, ed. Gawdat Gabra and Hany N. Takla (Cairo & New York: The American University in Cairo Press, 2008), 48.

63 Dunn, *Monasticism*, 33–34.

64 James E. Goehring, "2005 NAPS Presidential Address: Remembering Abraham of Farshut: History, Hagiography, and the Fate of the Pachomian Tradition," *Journal of Early Christian Studies* 14.1 (2006): 2.

65 The basilica church in Pbow is the only part of a Pachomian monastery that has been published to date. Elderen, "Second Season;" Elderen, "Nag Hammadi Excavation;" Grossmann, "Basilica;" Grossmann, "Faw Qibli." See also Goehring, "Pachomian Tradition," 4; Sheila McNally, "Transformations of Ecclesiastical Space: Churches in the Area of Akhmim," *Bulletin of the American Society of Papyrologists* 35 (1998): 91.

66 Besa Abbot of Athribe, *The Life of Shenoute*, trans. David N. Bell (Kalamazoo, Michigan: Cistercian Publications, 1983), 47.

67 Goehring, "Pachomian Tradition."

1.1.3 Social and Economic Diversity in Monastic Communities

The three general types of monasticism discussed above, i.e., the *apotactites*, the *anchorites* and the *coenobitic* communities, were never static and often included variations where monasteries combined different lifestyles within one congregation. Monasticism in its formative years was not fixed into a few simple forms, but could be manifested in a wide variety of physical expressions.

Lukas A. Schachner's appendix to his extensive study on the economic production of monasteries shows the range of settlement types.[68] It was not only the physical environment that varied, but also the perception of the ascetic practice and lifestyle. One of the main principles behind monastic asceticism was total abstinence from sexual relations, although the written sources suggest frequent transgressions among the monastics.[69] Ideals of abstinence from specific types of food seem to have varied between the different monastic groups.[70] Similarly, wine was forbidden for all but sick monks in the White Monastery, but papyri from, for example, Wadi Sarga suggests that wine was readily consumed.[71] It should be noted that our understanding of the monastic rules are limited, as only the Pachomian and Shenoutian rule systems have been preserved in some detail. It is possible that each monastery had their own set of rules, perhaps elaborated or simplified from other rule sets—this could have been the case of Abraham of Farshut's copying of the White Monastery rules.

Along similar lines, the ideal of voluntary poverty was subject to variation. The Pachomian foundation and the White Monastery required the aspiring monastic to give away all property before becoming a full member of the community.[72] In the *koinonia* the monks could transfer their worldly goods to relatives or to the monastery, while the White Monastery federation under Shenoute's rule required the novice to transfer all wealth to the *diakonia*—a structure that served the monastery's administration—within three months of joining the community. Once belonging to the monastery, it could not be reclaimed should the monk for one reason or another leave the community. The transferred property could consist of money, houses, land or farm animals and would therefore actively contribute to the wealth of the community. The acquisition of new monks was an important source of income for the monastery, resulting in the accumulation of property and finances over the years.[73]

Written sources suggest that other monasteries were more lenient than the White Monastery in their approach to the monastics' personal finances. Documentary sources from the Monastery of Apa Apollo at Bawit, from Bala'izah and from the archive of the monk Frange in Western Thebes provide a more nuanced view of the monks' personal wealth.[74] From these sources, we learn that the economy of monastic communities was as diverse as the circumstances under which the ascetics lived. In some communities, monastics were permitted to own land plots, livestock, houses, workshops and money even after they joined their congregation.[75] The property could be leased or be a continuing source of income for the monastic throughout his or her ascetic life or it could be bequeathed in a will to a family member

68 Schachner, *Monasteries.*

69 See for example Rebecca Krawiec, *Shenoute & the Women of the White Monastery: Egyptian Monasticism in Late Antiquity* (Oxford & New York: Oxford University Press, 2002) on the women of the White Monastery.

70 Mary, Harlow and Wendy Smith, "Between Fasting and Feasting: The Literary and Archaeobotanical Evidence for Monastic Diet in Late Antique Egypt," *Antiquity* 75 (2001): 758–768.

71 Dorota Dzierzbicka, "Wine Consumption and Usage in Egypt's Monastic Communities (6th–8th century)," in *Aegyptus et Nubia Christiana. The Włodzimierz Godlewski Jubilee Volume on the Occasion of his 70th Birthday*, ed. Adam Łajtar, Artur Obłuski, and Iwona Zych (Warsaw: Polish Centre of Mediterranean Archaeology, 2016), 102.

72 Layton, "Rules," 60; Wipszycka, "Resources," 172.

73 Wipszycka, "Resources," 166.

74 Boud'hors et al., *Monastic Estates in Late Antique and Early Islamic Egypt. Ostraca, Papyri, and Essays in Memory of Sarah Clackson* (Cincinnati: The American Society of Papyrologists, 2009); Sarah J. Clackson, *It is Our Father who Writes: Orders from the Monastery of Apollo at Bawit* (Cincinnati: American Society of Papyrologists, 2008) (Bawit); Wipszycka, "Resources," 183 (Western Thebes).

75 Wipszycka, "Resources," 163.

or to the monastery.[76] There are even examples of monks who owned and sold the cells in which they lived.[77] Documentary papyri from the eighth-century archive at the Monastery of Apa Apollo at Bawit reveal that the monastery would lease land to its own monks, thereby providing an income for both the monastery and the monks.[78]

Monasteries could receive gifts in the form of land, houses, money or objects.[79] Two of the more extravagant examples are the entire monastery of Tbew, which was gifted to the Pachomian foundation by the father of Patronios, possibly as part of the political negotiation of the foundation's leadership following Pachomius' death—Patronios was the immediate successor of Pachomius.[80] The other example is the church of the White Monastery federation, which, according to an inscription on a door lintel, was funded by a local Christian referred to as Caesarius, son of Candidianus.[81]

76 Wipszycka, "Resources," 163.

77 Roger S. Bagnall, "Monks and Property: Rhetoric, Law, and Patronage in the Apophtegmata Patrum and the Papyri," *Greek, Roman, and Byzantine Studies* 42 (2001): 7–24; Martin Krause, "Die koptischen Kaufurkunden von Klosterzellen des Apollo-Klosters von Bawit aus abbasidischer Zeit," in *Monastic Estates in Late Antique and Early Islamic Egypt. Ostraca, Papyri, and Essays in Memory of Sarah Clackson*, ed. Anne Boud'hors et al. (Cincinnati: The American Society of Papyrologists, 2009), 159–169; Ewa Wipszycka, "Monks and Monastic Dwellings: P. Dubl. 32–34, P.KRU 105, and BL MS.Or 6201–6206 Revisited," in *Monastic Estates in Late Antique and Early Islamic Egypt*, ed. Anne Boud'hors et al., 239–243. See also Brooks Hedstrom, "Divine architects," 371.

78 Tonio S. Richter, "The Cultivation of Monastic Estates in Late Antique and Early Islamic Egypt. Some Evidence from Coptic Land Leases and Related Documents," in *Monastic Estates in Late Antique and Early Islamic Egypt*, ed. Anne Boud'hors et al., 205–215.

79 Wipszycka, "Resources," 167-168.

80 Rousseau, *Pachomius*, 74.

81 Grossmann et al., "Monastery of Apa Shenute," 169. See also Andrew Crislip, "The Red Monastery in Early Byzantine Egypt," in *The Red Monastery Church. Beauty and Asceticism in Upper Egypt*, ed. Elizabeth S. Bolman (New Haven and London: Yale University Press, 2016), 8.

82 Grossmann, *Christliche Architektur*; Otto F. A. Meinardus, *Christian Egypt. Ancient and Modern* (Cairo: Cahiers d'Histoire Égyptienne, 1965); McNally, "Transformations."

1.2 A LOCAL MONASTIC GEOGRAPHY

There is ample evidence of a rich and long-lived tradition of Coptic Christianity in the region of the White Monastery. Most important for our understanding of the Late Antique monastic geography are the Pachomian monasteries, but other congregations also developed in the area. The quantity and quality of the evidence from Akhmim, however, are remarkably low compared to the White Monastery: most monasteries have not been excavated and only their churches have been studied in any detail.[82] There is almost no material available to date the foundations and in most cases, their temporal origins have been determined on a basis of architectural comparisons or traditional beliefs.[83] Textual sources are negligible and often mention monasteries by name without providing much further detail.[84] For these reasons, it is not possible to examine the monastic remains in depth, but Akhmim yields sufficient textual and archaeological material to form an impression of the local history and the monastic geography within which the White Monastery was founded and developed. Rather than presenting each archaeological site on its own, the available data have been summarised in table 2.[85]

83 McNally, "Transformations," 84.

84 The sources are summaries by Stefan Timm, *Das Christlich-Koptische Ägypten in Arabischer Zeit: Eine Sammlung Christlicher Stätten in Ägypten in Arabischer Zeit, unter Ausschluss von Alexandria, Kairo, des Apa-Mena-Klosters (Der Abu Mina), der Sketis (Wadi n-Natrun) und der Sinai-Region* (Wiesbaden: Reichert, 1984–2007), 89–90.

85 Table 2 is comprised by data obtained from the following publications: Roger S. Bagnall and Dominic W. Rathbone, *Egypt. From Alexander to the Copts* (London: The British Museum Press, 2004), 172–173; Réne-Georges Coquin, "Akhmim," in *The Coptic Encyclopedia*, ed. Aziz S. Atiya, (New York, Oxford, Singapore, Sydney: Maxwell Macmillan International, 1991); Réne-Georges Coquin, Peter Grossmann, and S.J. Maurice Martin, "Dayr Al-Sab'at Jibal," in *The Coptic Encyclopedia*, 732–733, Réne-Georges Coquin, Peter Grossmann, and S.J. Maurice Martin, "Dayr Sitt Dimyanah," in *The Coptic Encyclopedia*, ed. Aziz S. Atiya, 870–871; Réne-Georges and S.J. Maurice Martin, "Dayr al-Fakhuri," in *The Coptic Encyclopedia*, ed. Aziz S. Atiya, 802–805; Réne-Georges Coquin, S.J. Maurice Martin, and Sheila McNally, "Dayr Anba Bakhum," in *The Coptic Encyclopedia*, ed. Aziz S. Atiya,

Names in Coptic or Arabic and English (when applicable)	Location	Date of Foundation	Date of Disuse	Church	Enclosure wall	Well	Other Remains	Comments
- Tse/ Tasi	Akhmim Location unknown	4th cent.	-	-	-	-	-	Pachomian foundation
- Unkown	Akhmim Location unknown	4th cent.	-	-	-	-	-	Pachomian foundation
- Tesmine	Akhmim Location unknown	4th cent.	-	-	-	-	-	Pachomian foundation
- Deir Anba Bisadah al-Usquf - Monastery of St. Bisadah the Bishop	18 km S of Akhmim Located on edge of village al-Sawam'a Sharq	6th cent.	In use	Y	Y	-	Tomb of St. Bisadah, martyred in 4th cent.	Mentioned by al-Maqrizi
- Monastery of Harpokrates	Akhmim Location unknown	In use in 709	-	-	-	-	-	Known from Greek papyri
- Monastery of St. Christophorus	Akhmim Location unknown	In use in 709	-	-	-	-	-	Known from Greek papyri
- Deir Anba Bakhum - Monastery of St. Pachomius	8 km N of Akhmim In village Sawam' at al-Sharq	7th/8th cent. date of church	In use	Y	-	-	-	Mentioned by Abu al-Makarim Only church remains.
- Deir al-Shuhada (Deir al-Wustani) - Monastery of the Martyrs	6 km NE of Akhmim, near village of al- Hawawish Located by Coptic cemetery.	Late Antiquity	In use	Y	Y	-	Large courtyard with tombs Cells and storerooms –date unknown	Late Antique pottery and cemetery suggest early date for monastery
- Deir Anba Halbanah	Akhmim Location unknown	In use in 12th cent.	-	-	-	-	-	Mentioned by Abu al-Makarim
- Monastery of St. Paul	Akhmim Location unknown	In use in 12th cent.	-	-	-	-	-	Mentioned by Abu al-Makarim
- Deir Mar Tumas - Monastery of St. Thomas	Nag al-Deir, South of Akhmim	13th cent.	In use	Y	-	-	Tomb of St. Thomas	Only church remains
- Deir al-Malak Mikhail (Die Sabrah) - Monastery of Michael the Archangel	6 km NE of Akhmim, near villages of al- Hawawish and al-Salamuni	13th cent.	In use	Y	Y	Y	Animal pens, bakery, fountain house, residential areas All of modern date	Mentioned by al-Maqrizi.
- Deir al-Sab'at Jibal (Deir al-Madwid) - Monastery of the Seven Mountains Possibly same as: - Deir al-Sufsafah - Monastery of the Weeping Willow	Located about 1½ hours walk into Wadi bir al-Ayn, SW of Akhmim	In use in 15th cent.	-	-	-	Y	Cistern containing water from mountain stream Graffiti and hermitages	Mentioned by al-Maqrizi.
- Deir al Qurqas	Unknown	In use in 15th cent.	-	-	-	-	-	Mentioned by al-Maqrizi
- Deir Mar Jirjis al-Hadidi - Monastery of St. George	8 km S of Akhmim	15th cent.	In use	Y	Y	-	Domestic houses of modern date	Now village church
- Deir Sitt Dimyanah	Akhmim city	16th cent.	In use	Y	-	-	-	Only church remains
- Deir al-Adhra - Monastery of the Virgin	5km NE of Akhmim, near village of al- Hawawish	16th cent.	In use	Y	Y	-	Cells and storage rooms All of modern date	
- Deir Abu Sayfayn	Akhmim city		In use	Y	-	-	-	Only church remains

Table 2. Monasteries in Akhmim.

1.2.1 Akhmim in Overview

The city of Akhmim lies on the east bank of the Nile, opposite Sohag and the White Monastery. Until the nineteenth century, Akhmim was the major city in the province, while Sohag was just a minor town. The introduction of the railway with a station on the Sohag side of the Nile markedly changed this configuration and meant that Sohag drastically expanded, while Akhmim somewhat stagnated.[86] Before this recent development, Akhmim had seen almost 6000 years of uninterrupted occupation, which has been documented through archaeological evidence and texts.[87]

Only a few excavations have been carried out in the city itself. Most of these were conducted by the SCA as precursors to major building projects and none of them have brought forth material from the monasteries in or nearby the city.[88] Excavations outside the city have focussed on the Pharaonic, Greco-Roman and Coptic necropolises, yielding abundant funerary materials—in particular textiles.[89] These archaeological finds along with textual sources confirm that Akhmim was an important centre for the textile industry.[90] Arabic authors such as Ahmed al-Yaqubi (ninth century) and Ali al-Masudi (tenth century) mention textiles produced in Akhmim and an inscription in a rug mentions that it was produced in an Akhmim factory in the year 818.[91] Even today, the textile industry forms an important part of the local economy.

The vast majority of texts procured from the area have their origin in the White Monastery and, therefore, only few sources provide insight into the city of

730–731, Réne-Georges Coquin, S.J. Maurice Martin, and Sheila McNally, "Dayr Anba Bisadah," in *The Coptic Encyclopedia*, ed. Aziz S. Atiya, 732–733, Réne-Georges Coquin, S.J. Maurice Martin, and Sheila McNally, "Dayr al-Malak Mikha'il," in *The Coptic Encyclopedia*, ed. Aziz S. Atiya, 823; Réne-Georges Coquin, S.J. Maurice Martin, and Sheila McNally, "Dayr Mar Jirjis al-Hadidi," in *The Coptic Encyclopedia*, ed. Aziz S. Atiya, 831–832, Réne-Georges Coquin, S.J. Maurice Martin, and Sheila McNally, "Dayr al-Shuhada," in *The Coptic Encyclopedia*, ed. Aziz S. Atiya, 865–866; Grossmann, *Christliche Architektur*, 539–546; Sheila McNally, "Dayr Al-Adhra," in *The Coptic Encyclopedia*, ed. Aziz S. Atiya, 713–714, Sheila McNally, "Dayr Mar Tumas," in *The Coptic Encyclopedia*, ed. Aziz S. Atiya, 835–836; McNally, "Transformations," 79–95; Meinardus, *Christian Egypt*, 295–299; Timm, *Das Christlich-Koptische Ägypten*, 80–96.

86 Sheila McNally and Ivancica D. Schrunk, *Excavations in Akhmim, Egypt: Continuity and Change in City Life from Late Antiquity to the Present*. British Archaeological Reports, International Series 590 (Oxford: Tempus Reparatum, 1993), 11.

87 Naguib Kanawati, *Sohag in Upper Egypt. A Glorious History* (Cairo: Ministry of Culture, Egypt, 1990), 8.

88 Roger S. Bagnall, "Public Administration and the Documentation of Roman Panopolis," in *Perspectives on Panopolis. An Egyptian Town from Alexander the Great to the Arab Conquest*, ed. A. Egberts, Brian Paul Muhs, Joep Van der Vliet (Leiden, Boston & Köln: Brill, 2002), 1; Bagnall and Rathbone, *Egypt*, 172–173. The University of Minnesota's project in the late 1970s and early 1980s and excavations carried out by the German Archaeological Institute were exceptions, see Klaus P. Kuhlmann, *Materialien zur Archäologie und Geschichte des Raumes von Achmim* (Mainz am Rhein: Verlag Philipp von Zabern, 1983); McNally and Schrunk, *Akhmim*. For excavations carried out by the SCA, see for example Yahia el-Masry, "Seven Seasons of Excavations in Akhmim," in *Proceedings of the Seventh International Congress of Egyptologists, Cambridge 3-9 September 1995*, ed. Christopher Eyre, 759–765 (Leuven: Peeters Publishers, 1998).

89 See for example Naguib Kanawati, *The Rock Tombs of El-Hawawish. The Cemetery of Akhmim I–X* (Sydney: Macquarie Ancient History Association, 1980–); Kuhlmann, *Achmim* (necropolises); Mark Depauw, "The Late Funerary Material from Akhmim," in *Perspectives on Panopolis. An Egyptian Town from Alexander the Great to the Arab Conquest*, ed. A. Egberts, Brian Paul Muhs, Joep Van der Vliet, 71-81 (Leiden, Boston & Köln: Brill, 2002); Cäcilia Fluck, "Akhmim as a Source of Textiles," in *Christianity and Monasticism in Upper Egypt*, ed. Gabra and Takla, 211–223; Sheila McNally, "Syncretism in Panopolis? The Evidence of the 'Mary Silk' in the Abegg Stiftung," in *Perspectives on Panopolis*, ed. Egberts, Muhs, Van der Vliet, 145–164 (textiles).

90 Fluck, "Akhmim," 211; Robert Forrer, *Über Steinzeit-Hockergräber zu Achmim, Naqada etc. in Ober-Ägypten und über Europäische Parallelfunde* (Achmim-Studien I) (Strassburg: von E. Birkhäuser, 1891).

91 Fluck, "Akhmim," 211.

92 Bagnall, "Public Administration," 1; Peter van Minnen, "The Letter (and other Papers) of Ammon: Panopolis in the Fourth Century A.D.," in *Perspectives on Panopolis. An Egyptian Town from Alexander the Great to the Arab Conquest*, ed. A. Egberts, Brian Paul Muhs, Joep Van der Vliet (Leiden, Boston & Köln: Brill, 2002), 177–199.

Akhmim.[92] An exception is the archive of Ammon, a fourth-century lawyer (*scholastikos*), whose collection of texts tells us that the city contained temples and churches, a festive hall, a theatre, a gymnasium with an attached bathhouse, two other public bathhouses and a philosophical school.[93] These and other documents reveal that in Late Antiquity, Akhmim was a centre for classical education, philosophy and poetry.[94]

It was in this environment that a fourth-century bishop invited Pachomius to organise a monastery—forming the area's first *coenobitic* community—which soon led to the organisation of two further monasteries (Tse and Tsemine), one of which was a congregation for female monastics.[95] Efforts to determine the precise location of these monasteries have proven fruitless.[96] The three Pachomian foundations were probably not the first monastic communities in the city, but they were the first monasteries that were a part of a federation organised under one set of rules and led by a supreme leader.

Medieval authors generally focused on the textile industry and the remains of the Pharaonic temples with very little to say about the monasteries.[97] Abu al-Makarim, however, mentioned that until 1157 there were 70 churches in and near the city.[98] Only four monasteries are mentioned by name (see table 2). Their physical appearance is not described in any detail, but Abu al-Makarim associated several miraculous stories with the sites.[99] Taqi al-Din Al-Maqrizi named five monasteries in the vicinity of Akhmim, but these are not the same as those mentioned by Abu al-Makarim.

1.2.2 The Monasteries of Akhmim

Today, there are nine functioning monasteries in the Akhmim area on the east side of the Nile. Most of these are located in or on the edge of Akhmim or nearby villages, which means that their primary function has become that of village churches.[100] One further monastery is in ruins, and the location of another eight monasteries referred to in texts remains unknown.

The monasteries are distributed within an area that stretches from 8 km north of Akhmim to 18 km south of the city. The northernmost foundation is the Monastery of Pachomius—not the founder of *coenobitic* monasticism, but a martyr of the same name. The monastic church has been dated by Grossmann to the seventh or eighth century.[101] The southernmost foundation is the Monastery of Bisadah the Bishop, supposedly a fourth-century martyr, whose remains are said to be kept in a tomb in the church. The church has been dated by Peter Grossmann to the sixth century.[102] Three monasteries are clustered near the Late Antique cemetery by the village of al-Hawawish, some 6 km to the north of Akhmim. These are the Monastery of the Martyrs, the Monastery of Michael the Archangel and the Monastery of the Holy Virgin. The remaining three monasteries lie 8 km south of Akhmim (the Monastery of St George) and within the city of Akhmim (Deir Sitt Dimyanah and Deir Abu Sayfayn). A ninth monastery (the Monastery of the Seven Mountains) is located in ruins about one and a half hour's walk into the Wadi Bir al-Ayn.

It is not clear if these monasteries were founded near villages in the first place or the villages grew

93 Bagnall, "Public Administration," 1; Minnen, "Letter."
94 Alan Cameron, "Poets and Pagans in Byzantine Egypt," in *Egypt in the Byzantine World 300–700*, edited by Roger S. Bagnall (Cambridge: Cambridge University Press, 2007), 21–46; Raffaella Cribiore, "Higher Education in Early Byzantine Egypt: Rhetoric, Latin, and the Law," in *Egypt in the Byzantine World 300–700*, ed. Roger S. Bagnall, 47–66.
95 Goehring, "Pachomius," 48; Timm, *Das Christlich-Koptische Ägypten*, 80.
96 Coquin, "Akhmim," 78.
97 Kuhlmann, *Achmim*, 25–37; McNally and Schrunk, *Akhmim*, 10.
98 This work is thought to be the result of a collective authorship including Abu al-Makarim. See Johannes Den Heijer, "The Composition of the History of the Churches and Monasteries of Egypt: Some Preliminary Remarks," in *Acts of the Fifth International Congress of Coptic Studies*, ed. David Johnson (Rome: C.I.M., 1993), 209–219.
99 Abu Salih the Armenian, *The Churches & Monasteries of Egypt and Some Neighbouring Countries*, trans. B.T.A. Evetts (Oxford: The Clarendon Press, 1895), 242–244; Timm, *Das Christlich-Koptische Ägypten*, 89–90.
100 McNally, "Transformations," 82–84.
101 McNally, "Transformations."
102 McNally, "Transformations."

up around the monastic complexes. In the Pachomian tradition, monasteries were tightly linked with, and took their names from, the villages in which they were placed. This practice could have continued in non-Pachomian foundations as the monasteries relied on the villages for economic exchange and perhaps also served the spiritual needs of their populations.

It is not possible to discuss the monasteries' internal organisation, but it is relevant to emphasise that all but the three Pachomian foundations and the Monastery of the Seven Mountains were associated through their names with saints, martyrs or biblical figures. Two monasteries (the Monastery of the Martyrs and the Monastery of Bisadah the Bishop) contain the tombs of the martyrs with which they are associated. The association with saints through either the names of the monasteries or through relics kept within the monastic churches could imply that the majority (thirteen of seventeen) of monasteries in Akhmim to some extent were a part of Egypt's Medieval-period pilgrimage industry and relied on Christian visitors for revenue. Visitation to monastic sites is elaborated in Chapter 4.3.

Looking at the diachronic development of the congregations, Sheila McNally sees the construction of monasteries in the Akhmim area as intermittent into the Fatimid period (tenth–twelfth century). She described a gap in the Mamluk period (mid thirteenth–early sixteenth century) with renewed activity in the Ottoman period (sixteenth–nineteenth century), after which construction continued at a slower pace until the present.[103] It will be demonstrated in Chapters 3.9 and 5 that this development is consistent with the usage of the White Monastery federation.

1.3 THE ARCHITECTURE OF MONASTICISM

Life in the *coenobitic* communities was governed through extensive corpora of written rules. This is particularly evident in the White Monastery federation where Layton has identified more than five hundred rules among the surviving body of Shenoute's writings.[104] These rules regulated hierarchical roles, bodily behaviour in all contexts, attitudes and terminology.[105] They constituted an enormously complex social order and Layton has convincingly argued for a total re-socialization into the monastic world—a world replacement—in which the new monastic 'had to erase the structure of his or her former, non-monastic life and enter into this new, carefully ordered structure.'[106] This adopted way of life also affected the layout and forms of architecture within the monastic built environment, as certain structures were required to sustain this type of monastic lifestyle.

Much past archaeological research has focused on identifying and describing buildings considered relevant to the monastic lifestyle. Although my aim is to move beyond these studies of individual architectural units by applying a holistic approach, it is necessary to first discuss which buildings have traditionally been perceived as particular to monasticism, as well as define what architectural remains we can expect to find on the archaeological sites.[107] A brief overview of the organisation of the built environment in *coenobitic* monasteries with a generalised description of each component follows below. The purpose of this part of the chapter is to give a sense of the built environment with a few illustrative examples, rather than to provide an exhaustive list of features of the monasteries in which they occur.

1.3.1 The Organisation of the Built Environment

The term *coenobitic* has been used as a synonym for communal monasticism to make a distinction from other monastic forms. Some scholars have defined the *coenobitic* communities through their leadership and internal organisation, while others have sought a physical expression. In Schachner's definition, it was the wall, as an element of separation, and com-

103 McNally, "Transformations," 84.
104 Layton, "Social Structure;" Layton, "Rules;" Layton, *Canons of Our Fathers*.
105 Layton, "Rules," 59.
106 Layton, "Rules," 59.
107 By for example Grossmann, *Christliche Architektur*, and Walters, *Monastic Archaeology*.

munal participation in the table, prayer, liturgy and labour that stood apart from other forms of monasticism.[108] Emmel & Layton defined *coenobitism* as 'a communal monastery with an all-powerful abbot, communal worship and common food service, a rigid schedule of work and worship, an elaborate walled physical installation, and written rules.'[109] Svetlana Popovic further elaborated on the architectural components of a *coenobitic* monastery's built environment. She suggested that the monasteries should be divided into three functional zones that often were clustered into groups.[110] These are:

- a zone reserved for religious worship (churches, chapels and refectories);
- a zone for dwellings (cells, dormitories and structures to uphold the daily non-religious aspects of life);
- a zone for economic activities.

Beyond the rules and physical environment, a *coenobitic* monastery should be considered as a functional unit within society that housed, maintained and supported all needs of the monastics and at least to some degree was economically self-sufficient. The *Epistula Ammonis 20*—a trustworthy source, according to Wipszycka—claims that the Pachomian monastery in Pbow was home to no less than 600 monks in the 360s.[111]

Maintaining the monastic lifestyle of such a large population required a highly organised community, which contained structures to facilitate religious needs and required a functioning infrastructure. The most important element of the infrastructure was the water supply, which not only was used for drinking and food preparation, but also supplied various industrial processes and sanitary installations. Secondly, the network of thoroughfares and passageways linked the different parts of the monastery, which facilitated communication, the transport of goods and movement from one area to the next. The communal usage of the *coenobitic* monasteries and the number of monastics present in the communities meant that these aspects had to be planned in detail—the monastery could not be expanded in the same way as a household in a village, where an increase in numbers could mean constructing a new house with separate water supply, kitchen and sanitation. This would not be possible in a monastery where all members were expected to take a daily meal in the same area and attend the same church. I use the term *coenobitic* only in relation to monasteries belonging to either the Pachomian or the Shenoutian traditions.

1.3.2 *Individual Components*

The architectural elements discussed in this section are enclosure walls; keeps; churches; cells and dormitories; refectories, kitchens, and storerooms; latrines and baths; guesthouses and infirmaries; *scriptoria* and other workshops; gardens and orchards.[112]

ENCLOSURE WALLS

According to the *Life of Pachomius*, the monastic community at Tabennese enclosed the settlement with a wall before the church was built.[113] The story may not be historically accurate, but it nonetheless reflects the Pachomian emphasis upon the physical separation of the community from the outside world. With only one point of access—a gatehouse, guarded by a monk—the wall served to control the movement of the monastics as well as restrict and

108 Schachner, *Monasteries*, 1–2.
109 Emmel & Layton, "Pshoi."
110 Svetlana Popovic, "The 'Trapeza' in Cenobitic Monasteries: Architectural and Spiritual Contexts," *Dumbarton Oaks Papers* 52 (1998): 282. See also Svetlana Popovic, *The Architectural Iconography of the Late Byzantine Monastery* (Toronto: Canadian Institute of Balkan Studies, 1997); Popovic, "Byzantine Monastery;" Svetlana Popovic, "Dividing the Indivisible: The Monastery Space – Secular and Sacred," *Recueil des travaux de l'Institut d'études byzantines* XLIV (2007): 47–65.
111 Wipszycka, "Resources," 187.
112 For further elaboration of the monastic built environment, see also Brooks Hedstrom, *The Monastic Landscape*, 180–222.
113 Rousseau, *Pachomius*, 57–77.

record access. An enclosure wall is also mentioned in the writings of Shenoute.[114]

These enclosure walls were, according to Grossmann, not built for protective purposes but to demarcate the monastery and the lives of the monastics from the contemporary world. It was only at a later point in Egypt's history that the enclosure wall became fortified and began to serve as protection against raids and military instability.[115] Grossmann based his interpretation on a ninth-century reference to the fortification of the monasteries of Wadi Natrun by the Patriarch of Alexandria, Shenoute I (r. 859–880).[116]

The remains of enclosure walls have been excavated, for example, at the Monastery of Apollo at Bawit, at the monastery at Kom al-Nana at Amarna and at the Monastery of Jeremias at Saqqara,[117] but the best example is found at the monastery at Bala'izah, where the lower courses of the wall in most parts are preserved *in situ*. The monastery was built on a hillside and employed the vertical cliff as its western border. The three other sides of the settlement were enclosed by a wall, where a single gate in the south side gave access to the monastery.[118] According to Grossmann, the enclosure walls from Apa Apollo, Jeremias, and Bala'izah date to the seventh century.[119]

KEEPS

Towers of refuge or keeps are found in monasteries in all parts of Egypt. They served to protect the monastic inhabitants against violent intruders and were built in response to periods of increased raids and military instability.[120] The towers would normally consist of a square ground plan with several storeys. They were accessed via an inner staircase, ladder or drawbridge, which gave access to a doorway on the first floor.[121] The early version would commonly not contain a separate water supply, but this became essential in later versions of the towers. Some versions were also equipped with latrines and storage units for food.

More than thirty towers of refuge were found at Kellia, most dating to the first half of the fifth century.[122] Other examples are found in Wadi Natrun, Deir el-Muharraq, Deir Anba Hadra, St Anthony's, St Paul's, Kom al-Nana and Deir al-Fahuri (fig. 3).

CHURCHES

The churches served as the focal point of the monastery's religious life and as a gathering point for all monastics several times each day. Grossmann has dedicated a large part of his career to the study of churches in Egypt and has provided substantial evidence for their layout, use and development.[123] In the study of the life that unfolded within the enclosure walls, churches are essential, as they can inform us about the importance of the community, the wealth of the patrons, as well as suggest whether the church served members of non-monastic society, e.g., for baptism or pilgrimage.[124] This debate is further explored in Chapter 4.3.

114 Layton, "Rules," 69–70, 73.
115 Grossmann, *Christliche Architektur*, 307–315.
116 Mark N. Swanson, *The Coptic Papacy in Islamic Egypt 641–1517* (Cairo & New York: The American University in Cairo Press, 2010), 35.
117 Grossmann, *Christliche Architektur*, 307–308; Barry Kemp, "Kom el-Nana," in Anonymous, Editorial foreword, *Journal of Egyptian Archaeology* 80 (1994): vii–ix.
118 Grossmann, *Christliche Architektur*, fig. 147.
119 Grossmann, *Christliche Architektur*, 307–311.
120 Grossmann, *Christliche Architektur*, 303.
121 Grossmann, *Christliche Architektur*, 302.
122 Georges Descœudres, "Wohntürme in Klöstern und Ermitagen Ägyptens," in *Themelia: Spätantike und Koptologische Studien Peter Grossmann zum 65. Geburtstag*, ed. Martin Krause and Sofia Schate (Wiesbaden: Ludwig Reichert Verlag, 1998), 69–79.
123 See for example Peter Grossmann, *Kirche und spätantike Hausanlagen in Chnumtempelhof: Beschreibung und Typologische Untersuchung* (Mainz am Rhein: von Zabern, 1980); Peter Grossmann, *Mittelalterliche Langhauskuppelkirchen und verwandte Typen in Oberägypten: eine Studie zum mittelalterlichen Kirchenbau in Ägypten* (Glückstadt: J.J. Augustin, 1982); Peter Grossmann, *Abu Mina. I, Die Gruftkirche und die Gruft* (Mainz am Rhein: von Zabern, 1989); Grossmann, *Christliche Architektur*.
124 For a general discussion of the usage of churches, see Ann Marie Yasin, *Saints and Church Spaces in the Late Antique Mediterranean. Architecture, Cult and Community* (Cambridge: Cambridge University Press, 2009).

Fig. 3. Seventh-century keep at the Monastery of St Antony. Note drawbridge (photograph by the author).

CELLS AND DORMITORIES

The archaeological remains of dwellings are best documented in the *anchorite* societies where sites such as Esna, Kellia and the monastery of John the Little at Wadi Natrun offer extensive insights into the organisation of the monastics' daily life.[125] At Kellia, some monastic dwellings (*manshubiyat*) contained a kitchen and storage rooms, sleeping quarters, a room for receiving visitors, an oratory, rooms for a servant or disciple, a toilet and perhaps a small garden.[126] The cells of the monastics in the *coenobitic* monasteries are less well-documented. Shenoute's rules dictate that two to three monastics should share a single cell.[127] However, the lack of furniture in the archaeological record means that cells or dormitories can be difficult to identify and are easily mistaken for storerooms and vice versa. Some features, such as niches, could be expected, as they were used by the monastics to store personal items, but their presence

125 Nicola Aravecchia, "Hermitages and Spatial Analysis: Use of Space at the Kellia," in *Shaping Community: The Art and Archaeology of Monasticism*, ed. Sheila McNally (Oxford: Archaeopress, 2001); Stephen Davis et al., "Yale Monastic Archaeology Project: John the Little. Season 1 (June 7–27, 2006)," *Mishkah: The Egyptian Journal of Islamic Archaeology* 3 (2009): 47–52; Stephen Davis et al., "Yale Monastic Archaeological Project. Pherme (Qusur Higayla and Qusur 'Erayma). Season 1 (May 29–June 8, 2006)," *Mishkah: The Egyptian Journal of Islamic Archaeology* 3 (2009b): 53–5; Stephen Davis et al., "Yale Monastic Archaeology Project: John the Little, Season 2 (May 14–June 16, 2007)," *Mishkah: The Egyptian Journal of Islamic Archaeology* 3 (2009): 59–64; Serge Sauneron, Jean Jacquet and Helen Jacquet-Gordon, *Les Ermitages Chrétiens du Désert d'Esna* (Cairo: Institut français d'archéologie orientale du Caire, 1972).

126 See Gillian Pyke and Darlene L. Brooks Hedstrom, "The Afterlife of Sherds: Architectural Reuse Strategies at the Monastery of John the Little, Wadi Natrun," in *Functional Aspects of Egyptian Ceramics within their Archaeological Context*, ed. Bettina Bader and Mary Ownby (Leuven: Peeters, 2012), 307–326 for a description of a *manshubiya* at John the Little, Wadi Natrun.

127 Grossmann, *Christliche Architektur*, 272.

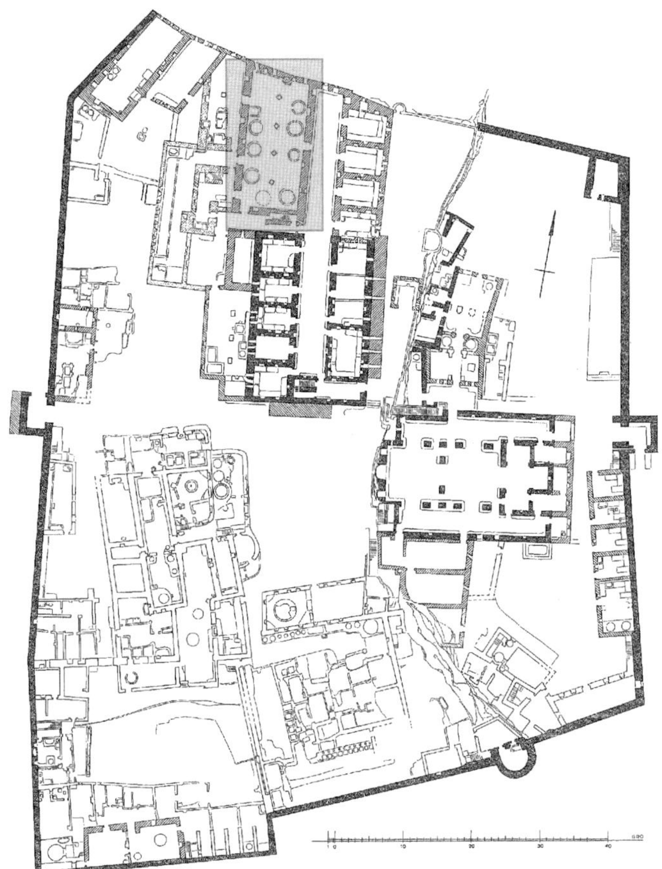

Fig. 4. Deir Anba Hadra, Aswan. Emphasis on refectory (modified from Monneret de Villard, *Les Couvents*, fig. 87).

is not requisite. Niches are also found in, e.g., oratories and refectories and therefore cannot act as a sole identifier: the location of the room in question and its proximity to other rooms or buildings with a known purpose must also be taken into consideration. A monastery in Ansina contains a structure that has been interpreted as a dormitory based on the structure's layout and location. It consists of eleven rectangular rooms, each measuring some 4 m by 10 m and each containing up to twelve wall niches. Following Grossmann's reconstruction, the larger of the rooms could contain up to eleven monastics.[128]

REFECTORIES, KITCHENS AND STOREROOMS

The refectory was an important centre for communal life in the *coenobitic* monasteries. The refectories were used for the consumption of food and in Shenoute's federation, all monastics would share a single daily meal at a fixed time. At other times of the day, a light meal (mostly bread) would be consumed in the cells.[129] The refectory can be identified in the archaeological record either through the presence of fixed benches and tables or by its proximity to the kitchen.

Grossmann suggests two basic layouts for the refectory. The first type consists of a room with fixed circular benches (fig. 4). Often, the benches were found within an open hall with a roof or second floor supported by pillars and with two or more aisles. Such refectories have been found in St Jeremias, Atripe, Deir Anba Hadra, and at Deir al-Bachit. Rooms with a similar layout, but without the remains of seating arrangements have in some cases been interpreted as refectories. This is the case at, for example, Deir al-Fahuri near Esna and at Bala'izah.

Grossmann's second type consists of a long hall with two long benches running parallel to a central table. Refectories of this type are found, for example, in the monasteries of St Antony and St Paul (fig. 5). The chronological development of the monasteries suggests that the former type—the large hall—was more commonly found in the earlier monasteries, although this form continued to be in use at least into the ninth century. The other type is of a later date and would be suitable for a monastery with fewer monastics.[130]

The *coenobitic* monastics' communal eating habits made further demands on the built environment.

128 Brooks Hedstrom has worked extensively on the monastic cell. See for example Darlene L. Brooks Hedstrom, "Your Cell will teach you all Things:" The Relationship between Monastic Practice and the Architectural Design of the Cell in Coptic Monasticism, 400–1000. Unpublished PhD, Miami University, 2001; Brooks Hedstrom, "Divine architects;" Darlene L. Brooks Hedstrom, "The Geography of the Monastic Cell in Early Egyptian Monastic Literature," *Church History* 78.4 (2009): 756–791.

129 Layton, "Rules," 48.

130 Grossmann, *Christliche Architektur*, 287.

In Shenoute's federation, where all members of the community were expected to take their main daily meal at the same time, sizeable facilities were required for food preparation and for the storage of food. Sustaining a population of several hundred monastics—even on an ascetic diet—made extensive demands on the capacity and organisation of the kitchen facilities in terms of obtaining, storing and managing the food supply. Unfortunately, these intricate aspects of monastic life have, in most cases, been overlooked in the archaeological record or superficially referred to without further exploration. An exception is Herbert E. Winlock and colleagues' monograph on the Monastery of Epiphanius.[131]

Similarly, storage rooms are often not identified in the archaeological record or are confused with dormitories or refectories. The architectural forms associated with these two structures—a large open pillared hall or a building constituted by several equally shaped rooms on either side of a long hall—could also have been used for storage or, in the case of the former type, for communal activities that left no physical traces behind. Shenoute refers in his writings to the *diakonia*, which was an administration that also served as a storage place for foodstuffs. This building is discussed in Chapter 4.1.1.

Fig. 5. Seventh century refectory in the Monastery of St Antony (photograph by the author).

LATRINES AND BATHS

Latrines were presumably a necessity in the larger *coenobitic* communities in order to maintain a basic standard of hygiene. Unfortunately, latrines are rarely found in the archaeological record and neither Shenoute nor Pachomius offer advice on this subject.

John Moschos' reports on the death of Nestorius, who was archbishop of Constantinople from 428, but condemned for heresy in 431 and exiled to the Kharga Oasis.[132] According to Moschos, Nestorius died on his privy, which is described as a small room set apart from the rest of his living quarters. Here, Nestorius was found by his guards, seated and dead. As such, Moschos' description corresponds with the few archaeological examples found in Egypt. At Kellia, latrines were located in the cells in the far corner of the courtyards, opposite the main living area and at the North Tombs Settlement at Amarna, a small square structure was found fifteen metres from the main dwelling above an almost vertical drop. Deir Anba Hadra near Aswan contained a latrine with seats placed in stalls immediately next to each other. The latrine was flushed with water from the drains of the monastic baths. This is the only known example of a monastic bath, with the possible exception of the White Monastery (see Chapter 3.6).[133]

131 Winlock, Crum and Evelyn-White, *Monastery*, 53–55.
132 John Moschos, *The Spiritual Meadow (Pratum Spirituale)* (Kalamazoo, Michigan: Cistercian Publications, 1994), 197–198. See also Crislip, "The Red Monastery," 5.
133 Ugo Monneret de Villard, *Il Monastero di S. Simeone presso Aswan* (Milano: Tipografie e Libreria Pontificia Arcivescovile S. Giuseppe, 1927), 25–33.

The general lack of latrines in the archaeological record is very likely a result of a focus on the nucleus of settlements by past excavators. In the few known examples, the latrines are located at the community's periphery, where the unpleasant smells would cause a minimal discomfort for the monastics. This was the case in the Monastery of Martyrius in the Judean desert, where a rectangular room by the entrance to the monastery served as a latrine.[134] Here, an open conduit ran along the side of the room, which allowed the waste to be drained outside the monastery's wall. The hot and dry climate in Egypt's deserts means, however, that most monasteries would not have had the capacity to drain the latrines with water. Therefore, cesspits were used that would collect the sewage and be emptied manually from time to time. A newly discovered latrine in the monastery in Ghazali, Sudan, consists of fifteen stalls with cesspits located immediately next to each other, but separated by walls.[135] Here, wooden seats were placed on top of ceramic pipes that gave access to the cesspits.

GUESTHOUSES AND INFIRMARIES

Guesthouses and infirmaries are known from the monastic rules. Pachomius' *Rules* refers to guesthouses where prospective monks as well as visitors to the *koinobion* would stay. From the sixth century onwards, these guesthouses possibly also housed pilgrims visiting the monasteries. In Pachomius' *koinonia* these houses were located on the outside of the walls. As such, they are seldom found in the archaeological record as excavations tend to focus on the intra-mural remains. A building interpreted as a guesthouse has been identified just south of the entrance to Deir al-Bala'izah.[136] According to Shenoute's writings, prospective monastics, tradesmen and visitors to his federation would stay in the gatehouse, which may have meant that in the early version of the White Monastery, there would not have been a need for a separate guesthouse.

Infirmaries for sick monastics are also found in references, but are difficult to identify in the archaeological record as their layout could just as well be interpreted as cellblocks, refectories or storage facilities. Andrew Crislip has worked extensively on the textual references to the monastic hospitals, but did not include archaeological remains in his study.[137]

SCRIPTORIA AND LIBRARIES

In Late Antiquity, the production of books was primarily if not exclusively carried out in the monasteries.[138] The monks copied, illustrated, and bound the books for the use of individual monks, for the community as a whole and for non-monastics in return for commissions.[139] The requirements of the built environment were a *scriptorium* and a library although books were also produced and stored in less official surroundings.[140] In the Pachomian monasteries, the monks were compelled to learn how to read upon joining the monastic community. Each monastery

134 Yizhar Hirschfeld, *The Judean Desert Monasteries in the Byzantine Period* (New Haven & London: Yale University Press, 1992), 97.
135 Artur Obłuski, personal communication with author, 2014. See also Włodzimierz Godlewkski, "Monastic Life in Makuria," in *Christianity and Monasticism in Aswan and Nubia*, ed. Gawdat Gabra and Hany N. Takla (Cairo & New York: The American University in Cairo Press, 2013), 173.
136 Grossmann, *Christliche Architektur*, fig. 147.
137 Andrew Crislip, *From Monastery to Hospital: Christian Monasticism and the Transformation of Health Care in Late Antiquity* (Ann Arbor: University of Michigan Press, 2005). See also Andrew Crislip, *Thorns in the Flesh: Illness and Sanctity in Late Antique Christianity* (Philadelphia: University of Pennsylvania Press, 2013).
138 Chrysi Kotsifou, "Books and Book Production in the Monastic Communities of Byzantine Egypt," in *The Early Christian Book*, ed. William E. Klinhshirn and Linda Safran (Washington, DC: The Catholic University of America Press, 2007), 50; Chrysi Kotsifou, "Bookbinding and Manuscript Illumination in Late Antique and Early Medieval Monastic Circles in Egypt," in *Eastern Christians and their Written Heritage: Manuscripts, Scribes and Context*, ed. Juan P. Monferrer-Sala, Herman G.B. Teule and Sofia Torallas Tovar (Leuven, Paris & Walpole, MA: Peeters, 2012), 213–244.
139 Kotsifou, "Books and Book Production," 66.
140 Kotsifou rejects the use of the term *scriptorium*, due to its connotation with Western Monasticism. She argues that such institutions were not found within Late Antique Egyptian monasteries (Kotsifou, "Bookbinding," 216).

contained a library from which the monastics could borrow a book to read in their cell.[141]

Colophons document that manuscripts were given as gifts from one monastery to another. The White Monastery, for example, received manuscripts from the Monastery of St Michael at Pantoou in the Fayoum, while at the same time producing manuscripts for other monasteries, such as the Monastery of the Virgin in the desert of Apa Shenoute, as stated in a colophon.[142] Libraries have been attested through colophons or other textual sources in, for example, the Monastery of Phoibammon, in the Pachomian monasteries, in Nag Hammadi, in the Fayoum, at the White Monastery, at Bala'izah and in Wadi Natrun.[143] The library in the Monastery of St Macarius seems to have been particularly important as it received annual funds from the Emperor.[144] In relation to the monasteries of Wadi Natrun, Evelyn-White noted that the library was located in the church during the early history of the monastery, but was moved to a room on the second floor of the tower of refuge to protect the books from raids.[145] Evelyn-White also suggested that binding and repairing was carried out in an adjoining workroom, while book copying took place in a common room, perhaps in the library itself, in the large hall of the tower or perhaps even in the cells of the monks.[146]

Neither *scriptoria* nor libraries demanded specific requirements in their architectural layout and all materials used were portable. These rooms are very difficult to identify in the archaeological record, unless painted inscriptions on the walls suggest that the room was used to store manuscripts, as was the case in the White Monastery (see Chapter 2.3).

OTHER WORKSHOPS

Evidence for the production of wine, oil, pottery, textiles and other goods is found among archaeological remains as well as referred to in literary and documentary sources. The monasteries needed such products to sustain daily life, but they were also produced at a larger scale to provide an income for the monasteries. Such production is dealt with in Chapters 4 and 5 and will, therefore, not be further elaborated here.

GARDENS AND ORCHARDS

Gardens and orchards are frequently referred to in hagiographies and in other literary sources.[147] The only example identified through archaeological excavation comes from the Monastery at Kom al-Nana, Amarna, where 'a substantial area [was] given over to the cultivation of trees, so forming an artificial oasis.'[148] Within an enclosed area, trees were planted in small square plots separated by furrows for the equal distribution of water.[149] It has not been pos-

141 Martin Krause, "Libraries," in *The Coptic Encyclopedia*, edited by Aziz S. Atiya (New York: Macmillan Publishing, 1991b), 1447–1450.

142 Réne-Georges, Coquin and Maurice Martin, S.J, "Dayr Anba Shinudah. History," in *The Coptic Encyclopedia*, ed. Aziz S. Atiya, 763; Stephen Emmel, "The Library of the Monastery of the Archangel Michael at Phantoou (al-Hamuli)," in *Christianity and Monasticism in the Fayoum Oasis*, ed. Gawdat Gabra, (Cairo & New York: The American University in Cairo Press, 2005), 68.

143 Paul E. Kahle, *Bala'izah. Coptic texts from Deir el-Bala'izah in Upper Egypt* (London: Oxford University Press, 1954); Krause, "Libraries."

144 Krause, "Libraries," 1449. Krause does not mention which emperor.

145 Evelyn-White & Hauser, *Monasteries*, xliv.

146 Evelyn-White & Hauser, *Monasteries*, xlv–xlvi.

147 In relation to the White Monastery see Besa, *Life*, 82; Abu Salih the Armenian, *The Churches & Monasteries*, 237.

148 Kemp, "Kom el-Nana," vii–ix. See also Barry Kemp, "Amarna's other Period," *Egyptian Archaeology* 3 (1993): 13–14, Barry Kemp, "Kom el-Nana," in Anonymous, Editorial foreword, *Journal of Egyptian Archaeology* 79, (1993): vi–vii; Barry Kemp, "Tell el-Amarna, 2000," in "Fieldwork, 1999–2000: Sais, Memphis, Tell el-Amarna, Tell el-Amarna Glass Project, Qasr Ibrim," ed. Penelope Wilson, David Jeffreys, Janine Bourriau, W. Raymond Johnson, Barry Kemp, Paul T. Nicholson and Pamela Rose, *Journal of Egyptian Archaeology* 86 (2000): 12–14.

149 Anna Stevens, personal communication with author, 2008.

sible to identify what was planted in the gardens of Kom el-Nana, although Wendy Smith has provided a thorough study of the archaeobotanical remains from the monastery.[150]

150 Wendy Smith, *Archaeobotanical Investigations of Agriculture at Late Antique Kom el-Nana (Tell el-Amarna)* (London: Egypt Exploration Society, 2003).

Chapter 2

FRAMING THE WHITE MONASTERY
HISTORY, HISTORIOGRAPHY, AND ARCHAEOLOGY

This chapter examines earlier scholarship on the White Monastery and reconstructs the history of the complex by employing a variety of sources, including writings by Christian and Muslim authors (among these the extensive textual corpus that is associated with the White Monastery library), inscriptions left by monastics and visitors, archaeological remains, travelers' accounts and photographic material. The scarce nature of the sources means that it is not possible to separate history from historiography and the two are therefore discussed together. The sources are addressed chronologically according to their subject rather than their date of origin.

I begin with the foundation of the monastery and the first five abbots (Chapter 2.2), followed by a summary of its history from the sixth to the sixteenth century (Chapter 2.3). Chapter 2.4 contains an analysis of the observations made by European travelers from the seventeenth century onwards, and Chapter 2.5 addresses the first systematic exploration of the monastery. The last part of the chapter revisits the two archaeological missions that preceded the White Monastery Project. A historical overview has been summarised in table 3.

The textual sources on the White Monastery are biased towards the monastery's early history. As a consequence, most scholarly attention has been directed at the works of Shenoute, and the organisation of the early monastery has been well-studied, while little is known about its later developments. Here, I will attempt to reconstruct a historical trajectory from the textual sources that will provide a contextual setting for the archaeological remains. I will begin with a brief review of the context in which the White Monastery was formed.

2.1 THE WHITE MONASTERY BEFORE THE MONKS

The occupational history of the area before the Pharaonic period (3100–332 BCE) is scarce, but the archaeological findings of a number of pre-dynastic slate palettes along with contemporary pottery at Akhmim, suggests that a settlement existed here in the Neolithic period (6000–3200 BCE).[151] The archaeological exploration of the White Monastery has not yielded material of such an early date, but from the Pharaonic period onwards, material remains are found in abundance on both sides of the Nile. These remains include a series of rock-cut tombs that line the cliff-face immediately west of the White Monastery and numerous re-used building blocks found throughout the archaeological site.[152] These Pharaonic remains led Herman Kees to suggest that the

151 McNally and Schrunk, *Akhmim*, 1.

152 Yahia El-Masry, "Recent Explorations in the Ninth Nome of Upper Egypt," in *Egyptology at the Dawn of the Twenty-First Century, Proceedings of the Eight International Congress of Egyptologists, Cairo 2000*, ed. Zahi Hawass and Lyla Pinch Brock (Cairo: The American University in Cairo Press, 2002), 331–338.

YEAR	EVENT
The foundation of the White Monastery and its first five abbots	
c. 350	Foundation of the White Monastery by former Pachomian monk Pcol.
370s	White Monastery led by monk named Ebnoh.
385	Shenoute assumes leadership of the White Monastery and its federation.
5th cent.	Shenoute reports on providing for 20.000 refugees for three months.
466	Death of Shenoute. Besa assumes leadership of the White Monastery federation.
5th/6th cent.	Death of Besa. Zenobios, a former physician and secretary to Shenoute, now lead the White Monastery.
The White Monastery in the Medieval period	
567	A monk named Peter is mentioned as priest and *archimandrite* of the Monastery of St. Shenoute.
6th cent.	Koursios, son of Joseph is mentioned in a papyri as an administrator of the monastery.
709	Papyrus refers to the monastery of St. Shenoute in the nome of Panopolis.
8th cent.	Apa Seth is mentioned as *archimandrite* of the monastery of St. Shenoute. The unfortunate visit of al-Qasim ibn Ubaydallah to the White Monastery is recorded.
866	The Abbasid civil war affected the Monastery of St. Shenoute. No details are recorded.
927–940	Chael is mentioned as *archimandrite* in two colophons. A contemporary colophon mentions Basil as steward of the White Monastery.
10th cent.	Apa Ioustos is mentioned as ruler of the monastic congregation.
11th cent.	Relics of the two apostles Bartholomew and Simon the Zealot are reported by HPA to be kept in the White Monastery.
1124	Paintings in church domes by Armenian artist.
1137–1139	Bahram, former vizier, retired to the White Monastery. Possible Armenian community in the monastery.
1167	Manuscripts were looted from the White Monastery during the Ayyubid incursion. According to Abu al-Makarim, the body of Shenoute was hidden during the invasion.
1259	Structural repairs in church after earthquake, under the leadership of John the *archimandrite*.
13th cent.	Yaḳut refers to the White Monastery, using this name for the first time.
1301	A monk named Macurius visits the monastery.
14th/ 15th cent.	The White Monastery is described to be in ruins with only the church standing.
1563	Ethiopian inscription in ciborium in church nave witness settlement in nave and perhaps also Ethiopian caravan station.
The White Monastery 'discovered': European Travellers on the Nile	
1673	Vansleb visited the White Monastery. He referred to monks residing inside the church.
1731	Granger visited the White Monastery.
1737	Pococke visited the White Monastery.
1738	Members of the exhibition led by Norden visited the White Monastery.
1742	Perry visited the monastery and associated, for the first time, the monastery with a large corpus of Coptic manuscripts.
18th cent.	Cardinal Stefano Borgia purchased folios and fragments from the White Monastery library without realising their provenance.
c.1800	Denon visited the White Monastery the day after an attack by a group of 'Mamlukes'.
1802	Collapsed SW corner of church was rebuilt.
1812	Raid on monastery, recorded by Curzon.
1833	Curzon visited the White Monastery.

Table 3. Overview of the history of the White Monastery.

YEAR	EVENT
1847	Wilkinson included the White Monastery in a handbook for travellers in Egypt.
The continued Legacy: Modern Exploration and Re-appropriation	
1858	Construction of railway on the western side of the Nile with a station in Sohag permanently changes the local demography. Sohag rapidly grows, while Akhmim stagnates. Access to the White Monastery is now easily obtained.
19th cent.	Maspero purchased 3500 folios and fragments from the White Monastery. Somers Clarke visits the White Monastery on several occasions in the late 19th and early 20th centuries. This resulted in the beginning interest in the monastery and in major publications by among others Amélineau and Leipoldt.
1901	De Bock visits the White Monastery.
1906	The Comité purchased the White Monastery church.
1907	Petrie excavates at the White Monastery.
1907-1911	The Comité restores the White Monastery Church and evicts the villagers who lived within the nave. As a part of this work, Monneret de Villard produced the first detailed plan of the church.
1962	The Technical Institute of Darmstadt, Germany carried out a structural survey, producing plans and scale models of the monastic church.
1980s	Meinardus reports that the church has once again been transformed into a village.
1985	The SCA begins their work at the archaeological site.
1993	Emmel submitted his doctoral thesis on the codiocological reconstruction of Shenoute's literary corpus.
1996	Pope Shenoute III re-established the White Monastery with Wissa, the current abbot, as head of the monastery.
2000	Emmel and a team of international scholars began to translate and interpret Shenoute's writings.
2005	The White Monastery Project commenced.

Table 3 (cont.). Overview of the history of the White Monastery.

White Monastery was constructed on the site of an earlier temple dedicated to the Egyptian god Horus, but the archaeological evidence does not support this interpretation.[153] On the contrary, David Klotz has identified the origin of the building blocks as Abydos, Nag al-Mesheyeki, Ptolemais, and the temple of Repyt at nearby Atripe.[154] He dates the earliest blocks to the ninth century BCE, while the majority is of Ptolemaic origin (323–30 BCE).

Written sources create a vivid image of Akhmim in the Roman period, but do not report on any settlement in the area of the White Monastery.

2.2 THE FOUNDATION OF THE WHITE MONASTERY AND ITS FIRST FIVE ABBOTS (FOURTH TO SIXTH CENTURIES)

The main sources associated with the early history of the White Monastery are the writings of Shenoute, the monastery's third leader, and the writings of his successor Besa.[155] Further information may be obtained from the Coptic list of saints (the *Synaxarion* of Upper Egypt), from *typika*, chronicles

153 Hermann Kees, "Kulttopographische und Mythologische Beiträge," *Zeitschrift für ägyptische Sprache und Altertumskunde* 63–64 (1929): 266–282; David Klotz, "Triphis in the White Monastery: Reused Temple Blocks from Sohag," *Ancient Society* 40 (2010): 199.

154 Klotz, "Triphis;" David Klotz, "A Naos of Nectanebo I from the White Monastery Church (Sohag)," *Göttinger Miszellen* 229 (2011): 37–52. See also Petrie, *Athribis*; Rafed El-Sayed, "Schenute und die Tempel von Atripe. Zur Umnutzung des Triphisbezirks in der Spätantike," in *Honi soit qui mal y pense. Studium zum Pharaonischen, Griechisch-Römischen und Spätantiken Ägypten zu Ehren von Heinz-Josef Thissen*, ed. Hermann Knuf, Christian Leitz and Daniel von Recklinghausen (Leuven & Walpole, MA: Peeters, 2010), 519–539.

155 Emmel, *Shenoute*; Karl H. Kuhn, *The Works of Besa, from a MS in the British Museum* (Unpublished Ph.D. thesis, University of Durham, 1952); Karl H. Kuhn, "A

and hagiographies that refer to the first leaders of the monastery. These latter sources, however, postdate the monastery's first five abbots and should be approached with the caution that their long and complex history of transmission warrants.

The White Monastery was founded by the monk Pcol around the middle of the fourth century. From a chronicle, referred to by Emmel and Layton, it seems that Pcol had been a monk in a Pachomian monastery.[156] He left his monastic community for reasons unknown, founded a new monastery and rewrote the rules of Pachomius by adding new rules and making the existing rules more ascetically severe.[157] Shenoute—our main source for the early monastery—does not mention the first leader by name, but simply refers to a first father, who was a direct disciple of Pachomius.[158] He does, however, name a man called Ebonh as the successor of the first father. Ebonh appears to have led the community during the 370s, but was replaced by Shenoute following a crisis in the monastic leadership.[159]

A hagiographic text known as the *Life of Shenoute* and attributed to Shenoute's successor Besa (the validity of this source is discussed below) reports that Shenoute was born around 347 in Shandawil, a village on the west bank of the Nile in the region of Akhmim.[160] He entered monastic service as a child, supposedly becoming a monk around 370 and assuming the role of the third abbot of the White Monastery in 385.[161]

From Shenoute's own letters we know that during his leadership he was in contact with four patriarchs of Alexandria: Timothy I (r. 380–385), Theophilus (r. 385–412), Cyril I (r. 412–444) and Dioscorus (r. 444–451).[162] The *Life* further reports that he accompanied Cyril I to the Council of Ephesus in 431, to bear witness against the archbishop of Constantinople, Nestorius (r. 428–431), who was exiled to Egypt.[163]

The fame of the White Monastery as a bastion of Egyptian monasticism results directly from Shenoute's reputation, and the early history of the White Monastery is intimately linked to his character. Under Shenoute's rule, the monastery played the role of the leading partner of three federated *coenobitic* communities.[164] Aside from the White Monastery, the federation included a women's foundation in the village to the south in the ruined Ptolemaic temple site of Atripe and a smaller men's congregation to the north, commonly known in Western scholarship as the Red Monastery. The federation also included male and female hermits living alone in the desert and for part of his life Shenoute followed this lifestyle.[165] Johannes Leipoldt estimated that the monas-

Fifth Century Egyptian Abbot. I. Besa and his Background," *Journal of Theological Studies* (1954): 36–48; Karl H. Kuhn, "A Fifth Century Egyptian Abbot. II. Monastic life in Besa's Day," *Journal of Theological Studies* (1954): 174–187; Karl H. Kuhn, "A Fifth Century Egyptian Abbot. III. Besa's Christianity," *Journal of Theological Studies* (1955): 35–48; Karl H. Kuhn, *Letters and Sermons of Besa*, 2 vols. Corpus Scriptorum Christianorum Orientalium (Louvain: Imprimerie Orientaliste, 1956).

156 Emmel & Layton, "Pshoi," 12.

157 Emmel & Layton, "Pshoi," 12.

158 Tito Orlandi, "The Library of the Monastery of Saint Shenoute at Atribe," in *Perspectives on Panopolis. An Egyptian Town from Alexander the Great to the Arab Conquest*, ed. A. Egberts, Brian Paul Muhs, Joep Van der Vliet (Leiden, Boston, Köln: Brill, 2002), 211.

159 Emmel, *Shenoute*, vol. 2, 558–564; Stephen Emmel, "Shenoute's Place in the History of Monasticism," in *Christianity and Monasticism in Upper Egypt*, ed. Gawdat Gabra and Hany N. Takla (Cairo & New York: The American University in Cairo Press, 2008), 37. See also Stephen Emmel, "Shenoute the Monk: The Early Monastic Career of Shenoute the Archimandrite," in *Il Monachesimo tra editā e aperture: atti del Simposio "Testi e temi nella Tradizione del monachesimo Cristiano" per il 50 anniversario dell'Instituto Monastico di Sant'Anselmo. Roma, 28 maggio–1 giugno 2002*, ed. Maciej Bielawski and Daniel Hombergen (Rome: Centro Studi Sant' Anselmo, 2004), 151–174.

160 Besa, *Life*, 42.

161 Besa, *Life*, 8.

162 Samuel Moawad, "The Relationship of St. Shenoute of Atripe with his Contemporary Patriarchs of Alexandria," in *Christianity and Monasticis*, ed. Gabra and Takla, 109. See also Crislip, "The Red Monastery."

163 Besa, *Life*, 47, 78; Emmel, *Shenoute*, 8; David W. Johnson, "Nestorius," in *The Coptic Encyclopedia*, ed. Aziz S. Atiya (New York: Macmillan Publishing Company, 1991), 1786.

164 Layton, "Social Structure," 26.

165 Besa, *Life*, 82; Layton, "Rules," 47; Johannes Leipoldt, *Schenute von Atripe und die Entstehung des national aegyptischen Christentums* (Leipzig: J.C. Hinrichs, 1903), 95–96.

tic landholdings under Shenoute amounted to more than 50 km^2.[166] The *Life* reports that at the time of Shenoute's death in 465, at the improbably advanced age of 118, the monastic federation had expanded to include 2200 monks and 1800 nuns.[167] My research suggests that this number is highly inflated—this issue will be addressed in Chapters 4 and 5.

Shenoute's fame in modern scholarship derives from his extensive writings. Emmel has concluded that Shenoute's work was transmitted in two main collections: in nine volumes of Canons (letters) and eight volumes of Discourses (public sermons).[168] This extensive corpus played an important part in the formation of the Coptic literary tradition.[169] Although Shenoute was not the first author to use Coptic extensively, he 'brought the language to a peak of literary quality which subsequent authors would struggle to attain.'[170] The codices survived through continuous copying over the centuries—the versions preserved today date mainly from the tenth to the twelfth centuries and preserve about 10–15% of the original texts.[171] They provide an extraordinarily detailed picture of Christian life in the period from 385 to 466, and offer a unique insight into aspects of monastic life and organisation. However, the nature of the texts and the purpose of their transmission mean that there are no documentary sources pertinent to the monastery's economic life.[172]

The interest in Shenoute's writings began in the late eighteenth century with the dispersal of the White Monastery library collection (see Chapter 2.5). Georg Zoega was the first to acknowledge Shenoute's writings as an important topic in the early nineteenth century,[173] and some one hundred years later, Emile Amélineau undertook a massive publication project of Shenoute's own work,[174] as well as texts that were relevant to Shenoute.[175] Leipoldt published a monograph on Shenoute's life in 1903. This monumental work resulted in the general scholarly assumption that everything that could be said about Shenoute had been said—an assumption that lasted into the 1980s and only changed with the completion of Emmel's doctoral dissertation on the codicological reconstruction of Shenoute's literary corpus.[176] In 2000, a team of international scholars, led by Emmel, set out to edit, translate and interpret Shenoute's writings.[177] This project is now drawing towards its end, but several publications are still forthcoming. So far, Anne Boud'hors' edition has been published.[178]

Emmel's work has inspired a renewed interest in Shenoute, which has led to a variety of thematic studies. These include, but are not limited to, Shenoute's relation to the women of the White Monastery, monastic perspectives on the body, the care of the sick, attitudes towards poverty, and pilgrimage.[179] Of particular importance for this study is the work

166 Leipoldt, *Schenute*, 95–96; Kuhn, "Besa and his Background," 37.
167 Emile Amélineau, *Monuments pour servir à l'histoire de l'Égypte chrétienne* (Paris: Ernest Leroux, 1888–1895), 331; Leipoldt, *Schenute*, 93–94.
168 Emmel, *Shenoute*, 4; Layton, "Rules," 45–46.
169 Orlandi, "Library," 224.
170 Heike Behlmer, "Do not believe every word like the fool…! Rhetorical Strategies in Shenoute, Canon 6," in *Christianity and Monasticism in Upper Egypt*, ed. Gabra and Takla, 1.
171 Emmel, "Shenoute's Place," 33.
172 Wipszycka, "Resources," 235.
173 Georg Zoega, *Catalogus Codicum Copticorum Manu Scriptorum Qui in Museo Bordiano Velitris Adservantur* (Repr. ed. Hildesheim & New York: Georg Olms Verlag [1973]: 1810).
174 Emile Amélineau, *Œuvres de Shenoudi: Texte Copte et Traduction Francaise*, 2 vols. (Paris: Ernest Leroux, 1907–1914).
175 Amélineau, *Monuments.*
176 Submitted to Yale University in 1993, published 2004 (Emmel, *Shenoute*).
177 The editorial team consists of Heike Behlmer, Anne Boud'hors, David Brakke, Andrew Crislip, Jean-Louis Fort, Bentley Layton, Samual Moawad, Zlatko Pleše, Tonio Sebastian Richter, Tito Orlandi, Sofia Torallas Tovar and Frederik Wisse. For an overview of the project, see Emmel, "Shenoute's Place," 34.
178 Anne Boud'hors, *Le Canon 8 de Chénouté: d'après le Manuscrit IFAO Copte 2 et les Fragments Complémentaires* (Cairo: Institut Français d'Archéologie Orientale, 2013); See also Layton's reconstructed corpus of monastic rules (Layton, *Canons*).
179 Krawiec, "Shenoute & Women;" Rebecca Krawiec, "The Role of the Female Elder in Shenoute's White Monastery," in *Christianity and Monasticism in Upper Egypt*, ed. Gabra and Takla, 59–71 (women); Caroline T. Schroeder, *Monastic Bodies: Discipline and Salvation in Shenoute of Atribe* (Philadelphia: University of Pennsylvania Press,

of Layton, who has examined the monastic organisational structure and its everyday life.[180]

Returning to the *Life of Shenoute*, a single complete version of this text has survived the centuries. This version was written in Bohairic—the Coptic dialect spoken in northern Egypt, and in the Medieval-period the lingua franca of Coptic liturgy—and entrusted to the library of the Monastery of St Macarius in Wadi Natrun in 935.[181] It bears the full title *A few of the miracles and marvels which God effected through our holy father the prophet Apa Shenoute, the priest and archimandrite, which the holy Apa Besa, his disciple, witnessed.*[182] Fragmented versions of the *Life* have also survived in Sahidic (the Coptic dialect spoken in southern Egypt), Arabic, Ethiopic and Syriac.[183] The Arabic version is more than double the length of the Bohairic as it contains material that does not exist in the other version, including several miracle accounts and further elaborations on existing stories.[184] Ascribed to Shenoute's successor Besa, its presumed antiquity gave the text great authority among modern scholars in the study of Shenoute's life and the early history of the White Monastery.

Recently, however, Nina Lubomierski has shown that Besa was not the author of the *Life*.[185] Instead, she argues, the many versions reflect a complex process of elaboration in and through liturgical practices, put together from eulogies that contained episodes of Shenoute's life, many of which were the product of his followers' 'pious imagination.'[186] Lubomierski convincingly argues that the attribution to Besa was made at some later (undated) stage, to give authority to the text.[187]

The purpose of the text was to convey the wonders of Shenoute's biography, rather than provide an accurate historical account of events that could be of interest to future researchers studying Egyptian monasticism. The *Life* should accordingly be acknowledged as a hagiographical composition and used with caution.[188] It is possible to extract circumstantial information from the *Life* that relates to aspects of monastic organisation and structure that very likely could be found within the monastery, but cannot be precisely dated. The text should be seen as reflecting evolving monastic realities over the extended period of the text's liturgical formation rath-

2007) (the body); Andrew Crislip, *From Monastery to Hospital*; Andrew Crislip, "Care for the Sick in Shenoute's Monasteries," in *Christianity and Monasticism in Upper Egypt*, ed. Gabra and Takla, 21–30 (the sick); Ariel G. Lopez, *Shenoute of Atripe and the Uses of Poverty: Rural Patronage, Religious Conflict and Monasticism in Late Antique Egypt* (Berkeley, CA: University of California Press, 2013) (poverty); David Frankfurter, *Religion in Roman Egypt. Assimilation and Resistance* (Princeton: Princeton University Press, 1998); Janet Timbie, "A Liturgical Procession in the Desert of Apa Shenoute," in *Pilgrimage and Holy Space in Late Antique Egypt*, ed. David Frankfurter (Leiden, Boston Köln: Brill, 1998), 415–444; Janet Timbie, "Once More into the Desert of Apa Shenoute: Further Thoughts on BN 68," in *Christianity and Monasticism in Upper Egypt*, ed. Gabra and Takla, 169–17; Peter Grossmann, "Zum Grab des Schenute," *Journal of Coptic Studies* 6 (2004): 83–103 (pilgrimage).

180 Especially Layton, "Social Structure;" Layton, "Rules;" Layton, *Canons*.

181 Stephen J. Davis, "Shenoute in Scetis: New Archaeological Evidence for the Cult of a Monastic Saint in Early Medieval Wadi al-Natrun," *Coptica* 14 (2015): 16.

182 Emmel, "Shenoute's Place," 35; Nina Lubomierski, "The Coptic Life of Shenoute," in *Christianity and Monasticism in Upper Egypt*, ed. Gabra and Takla, 91.

183 Bohairic: Amélineau, *Monuments*, 1–99; Johannes Leipoldt, *Shenithii Archimandritae Vita et Opera Omnia*, 3 vols, Corpus Scriptorum Christianorum Orientalium 41, 42, 73 (Paris: Imprimerie Nationale, 1906–1913). Sahidic: Arthur F. Shore, "Extracts of Besa's Life of Shenoute in Sahidic," *Journal of Egyptian Archaeology* 65 (1979): 134–139. Arabic: Amélineau, *Monuments*, 289–480. Ethiopic: Gérard Colin, *La Version Éthiopienne de la Vie de Schenoudi*, Corpus Scriptorum Christianorum Orientalium 444, 445 (Leuven: Peeters, 1982). Syriac: François N. Nau, "Une version syriaque inédite de la Vie de Schenoudi," *Revue sémitique d'épigraphie et d'histoire ancienne* 7 (1899): 357–363; 8 (1900): 153–167, 252–265.

184 Lubomierski, "Coptic Life," 92.

185 Emmel, "Shenoute's Place," 36; Nina Lubomierski, *Die Vita Sinuthii: Form- und Überlieferungsgeschichte der hagiographischen Texte über Schenute den Archimandriten*, Studien und Texte zu Antike und Christentum 45 (Tübingen: Mohr Siebeck, 2007), Lubomierski, "Coptic Life."

186 Lubomierski, "Coptic Life," 96–97. See also Davis, "Shenoute," 16.

187 Lubomierski, "Coptic Life," 97.

188 Besa, *Life*, 6.

er than as an empirical account of events that took place in Shenoute's lifetime.

Some passages in the *Life* are, however, of interest to this study, either because they are repetitions or variations of stories found within Shenoute's own writings or because they relate to the monastery's built environment and can be viewed alongside the physical remains of the site. References to Shenoute's extensive building programme, for example, are frequent and include the mention of a well and a church.[189] Both structures feature prominently within the archaeological remains and their foundation is attested in Shenoute's own writings. Several miracle stories involve the production and distribution of bread. One mentions a grain mill and the making of flour within the monastic walls, while another speaks of eleven bread ovens that produced bread for the entire congregation.[190] Two stories refer to the bread-store and to the brother in charge of the structure.[191] Bread was an essential part of the monastic diet, so it is not surprising to find that the continuous supply would have been a concern for the monastics and thus a subject for miraculous stories.[192] Other stories mention a vegetable garden, nearby orchards and fields that were cultivated by the monastery and some even refer to the consumption of wine in the monastery, although there is no reference to its production.[193]

A couple of stories mention charitable work carried out by Shenoute and the White Monastery. In one, several hundred people took refuge in the complex and were fed during a drought. On another occasion, Shenoute rescued captives from the Blemmyes,[194] brought them to the monastery and provided them with subsistence before he sent them back to their homes.[195] Shenoute himself provides a somewhat more detailed account of the story. He mentioned 20,000 captives (including women and children) and reports that they remained in the monastery for three months.[196] His account describes in detail what food was provided by the monastery and states that physicians and medicines were supplied to the injured and recounts the number of deaths and babies born.[197] Ariel G. Lopez has calculated that the total amount spent on this refugee-crisis was 2384 *solidi*.[198] Even though these numbers may be inflated, they offer an important indication of the economic potential of the White Monastery.

The character and activities of Shenoute's successor Besa are somewhat obscure compared to his predecessor. The dates of his birth and death remain unknown and no *Life* has survived.[199] The little information we do possess comes from Besa's own writings, comprising a corpus of letters and sermons, which offers a series of fragmentary glimpses into life in the monastery under his rule.[200] Karl H. Kuhn emphasises that an indirect testimony to the abbot's reputation is that fresh copies of his writings were continuously made over the centuries.[201]

Besa's writings give account of a famine in 471, in which more than 5000 people sought refuge in the monastery.[202] During their stay, they were given

189 Besa, *Life*, 49, 51.
190 Besa, *Life*, 48, 51.
191 Besa, *Life*, 50 & 81.
192 Layton, "Social Structure;" Layton, "Rules."
193 Besa, *Life*, 82 (vegetable garden), 53 (orchards and fields), 67 (wine).
194 Blemmye is a general Coptic reference to a group of nomadic tribes, referred to in Arabic as the Beja (William Yewdale Adams, "Beja Tribes," in *The Coptic Encyclopedia*, ed. Aziz. S. Atiya [New York: Macmillan Publishing Company, 1991], 373).
195 Besa, *Life*, 68.
196 Emmel, "Shenoute's Place," 35.
197 Emmel, "Shenoute's Place," 32; Layton, "Social Structure," 27.
198 Lopez, *Shenoute*, 57–63.
199 Kuhn, "Besa and his Background," 37–39.
200 Letters and sermons translated in Kuhn, *Works of Besa*; Kuhn, "Letters and Sermons;" and discussed thematically in Kuhn, "Besa and his Background;" Kuhn, "Monastic life;" and Kuhn, "Besa's Christianity;" and summarised in Karl H. Kuhn, "Besa," in *The Coptic Encyclopedia*, ed. Aziz S. Atiya (New York: Macmillan Publishing, 1991), 378–379.
201 Although the majority of Besa's work was written around the end of the 5th century, the surviving manuscripts are much later. According to Kuhn, it is not possible to determine their precise date (Kuhn, "Besa's Christianity," 40).
202 Emmel, *Shenoute*, 11.

food, baths and medical treatment, and those who died (about 128) were buried.[203] The story accounts for the continuous charitable role of the monastery, but is also remarkably similar to the just discussed stories pertinent to Shenoute's life, although the number of people who sought refuge during Besa's time was much smaller. It is worth considering if the story was a doublet modelled on Shenoute's giving of refuge in time of drought, which served to legitimise Besa's succession as well as glorify Shenoute through his greater achievement.

The last of the first five abbots was Zenobios, a physician and secretary to Shenoute, who followed Besa as monastic leader.[204] According to the *Synaxarion* (a much later source, possibly compiled in the twelfth century although some components are earlier), Zenobios founded a convent of nuns at al-Mara'igh near Akhmim, perhaps adding a fourth monastic community to the White Monastery federation.[205] A *Life of Zenobios* was composed, but has survived only in fragments.[206] The early histories of the Red Monastery and the female congregation at Atripe are recounted in Chapters 5.1 and 5.2.

2.3 THE WHITE MONASTERY FROM THE SIXTH TO THE SIXTEENTH CENTURY

Following the first five abbots, the written history of the White Monastery disappears into obscurity for centuries. A variety of fragmented sources, however, gives some evidence of the activities that continued during this period and allows us to link individual names and dates to the monastery. The sources combined in this section are papyri (sixth to ninth centuries), manuscripts (tenth to twelfth centuries), inscriptions (twelfth and thirteenth centuries) and external sources, such as Arab travellers' accounts and histories. These sources cover the period up to the arrival of the first European travellers in the seventeenth century. Stefan Timm has provided an overview of the sources pertinent to this period and Réne-Georges Coquin and S.J. Meurice Martin have synthesised aspects of the White Monastery's history in their entry in *The Coptic Encyclopedia*.[207]

The few details that survive from the period between the sixth and the eighth centuries come mostly from the papyri.[208] A papyrus refers to Peter, priest and *archimandrite* of the Monastery of St Shenoute in the year 567. This reference is important, as it is the earliest record of Shenoute as the monastery's patron saint.[209] Another papyrus from the sixth century mentions an administrator, named Koursios, son of Joseph,[210] and a papyrus dated to 709 refers to the Monastery of St Shenoute in the nome of Panopolis (Akhmim).[211] Such brief notions do not enrich our understanding of the monastery, but serve as a witness to its continuous use.

From the eighth and ninth centuries, *The History of the Patriarchs of Alexandria* offers the best insight into events associated with the White Monastery.[212] The *History* was compiled and edited in the eleventh century by the Alexandrian ecclesiastic,

203 Kuhn, "Besa and his Background;" 38, Kuhn, "Monastic life," 178-179.
204 Kuhn, "Besa and his Background," 38.
205 Réne-Georges Coquin, "Zenobios," in *The Coptic Encyclopedia*, ed. Aziz S. Atiya (New York, Oxford, Singapore, Sydney: Maxwell Macmillan International, 1991b), 2371–2373; Muhammad Ramzi, *Al-Qamus al-Jughrafi lil-Bilad al Misriyyah*, 3 vols (Cairo: Matba'at Dār al-Kutub al-Misrīyah, 1953–1968), vol. 2, 4, 124.
206 Coquin, "Zenobios," 2371.
207 Coquin and Maurice Martin, "Dayr Anba Shinudah," 761–766; Timm, *Das Christlich-Koptische Ägypten*, 601–625.
208 Coquin and Maurice Martin, "Dayr Anba Shinudah," 762.
209 Grigoriĭ F. Zereteli and Peter Jernstedt, *Papyri russischer und georgischer Sammlungen*, 5 vols (Tiflis: Universitätslithographie, 1925–1935), vol 3, 48. See also Arietta Papaconstantinou, "The Cult of the Saints: A Haven of Continuity in a Changing World?" in *Egypt in the Byzantine World 300–700*, ed. Roger S. Bagnall (Cambridge: Cambridge University Press, 2007), 356–357 for a discussion of the general tendency for monasteries from the sixth century onwards to be referred to by their patron saint.
210 Zereteli and Jernstedt, *Papyri*, vol 3, 48.
211 Harold I. Bell, *Greek Papyri in the British Museum*, vol. 4 (London: British Museum, 1910), 1460.
212 Johannes Den Heijer, "History of the Patriarchs of Alexandria," in *The Coptic Encyclopedia*, ed. Aziz S. Atiya (New York: Macmillan Publishing Company, 1991), 1238–1242; Christian F. Seybold, *Alexandrinische Patriarchengeschichte von S. Marcus bis Michael I., 61–767:*

Mawhub ibn Mansur ibn Mufarrij (1025–1100), who collected texts from the archives of the Monastery of the Blessed Virgin at Nahaya, the Monastery of St Theodore in the Fayoum and the Monastery of St Macarius in Wadi Natrun.[213] The focus on the Coptic Patriarchate means that the *History* mostly is pertinent to Alexandria and the Delta, but some references concern the monasteries of other regions in Egypt. Apa Seth, *archimandrite* of the monastery of St Shenoute, on the mountain of Adribah, is mentioned in a notice on the 43rd patriarch of Alexandria, Alexander II (r. 702–729). Apa Seth is also mentioned in the *Synaxarion*, which tells us that his feast day was on 29 Tubah (23rd January).[214] On this day, he was commemorated for his piety, ascetic practice, humility and monastic teachings as well as his success in persuading the Muslim authorities not to impose new taxes on the monastery.[215] The reference to feast days is an important indicator of the liturgical life in the monastery, where the former leader very likely would have been commemorated in a service involving just the monastics, or in a feast accommodating visitors to the monastery (see Chapter 4.3).

The *History of the Patriarchs* further recounts an event in the time of Kha'il, the 46th patriarch (r. 744–767), during whose reign al-Qasim ibn Ubaydallah, who at the time was Egypt's financial director under the Umayyads, visited the monastery accompanied by his troops and his favourite mistress.[216] The story recounts how al-Qasim insisted on entering the church on horseback accompanied by his retinue. An old monk pleaded with al-Qasim not to 'enter with such pride into the house of God, above all in the company of this woman; for never from the beginning has any woman entered into this church!'[217] Al-Qasim ignored his plea and entered the church without dismounting, which according to the account, led to the death of his mistress, whose horse fell to the ground, both horse and rider dying instantly. Al-Qasim gave 400 *dinars* to the monastery as an offering and later added another 300 *dinars* when thirty of his men attempted to steal a chest, which belonged to the monastery. The thirteenth-century Coptic priest Abu al-Makarim later paraphrased these events in his *History of Churches and Monasteries in Egypt and some Neighbouring Countries* (compiled between 1170 and 1240).[218]

The historicity of the account is questionable and the reason behind al-Qasim's provocative act may reflect contemporary problematic relations between Muslims and Christians in Egypt rather than an actual situation. The story does, however, contain a few useful references to the monastery. The Muslims' entry into the monastery is described as follows: '… and they passed through the first door, and through the second which leads into the enclosure of the church; and they went as far as the door which forms the entrance into the church.'[219] The first door could refer to the entrance to the monastery, perhaps to the gatehouse in the enclosure wall,[220] while the second door most likely would refer to the narthex or south hall (fig. 6). This could mean that the procession entered through the west or the south door. The old monk informs us that only men used the church, the obvious inference being that women from the local congregation were not allowed to enter the building. Although somewhat speculative, two suggestions can be deduced from this information. Firstly, as the architectural evidence suggests, the western narthex gives access to a staircase, which led to the galleries above the aisles of the nave.[221] It is important to note that the old monk did not stop the

nach der ältesten 1266 geschriebenen Hamburger Handschrift (Hamburg: Lucas Gräfe, 1912).

213 James Howard-Johnston, *Witnesses to a World Crisis: Historians and History of the Middle East in the Seventh Century* (Oxford: Oxford University Press, 2010), 315.

214 Mark N. Swanson "An Eclipsed History. Towards a Framework for the Medieval History of the Red Monastery," in *The Red Monastery Church. Beauty and Asceticism in Upper Egypt*, ed. Elizabeth S. Bolman (New Haven and London: Yale University Press, 2016), 196.

215 Swanson "Eclipsed History," 196.

216 Seybold, *Alexandrinische Patriarchengeschichte*, 204.

217 Abu Salih the Armenian, *The Churches & Monasteries*, 238.

218 Abu Salih the Armenian, *The Churches & Monasteries*, 238.

219 Abu Salih the Armenian, *The Churches & Monasteries*, 238.

220 See Layton, "Rules," 46.

221 Michael Burgoyne, personal communication with author, 2012.

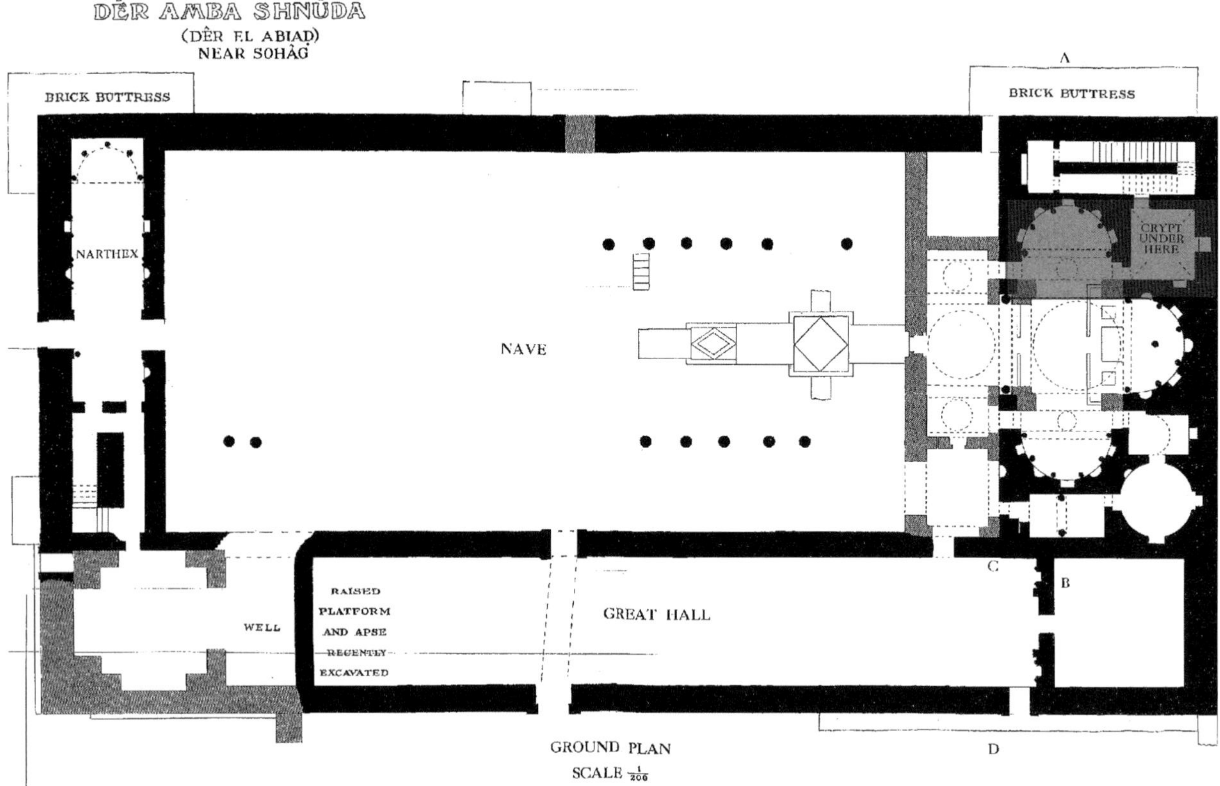

Fig. 6. Plan of the White Monastery church with an emphasis on the north conch and the adjacent room (modified from Clarke, *Christian Antiquities*, pl. XLV).

processions by the door to the narthex or south hall (or for that matter by the gate of the monastery), but by the door leading into the nave. Could this suggest that women were allowed in the galleries or in other side rooms? Secondly, the reference to an enclosure wall suggests that the White Monastery was not yet in ruins. The archaeological remains confirm this second point (see Chapter 3).

The *History of the Patriarchs* also notes that the Abbasid civil war between the brothers al-Mutazz and al-Mustain around 866 affected the Monastery of St Shenoute, but unfortunately further details are lacking.[222] The section on the patriarch Cyril II (r. 1078–1092) mentions a list of relics in Egypt and notes that the White Monastery was host to the remains of the two apostles, Bartholomew and Simon the Zealot.[223] The disruptive impact of civil war on regional economy and infrastructure is worth considering when exploring the archaeological remains, while the presence of relics could be a strong indicator that pilgrimage to the monastery was common (see discussion in Chapter 4.3).

A group of colophons found in or associated with the White Monastery's library and studied by Arnold Van Lantschot casts some light on the period from the tenth to the thirteenth centuries. This dataset mostly contains individual names and occasional dates with little or no further reference to events or circumstances surrounding the people mentioned. Chael the *archimandrite* is mentioned in two colophons. One dates to 927/928, the other to 939/940.[224] Another colophon mentions that Basil, steward of the White Monastery, wrote the associated manuscript in the first half of the tenth century,[225] while

222 Coquin and Maurice Martin, "Dayr Anba Shinudah," 762; Swanson "Eclipsed History," 198.

223 Coquin and Maurice Martin, "Dayr Anba Shinudah," 764.

224 Arnold Van Lantschoot, *Recueil des colophons des manuscrits chrétiens d'Egypte*, 2 vols. (Louvain: J.B. Istas, 1929), 84–86.

225 Van Lantschoot, *Manuscrits*, 126–127.

another copy was to be given to the Monastery of the Virgin (only known from written sources) located near the White Monastery, but it seems not to have reached its destination. The same colophon contains a prayer for the patriarch Cyril II, suggesting a tentative eleventh century date for the manuscript, while a tenth century colophon refers to Apa Ioustos as ruler of the monastic congregation.[226]

Two colophons (CI and CII) are of particular importance, as they formed part of codices that were looted during the Ayyubid incursion into Egypt, led by Shirkuh in 1167.[227] Abu al-Makarim added that when Shirkuh and his Ghuzz army invaded Egypt, the body of Shenoute was removed from its resting place and concealed in an unconsecrated chamber near the altar of a church on the mountain called Athribah.[228] In a brief account of the White Monastery, Abu al-Makarim described the church as spacious enough to contain thousands of people,[229] and mentioned a keep as well as an enclosure wall, which surrounded a garden full of 'all sorts of trees.'[230] This description is important for our understanding of the layout of the White Monastery, but we cannot be sure that it refers to the time of Abu al-Makarim and there is no reason to think that the author ever set foot in the monastery. To take one example from his account, the description of the church is vastly exaggerated in size.

Abu al-Makarim also refers to Bahram, an Armenian Christian,[231] who had been vizier in the caliphate of Al-Hafiz from 1135 to 1137, but retired to the 'White Monasteries' (*al-diyarat al-bid*) after he was banished from office and remained there until 1139.[232] The term 'White Monasteries' was, according to Mark N. Swanson, used collectively about the White and Red Monasteries by (mainly Arab) authors between the eleventh and thirteenth centuries.[233] Together with three painted inscriptions (*dipinti*) in Armenian in the church of St Shenoute, this note has given rise to the idea that the White Monastery for a short while served the Armenian community in Egypt and during this period housed Armenian monks.[234]

The Armenian inscriptions form a part of a larger corpus of *dipinti* in the sanctuary of the monastic church and its adjoining rooms dating from the twelfth and thirteenth centuries. Walter E. Crum studied and published some of these inscriptions, focusing on a group that was found in the northern part of the sanctuary's triconch.[235] The inscriptions were located in the apse, in associated niches, on the walls and in a room immediately to the east (fig. 6).[236]

From these inscriptions we learn that the paintings in the three domes were painted in 1124 and that extensive structural restoration was carried out in 1259.[237] The date of the paintings derives from an in-

226 Coquin and Maurice Martin, "Dayr Anba Shinudah," 763.
227 Van Lantschoot, *Manuscrits*, 171–177.
228 Abu Salih the Armenian, *The Churches & Monasteries*, 236.
229 Abu Salih the Armenian, *The Churches & Monasteries*, 235–240.
230 Abu Salih the Armenian, *The Churches & Monasteries*, 237.
231 Seta B. Dadoyan, *The Armenians in the Medieval Islamic World. Paradigms of Interaction. Seventh to Fourteenth Centuries*, 2 vols (New Brunswick & London: Transaction Publishers, 2011–2013), Seta B. Dadoyan, "Bahrām," in *Encyclopedia of Islam*, ed. Gudrun Krämer, Denis Matringe, John Nawas, and Everett Rowson (Brill Online, 2013).
232 Abu Salih the Armenian, *The Churches & Monasteries*, 238; Dadoyan, *Armenians*. Swanson believes that the plural from of White Monasteries refer to both the White and Red Monasteries (Swanson "Eclipsed History," 194).
233 Swanson "Eclipsed History," 194.
234 Marius Canard, "Un vizir chrétien à l'époque fatimide, l'arménien Bahram," *Annales de l'Institut d'etudes orientales de la Faculté des lettres d'Alger* 12 (1954): 84–113; Marius Canard, "Notes sur les Arméniens à l'époque fatimide," *Annales de l'Institut d'études orientales de la Faculté des lettres d'Alger* 13 (1955): 143–157; Dadoyan, *Armenians*, vol. 2, 120–122; Otto F. A. Meinardus, *Monks and Monasteries of the Egyptian Deserts* (Cairo: American University in Cairo Press, 1989), 181; Josef Strzygowski, *Die Baukunst der Armenier und Europa: Ergebnisse einer vom Kunsthistorischen Institute der Universität Wien 1913 durchgeführten Forschungsreise*, 2 vols (Vienna: A. Schroll & Co, 1918), 731–732.
235 Walter E. Crum, "Inscription from Shenoute's Monastery," *Journal of Theological Studies* 5 (1904): 552–569.
236 Orlandi, "Library," 212.
237 Crum, "Inscription," 552–556.

scription located immediately next to the depiction of Christ enthroned in the central apse that names the artist as Theodore and the year of his work as 1124. A slightly longer version in Armenian on the opposite side of the figure mentions that Theodore was a native of Kesun (located in the eastern part of modern Turkey) and states that the painting was executed while Paul was *archimandrite*, in the time of Bishop Gregory, bishop of the Armenian colony in Egypt.[238] Two other inscriptions mention the patriarch Cyril III ibn Laqlaq (r. 1235–1243), during whose reign the *archimandrite* was a monk named John; John is also mentioned in an inscription dated to 1259, which refers to the restoration of the church. Here, John is described as a master builder, who restored sections of the church after it had been damaged in an earthquake (probably around the middle of the 13th century).[239] The full effects of this earthquake on the adjoining monastic complex and on neighbouring sites are considered in Chapters 4 and 5. It is worth noting here that the Red Monastery church saw substantial rebuilding around the same time as the repairs were made to the church of the White Monastery (see Chapter 5.1.1). Lastly, a badly damaged painting of St Michael refers to Phoibammon as *archimandrite*, but does not provide a date.[240]

At least two visitors wrote their names in the Sanctuary. The first was 'Mercurius' the artist: this could be the same Mercurius, who inscribed his name in the neighbouring Red Monastery between 1300 and 1320. The second graffito is damaged with only the last part preserved. It ends 'and I entered this monastery on the 24th day of the month of Epip' (31st July) in 1237.[241]

A series of inscriptions in a room that is located immediately to the north of the sanctuary suggests that this room once served as the monastic library.[242] Lists of books inscribed on the walls in the Bohairic Coptic dialect may indicate the position once occupied by chests or shelves that housed these volumes. The lists include texts from the New Testament along the north side of the room, homiletic and historical works along the east wall and biographical works along the west wall with reference to the number of copies available. Unfortunately, the date of the inscriptions is unknown.[243] Extensive studies by Tito Orlandi of the content of the dispersed White Monastery library have led him to conclude that it grew to become the largest Coptic library ever known, with no less than 1000 codices averaging 200–300 pages each.[244] Of these, about 10% have survived in collections mainly in Europe.[245] Orlandi argues that this small chamber was not the original site of the library, but served as a storage space for manuscripts that were no longer in use.[246]

The traveller and scholar Yakut ibn 'Abd Allah Al-Hamawi (1179–1229) refers to the White Monastery but gives no further details, thus providing us with the earliest surviving reference to the site by this name.[247]

The White Monastery is mentioned in the fifteenth-century *History of the Copts in Egypt*, composed by the Arab historian and topographer al-Maqrizi (1364–1442). Al-Maqrizi has very little to

238 See Dadoyan, *Armenians*, for the Armenian community in Egypt.
239 Sofia Schaten and Jacques Van der Vliet, "Monks and Scholars in the Panopolite Nome: The Epigraphic Evidence," in *Christianity and Monasticism in Upper Egypt*, ed. Gabra and Takla, 137. See also Nicholas Ambraseys, *Earthquakes in the Mediterranean and Middle East: A Multidisciplinary Study of Seismicity up to 1900* (Cambridge: Cambridge University Press, 2009), 342.
240 Coquin and Maurice Martin, "Dayr Anba Shinudah," 764.
241 Crum, "Inscription," 557.
242 See Davis et al., "Left Behind: A Recent Discovery of Manuscripts Fragments in the White Monastery Church," *Journal of Coptic Studies* 16 (2014): 69–87; Catherine Louis, "The Fate of the White Monastery Library," in *Christianity and Monasticism in Upper Egypt*, ed. Gabra and Takla, 83–91; Orlandi, "Library" for discussion of the location of the monastic library.
243 Crum, "Inscription," 1904.
244 Orlandi, "Library," 213, 225–226.
245 See Louis, "Fate;" Orlandi, "Library," 227–230 for the dispersal of the White Monastery library.
246 Orlandi, "Library," 220.
247 Ibn 'Abd Allah al-Hamawi Yakut, *Geographisches Wörterbuch*, 6 vols, ed. Ferdinand Wüstenfeld (Leipzig: in Comission bei F.A. Brockhaus, 1866–1873), vol. 2, 641.
248 Ferdinand Wüstenfeld, *Macrizi's Geschichte der Copten* (Göttingen: Dieterichsche Buchhandlung, 1847), 96.

Fig. 7. *Ciborium*. View towards northwest (De Bock, *Matériaux*, pl. XIX).

say about the White Monastery except that it is an ancient monastery, built of stone, but in ruins with only the church remaining and he mentions it by both its names, i.e., the White Monastery and the Monastery of St Shenoute.[248] He states that the monastery is said to have had a property of 4¾ *feddans*, of which only one *feddan* remains (4200 m²).[249] This information is probably correct as agricultural land in the fourteenth and fifteenth centuries was taxed (and therefore carefully accounted for) according to size and type of crop.[250] Al-Maqrizi's very brief description would suggest that he did not visit the monastery himself, but perhaps copied his description from one or more sources.

There are no surviving documents that tell us when or how the monastic site came to be in ruins, although al-Maqrizi's description provides a *terminus ad quem*. The continuing use of the church is testified though the presence of an inscription in Ethiopic and a dated manuscript, both deriving from the sixteenth century. The inscription was found in a square *ciborium*—a structure resembling a canopy—built from stones and fired bricks that sheltered the pulpit in the nave of the church (fig. 7).[251] It has

249 Giovanni Ruffini, *Medieval Nubia. A Social and Economic History* (Oxford & New York: Oxford University Press, 2012), 81.

250 Noël Deerr, *The History of Sugar* (London: Chapman and Hall, 1949), 93.

251 Gustave Lefebvre, "Deir el-Abiad," in *Dictionnaire d'Archéologie Chrétienne et de Liturgie*, ed. Fernand R.D. Cabrol and Henri R.P.D. Leclercq (Paris: Librairie Letouzey et Ané, 1916), vol 4: col. 497; Carlo Conti Rossini, "Aethiopica III," *Rivista degli Studi Orientali* 9 (1923): 461–462.

been suggested that the inscription was made by a member of an Ethiopian caravan of pilgrims or that it was possibly even associated with a small Ethiopian community that lived for a short time in the White Monastery.[252] Based on its contents, Vladimir G. De Bock dated the inscription to 1730, while Carlo Conti Rossini believed that it was as early as 1563.[253] The latter interpretation is general accepted today.[254] Further evidence for activity at the White Monastery is found in two manuscripts. One called *The Rite for the Feast of the Desert of Apa Shenoute* has been estimated to date to the fifteenth or sixteenth century.[255] The other—a book of psalms—contains two colophons, one stating that it was completed in the White Monastery in 1587, the other documenting that it was presented to Deir Anba Bishoi 'in the desert of Abu Makar' in 1619 by a deacon called 'Shanudah'.[256]

The written sources of the Medieval period thus paint a picture of continuous activity at the White Monastery, although most of them—except that of Abu al-Makarim—refer only to individuals or to activities that took place within the church. The colophons indicate that both the White Monastery library and *scriptorium* were in use, and the major building programme carried out in the thirteenth century would suggest a significant presence at the site. The dates provided by the Arabic writers (Yakut, Abu al-Makarim and al-Maqrizi) are not particularly reliable and there is nothing in the texts to confirm that the authors visited the monastery themselves. It seems more likely that they were copying from sources that have since been lost. This means, for example, that we cannot be certain whether the monastic grounds fell into ruin at the time of al-Maqrizi's writing or whether they had already done so several hundred years before—or even earlier.

The last reliable data before the sixteenth century is Mercurius' visit in 1307, thus leaving an information gap of 250 years. Importantly, however, the two manuscripts dating to late sixteenth century identified the site by the same name (the Monastery of St Shenoute) that had been used centuries before: this indicates, if not continuous use, at least an unbroken memory of the earlier site and its function. Finally, the sixteenth century inscription in the *ciborium* that enclosed the pulpit reveals that already by this time, internal structures were being constructed in the nave of the monastic church.

2.4 THE WHITE MONASTERY 'DISCOVERED': EUROPEAN TRAVELLERS ON THE NILE (SEVENTEENTH TO NINETEENTH CENTURIES)

The White Monastery re-emerges in accounts from the late seventeenth century, when European visitors began to make their way up the Nile. The journals kept by these visitors mean that from this point, the White Monastery occurs more frequently and is portrayed in much greater detail than was the case for the 1100 preceding years. Johann M. Wansleben (or Vansleb) (1635–1679) visited the White Monastery in April 1673 as part of a mission for the French Government, which sent him to Egypt to gather manuscripts and antiquities for the royal collections.[257] He arrived on a Saturday afternoon and lodged in the monastery for the night, after the ordeal of having

252 Ethiopians had staging posts at Deir al-Muharraq, Wadi al-Natrun and in Cairo, as part of a pilgrimage route to Jerusalem (Coquin and Maurice Martin, "Dayr Anba Shinudah," 765).

253 Vladimir G. De Bock, *Matériaux pour servir à l'archéologie de l'Égypte chrétienne* (St. Petersburg: Tip. E. Tile Preemn, 1901), 54; Conti Rossini, "Aethiopica III," 462.

254 Coquin and Maurice Martin, "Dayr Anba Shinudah," 764.

255 See for example Stephen J. Davis, *Coptic Christology in Practice: Incarnation and Divine Participation in Late Antique and Medieval Egypt* (Oxford: Oxford University Press, 2008); Grossmann, "Schenute;" Timbie, "Liturgical Procession;" Timbie, "Once More."

256 Walter E. Crum, *Catalogue of the Coptic Manuscripts in the British Museum* (London: British Museum, 1905), no. 866.

257 Morris L. Bierbrier, *Who was who in Egyptology*, 4th revised edition (London: The Egypt Exploration Society, 2012), 566.

lost his donkey to robbers on the route from Tahta.[258] Vansleb described the Church of St Shenoute as one of the most magnificent structures in Egypt, but offered only little information about the building itself and its inhabitants. He provided a general (but faulty) description of the church, but significantly noted that five of the six doorways were blocked, and that the then current entrance—located in the south wall—had been reduced to the size of a man. Vansleb mentioned that the main gate, located in the west wall is referred to as Bab al-Baghl (the Mule Gate) in remembrance of 'what happened to a daughter of a heathen king, who offered to go into the church in contempt, riding upon a Mule and was swallowed up alive in a Pit that opened, to punish her insolence.'[259]

This tale provides evidence that a version of al-Qasim ibn Ubaydallah's visit to the White Monastery was still recalled in the seventeenth century. Vansleb made a few further remarks on the appearance of the church: he mentioned that all windows had been walled up and the inside of the church had been demolished, except from the sanctuary where the liturgy was performed. The roof of the nave had collapsed, and the pillars stood open to the sky. He noted the many reused stone blocks from the Pharaonic period and referred to the well located in the southwest corner of the building. The residents—who were described by Vansleb as monks—told him that the water was forty cubits deep (about twenty metres) and that it had been sanctified or blessed by 'our Saviour.' Vansleb recalled that the water was very sweet (as opposed to brackish) and that it rose and fell with the Nile, although there was no direct contact with the river.[260]

Vansleb's description is significant as it is the earliest firm account of how the monastic settlement had become confined within the church. He does not mention the area surrounding the church and it seems that he did not realise that the monastery was once of much greater size. The mention of monks living within the church is significant (although it should be noted that Vansleb may have mistaken priests for monks), as is the note revealing that travellers were able to lodge there for the night.

The French physician and traveller Claude Granger (1680–1734) visited the White Monastery in 1731 during a longer exploration of Upper Egypt.[261] Granger described the monastery as the least ugly (!) in Upper Egypt and we learn that three poor monks lived in houses within the monastery church (Vansleb did not mention the houses).[262] Just six years later in 1737, Richard Pococke (1704–1765) visited both the Red and White Monasteries.[263] Pococke described a church surrounded by remains of ancient pillars and stones of red granite and thus assumed that the monastery was built on the ancient site of Crocodilopolis. The grandeur of both churches, along with the combination of what he described as Greek and Egyptian architectural styles, led him wrongly to ascribe the construction of the monastic church to Empress Helena (250–330). Pococke did not mention any residents at the White Monastery, but described his experience of lodging in the Red Monastery, where the priests made coffee for him in the morning and offered to slaughter a sheep for an evening feast.

The tale of Empress Helena's building activities was repeated again in 1738 when the Danish naval captain Frederik L. Norden (1708–1742) landed in Meschie (modern Sohag).[264] Norden did not visit

258 Johann M. Vansleb, *The present state of Egypt or a new relation of a late voyage into that kingdom, performed in the years 1672 and 1673* (Farnborough: Gregg International Publishers, 1972 (first published in 1678), 222–228.

259 Vansleb, *Egypt*, 224.

260 Vansleb, *Egypt*, 225.

261 Bierbrier, *Who was who*, 220.

262 Claude Granger, *Relation du Voyage fait en Égypte par le sieur Granger en l'année 1730. Oú l'on voit ce qu'il y a de plus remarquable, particulièrement sur l'Histoire naturelle* (Paris, 1745), 92–96; Cédric Meurice, "L'intervention du Comité de conservation des monuments de l'art arabe au couvent Blanc de Sohag," in *Études coptes XI, Treizième journée d'études (Marseille, 7–9 juin 2007)*, ed. Anne Boud'hors and Catherine Louis (Paris: Cahiers de la Bibliothèque copte 17, 2009), 277.

263 Richard Pococke, *A Description of the East and some other Countries* (London: printed for the author by W. Bowyer, 1743), 79.

264 Frederik L. Norden, *Voyage d'Égypte et de Nubie*, 3 vols, ed. L. Langlès (Paris: P. Didot, 1795–1798). Denon and Curzon (see below) also report on a local tradition of as-

Fig. 8. Denon's drawing of the White Monastery (Denon, *Travels*, pl. XVII, fig. 2).

the White Monastery himself, but a group of men from his company reported that they saw a cross, which came from an old church. In 1742, Charles Perry (1698–1780), a British traveller and medical writer visited the monastery and for the first time mentioned the existence of a large corpus of Coptic manuscripts.[265]

Dominique-Vivant Denon (1747–1825), a French antiquarian, artist and author, who accompanied Napoleon's troops in their conquest of Egypt, reported on the state of the Red and White Monasteries towards the end of the 18th century.[266] Denon wrote an account of his journey and contributed with more than 150 drawings of Egyptian monuments that were published in the *Description de l'Égypte*—among these, a drawing of the White Monastery (fig. 8).[267] The company arrived in 1798, the morning after a group of 'Mamelukes' had set fire to the two communities. The Red Monastery was apparently still burning when Denon arrived, preventing him from entering the church. The White Monastery had also been torched, the priests had fled and only monks remained, apparently clothed in rags and attempting to save what they could from the ruins.[268] Denon noticed fragments of walls and blocks of granite in the immediate vicinity and concluded that a larger monastery was once attached to the church. He noted, however, to his dismay that since the destruction of the site, the monks had 'made their dwelling in the lateral gallery of the church, if dwellings they might be called, which were only wretched huts, set up under those splendid porches; it was misery in the very palace of pride.'[269]

In the early nineteenth century, the southwest corner of the church above the area of the well collapsed. The collapse of this part of the building

cribing the construction of the two monasteries to Empress Helena: Robert Curzon, *Visits to Monasteries in the Levant* (London: Arthur Barker, 1955), 139–140; Vivant Denon, *Travels in Upper and Lower Egypt, in Company with several Divisions of the French Army during the Campaigns of General Bonaparte in that Country*, trans. Arthur Aikin (London: Longman and Rees, 1803), 15.

265 Charles Perry, *A View of the Levant: Particularly of Constantinople, Syria, Egypt, and Greece. In Which Their Antiquities, Government, Politics, Maxims, Manners, and Customs, (with Many Other Circumstances and Contingencies) Are Attempted to be Described and Treated on* (London: T. Woodward, C. Davis, and J. Shuckburgh, 1743), 370.

266 Bierbrier, *Who was who*, 150.

267 Edme F. Jomard and Charles L.F. Panckoucke, *Description de l'Égypte: ou, Recueil des observations et des recherches qui ont été faites en Égypte pendant l'expédition de l'Armée française* (Paris: C.L.F. Panckoucke, 1821).

268 Denon, *Travels*, 14–17.

269 Denon, *Travels*, 16.

must have affected the community living inside the church, and possibly, for this reason, it was rebuilt soon after in 1802.[270]

The nineteenth century also saw a succession of travellers. In 1847, the British Egyptologist Gardner Wilkinson (1797–1875) published a handbook for travellers in Egypt. He described the remains of the White Monastery in an account of an itinerary from Cairo to Thebes. He noted that the monastery at this time had been transformed into a Christian village, inhabited by families living in what once formed the aisles of the nave.[271] Unlike his predecessors, Wilkinson briefly noted that brickwork remained to the south, west and north of the church, while the area eastwards (in the cultivated Nile Valley) was used for agriculture—a small portion of this land was cultivated by the 'monastic inmates.'[272] Wilkinson noted that certain precautions had been taken to secure the building against assaults from the Muslims in turbulent times. The inhabitants of the church had transformed St Shenoute into a Muslim sheikh bearing the name of 'Sheykh Aboo Shenóodeh.'[273]

This story is repeated by Robert Curzon (1810–1873), who visited the White Monastery in 1833, as part of a tour through Egypt, Syria and Palestine, in search of manuscripts in monastic libraries.[274] Curzon vividly retold how he arrived at the White Monastery on the back of a donkey after an hour and a half's canter from Sohag. He described how the monastery had been ruined and sacked over and over again, most recently in 1812.[275] The monks had returned one by one and were repairing the monastery. The interior had been gutted by the attackers, but the 'immense strength of the outer walls had resisted all their efforts to destroy them.'[276] Curzon provided a brief description, but repeated the accounts of past travellers and showed remarkably little interest in the actual functions of the building. Of some importance is a brief description of his difficulty in gaining access to the church. Curzon banged the door repeatedly, until he was finally let in by a monk, after stating that he and his companions were Christians and meant no harm. Upon entering the church through a tunnel that led from a 'small doorway in the south wall, he found himself surrounded by ruined buildings of various ages. He described how the nave, now open to the sky, was host to chickens and goats and how Coptic women were peeping at him from the windows of 'some wretched hovels of mud and brick.'[277]

Other travellers made it to the White Monastery, but the accounts mentioned above are the richest and most influential descriptions from the seventeenth to the nineteenth century.[278] It is clear from these descriptions that the surrounding site was completely derelict and the focus of the settlement was now on the church, but even here, the community is described as far removed from past glory. Especially vivid are the accounts of Denon and Curzon for their descriptions of a dilapidated community inside the church. These descriptions, however, should be considered within the context of European attitudes towards the Orient. It seems significant that the community rebuilt the southwest corner of the church after it collapsed, suggesting either a financial surplus within the community itself, the ability to raise the funds or a donation of materials and time by local Christian workmen. Either way, the White Monastery was not nearly in as bad shape as it would appear in the accounts of these travellers.

270 George Somers Clarke, *Christian Antiquities in the Nile Valley. A Contribution towards the Study of the Ancient Churches* (Oxford: Clarendon Press, 1912), 154.
271 Gardner Wilkinson, *A Handbook for Travellers in (lower and upper) Egypt. Handbook for Egypt and the Sudan. Being a new ed. of 'Modern Egypt and Thebes'*, 2 vols (London: John Murray, 1847), 428–429.
272 Wilkinson, *Handbook*, 429.
273 Wilkinson, *Handbook*, 429.
274 Curzon, *Monasteries*, 138–139.
275 Curzon, *Monasteries*, 137.
276 Curzon, *Monasteries*, 137.
277 Curzon, *Monasteries*, 138–139.
278 See also Elisabeth R. O'Connell, "The Discovery of Christian Egypt. From Manuscript Hunters towards and Archaeology of Late Antique Egypt," in *Coptic Civilization: Two Thousand Years of Christianity in Egypt*, ed. Gawdat Gabra (Cairo: The American University in Cairo Press, 2014), 163–176.

2.5 THE CONTINUED LEGACY: MODERN EXPLORATION AND RE-ESTABLISHMENT (NINETEENTH TO TWENTY-FIRST CENTURIES)

Scholarly interest in the White Monastery greatly increased with the European discovery of a large part of the monastic library towards the end of the nineteenth century. Already in the late eighteenth century, Cardinal Stefano Borgia (1731–1804) had purchased several folios and fragments relating to the White Monastery, without knowledge of their provenance (this collection is kept in the Vatican library).[279] During the 50 years following Borgia's purchase, many more unprovenanced texts were acquired by museums and libraries.[280] However, it was not until the late nineteenth century that Gaston C.C. Maspero (1846–1916), at the time head of the *Institut Français d'Archéologie Orientale*, purchased a collection of manuscripts from a dealer in Cairo, who claimed to have obtained them from a monk at the White Monastery. Among these were folios that clearly were similar to the ones bought by Cardinal Borgia, and that appear to have originated in a hidden room within the monastery.[281] From this collection, Maspero bought 3500 folios and fragments of parchments for the *Bibliothèque Nationale de France*. Despite a desire for secrecy, the news reached the antiquities market, resulting in museums, including the British Museum, sending their representatives to purchase manuscripts.[282]

This new scholarly interest led to increased attention in the remains of the White Monastery. With the introduction of the Upper Egyptian railway in 1858, access to the monastery was much improved and the number of visitors soared. The invention of photography meant that the visual records of the monastery began to increase at this time. The following remarks do not aim at an exhaustive analysis of the material available, but rather focus on the most significant episodes in the modern history of the White Monastery.

The Russian art historian and archaeologist De Bock (1850–1899), who visited the monastery towards the end of the nineteenth century, carried out the first systematic study of the church. He produced a plan, photographs and a complete architectural description.[283] In his publication of the site in *Matériaux pour servir à l'archéologie de l'Égypte Chrétienne*, De Bock focused his attention on what he described as the appalling state of the White and Red Monasteries. He stated how the monasteries were in ruins—overbuilt by overcrowded houses, occupied by four priests, their families and several farmers (*fellaheen*) who were engaged to cultivate the monasteries' land (fig. 9). In De Bock's opinion, the presence of the houses not only made it impossible to understand the building, they were also the direct cause of a rapid decay of the original church architecture. In this way, De Bock was the first person to criticise the settlement within the church—not for the state of its building, but with the scholarly concern of the ancient monument in mind.

Sharing De Bock's concerns was George Somers Clarke (1841–1926), an English architect and archaeologist who visited the White Monastery on several occasions during the late nineteenth and early twentieth centuries, and who published important descriptions of the church, its layout and architecture.[284] Describing his arrival at the monastery from

279 Emmel, *Shenoute*, 24.
280 Louis, "Fate," 83.
281 Louis, "Fate," 83.
282 For a detailed account of the dispersal of the library: Emmel, *Shenoute*, 18–24; Davis et al., "Left Behind," 79–80; Louis, "Fate;" Orlandi, "Library;" Hany N. Takla "The Library of the Monastery of St. Shenouda the Archimandrite," *Coptica* 4 (2005): 43–51; Hany N. Takla, "Biblical Manuscripts of the Monastery of St. Shenoute the Archimandrite," in *Christianity and Monasticism in Upper Egypt*, ed. Gabra and Takla, 155–168.
283 De Bock, Matériaux, 39-60.
284 Clarke, *Christian Antiquities*, 145–161; Charles R. Peers, "The White Monastery near Sohag, Upper Egypt," *The Archaeological Journal* LXI, 242 (1904): 131–153. See also Nicholas Warner, "An Architect Abroad. The Life and Work of Somers Clarke in Egypt," *Mitteilungen des Deutschen Archäologischen Instituts Abteilung Kairo* 68 (2012): 237–261.

Fig. 9. Domestic houses in nave of the White Monastery church c. 1900. View towards east (De Bock, *Matériaux*, pl. xx).

the south, Clarke recounted seeing a massive rectangular block of limestone masonry that stood among mounds of ruined brick buildings. Importantly, he noted that the church was surrounded on its north, west and south sides by large amounts of debris from buildings, containing both fired and unfired bricks. He wrote that when viewed from the top of the walls of the church, the area covered by debris appeared to be roughly in the shape of a rectangle with its longest extent towards the north and south.

He was aware (and explicitly stated) that the building commonly referred to as the monastery (*Deir*), was only the monastic church, while the original monastery and all its facilities were in ruins.[285] Clarke mentioned that the monastic enclosure wall could not easily be made out—a rather interesting statement considering the clarity with which it is marked on Petrie's plan (see discussion of the archaeological exploration of the site below).[286] Clarke entered the church of St Shenoute through the same doorway and tunnel in the south wall as Curzon had some 70 years earlier—not much had changed during the intervening time. Clarke stated that many people lived within the boundaries of the church with all their livestock, and to his great dismay, the west narthex was filled with rubbish. In a rather harsh tone, he noted that 'this part of the church was until recently the refuse pit of the miserable and degraded community living within its walls, a pitiable sight.'[287] In the same year, an expedition led by Petrie

285 Clarke, *Christian Antiquities*, 146.
286 Clarke, *Christian Antiquities*, 146.
287 Clarke, *Christian Antiquities*, 149–150.

(1853–1942) carried out the first extensive excavation of the site, which included large-scale excavations to the south of the church (see Chapter 2.6)

Clarke repeatedly contacted the authorities responsible for Coptic and Islamic antiquities in Egypt, the *Comité de Conservation des Monuments de l'Art Arabe* (the Comité, for short), to report on the state of the church, and he recommended that immediate action be taken to improve this situation.

In 1906, the Comité bought the monastic church and in 1907 responded to the demands for intervention and architectural restoration at the White and Red Monasteries.[288] The Comité was heavily engaged with the restoration of monuments in Cairo, but from 1907 to 1911, it undertook an extensive programme of work at the two monasteries in Sohag and at Deir Anba Hadra in Aswan.[289] The focus was on restoration rather than conservation, which involved extensive cleaning and removal of elements that were not considered to be part of the original structure.[290] Walls were taken down, blocks were recut and then reassembled. Paint, plaster and other encrustations were removed from the nave and all but two houses were cleared: the inhabitants were rehoused in a nearby village, possibly in the immediately adjacent Nag al-Deir located to the north of the church. In 1935, however, the two houses were still to be found within the nave and in 1947, yet another house had been built.[291]

Integral to the work of the Comité was an extensive photographic survey, carried out by Jean Clédat (1871–1943) before and after the restoration, while Georges Lefebvre (1879–1957) copied inscriptions.[292] The architectural preservation involved consolidating the outer walls, stairs and brickwork. The mounds to the south of the church were thought to be important to the history of the monastery. The Comité, therefore, decreed that all activities, most importantly construction, should be forbidden within 50m of the church walls.[293] Alongside and subsequent to the work of the Comité, the Italian architectural historian Ugo Monneret de Villard (1881–1954) produced a two-part account of the White and Red Monasteries—by far the most detailed description compiled to date and the first attempt to interpret the architectural history of the building.[294]

In 1962, the Technical Institute of Darmstadt, Germany, carried out a five-day structural survey, preparing plans of all architectural elevations of the two monastic churches, which then were turned into scale models and put on exhibition.[295] Both reconstructions were modelled on Egyptian-style religious architecture, rather than the basilica type model. This meant that the nave was depicted as an open courtyard instead of a roofed aisle lit through a clerestory, as Monneret de Villard had proposed. The models were incomplete, as part of the complex remained obstructed by the presence of three domestic houses in the nave. The situation had not changed markedly when James Wellard visited the White Monastery in the late 1960s.[296] Some 20 years later, Otto Meinardus mentioned that one monk, Father Basilius al-Bishoi, and three novices occupied the church, and that the nave had once again been transformed into a village.[297]

Graffiti found in the nave of the church testify to its continued use as domestic housing in the 1970s

288 For an extensive discussion of the work of the Comité at the White and Red Monasteries, see Meurice, "Intervention."

289 Meurice, "Intervention," 278. The work of the Comité at the White Monastery was reported in the Comité's bulletins from 1901, 1903, 1904, 1906, 1907, 1908, 1910 and 1912 (available online: http://www.islamic-art.org/comitte/BArchMain.asp)

290 http://www.islamic-art.org/comitte/Comite.asp

291 Meurice, "Intervention," 285.

292 Lefebvre, "Deir el-Abiad," vol 4: col. 459–502; Meurice, "Intervention," 280. See also Cédric Meurice, *Jean Clédat en Égypte et en Nubie (1900–1914)* (Cairo: Institut français d'archéologie orientale, 2014).

293 Meurice, "Intervention," 281–282.

294 Ugo Monneret de Villard, *Les Couvents près de Sohag*, 2 vols (Milan: Tipografia Pontificia e Arcivescovile S. Giuseppe, 1925–1927).

295 Hans-Gerard Evers and Rolf Romero, "Rotes und Weisses Kloster bei Sohag, Probleme der Rekonstruktion," in *Christentum am Nil*, ed. Klauss Weisses (Recklinghausen, 1964), 175–194.

296 James Wellard, *Desert Pilgrimage* (London: Hutchinson & Co, 1970), 129–133.

297 Meinardus, *Monks*, 181.

and 1980s.[298] The church was finally cleared of the remaining houses in 1985 by the local department of the Supreme Council of Antiquities. The following year, they commenced excavations to the south and east of the church in order to examine the early monastic complex (see further comments below). In 1973, Pope Shenoute III (r. 1971–2012) visited the White and the Red Monasteries, expressing a wish to revive monastic life at the two sites. In 1986 Pope Shenoute sent Father Basilius al-Bishoi to Sohag to re-establish a monastic community at the White Monastery, but it was only in 1997 that the Holy Synod of the Coptic Church officially acknowledged the Monastery of St. Shenoute as a fully recognised monastic community.[299] During the past 20 years, the modern monastery has developed into a thriving community with about 25 resident monks and 30 novices. The complex attracts a large gathering of pilgrims, particularly around July 1, when Shenoute is celebrated in accordance with the Coptic calendar and the *Synaxarion*.[300] The White Monastery Project was instigated in 2005 and the results of the project are the main focus of the next chapter.

2.6 THE ARCHAEOLOGICAL EXPLORATION OF THE WHITE MONASTERY (TWENTIETH AND TWENTY-FIRST CENTURIES)

The archaeological exploration of the White Monastery began in the early twentieth century as a part of a contemporary interest in the monastic environment by Clarke, Peers, De Bock and the Comité. The first mission was undertaken in 1907 by Petrie and his team of British archaeologists. After the completion of the restoration of the church, interest in the White Monastery faded and archaeological exploration was discontinued until 1985, when the Supreme Council of Antiquities (SCA) took an interest in the site. My account below presents an overview of the work carried out by the two missions and the circumstances under which the projects operated. Particular focus is placed on material remains that have not been accessible for re-examination by the White Monastery Project.

2.6.1 Petrie's Mission to Atripe (Athribis) in 1907

Petrie began the archaeological exploration of the White Monastery in 1907. He first visited the Sohag region in 1900 and returned seven years later with the principal objective of excavating a Ptolemaic and Roman temple at nearby Atripe—the site of the female monastic congregation. During the season, members of Petrie's team excavated and mapped a larger area to the south of the monastic church. Edwin Ward, a junior officer at Edinburgh's Royal Scottish Museum with no previous archaeological experience, led the team.[301] During the course of two weeks, Ward and his 'regiment of Arab diggers and carriers' exposed an area of approximately 160 m by 100 m (16,000m^2), containing a rich variety of mud brick and fired brick buildings.[302] Much of the following two weeks was spent drawing plans of the architectural remains brought forth from the excavations (fig. 10). Petrie visited the site twice—once at the beginning of the season and again towards

298 These inscriptions have been studied in detail by G. Pyke in cooperation with the SCA as a part of the White Monastery Project. Publication is forthcoming. See also, Gillian Pyke, Stephen J. Davis, Gaber Ahmed Hafez, Rashed Mohammad Badary & Sayed Mohammad Mahmoud,* "White Monastery 2011: Window Inscriptions" (Yale Monastic Archaeology Project [South] interim report, 2011).

299 Maximous El-Antony, "Prologue. The Renaissance of the Red Monastery," in *The Red Monastery Church: Beauty and Asceticism in Upper Egypt*, ed. Elizabeth S. Bolman (New Haven and London: Yale University Press, 2016), xviii.

300 Réne-Georges Coquin, "Le Synaxaire des Coptes: Un nouveau témoin de la recension de Haute Egypte," *Analecta Bollandiana* 96 (1978): 351–365.

301 Alice Stevenson, personal communication with author, 2013. See also Alice Stevenson, "Artefacts of Excavation. The British Collection and Distribution of Egyptian Finds to Museums, 1808–1915," *Journal of the History of Collections*. Advance Access (August 23, 2013), 5.

302 Anonymous, "Royal Scottish Museum," *Museums Journal* 6.4 (1906): 154.

the conclusion of the work. Based in part on Ward's notes and in part on Petrie's own observations, the results of the campaign were published in two pages of text and a single plan in Petrie's volume on Atripe.[303]

Here I provide a full thematic account of the information that can be extracted from the publication. Such a detailed account is necessary, as no other record exists of the excavations to the south of the church: the area was later backfilled, bulldozed and in part overbuilt in the process of refurbishing the site for the use of the modern monastery.

Petrie's interest in the White Monastery was kindled by what he described as large heaps of ceramics dating to the time of the emperor Constantine (r. 303–337). To Petrie, this material evidence suggested that the site predated formalised monasticism and represented a *coenobitic* establishment from the formative phase of Egyptian Christianity.[304] The main architectural features exposed by the team included (1) an enclosure wall with three entrances; (2) a large slag-heap, which according to Petrie resulted from lime burning; and (3) an area of brick buildings with associated ceramic emplacements (fig. 10). Finally, the main monastic church was briefly described.

Two phases of the enclosure wall were exposed—an inner section immediately south of the main church along with sections of the south and west sides of an outer wall. Petrie interpreted the former as the north wall of a smaller *coenobitic* congregation that predated the construction of the church. Judging from the plan and the intersection of this north wall with the western enclosure wall, this is clearly not the case and has been refuted by Grossmann.[305] No traces were found of the eastern wall that would have run alongside the edge of the cultivated area outside the complex.

Three gateways or doorways were excavated—one in each section of the enclosure wall (inner south wall, outer south wall and west walls). Petrie describes the opening in the south wall as five metres wide with a threshold of large irregular blocks.

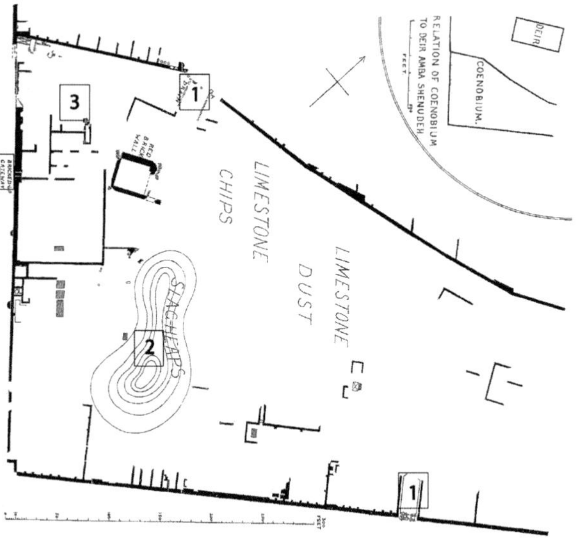

Fig. 10. Petrie and Ward's plan of the excavation at the White Monastery. 1. Enclosure wall and entrances; 2. Limestone slag heap; 3. Area of brick buildings (modified from Petrie, *Athribis*, pl. XLIII).

The gateway in the north wall was placed where two sections of the wall met. This opening was no less than seven metres wide and was flanked by two ceramic pipelines. Petrie correctly noted that such pipelines are unlikely to have run underneath houses, but were probably sunk below the surface at the sides of a road, thus indicating its width. The third opening, which is found in the northern half of the western wall and measures 1.3 m in width went out of use at some point and was blocked up.

Petrie's expedition took a particular interest in a large heap of limestone slag, chips and dust. According to Petrie, the size of the heap proved that a considerable building of limestone—a church dating to the time of Constantine—once stood here, although nothing remained of any built structure. He saw the distribution of waste deposits as proof of a systematic dismantling of the building, suggesting that the chips and dust remained from its construction, while the slag was the result of unsuitable building stone that had been burned to plaster.[306] Following

303 Petrie, *Athribis*, 2, 13–15.
304 Petrie, *Athribis*, 13.
305 Mahmoud A. Mohammed and Peter Grossmann, "On the Recently Excavated Monastic Buildings in Dayr Anba Shinuda: Archaeological Report," *Bulletin de la Sociéte d'Archéologie Copte* 30 (1991): 53–63.
306 Petrie, *Athribis*, 13.

the current interpretation of the site by the White Monastery Project, it seems equally possible that this area was used to prepare the limestone blocks used in the construction of the White Monastery church.

A collection of brick and mud brick features in the northwestern part of the enclosed area received special attention in the publication. Petrie described the area as consisting of a series of walls that ran either perpendicular or parallel to the western enclosure wall. A few individual rooms were identified, but in most cases too many portions of the walls were missing to make sense of their organisation. In summary, three smaller chambers were identified in the centre of the west wall. The southernmost contains a large ceramic vat. These rooms are very likely identical to buildings examined by the White Monastery Project (see Chapter 3.8). A vaulted chamber in the corner formed by the western and northern enclosure wall could be accessed by a staircase. A barrel-vaulted passage ran east from the chamber and is accessed from the surface by a flight of steps. A series of walls ran perpendicular to the north face of the north wall. It is not clear whether these walls were bonded and thus contemporary to the construction of the north wall, or whether they were abutting and, therefore, a later addition. In the area closest to the gate, two niches were found along with three ceramic emplacements.

Petrie also noted a large brick building that was located about 30 m south of the north gate. The building's exterior measurements were 11 m by 12 m and the walls are about 2 m thick. The size and solidity of the construction prompted Petrie to suggest that it served some important purpose, but he was unable to identify its function.

A few other buildings were mentioned in passing. Petrie stated that the majority of buildings on site were constructed from mud bricks with the exception of structures such as baths and cisterns, which were constructed from fired brick and cement.[307] The reference to a bathhouse—monastic or otherwise—is important as this could illuminate a little-understood aspect of monastic life, but unfortunately this structure was not elaborated further in the text or indicated on the plan.[308]

In terms of chronology, Petrie identified two main phases. According to his interpretation, the first use of the area took place under Constantine, where a large church was built, surrounded by a considerable Christian settlement or *koinobion*. Petrie saw the walls and features in the northwest part of the enclosure wall as a part of this early use and as contemporary with the three enclosure walls. The second phase took place in the age of Theodosius (r. 379–395) under the leadership of Shenoute.[309] Re-useable building material from the first church was used in the construction of the new building, which accounted for the large slagheap and the areas of limestone chips and dust. This new church became the centre for a new settlement located around the church, where a series of new dwellings were built, while the buildings of the original monastery remained in use.[310] Petrie believed that the northernmost extension of the west wall was added in this second phase, when the enclosure wall was expanded to include the newly constructed church. Petrie's suggestion derived from his observation of the northernmost extension, abutting rather than being bonded to the southern part of the wall. Unfortunately, he failed to observe that this particular building technique was applied to long stretches of wall throughout the White Monastery, where walls were constructed in sections to avoid strain and collapse of larger areas, to ease repair and to allow for expansion and contraction of the wall due to rise and fall in the temperatures. This technique is commonly applied in Egypt and is also found in the construction of temple enclosure walls of the Pharaonic period.[311]

307 Petrie, *Athribis*, 13.
308 Petrie, *Athribis*, 15.
309 Petrie, *Athribis*, 15.
310 This is the first mention of other buildings, which suggests that they were not visible, but just believed by Petrie to exist.
311 Jeffrey A. Spencer, *Brick Architecture in Ancient Egypt* (Warminster: Aris & Phillips, 1979), 112–118, 130–135.

A SUMMARY OF PETRIE'S AND WARD'S EXCAVATION

The pages above summarise the results of Petrie and Ward's two-week excavation season as they were presented in just two published pages of text and a single plan. Considering the size of the excavated area and the quantity of material unearthed, the publication is superficial and reveals several shortcomings. Some of these shortcomings were inevitable given the circumstances of the excavators' campaign, but the vast majority were methodological.

From 1905–1910, Petrie found himself in a transitional phase between terminating his collaboration with the Egypt Exploration Fund and establishing the British School of Archaeology in Egypt.[312] During this time, Petrie lacked proper financial support as well as qualified assistants, which meant that his documentation was often lacking and, at times, he left no clear account of the precise places he worked within a site.[313] The mission to Atripe and Sohag took place during this transitional period and the publication reflects Petrie's schematic recording as well as Ward's lack of archaeological experience.[314] Finds from the mission, now in the Petrie Museum, were sporadically recorded and sometimes objects from the White Monastery were labelled as found in Atripe.[315]

In addition to the unfortunate financial circumstances, Petrie's work at the White Monastery took place at a time where standard archaeological practice did not include stratigraphic excavation or contextual recording. The use of large numbers of workmen reflected a focus on object recovery and exposure of architectural remains on a large scale with the unfortunate consequence that meaningful deposits were removed without sufficient recording. Petrie's notebook lists the names of no less than 173 salaried workmen, but it is not clear if they were all employed at the same time, or whether they worked at one site or the other.[316] Neither the Petrie Museum nor Ward's archive at the National Museum of Scotland holds a record that relates exclusively to the White Monastery.[317] Furthermore, Petrie's diaries hold hardly any information pertinent to the excavations at the White Monastery.

The published architectural descriptions are minimal and most walls and features are either not mentioned or referred to with a single sentence. There was no record of building material, and no basic measurements or other characteristics that might hint at the function of the specific features, their internal relationship or their position within the site chronology. Indeed, Petrie gave no indication of sequential development, but simply referred to what he saw as the two main phases of construction. Lastly, Ward's lack of archaeological experience and the fact that the site plan was drawn during the course of just two weeks should mean that it was simplified at best and highly faulty at worst. At the very least, the scale is incorrect as will be demonstrated in Chapter 4.

2.6.2 *The Excavations by the Supreme Council of Antiquities from 1985 to 2011*

Almost 80 years after Petrie's excavations, the local department of the Egyptian Antiquities Organisation (later known as the Supreme Council of Antiquities [SCA]) commenced the second archaeological exploration of the White Monastery. Between 1985

312 Bierbrier, *Who was who*, 428–430.

313 Stephen Quirke, personal communication with author, 2013. See David G. Jeffreys and Harry S. Smith, *The Survey of Memphis* (London: Egypt Exploration Society, 1985), for the problems at Memphis, and Stephen Quirke, *Lahun Studies* (Reigate: SIA publishing, 1998), for the problems at Lahun.

314 I have consulted Petrie's notebooks, diaries and unpublished photos at the Petrie Museum with no further results, I have also been in contact with Margaret Maitland and Ine Castellano, curators of the Egyptian collection and librarian, respectively, at the National Museum of Scotland in Edinburgh that holds Ward's archive. Unfortunately, the archive does not contain any of Ward's documentation from his work at the White Monastery.

315 Alice Stevenson, personal communication with author, 2013.

316 William Matthew Flinders Petrie,* "Three Notebooks" (Petrie Museum, University College London, 1907).

317 Ine Castellano, personal communication with author, 2013.

and 2011, the SCA carried out a number of excavations in five distinct areas, the main excavation seasons taking place in 1985–1999 with additional excavations in smaller areas in 2005–2011. The combined area excavated by the SCA takes up some 19,500 m^2 and defines the current archaeological site, including the areas subsequently explored by the White Monastery Project (Chapter 3). This section will provide a brief overview of the work carried out by the SCA. It is based on published architectural reports compiled by, among others, Mahmoud Ali Mohamed and Grossmann.[318] The field work was supervised by Mohammed Abd el-Rassoul, who was the director of the local office and later became director of the Sohag regional office for Coptic and Islamic archaeology.[319]

The SCA began their exploration of the White Monastery in 1985 by clearing the remaining houses from the nave of the church, and started excavating the nave in 1985–1986. In 1988–1989 the nave was paved with the present limestone floor and the damaged northeast corner of the church was repaired. Finally, in 2001 conservation intervention was carried out at the north end of the west narthex.

The area immediately south of the church was excavated over three seasons in 1986, 1998–1999 and in 2003 (WM.5, see Chapter 3.6). The initial excavation took place as a test in a 20 m by 20 m square, prior to discarding materials from the demolition of the houses from inside the church into this test area. The excavations revealed a series of tanks connected by pipes along with four rooms that define the southern extent of a large rectangular building uncovered in 1998. In 1999 the area was expanded to the east and west, uncovering further rooms and a complex system of ceramic water pipes. The SCA report mentions the remains of two clay-lined fireplaces and ceramic tobacco pipes found during the first season of work. These finds indicate a prolonged use of the area, a point also demonstrated in Chapter 3.6.

The most extensive excavations took place immediately to the west of the church between 1987 and 2011 (WM.4, See Chapter 3.5).[320] This area covers some 100 m by 100 m and contains a complex architectural stratigraphy, which gives information on both the earliest and the most recent uses of the monastery. During the course of these excavations, a well in the northern end was identified with adjoining pipelines leading in all directions; a series of ovens, interpreted as pottery kilns and crushing basins, were found in the eastern part, as well as a large building interpreted as serving an administrative purpose. The complex picture revealed in this area of the site will be dealt with in detail in Chapter 3.5 and in Chapter 4.

Significant finds from the area to the west of the church includes two hoards of Late Antique gold *solidi* as well as 1185 single finds of copper coins. Hans-Christoph Noeske published the first hoard, although he was not given direct access to the coins, and relied on photographs supplemented by information provided by members of the SCA. The two remaining groups have not been published and information regarding their contents is only partially available.[321] The first hoard was discovered in 1987 in a ceramic vessel below a basin at the southeast outer corner of the large building, which has tentatively been ascribed an administrative role (fig. 11, a). This hoard, currently housed in the Coptic Museum in Cairo, included 400 coins, dated to the emperors Phocas (r. 602–610) and Heraclius (r. 610–641), all from the mint of Constantinople. A pottery disk that was used to cast imitations of *dodekannumi* dating to the reign of Phocas and naming Alexandria as the mint was found in the southeast corner of the adjacent building. Other finds from this building and its immediate surroundings include ceramic tobacco pipes, single-handed jars (possibly of modern date) and lamps dating to the Early Medieval, Medieval and Modern eras.

318 See Mohammed and Grossmann, "Dayr Anba Shinuda," 53–63; Grossmann et al., "Excavation;" Grossmann et al., "Monastery of Apa Shenute," 167–219.

319 Grossmann et al., "Excavation."

320 Grossmann et al., "Excavation;" Grossmann et al., "Monastery of Apa Shenute;" Mohammed and Grossmann, "Dayr Anba Shinuda."

321 Grossmann et al., "Monastery of Apa Shenute," 210–219.

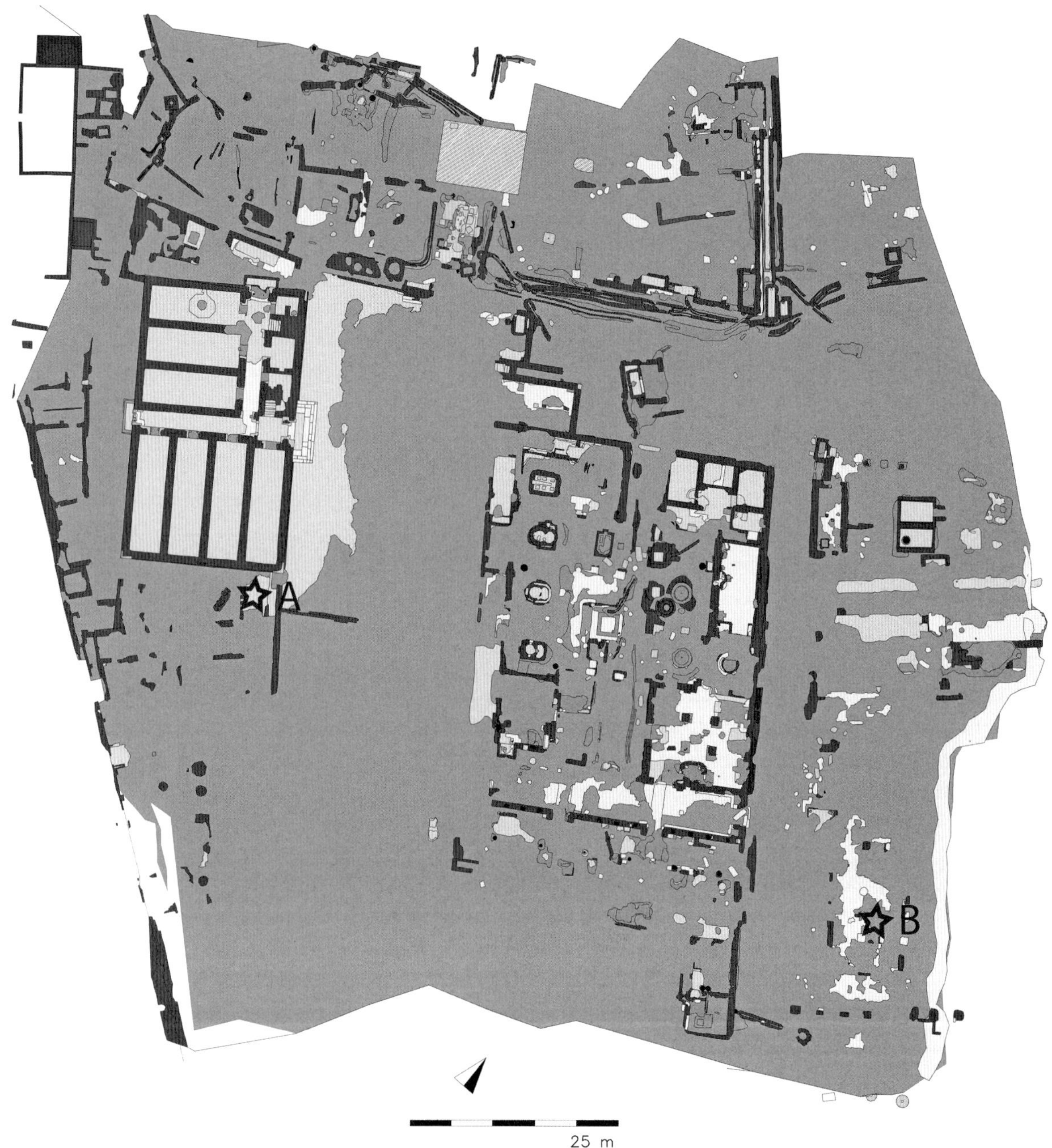

Fig. 11. Plan of excavation to the west of the White Monastery church (WM.4), showing approximate location of coin hoards A and B (map by Dawn McCormack and the author; © YMAP).

The second coin hoard was also found in 1987, in a pot below the floor, near the southernmost column of the western part of a peristyle hall, located to the west of the church (fig. 11, b). The find spot was confirmed by Grossmann during his collaboration with the SCA.[322] This hoard, currently housed in the Islamic Museum in Cairo, contained 420 gold coins, mostly gold *solidi*, including coins dating to Justinian I (r. 527–565) and several *semisses* dating to Constans II (r. 641–668). The single coin finds

322 Grossmann et al., "Monastery of Apa Shenute," 216.

were found in the general area to the west of the church (WM.4). This group contained 1185 copper coins from the reigns of Heraclius (r. 610–641) and Phocas (r. 602–610) and at least one further emperor who, unfortunately, is not specified, as well as a group that has been attributed to the Coptic patriarch Benjamin I (r. 626–665) with a possible mint in Akhmim.[323] Five further gold *solidi* were found while sieving the sand in the surrounding area. The hoards, their architectural context and their significance for our understanding of the use and history of this part of the White Monastery will be examined in Chapter 4.2.4.

2.7 SUMMARY

The written and archaeological sources discussed so far do not allow us to reconstruct the full history of the White Monastery. The dense textual record associated with Shenoute and Besa is mainly pertinent to the fourth and fifth centuries; thereafter, a variety of sources allow us to glimpse the history of the monastery up to the seventeenth century. We learn that the monastery was in use until some point in or before the fifteenth century and even after this point, the sources suggest a continuing use of the church. The sources associated with Shenoute and Besa are the most informative when it comes to the layout of the site and the organisation of monastic life during the monastery's early use. The sources deriving from the sixth to the sixteenth century only give sporadic indications of its use.

The history of the White Monastery amounts to more than sources pertinent to the foundation, early use and Medieval development. The travellers' accounts from the seventeenth century onwards and the scholarly exploration from the nineteenth century onwards are an almost equally important part of the monastery's history. The product of these early expeditions has formed not only our perception of the White Monastery, but also transformed the site itself. The priests and families who lived within the walls of the monastic church continued to use the surrounding site of the ancient monastery. At this time, however, it served as the outskirts of a village: for keeping animals, dumping garbage and as a source of re-useable building materials and fertiliser. Most recently, the modern monastery has redeveloped the ancient site for new purposes. This includes the construction of new buildings and levelling of the ground immediately next to the church with a bulldozer to create a stable surface for vehicles belonging to the many visitors. Therefore, it is impossible to analyse the development of the ancient monastery without also considering its recent development.

Based on the evidence presented in this chapter, I suggest that the White Monastery, or at least its church, has been in use continuously from its foundation in the fourth century to the present day. It is unclear from the travellers' accounts whether the White Monastery always housed monks, or at what stage it was transformed into a Christian village. The terms monastery and monk are used loosely: the former sometimes in reference to the church alone and the latter may on occasion have been used to refer to a priest. Curzon (1833), for example, refers to the site as a monastery and uses the term monks to describe some of its inhabitants, but also mentions Coptic women living within the nave. What seems clear is that the church of the White Monastery was in use in one form or another throughout the centuries and as such the site represents one of the longest-lived loci of Coptic Christianity.

323 Grossmann et al., "Monastery of Apa Shenute."

Chapter 3

AN ARCHAEOLOGY OF THE WHITE MONASTERY

This chapter provides an overview of the White Monastery based on the archaeological results obtained through the work of the White Monastery Federation Project (2005–2007) and the Yale Monastic Archaeology Project (South) (2008–ongoing). Some individual buildings have previously been discussed in publications by Grossmann and colleagues or in published excavation reports.[324] The results presented in these publications are re-evaluated in this chapter and discussed in a synthesised analysis of the site. The long history of the site means that not all architectural features can be reliably placed within a temporal or spatial framework. Such features will be briefly referred to for the sake of completeness, but otherwise omitted from the discussion.

In the following sections, I begin with an overview of the site as it appears today and a brief history of the White Monastery Project. Thereafter, each part of the archaeological site is introduced, and the main features described, focussing on stratigraphy and use, with particular attention to features that are relevant to the thematic discussion that follows in Chapter 4. These themes include the organisation of the monastic space, infrastructure and water supply and features associated with the monastic economy and production.

3.1 BACKGROUND TO THE STUDY OF THE WHITE MONASTERY

3.1.1 Layout and Overview

The current appearance of the White Monastery is a product of extensive excavations carried out by the SCA and the building activity associated with the modern use of the site. Most parts of the monastery are enclosed by a wall with only agricultural landholdings and the house of the current abbot located beyond the walls. Until recently, the villagers from the neighbouring Nag al-Deir had free access to the monastic grounds, but in 2005 this access was blocked by an extension to the enclosure wall.

324 Elizabeth S. Bolman, "The White Monastery Federation and the Angelic Life," in *Byzantium and Islam. Age of Transition 7th–9th Century*, ed. Helen C. Evans and Brandie Ratliff (New Haven & London: Yale University Press, 2012), 75–77; Bolman et al., "Late Antique and Medieval Painted Decoration at the White Monastery (Dayr al-Abiad), Sohag," *Bulletin of the American Research Center in Cairo* 192 (2007): 5–11; Bolman et al., "Shenoute and a Recently Discovered Tomb Chapel at the White Monastery," *Journal of Early Christian Studies* 18.3 (2010): 453–462; Bolman et al., "Tomb of St. Shenoute? More Results from the White Monastery (Dayr Anba Shenouda), Sohag," *Bulletin of the American Research Center in Egypt* 198 (2011): 31–38; Stephen J. Davis, "Archaeology at the White Monastery, 2005–2010," *Coptica* 9 (2010): 25–58; Grossmann, "Schenute;" Grossmann et al., "Excavation;" Grossmann et al., "Monastery of Apa Shenute;" Mohammed and Grossmann, "Dayr Anba Shinuda."

The enclosed area can roughly be divided into two parts: a public eastern half, which is accessible to visitors to the monastery and contains the archaeological remains, and a more private western half serving the needs of the monks. The area south and southwest of the church contains modern facilities for visiting pilgrims and archaeologists. This area includes accommodation, a kitchen, a refectory and a church. The western half of the monastery is dedicated to the monks and their facilities, including structures used as cells, a refectory, a church for the resident monks as well as workshops, offices and pens for livestock and chickens. Between the public east and the private west, a cemetery stretches almost the full length of the monastery. A photo published by Hans-Gerard Evers and Rolf Romero shows that the cemetery already was present in the early 1960s.[325]

The archaeological site can be described as six islands of architectural remains set within a sea of sand and debris and framed by the modern monastery. These islands include the monastic church, along with five larger areas of archaeological remains that lie to the south, west and northwest of the church, exposed by the SCA since 1985 (WM.1–2, WM.4–5, WM.7). Together they cover an area of approximately 19,500 m^2. Further areas were excavated by the White Monastery Project (WM.3, WM.6 and additions to WM.1, WM.2, WM.5 and WM.7) (pl. 2).

3.1.2 A History of the White Monastery Project

The White Monastery Project was instigated by the *Consortium for Research and Conservation at the Monasteries of the Sohag Region*—a group of international scholars with backgrounds in art history, archaeology and epigraphy along with members of the Egyptian Coptic community. The consortium was formed at the Coptic Congress in 2000, based on an initiative put forward by Elizabeth S. Bolman, Darlene L. Brooks Hedstrom and Bentley Layton.[326] Initially, the consortium focused on the conservation of the wall paintings of the Red Monastery, but in 2002 and 2003 work commenced at the White Monastery,[327] focussing at first on mapping and recording of the architectural remains that had been uncovered by the SCA.[328] In 2003, members of the consortium organised a conference on the White Monastery and its neighbourhood.[329] At this conference, Sheila McNally and Todd Brenningmeyer presented a preliminary analysis of satellite images of the monastic site, in which they identified substantial architectural remains preserved below the surface and thus recognised the opportunity to further our understanding of the ancient monastery.[330]

Building on the work of Grossmann, McNally and Brenningmeyer, the White Monastery Federation Project began in 2005 with Bolman, Brooks Hedstrom and Peter Sheehan as co-directors. The consortium saw the White Monastery as containing a unique combination of a rich archaeological record and an extensive textual corpus. Together, these different strands of data were perceived to offer a rare insight into early Egyptian monasticism. The project set out with three main research objectives:[331]

- to examine the archaeological remains that correlate to the writings of Shenoute, with the aim of creating a record of monastic life in the fifth and sixth centuries;
- to examine the development of a monastic community over time – especially material that could yield information on the process of the site's abandonment;

325 Evers and Romero, "Kloster bei Sohag," fig. 75.

326 Darlene L. Brooks Hedstrom, "An Archaeological Mission for the White Monastery," *Coptica* 4 (2005): 4; Emmel, "Shenoute's Place," 32.

327 The results of these two seasons were published in Grossmann et al., "Excavation;" Grossmann et al., "Monastery of Apa Shenute."

328 Brooks Hedstrom, "An Archaeological Mission," 4.

329 http://egypt.umn.edu/

330 Todd Brenningmeyer and Sheila McNally, "Analysis of Space at the White Monastery: Short Report on Methods and Techniques." *In Living for Eternity: The White Monastery and its Neighborhood. Proceedings of a Symposium at the University of Minnesota, Minneapolis, March 6 –9, 2003*, ed. Philip Sellew, http://egypt.umn.edu/Egypt/1-pb%20pdfs/Bren.pdf, 25–38; Brooks Hedstrom, "An Archaeological Mission," 5.

331 Brooks Hedstrom, "An Archaeological Mission," 7.

- to compare the White Monastery to other *coenobitic* communities, thus examining the impact of Shenoute's alterations to Pachomian rule and establish if the White Monastery and its monastic federation could be considered unique in the repertoire of early Egyptian monasticism.

I joined the project at the first season of archaeological work in 2005. The purpose of that season was to evaluate the site's potential and establish a working relationship with the SCA and the resident monks. The former was achieved by combining different strands of archaeological survey, these being topographical mapping combined with geophysical examinations (magnetometry, ground penetrating radar and resistivity). These non-intrusive methods were combined with excavations by way of small test trenches in areas not previously examined by the SCA.[332] Also in 2005, a conference on *Christianity and Monasticism in Upper Egypt* took place at the White Monastery. This was the Third International Symposium of the St Mark Foundation for Coptic History Studies and the St Shenouda the Archimandrite Coptic Society.[333]

In 2008, the consortium was dissolved and the White Monastery Project was transferred to Yale University's programme called *Yale in Egypt*, with Stephen J. Davis as executive director, Gillian Pyke as archaeological director, Bolman in charge of conservation projects concerning wall paintings and Layton directing the architectural documentation of the monastic church.[334] From this point onwards, the project was referred to as the Yale Monastic Archaeology Project (South), and continued with a focus primarily on areas that had already been excavated by the SCA with limited key-hole excavations adjoining these areas to cast further light on their use and development. The vast majority of the work presented in this chapter was carried out as a part of the Yale Monastic Archaeological Project (South). However, instead of differentiating between the two projects, I use the term White Monastery Project to distinguish the work carried out from 2005 onwards from the work of Grossmann, Petrie and the SCA.

3.1.3 Methodology and Constraints

The long history of the site is reflected in its built environment, which contains a complex palimpsest of building activity, modification, abandonment and reuse. For this reason, the archaeological remains that define the site today do not represent one specific period in time, but several overlapping and intertwined phases of use. This situation, combined with the previous excavation of the site, means that the process of interpreting the material remains, their use and their place in the monastic chronology has proved highly challenging. The main archaeological resource available for analysis is architectural, and access to stratified deposits and associated material culture is rare.

From the outset in 2005, the White Monastery Project was conceptualised as an international and interdisciplinary endeavour including several specialists and assistants and with a close collaboration with the local department of the SCA and the resident monks at the White Monastery. During the first two seasons on site (2005 and 2006), non-intrusive geophysical examinations were carried out by Polish geophysicist Tomasz Herbich and his team to examine areas of particular interest for further archaeological investigation.[335] Four main areas were examined; these were located to the southeast of the monastic church, immediately north of the church, at the northernmost extent of the site and outside the modern monastic enclosure wall. The principal method used was magnetometric survey, with two areas south and west of the church subjected

332 Brooks Hedstrom, "An Archaeological Mission," 5.
333 Gawdat Gabra and Hany N. Takla, *Christianity and Monasticism in Upper Egypt, Volume 1: Akhmim and Sohag* (Cairo: American University in Cairo Press, 2008).
334 https://egyptology.yale.edu/expeditions/current-expeditions/yale-monastic-archaeology-project-south-sohag
335 Darlene L. Brooks Hedstrom and Elizabeth S. Bolman, "The White Monastery Federation Project: Survey and Mapping at the Monastery of Apa Shenoute (Dayr al-Anba Shinuda), Sohag, 2005–2007," *Dumbarton Oaks Papers* 65/66 (2012): 333–364.

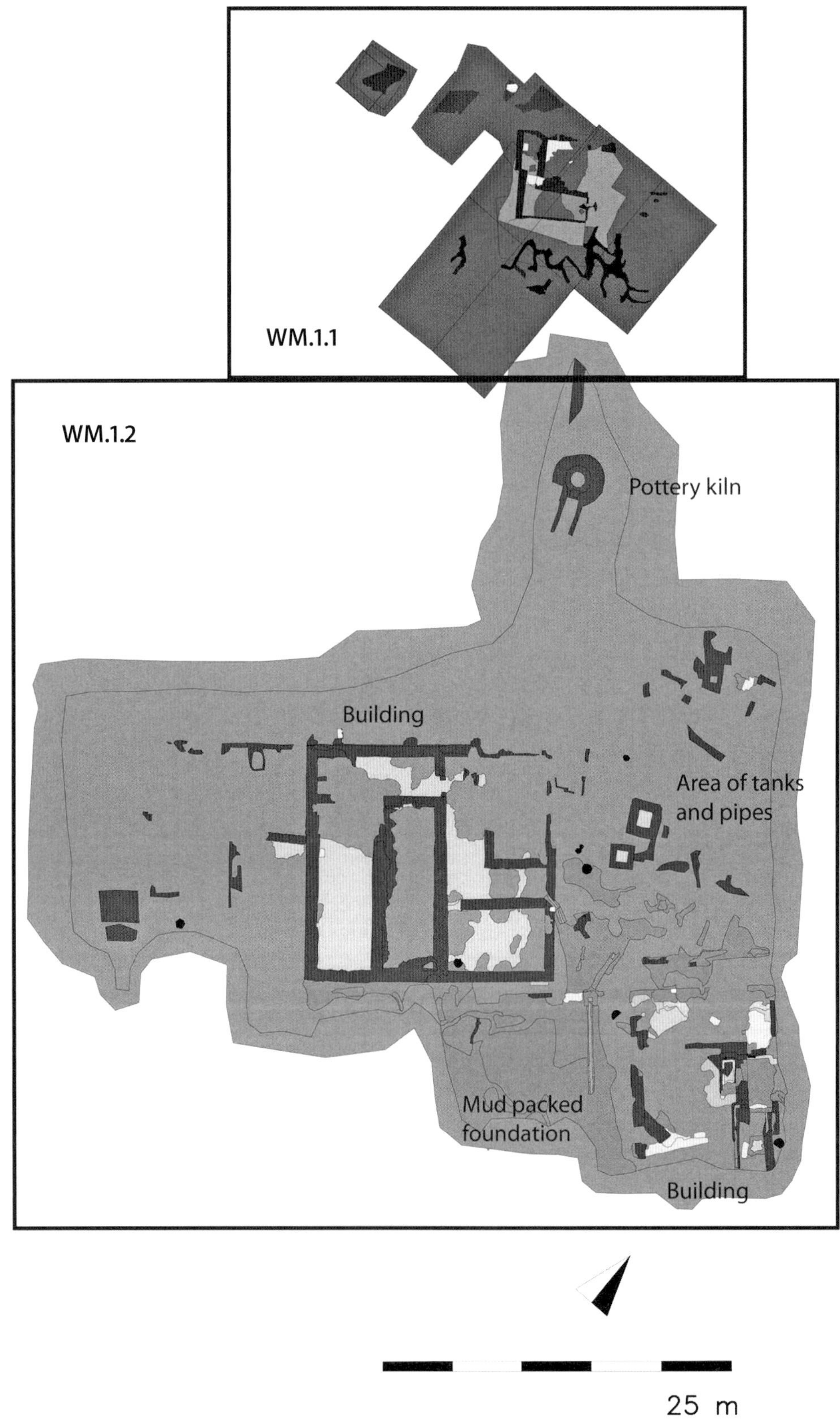

Fig. 12. Map of WM.1 identifying structures discussed in text (map by Dawn McCormack and the author; © YMAP).

to further analysis using resistivity survey.[336] Unfortunately, the magnetic survey was disturbed by the presence of modern buildings, iron water pipes, an extensive network of power lines and substantial deposits of rubbish including modern metal objects such as bottlecaps. The survey of WM.1 revealed a concentration of material remains in the southern half of the area, suggesting the presence of structural remains, although no distinct architectural structures could be defined. Better results were achieved with the resistivity survey, which revealed remains of structures in the area southeast of the church as well as a part of the enclosure wall.

The newly excavated areas were dug and recorded according to a version of the MoLAS single context recording system, specifically adjusted to the site.[337] This means that all deposits were drawn and photographed before removal and described in a context sheet during the process of excavation. All excavated material was sieved, and all finds were kept for further studies. The trenches and their architectural content were added to the maps of the White Monastery.

The areas previously excavated by the SCA were in most cases too large to allow the recording of every feature. For the purpose of this book, I subdivided these areas into zones and WM.4 was further subdivided into sections. Thereby, each area, zone or section is denoted with a unique identifier (see Appendix at the end of this chapter). Similarly, the archaeological phasing is discussed using a unique identifier pertinent to the area or zone under discussion. Phases are referred with Roman numerals (for example, WM.4.2.6.iii = White Monastery, area 4, zone 2, section 6, phase iii).

So far, the ceramic material, plaster fragments and all objects have been studied by Pyke, while Boud'hors and Pyke have examined the ostraca. Other find groups, such as glass, bone and archaeobotanical samples, have been omitted from this book as studies are still in progress. The ceramic assemblage referenced here is based on preliminary studies by Pyke with analysis yet to be completed ahead of publication.

3.2 WM.1 — THE NORTHERNMOST PART OF THE ANCIENT MONASTERY

WM.1 is located in the northernmost part of the White Monastery in an uninhabited sandy area defined to the north and east by the monastic enclosure wall, to the west by the cemetery and to the south by spoil heaps from SCA's excavations (fig. 12).[338] A preliminary survey of the ceramic surface scatter revealed a concentration of ceramics dating from the fifth to the ninth centuries with some modern fabrics in the mix. The scatter was concentrated in the southern end, while the northern two thirds contained few or no ceramic sherds. This distribution suggested that the northern section was natural desert and possibly never a part of the main monastic occupation (see Chapter 4.1.1). Following these results, excavations were carried out in WM.1.1 in 2005 and 2006 to determine the extent of the site towards the north and to look for indicators of chronology and use. A total of 300m^2 was excavated. Some 1700m^2 were excavated by the SCA immediately south of WM.1.1 in 2001 and 2010.[339]

336 Darlene L. Brooks Hedstrom*, "White Monastery Federation Project Excavation Report: Season 1 & 2, 2005–2007" (White Monastery Project interim report, 2007), 27–34.

337 Anonymous, *Archaeological Site Manual* (Museum of London Archaeological Service, 1994).

338 WM.1.2 is dealt with in Brooks Hedstrom and Bolman, "White Monastery;" Davis, "White Monastery," 36–37; Grossmann et al., "Monastery of Apa Shenute," 203; and in Gillian Pyke*, "White Monastery Project 2005 Preliminary Report" (White Monastery Project interim report, 2005); Gillian Pyke*, "White Monastery Project 2006. Preliminary Plaster Report" (White Monastery Project interim report, 2006); Gillian Pyke*, "White Monastery Pottery Report 2006" (White Monastery Project interim report, 2006); Gillian Pyke*, "White Monastery 2010: Pottery Report" (Yale Monastic Archaeology Project [South] interim report, 2010), 32–34.

339 Gillian Pyke*, "The Work of the Supreme Council of Antiquities at the White Monastery" (Yale Monastic Archaeology Project [South] interim report, 2011), 3.

3.2.1 WM.1.1 — Results and Stratigraphy

Five phases of use were identified in WM.1.1. The earliest use of the area (WM.1.1.i) was identified as a rectangular building (6.8 × 6.5 m) made from fired bricks with plaster-coated walls and floors laid with lime stone pavers. In its current state, three rooms are discernible, but the floor foundations suggest that the structure once continued further south and west. The foundational deposits were not excavated and no material evidence was retrieved that could assist in a dating of the structure. The building technique may, however, be indicative of the construction date: similar limestone floors are found in WM.2 and WM.4, while the chipped limestone floor foundation is found in WM.2 only. The comparable structures are all associated with use from the fifth to the seventh centuries. Indications of burning throughout the building suggests that phase WM.1.1.i was interrupted by an episode of conflagration, which resulted in a temporary abandonment of the building.

Phase WM.1.1.ii saw a refurbishment of the brick building, during which the original fired brick walls were replaced with mud bricks. The same type of reuse was found in WM.2 and WM.4. There were no datable remains associated with this phase and neither the organisation nor its finds gave any clues as to the use of the structure. It is very likely that this phase correlated with a series of mud brick walls, located east of the structure, defining two sides of a small room with a stamped mud floor.

During phase WM.1.1.iii, the now abandoned building was used as a midden for discarded ceramic sherds. Three large pottery middens were found adjacent to each other. The ceramic assemblage dates to the seventh to ninth centuries, thus supporting a Late Antique use of the area.[340] Hereafter, WM.1.1 fell into disuse for several centuries.

Phase WM.1.1.iv consisted of crudely constructed pens made from mud and animal faecal matter. The date of the associated ceramic material suggests that this area was used for tethering and keeping animals by the inhabitants of the nearby village. In the most recent past (Phase WM.1.1.v), the SCA used the area as a spoil heap for their excavations.

WM.1.1 — FINDS

The ceramic material from the WMP excavations in WM.1.1 ranged in date from the fifth to the eighth centuries with some additional material from the ninth to the twelfth centuries and from the modern periods.[341] Overall, the pottery displayed a close association with food consumption and, to a lesser extent, storage and food preparation.[342] Of particular interest were fragmented *saqiya* pots that could have been discarded from the nearby well in WM.4, a large number of amphora, both locally produced and imported, and finally table wares including vessels from Tunisia and Aswan made in the sigillata tradition.[343]

3.2.2 WM.1.2 — Results and Stratigraphy

WM.1.2 was excavated by the SCA in 2001 and 2010 and was mapped by the WMP in 2005 and again after the final excavation in 2010 (fig. 12).[344] The excavation covered a maximum extent of 48 m NS × 54 m EW. The most prominent feature is a roughly square building (16.5 m NS × 18 m EW), which contains at least six rooms that are organised around a central corridor. The building went through two phases of use, equivalent to WM.1.1.i and WM.1.1.ii. Phase WM.1.2.i saw the construction of the building with fired brick walls and plaster floors. After an episode of conflagration, the walls were replaced by mud bricks (WM.1.2.ii) and the building was expanded towards the west by constructing several mud brick walls with plaster floors.

Grossmann interpreted the building as a residential unit and identified a staircase leading to a second floor.[345] No traces, however, remained of the stair-

340 Pyke*, "White Monastery Pottery Report 2006."
341 Pyke*, "White Monasetry Project 2005 Preliminary Report;" Pyke*, "White Monastery Pottery Report 2006."
342 Pyke*, "White Monastery Pottery Report 2006," 1.
343 Pyke*, "White Monasetry Project 2005 Preliminary Report," 4.
344 WM.1.2 was briefly referred to by Grossmann et al., "Monastery of Apa Shenute," 203.
345 Grossmann et al., "Monastery of Apa Shenute," 203.

Fig. 13. WM.1.2. Pottery kiln. View towards north (photograph by the author; © YMAP).

case when the building was re-examined in 2005 and 2010.

The eastern half of the area contains a series of tanks and pipes. The tanks are coated on the inside with a water-proof *opus signinum* plaster. Unfortunately, the preservation of the area is somewhat patchy, so it has not been possible to determine the purpose of the tanks and pipes.

A hard-packed Nile silt deposit is found south and east of the tanks. Comparisons to WM.4 and WM.5 show that such deposits commonly were used as floor foundations, thus providing some indication of the density of the built environment. Further evidence is provided by the remains of a square building in the southeast corner of WM.1.2.

Finally, a pottery kiln is found in the northernmost part of the excavation (fig. 13). The presence of tanks and pipes along with the kiln suggest that the main purpose of this part of the site included some type of production.

WM.1.2 — FINDS

The ceramic material from the SCA excavation in WM.1.2 was retrieved from three deposits: a systematic sampling of the surface selection; a levelling layer associated with the construction of the mud brick walls (phase WM.1.2.ii) in the square building; and a collection of sherds gathered by the SCA in 2010.[346] The first group (the surface sample) contained mainly sherds of a fifth to eighth century date, with few sherds as late as the twelfth century. The second group (the levelling layer) provided a *terminus post*

346 Gillian Pyke*, "White Monastery Pottery Report 2007" (White Monastery Project interim report, 2007), 5; Pyke*, "White Monastery 2010: Pottery Report," 32–33.

quem in the sixth century for the construction of the mud brick walls WM.1.2.ii. The third group (the SCA collection) contained in most parts material dating from the fifth to the eighth centuries.

The composition of the ceramic material in WM.1.2 differed somewhat from the material retrieved from WM.1.1 with few wares associated with food consumption, while ceramics used in industrial production, such as tanks, pipes and basins, were plentiful.

3.2.3 WM.1 — Summary

Based on the ceramic assemblage and its stratigraphic relations to the architectural remains, the primary use of WM.1 took place from the fifth to the eight centuries with some secondary activity in the ninth to twelfth centuries as well as in recent times.[347] The two main construction phases were found in both WM.1.1 and WM.1.2 and consisted of fired brick structures with limestone or plaster floors (WM.1.1.i & WM.1.2.i), replaced by mud brick walls (WM.1.1.ii & WM.1.2.ii) after an episode of conflagration. Grossmann has suggested that the conflagration resulted from the Persian invasion in 619.[348] This interpretation is discussed in Chapter 3.9.

3.3 WM.2 — THE FUNERARY CHAPEL

WM.2 is located south of WM.1 between the SCA spoil heaps to the east and the modern cemetery to the west (fig. 14). WM.2 measures 35 m NS × 21 m EW and features a funerary chapel, the tomb element of which has recently been proposed to be that of St Shenoute, and a pillared hall immediately to the south.[349] WM.2 was excavated by the SCA in 2002 and from 2006 to 2009 it was recorded by the WMP.[350] WMP's work entailed expanding the area

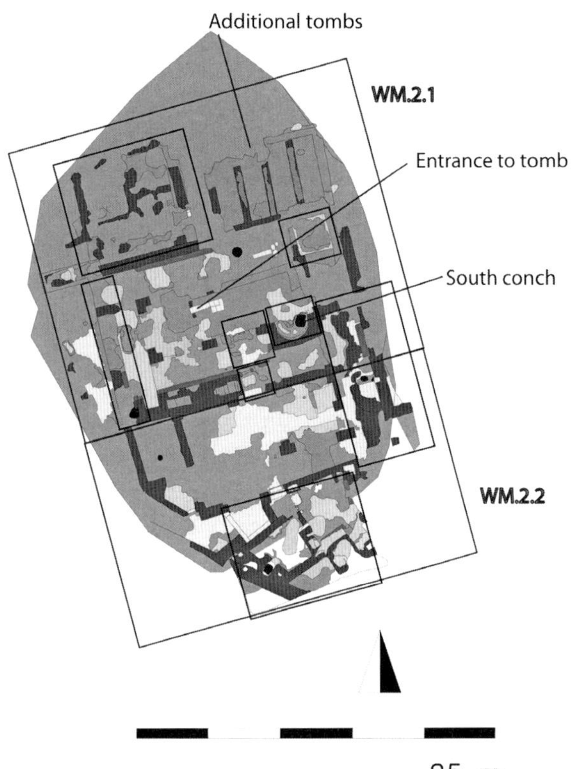

Fig. 14. Map of WM.2 showing main features discussed in text with emphasis on areas excavated by WMP (map by Dawn McCormack and the author; © YMAP).

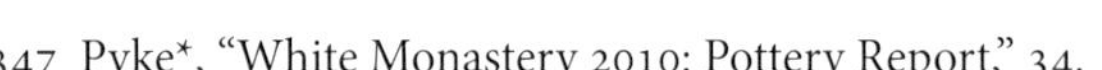

347 Pyke*, "White Monastery 2010: Pottery Report," 34.

348 Grossmann et al., "Monastery of Apa Shenute," 203.

349 See discussions in Bolman et al., "Shenoute;" Grossmann, "Schenute."

350 WM.2 has been published by Bolman et al., "Shenoute;" Davis, "White Monastery," 34–36; Grossmann, "Schenute;" Grossmann et al., "Monastery of Apa Shenute," 203–204; and has been dealt with in the following reports: Louise Blanke*, "White Monastery federation Project 2008. Area 1 Unit N. triconch Funerary Chapel, Excavation of Unit N3 and N4. Excavations and further Observations in the triconch Funerary Chapel" (Yale Monastic Archaeology Project [South] interim report 2008); Louise Blanke*, "White Monastery Project 2009. Area 1 Unit N. Excavation of Unit N6, N7, N8 & N9. Micro Excavation and Observation in the Triconch Funerary Chapel" (Yale Monastic Archaeology Project [South] interim report, 2009); Wendy Dolling*, "White Monastery Sohag. Tri-conch Funerary Chapel & South Hall. Archaeological Excavations Trench N1 – October 2008. Brief Report" (Yale Monastic Archaeology Project [South] interim report, 2008); Wendy Dolling*, "White Monastery Sohag. Archaeological Excavations Trench N5, Nov/Dec 2009. Preliminary Report" (Yale Monastic Archaeology Project [South] interim report, 2009); Gillian Pyke*, "White Monastery Project: Pottery Report. Autumn 2008" (Yale Monastic Archaeology Project [South] interim report, 2008); Gillian Pyke*, "White Monastery Triconch Funerary Chapel: Painted Plaster Report. October 2008" (Yale Monastic Archae-

Fig. 15. WM.2.1. Overview of funerary chapel showing entrance to tomb centrally placed in the nave. View towards east (photograph by Peter Sheehan; © YMAP).

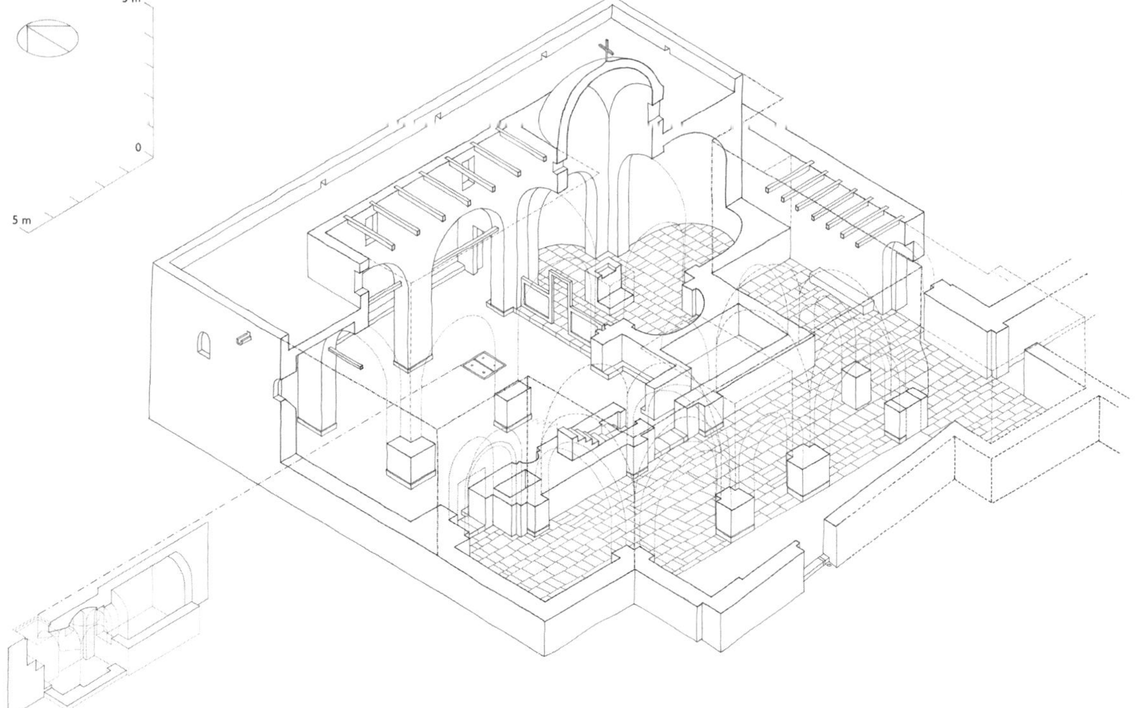

Fig. 16. WM.2.1. Isometric view of funerary chapel (drawing by Nicholas Warner; © YMAP).

through excavations to the north, east and south as well as clarifying structural relationships inside the church in six small trenches. WM.2 is the most detailed recorded area within the White Monastery, documenting the history of this part of the site from its construction to its modern use.

3.3.1 *WM.2 — Results and Stratigraphy*

The use of WM.2 developed over five phases. The earliest, phase WM.2.i, predated the construction of the chapel and consisted of mud brick walls found in excavations to the east of the church as well as below the church and the adjacent pillared hall.[351]

Phase WM.2.ii saw the construction of the funerary chapel (WM.2.1) and the adjoining pillared hall (WM.2.2). The chapel measures 11 m NS × 20.5 m EW and is constructed from fired bricks and lime-based mortar with plaster-coated walls. The chapel is orientated on an east–west axis with three aisles and a triconch apse at its east end (figs. 15 & 16). A possible narthex is located at the building's western end. The walls of the building have been thoroughly dug out in many places; often their layout is only preserved through the infill of the robber trenches, commonly consisting of small fragments of discarded building materials.

The north and south aisles gave access to rooms located next to the sanctuary, which were preserved only as foundations. Slightly off-centre in the chapel nave, a flight of steps givse access to a two-roomed barrel-vaulted structure below. No skeletal remains were found during the initial excavations in 2002, but the tomb was identified as dedicated to Shenoute, on the basis of an analysis of the decorative programme and the specific contents of the inscription (fig. 17).[352] Bolman studied the iconography and suggested a date between the fourth and the sixth century, based on comparisons with the nearby Red Monastery and the monasteries of Apollo at Bawit and Jeremias at Saqqara, thus providing a possible temporal framework for the construction of the building.[353] This interpretation corresponds with Davis' epigraphic analysis, which led the authors to propose that the tomb was designed for Shenoute himself in the fifth century.[354] Four rectangular rooms along the north side of the chapel may have served as additional tombs for benefactors or important members of the monastic community, who wanted to be buried close to the saint.

Fig. 17. WM.2.1. Figural representation of Shenoute in the *orans* pose (photograph by Gillian Pyke; © YMAP).

ology Project [South] interim report, 2008); Gillian Pyke*, "White Monastery 2009: Pottery Report" (Yale Monastic Archaeology Project [South] interim report, 2009); Gillian Pyke*, "White Monastery 2010: Pottery Report;" Peter Sheehan*, "Dayr Anba Shenouda/The White Monastery, Sohag. Archaeological Observations at the Tri-conch Funerary Chapel, January 2007" (White Monastery Project interim report, 2007); Anna Stevens*, "White Monastery Project 2008. Report on Excavations North of the Triconch Funerary Chapel, Area 1, Unit 2 (Trench 2). 30th September – 15th October 2008" (Yale Monastic Archaeology Project [South] interim report, 2008).

351 Dolling*, "Trench N1;" Sheehan*, "Dayr Anba Shenouda."

352 See Bolman et al., "Shenoute," 2011 for details.

353 Bolman et al., "Shenoute," 459.

354 Bolman et al., "Shenoute," 459–462.

The south hall is somewhat poorly preserved. It contains four freestanding, roof-supporting brick piers (originally there would have been at least six) and an abutting limestone floor. Rooms to the south showed some extensions of building activity in this direction.

Phase WM.2.iii involved modifications to the funerary chapel and to the adjoining pillared hall. A structural collapse, possibly following a period of abandonment took place throughout the building. After the collapse, WM.2 was used as a source of building material for construction elsewhere.

Phase WM.2.iv saw the church complex transformed to be used for seemingly domestic purposes. Ceramic vessels were inserted into the floor of the triconch, a door was blocked, and the floor was repaired in several places. Excavations immediately north and south of the chapel and the hall uncovered mud brick walls forming rooms that were contemporary with phase WM.2.iv.

Once again WM.2 fell into disuse and was subjected to several sequences of unsystematic pitting. In the final pre-modern use of the area (phase WM.2.v), the building was used as a cow-shed, evidenced by patches of dung in all parts of the building.

WM.2 — FINDS

As the long history of WM.2 entailed extensive sequences of reuse as well as excavation prior to the work of the WMP, no finds could be reliably associated with the first two phases. As a result, there is an absence of dating evidence with which to establish a foundation date for the WM.2 structures. The excavations to the south, east and west of the chapel and hall displayed a complete mix of material, where medieval and modern ceramics were found alongside the Late Antique sherds.[355] However, the general composition of the ceramic assemblage attests to the principal use of the buildings from the fifth to the ninth centuries (phases WM.2.ii–iii), with the domestic phase WM.2.iv around the twelfth to fourteenth centuries and the final phase (WM.2.v) in the modern period.[356]

A significant difference in the type of material provides important information about the wealth of the community living on site in these different periods. The sixth to ninth century assemblage commonly contains sherds of table ware produced in Aswan as well as a large proportion of transport vessels from Egypt, Tunisia and Gaza. This assemblage suggests that fine and utilitarian pottery as well as oil and wine were readily available, with no pressing need to recycle or mend broken vessels—even the finer table wares. This collection of sherds does, however, not necessarily resemble activities that took place within the church, but should be considered within the wider context of the White Monastery. In comparison, the assemblage from the domestic reuse contained hardly any fine wares or vessels used in the transportation of commodities, perhaps suggesting that these ceramic vessels were better looked after.[357]

Other finds of particular importance include two coins retrieved from the spoil heap that came from SCA's excavation of WM.2. One copper coin was struck by the Umayyad financial director, al-Qasim ibn Ubaydallah (r. 734–741) (see Chapter 2.3 for the story of his visit to the monastery). The other is too worn to read, but stylistic assessments and traces of the *shahada* might also indicate a date in the Umayyad period.[358] Although the coins were not found *in situ*, they indicate a presence on the site during the Umayyad period.

3.3.2 WM.2 — Summary

The development of WM.2—beginning when the chapel formed an integral part of the monastery (phase WM.2.ii), to its final pre-modern use as an animal stable (phase WM.2.v)—serves as an important comparison with other, less well-studied parts of the site. The economic prosperity of the site in the sixth to the eighth centuries is evident through the composition of finds and the use of building materials. During this prolonged use, the chapel and adjacent south hall were constructed from fired bricks with at least two full decoration programmes, one

355 Pyke*, "White Monastery 2009: Pottery Report."
356 Pyke*, "White Monastery 2009: Pottery Report."
357 Pyke*, "White Monastery 2009: Pottery Report," 7.
358 Luke Treadwell, personal communication with author, 2013.

partly replacing the other, as well as marble and limestone floors. The later phase WM.2.iv saw the use of mud bricks along with floor repairs, where re-used material was used to fill in the pitted areas.

3.4 WM.3 — NORTH OF THE WHITE MONASTERY CHURCH

WM.3 is a roughly rectangular area (20 m NS × 15 m EW) located immediately north of the monastic church (fig. 18).[359] The surface is covered in hard-packed gravel, which was deposited as a part of the modern use of the monastery. A two-room fired brick structure was excavated by the SCA immediately west of WM.3—each compartment measuring 8.8 m NS × 2.7 m EW.

WM.3 was chosen for excavation despite the negative results from the magnetometry survey. The lack of material remains recorded in this survey was considered worthy of investigation, in order to throw some light on why so little information was obtained from the geophysical examinations.[360] Another reason for excavating in this area was the suspected existence of a north–south route between the White and the Red Monasteries (some 3.5 km to the north). The presence of two doorways in the north wall of the White Monastery church and the alignment of the main street in the village of Nag al-Deir supported this idea. At the same time, the proximity to the church would facilitate an examination of its constructional history. For these reasons, excavations were carried out in 2005 and 2006 immediately north of the monastic church.[361]

3.4.1 WM.3 — Results and Stratigraphy

The excavation in WM.3 was continued to the level of natural sand and revealed no traces of architectural remains. However, other features that yielded information on the history of the monastery were

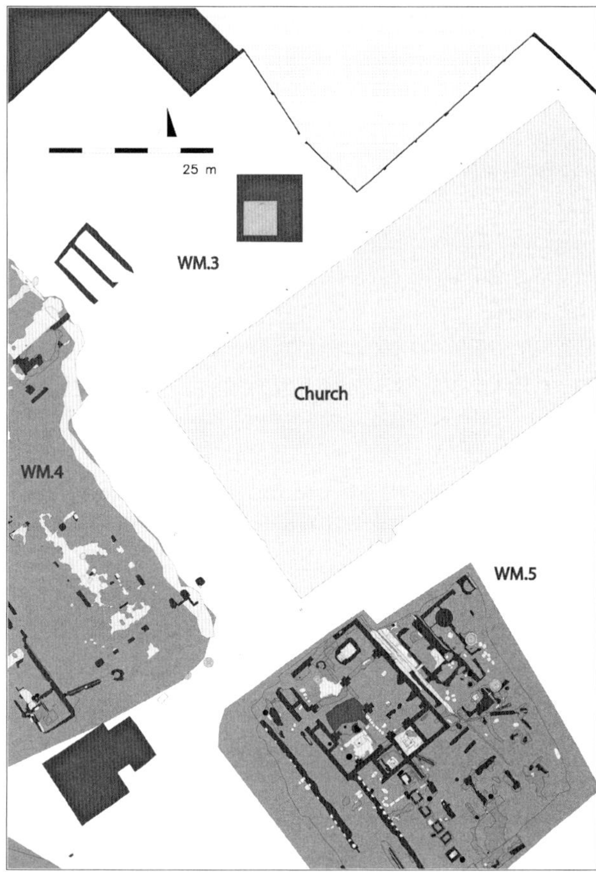

Fig. 18. WM.3 (map by Dawn McCormack and the author; © YMAP).

uncovered, thereby making the work in WM.3 of value. Three main phases of use were identified. The earliest occupational layer (phase WM.3.i) consisted of a compacted mud surface with two burials and several post holes dug into the natural sand from this surface. The two burials were of a young child (estimated at between 4 to 6 years old), wrapped in a reed mat and laid in a wooden casket, and of an adolescent, also wrapped in a reed mat, but entombed within a low vaulted brick tomb.

Phase WM.3.ii consisted of a large shallow pit that truncated the compacted mud surface as well as the brick tomb. The pit contained a dump with some

359 Bolman et al., "Painted Decoration;" Peter Sheehan*, "White Monastery Project. Unit D" (White Monastery Project interim report, 2005); Louise Blanke*, "Square Summary. Area 2, square G" (White Monastery Project interim report, 2006); Pyke*, "White Monastery Project 2006. Preliminary Plaster Report."

360 Sheehan*, "Unit D," 1.

361 Excavations were carried out by Peter Sheehan and by Louise Blanke: Sheehan*, "Unit D;" Blanke*, "Area 2, Square G." See also Bolman et al., "Painted Decoration."

3500 pieces of monochrome and polychrome plaster fragments, some of which were linked through comparative study by Pyke with plaster still *in situ* in the monastic church. Large amounts of discarded building materials mixed with some pottery and other finds were also retrieved from the deposit. Coins dated to the early 1920s were found in a deposit immediately above the dump, while glass fragments from the early twentieth century provided an approximate date for the deposition of the dump. The dateable material combined with the nature of the deposits would suggest that this dump was the result of the clearing of the church by the Comité in the early 20th century (see Chapter 2.5).

Excavations were carried out in 2006 to recover the rest of the material from the dump and obtain all plaster fragments in order to compare them with *in situ* remains and, thereby, study the church's decoration-programme.[362] This study drew attention to plaster fragments that were associated with the earliest use of the church as well as to plaster that was associated with the thirteenth-century restoration (see Chapter 2.3).[363]

The modern use of the area (WM.3.iii) contained activities associated with the work of the SCA and the modern occupation of the monastery. It included several sequences of levelling, where sand and gravel was spread across the area with a bulldozer. The disruptive consequences of this activity are clear from the amount of disarticulated human bones found within the deposit. The bulldozed surfaces were truncated by post holes that could be associated with the annual celebration of Shenoute during the festival (*moulid*) in July.

WM.3 — FINDS

The preliminary analysis of the ceramic assemblage from the dump (WM.3.ii) revealed that it contained Late Antique to Early Medieval wares, as well as modern material remains.[364] The deposits on top of the dump also contained a mixed assemblage representing all periods.

3.4.2 WM.3 — Summary

Three important observations were made from the examinations of WM.3. Firstly, the lack of activity associated with the Late Antique use of the monastery suggests that WM.3 was left open, serving either as a part of a road or as an open square. Secondly, the compacted mud surface represented the earliest use of the area. Unfortunately, there is no dateable material associated with the burials except the construction technique applied to the tomb, as the reused fired bricks would suggest that it post-dated the abandonment of the site. This point will be further explored below. The mud surface predated the Comité's work, and it is possible that the graves were part of a cemetery that served the community living in the church's nave. Thirdly, the dump from the Comité's work brings an important archaeological perspective to the modern history of the site, as does the extensive modern development, witnessed through bulldozed deposits, deriving firstly from the restorative work of the Comité and the SCA, and more recently from the preparation of the area for use by the modern monastic community.

3.5 WM.4 — WEST OF THE WHITE MONASTERY CHURCH

WM.4 is located immediately to the west of the monastic church. It was excavated by the SCA from 1989 to 1990, in 2002 and 2011 and takes up 115 m NS × 120 m EW (pl. 3). Grossmann has published three co-authored articles that address the archaeological remains from this area, based on observations made after the initial excavations and again in 2002–2003. He argued for the identification of specific buildings as refectories, residences, as well as areas designated for specific types of production.[365] In 2011 and 2012,

362 The results are published in Bolman et al., "Painted Decoration."
363 Pyke*, "White Monastery Project 2006. Preliminary Plaster Report."
364 Sheehan*, "Unit D," 3.
365 Grossmann et al., "Excavation;" Grossmann et al., "Monastery of Apa Shenute;" Mohammed and Grossmann, "Dayr Anba Shinuda." See also, Brooks Hedstrom and Bolman, "White Monastery;" Brooks Hedstrom, "An Archaeological Mission;" Davis, "White Monastery."

the area was further examined by the White Monastery Project.[366] While all zones and sections are presented below, only the architectural remains relevant to the analysis in Chapter 4 will be dealt with in detail. The overview of WM.4 provided in this Chapter (and the analysis in the next) represents the first attempt to analyse all material remains collectively.

WM.4 has been subdivided into seven zones based on either use or location (pl. 3). These are:

- WM.4.1: a thoroughfare and structures west of the church;
- WM.4.2: a kitchen to the west of the thoroughfare;
- WM.4.3: a food-processing area located immediately north of the kitchen;
- WM.4.4: an open square and a building on its west side;
- WM.4.5: the monastery's main well;
- WM.4.6: structures to the east of the well;
- WM.4.7: structures to the west of the well.

Architectural remains that cannot be stratigraphically or contextually associated with their surroundings are abundant throughout WM.4. In the following overview, these will be mentioned in passing, but are not subjected to any further study given their indistinct status.

3.5.1 WM.4.1 — The Thoroughfare and Structures West of the Church

WM.4.1 comprises a thoroughfare and four structures immediately west of the church (pl. 4). They represent some diversity in construction technique, use and date, but have been grouped together based on their proximity. Their presence in an area assigned to food production offers some hints towards the general use of the structures. Located immediately adjacent to the monastic church, this area is among the most exposed and therefore the least well-preserved in WM.4.

Fig. 19. WM.4.1.17. Overview of thoroughfare. View towards south (photograph by the author; © YMAP).

WM.4.1.17

In its current state of preservation, the thoroughfare stretches from the southern boundary of WM.4 two-thirds of the way towards the northern boundary, being 75 m long and 5 m wide (fig. 19). The alignment of structures further to the north suggests that the thoroughfare once ran the full length of WM.4. Doorways along the western façade gave access to a hallway (WM.4.2.4) that separated the kitchen (WM.4.2) from the food-processing area (WM.4.2.4) and to a storage facility (WM.4.3.15). The poor preservation of the buildings on the east side of the thoroughfare means that no doorways remain here. Nothing remains of the street's original surface, but sections of wall foundations that are vis-

366 Louise Blanke*, "White Monastery Project 2011. Area Q" (Yale Monastic Archaeology Project [South] interim report, 2011); Louise Blanke*, "White Monastery project 2012, Area Q" (Yale Monastic Archaeology Project [South] interim report, 2012); Gillian Pyke*, "White Monastery 2011: Pottery Report" (Yale Monastic Archaeology Project [South] interim report, 2011).

Fig. 20. WM.1.16. Overview of building identified as refectory. View towards southeast (photograph by the author; © YMAP).

ible along the western façade would suggest a surface level some 0.30 m above the current ground level.

WM.4.1.16

The pillared hall in the southeast corner of WM.4 measures 45 m NS × 20 m EW (pl. 4 & fig. 20). Traces of the outer walls of the original building (phase WM.4.1.16.i) are found along the building's north, south and west sides. Internally, the building consists of a large rectangular hall with a series of roof-supporting pillars that form a central rectangle. The floor is paved with limestone and a square plastered room is found in the northwest corner of the building. A *terminus ante quem* was provided by the coin hoard found below a floor paver, dating to the early seventh century. This means that the building must have been constructed before the date of the coins' deposition. Later use (phase WM.4.1.16.ii) consists of walls built from composite material that were constructed next to and around the pillars.

Grossmann referred to WM.4.1.16 as a peristyle hall and interpreted its function as a refectory based on the layout of the rooms and its proximity to the church.[367] His interpretation fits in general terms with my identification of the adjacent WM.2 as (one of) the monastery's kitchens. It also corresponds with studies of Byzantine monasteries by Popovic, who has suggested that the refectory played an important role in the religious practice in monasteries and therefore often was located immediately adjacent to the main church.[368]

367 Grossmann et al., "Excavation," 373.

368 Popovic, "Trapeza;" Popovic, "Dividing the Indivisible."

Fig. 21. WM.4.1.18. Overview of building. Note central hallway with catchment pits at north and south ends. View towards east (photograph by the author; © YMAP).

WM.4.1.18

WM.4.1.18 consists of five rectangular rooms that were accessed from a central hallway (pl. 4 & fig. 21). The outer walls are not preserved; rather, the building is defined by its floors and measures 15.8 m NS × 26 m EW. Two entrances (north and south), of which only the catchment pits remain, gave access to a narrow limestone-paved corridor from which a number of symmetrically-arranged rooms could be accessed. The catchment pits are preserved as shallow vats on the exterior side of the doors, where they according to Grossmann served to keep out rodents and vermin.[369] Four rooms are floored with an *opus signinum* plaster and one room is floored with limestone pavers. The room in the southeast corner contains the remains of a staircase from which either a second storey or the roof could be reached.

Grossmann suggested that WM.4.1.18 served as a residential hall—an interpretation based on similarities with WM.4.4.22 (see below).[370] I argue in Chapter 4 for an alternative interpretation as an administrative centre and a storage facility.

WM.4.1.19

A two-room fired brick building with an adjoining opus signinum surface defines WM.4.1.19 (pl. 4 & fig.

369 For a more general discussion of the use of catchment pits at the White Monastery, see Grossmann et al., "Excavation," 172.

370 Grossmann et al., "Excavation," 378–379; Grossmann et al., "Monastery of Apa Shenute," 169–172.

Fig. 22. WM.4.1.19. Overview of building identified as cold store. Note entrance in bottom right side and mud brick lining along walls. View towards west (photograph by the author; © YMAP).

Fig. 23. WM.4.1.20. Note possible doorway and catchment pit in foreground. View towards south (photograph by the author; © YMAP).

22). The building measures 6.5 m NS × 4.6 m EW and is accessed by a sloping ramp that leads from the surface level to a doorway in the north room. The floor level of the two rooms is found 0.5 m below the door's threshold. The two rooms are connected through a doorway with a now removed lintel and the south room contains a ceramic storage vessel with a depth of 1.05 m, which has been inserted into the floor. Both rooms were once roofed by barrel vaults, as seen from the vault-springs along the north and south walls. All walls have been reinforced by mud brick masonry on their exterior sides, which is known for its insulating properties, thereby suggesting that the rooms were once a cold store.[371]

WM.4.1.20

WM.4.1.20 contains the remains of two buildings (pl. 4 & fig. 23). The south room is built from mud brick walls with a limestone floor—a fireplace is found in

371 Grossmann et al., "Excavation," 378–379; Alfred Lucas and John R. Harris, *Ancient Egyptian Materials and Industries* (London: E. Arnold, 1962), 50.

Fig. 24. Map showing access routes in olive pressing area. Full lines go through preserved doorways or passages, dotted lines indicate where doorways could have been located (map by Dawn McCormack and the author; © YMAP).

Fig. 25. WM.4.2.4. Overview of hallway. View towards east (photograph by the author; © YMAP).

the southern end. Features to the north of the mud brick room have a slightly different orientation. They consist of a fired brick wall, a catchment pit and a granite threshold, thus constituting the entrance of a building of which nothing else remains. The building is cut by the mud brick room to the south, meaning that the latter is a more recent construction.[372]

WM.4.1 — SUMMARY

Very little dateable evidence can be associated with WM.4.1. The coin hoard found beneath the floor of the refectory (WM.4.1.16) suggests that the building was in use in the early seventh century and most likely also before. The northern end of WM.4.1 currently appears as if it was empty of buildings, but the few remains suggest the opposite: that the area was densely built over. The use of the southern part of WM.4.1 for a refectory and the northern part for food storage raises doubts about Grossmann's interpretation of WM.4.1.18 as a residential unit. Considering its immediate surroundings, it seems more likely that this building served as a storage facility. This point will be further discussed in Chapter 4.

3.5.2 WM.4.2 — A Kitchen to the West of the Thoroughfare

Several features identified as components of a monastic kitchen are located west of the thoroughfare in the southernmost part of WM.4 (pl. 3). These features include eight ovens, water boilers, storage bins, tanks and a cistern—together they measure 28 m NS × 32 m EW. The kitchen was a part of a larger enclosed compound that was used for the production

372 Grossmann et al., "Monastery of Apa Shenute," 195–197.

Fig. 26. WM.4.2.4. View of hallway. Note change of direction of limestone pavers to mark location of doorways. View towards north (photograph by the author; © YMAP).

and storage of food. The compound was divided in two by the corridor WM.4.2.4, which gave access to both the kitchen and the food production areas.

WM.4.2.4

The corridor served as an internal passageway, which connected the thoroughfare WM.4.1.17 with buildings in the western part of WM.4 and at the same time gave access to the kitchen (WM.4.2) and the food production area (WM.4.3) (figs. 24 & 25).[373] WM.4.2.4 measures 5 m NS × 32 m EW and developed through four main phases. Only few traces remain of the earliest use (phase WM.4.2.4.i), but a distinct brown mud brick wall with a cream-coloured mortar was found by the east and west doorways. WM.4.2.4.ii comprised the corridor's main phase which consisted of fired brick walls with limestone pavers. It is significant that the limestone pavers were laid out to follow the east–west orientation of the room, except where four symmetrically placed doorways provided access to WM.4.3.6, WM.4.3.8 and WM.4.2.3. Here, the limestone pavers changes direction to follow the north–south orientation of the adjoining rooms (fig. 26). Phase WM.4.2.4.iii saw the insertion of pipes that intersected the corridor through the doorways, and the somewhat haphazard repair of the floors in these areas. Thereafter, WM.4.2.4 was abandoned and used as a source of building materials. The final use, phase WM.4.2.4.iv, saw the reuse of the corridor with construction of

373 Blanke*, "White Monastery Project 2012. Area Q," 13–16; also discussed briefly in Grossmann et al., "Excavation," 381.

mud brick walls by the east entrance as well as repairs to the floor. At some point thereafter, WM.4.2.4 fell out of use.

Grossmann suggested that the corridor could have been used as a monastic sleeping hall.[374] The examinations that I have carried out as a part of the WMP, however, demonstrated that this could not have been the case. Grossmann's interpretation most likely resulted from looking at the corridor in isolation from surrounding buildings where the identification of a complex consisting of the kitchen (WM.4.2) to the south and the area for food processing and storage (WM.4.3) to the north emphasise the function of the hallway as an internal thoroughfare providing access to both parts of the complex as well as allowing movement to other parts of the monastery.

WM.4.2.3

WM.4.2.3 is a long hall that measures 7 m NS × 32 m EW located immediately south of the corridor (WM.4.2.4), and from which it could be accessed through the two doorways. The width, however, includes storage bins along the north wall and ovens and boilers along the south wall—the actual floor of the hall is only 2.5 m wide (pl. 4).[375] The development of the hall followed the phasing sketched above in relation to WM.4.2.4 and will therefore not be repeated in detail. The main phase (same as WM.4.2.4.ii) involved the construction of fired brick walls and limestone floors. The north wall was constructed with eleven ceramic storage vessels inserted into the wall (fig. 27). Each vessel measured 0.6 m (original height) and 0.5 m (diameter) and could be closed with a lid. Adjacent to each vessel, one or two niches can be found. These niches were intended for further storage or for placing a lamp when retrieving the stored material from the ceramic vessels. Plastered square bins were constructed in front of the ceramic vessels; each bin measures 0.5 m × 0.6 m (depth unknown) (fig. 28).

Fig. 27. WM.4.2.3. Ceramic storage vessel built into north wall. Note vessel rim, possibly intended for lid. View towards north (photograph by the author; © YMAP).

Eight bread ovens were identified on the south side of the south wall (the bread ovens are discussed in detail in Chapter 4.2.2). They consisted of circular structures with a plastered interior set within a frame of bricks with an internal diameter of 1.15 m and an exterior diameter of 1.4 m.

Separated from the ovens by a brick wall, tall and narrow ceramic vessels were built into the north side of the wall. Thick deposits of limescale found inside the vessels revealed that the installations were used for heating water and perhaps for cooking (fig. 29).[376] None of the vessels were preserved to their full height, but a single vessel was found preserved to a height of 0.9 m with a diameter of 0.5 m. The eight oven/vessel installations were separated by limestone blocks, possibly to prevent further transfer of heat through the wall.

374 Grossmann et al., "Excavation," 381.
375 Blanke*, "White Monastery Project 2012. Area Q," 8–13.
376 Mary F. Ownby*, "Preliminary Petrographic Analysis of Plasters and Mortars from the Triconch Church Project, White Monastery, Sohag" (Yale Monastic Archaeology Project [South] interim report, 2012).

Fig. 28. WM.4.2.3. Remains of storage bins built against north wall. View towards north (photograph by the author; © YMAP).

Fig. 29. WM.4.2.3. Example of oven/boiler installation. Note lime scale in ceramic vessel. View towards southwest (photograph by the author; © YMAP).

Fig. 30. WM.4.2.1. Overview of rooms identified as kitchen. Note cistern at the back of the photo. View towards south (photograph by the author; © YMAP).

WM.4.2.3.iii–iv saw the gradual decline of WM.4.2.3, where less expensive building materials were used for repairs and modifications until the hall was abandoned.

WM.4.2.5

WM.4.2.5 is located immediately west of WM.4.2.3 (pl. 4). The section contains a plaster-lined fired brick tank, a fired brick wall and remains of a plastered floor. The section has been thoroughly pitted and therefore the features cannot be meaningfully contextualised.

WM.4.2.2

WM.4.2.2 is located immediately south of the hall with the bread ovens (WM.4.2.3). The full size of the section is unknown, as is its internal organisation—only the south and east walls are preserved (pl. 4).[377] In its current condition, WM.4.2.2 measures 5.5 m NS × 15.6 m EW and comprises two areas of architectural remains. The eastern part consists of a fired brick wall, abutted by an *opus signinum* floor. The western part consists of two fired brick sub-floors set on top of each other, and a pipe that runs for a stretch of 3.8 m below the earlier subfloor. The diameter of the pipe is 0.21 m, making it among the thickest pipes on site. A local fire damaged this section, but does not seem to have reached adjoining sections.

WM.4.2.1

WM.4.2.1 is the southernmost excavated part of the kitchen (pl. 4 & fig. 30).[378] The section contains a

377 Blanke*, "White Monastery Project 2012. Area Q," 6–8.

378 Blanke*, "White Monastery Project 2012. Area Q," 3–6.

Fig. 31. WM.4.3.6. Overview of four-pillared hall. View towards east (photograph by the author; © YMAP).

small cistern, which was set within a small square room, three ceramic vessels that were integrated in the architectural layout, one of which was fed by a pipe that led from the cistern, and a basin, which was found covered in limescale. It measures 10.5 m NS × 6.5 m EW.

Measured from the top of the opening, the cistern is 1.35 m deep. Internally it is shaped like a flat-bottomed dome—walls and floors coated in *opus signinum* (similar in design to the cistern in WM.5.2). The floor was built with a significant slope towards the centre, where a small open-formed granite vessel is found. It served as a sump, allowing the cistern to be emptied for cleaning or repairs. The internal measurements of the cistern are 1.37 × 1.93 m, while a limescale line 0.97 m above floor level indicates the height of the water. Thereby, the total capacity of the cistern was less than 2.2 m^3. Two pipes are found inside the cistern—one served as an inlet and the other as an overflow. There are no indications of a mechanical water lifting system and given the small quantity of water used, manual lifting would have been sufficient.

WM. 4.2 — SUMMARY

The activities that took place in the northern part of the kitchen were identified from the remains of ovens, boilers, storage jars and bins. The southern part (WM.4.2.1) appears to have been the kitchen's main water source from which water was collected and distributed to the tanks and boilers. The earliest use of the area (same as WM.4.2.4.i and WM.4.2.3.i) is enigmatic, but thereafter, the kitchen maintained its layout and function. Unfortunately, the lack of stratified material remains means that it has not been possible to offer reliable dates for the phases.

3.5.3 *WM.4.3 — A Food-processing Area located immediately North of the Kitchen*

A zone designed for food production and storage is located immediately north of the dividing corridor (WM.4.2.4) (pl. 3). WM.4.3 measures 37.7 m NS × 34 m EW and has been divided into eleven sections. The sections are examined below according to their internal organisation as they would have been accessed from WM.4.2.4, beginning with WM.4.3.6, WM.4.3.9, WM.4.3.14, WM.4.3.13, WM.4.3.15, WM.4.3.29, WM.4.3.11, WM.4.3.10, WM.4.3.8, WM.4.3.7, then WM.4.3.12 (see pl. 4).[379]

WM.4.3.6

WM.4.3.6 consists of a roughly square room measuring 10.8 m NS × 12.6 m EW, which saw five phases of use (pl. 4 & fig. 31).[380] WM.4.3.6.i included walls constructed in the distinctive dark brown mud brick also found in WM.4.2.3 and WM.4.2.4, which was abutted by an *opus signinum* plaster floor. Phase WM.4.3.6.ii saw the floor replaced by limestone pavers. A major refurbishment took place in phase WM.4.3.6.iii, which included replacing the mud brick walls with fired bricks. The limestone floor remained in use and the lower part of the mud brick walls were employed as foundations for the brick walls. Two rows of four piers were inserted to support the roof.

Phase WM.4.3.6.iii was followed by a temporary disuse. During this disuse the building was either dismantled or became derelict to a point where the walls and roofs collapsed.

In phase WM.4.3.6.vi, mud brick walls replaced the fired brick walls. Once again, this phase was followed by disuse and possibly also removal of building materials for use elsewhere. Phase WM.4.3.6.v saw the final use of the area, in which the south wall was replaced by a composite wall of mixed building materials that probably were harvested from the site as well as a semi-circular enclosure abutting the south wall.

Grossmann interpreted WM.4.3.6 as a refectory (on the basis of its layout) and its date of construction to the middle of the seventh century.[381] Considering the function of the adjacent rooms (WM.4.3.9 and WM.4.3.14), which contained crushing basins, possibly for the production of olive oil, this interpretation seems somewhat unlikely. I explore the use of zone WM.4.3 and section WM.4.3.6 in Chapter 4.2.2.

WM.4.3.9

WM.4.3.9 was accessed through a doorway from WM.4.3.6. The section is composed of two similar sized rooms—each measuring about 5.5 m NS × 6 m EW (pl. 4 & fig. 32).[382] Centrally placed in the western room is a granite crushing basin, while a circular limestone foundation in the eastern room shows where a second crushing basin would have been. The walls were built from fired bricks, but the section's northwest corner was reinforced by limestone ashlars, most likely to support a beam holding the central pivot for the crushing basin. The shape of the pillars suggests that both rooms were roofed by vaulting. WM.4.3.9 underwent a similar development to WM.4.3.6 with sequences of abandonment, removal of building material and construction of mud brick walls. The integrity of the layout and perhaps also function appears to have been maintained through most of its use.

WM.4.3.14

Section WM.4.3.14 contains a granite crushing basin, a cistern and two tanks and measures 12.7 m NS × 8.1 m EW (pl. 4 & fig. 33).[383] The shared function of WM.4.3.9 and WM.4.3.14 suggests that the two rooms were once connected although this cannot be confirmed through the archaeological remains. The section underwent five phases of architectural de-

379 This area was discussed in some detail in Brooks Hedstrom and Bolman, "White Monastery."

380 Blanke*, "White Monastery Project 2011. Area Q," 3–5; Grossmann et al., "Excavation," 380–381.

381 Grossmann et al., "Excavation," 381.

382 Blanke*, "White Monastery Project 2011. Area Q," 6–9.

383 Blanke*, "White Monastery Project 2011. Area Q," 25–28.

Fig. 32. WM.4.3.9. Overview of room with installations for oil production. Note foundation for crushing basin in foreground. View towards west-southwest (photograph by the author; © YMAP).

Fig. 33. WM.4.3.14. Overview of room with crushing basin and cistern. View towards north-northeast (photograph by the author; © YMAP).

Fig. 34. WM.4.3.14. Crushing basin. Note incised image resembling two pillars spanned by a double arch. View towards west (photograph by the author; © YMAP).

velopment. The crushing basin was inserted during the second architectural phase (phase WM.4.3.14.ii), during which a tank was disassembled to facilitate the new use of the room. The crushing basin is similar in size to the one remaining in WM.4.3.9, with an exterior diameter of 2.38 m and a height of 0.78 m. The outline of two incised images can be seen on the side of the basin. A cross is found on the north side, while an image on the east side resembles two columns spanned by a double arch (fig. 34). The purpose of these images is unknown, but they could perhaps be associated with the manufacturer.

Several tanks are located in the northern end of the room, but their function is not understood. Phase WM.4.3.14.iii saw the insertion of a cistern immediately southwest of the crushing basin (fig. 33), which would have obstructed the treading path around the basin and would indicate that it had gone out of use. The cistern was fed by a pipe, which can be traced in fragments from the northernmost part of zone WM.4.3.

The two final phases of use resemble the development already described in relation to WM.4.3.6.

WM.4.3.13

A rectangular room (WM.4.3.13) is located immediately east of WM.4.3.14 and could be entered through a doorway placed centrally between these two sections.[384] The room comprises several limestone floors laid on top of one other (fig. 35). The north and east extent of the room is defined by mud brick walls, internally framed by thin fired brick walls. The south and west walls have been removed to the level

384 Blanke*, "White Monastery Project 2011. Area Q," 20–24. Grossman et al., "Monastery of Apa Shenute," 191–195.

Fig. 35. WM.4.3.13. Overview of room. Note veneer of fired bricks inserted into the mud brick wall along the right edge of the photo. View towards north (photograph by the author; © YMAP).

of their foundations. Three niches can be seen in the east wall and a sunken tank is located in the southwest corner. Within this tank, a lead pipe fed into a ceramic vessel set into the limestone floor. This vessel is a keg, set on one of its rounded ends. Both ends have been trimmed off to open the container at the top and the bottom, and the neck has been blocked with mortar. The trimming of the lower part of the pot would suggest that it was a soak-away.[385]

The rooms developed over nine phases during which the level of the floor was raised by 0.5 m. Ceramic evidence embedded in a foundation provides a *terminus post quem* for the phase WM.4.3.13.iv to the seventh century, but otherwise no further dateable material could be tied to the room.[386]

Grossmann suggested that this room was utilized for the production of *garum*— a fermented fish sauce.[387] I do not support this interpretation, as the production of *garum* in most archaeological contexts was shown to require containers far larger in size than the single ceramic vessel found in WM.4.3.13. According to Roman recipes, *garum* fermented while placed in the sun and the strong smell that accompanied the fermentation meant that the production was often placed on the outskirts of settlements.[388] I would instead propose that the room should be considered in relation to the crushing basins found immediately to the south and west. A full discussion of this issue will follow in Chapter 4.2.2.

WM.4.3.15

WM.4.3.15 is comprised by five adjoining rooms in the northeast corner of the food production zone (pl. 4 & fig. 36).[389] WM.4.3.15 is well-preserved in the north end, but the southwest part has been removed to the level of natural sand. The early wall phase, constructed from the brown mud brick and cream-coloured mortar already mentioned in relation to zones WM.4.2 and WM.4.3, is extensively represented in the two outer walls (north and east). Significantly, the remains of an earlier mud brick wall can be seen below the courses of the north wall. Whether this wall represents a local variation or an early phase across the complex is unknown. The internal walls are not very well-preserved, but variations in their thickness demonstrate how one could move from one room to the next (fig. 24). The rooms are connected internally through a central dividing room and the complex could be externally accessed through a doorway from the thoroughfare, WM.4.1.17. In all likelihood, a second doorway would have provided access from WM.4.3.14 in the south, although this cannot be confirmed by the

385 Pyke*, "White Monastery 2011: Pottery Report," 13–18.
386 Pyke*, "White Monastery 2011: Pottery Report," 13–18.
387 Grossmann et al., "Monastery of Apa Shenute," 195. See also Brooks Hedstrom and Bolman, "White Monastery," 355–357.
388 Robert I. Curtis, *Garum and Salsamenta: Production and Commerce in Materia Medica* (Leiden: Brill, 1991).
389 Blanke*, "White Monastery Project 2011. Area Q," 29–33; Grossmann et al., "Monastery of Apa Shenute,"191–195.

Fig. 36. WM.4.3.15. Overview of rooms. View towards south (photograph by the author; © YMAP).

Fig. 37. WM.4.3.11. Type one vat. Note six limestone blocks and central slot. View towards north-northwest (photograph by the author; © YMAP).

archaeological remains. All five rooms contain evidence of prolonged use as seen through extensive sequences of either plaster or stone floors.

Pyke examined ceramic material obtained from seven different locations: embedded within the floor foundations (five sample areas) and from surface deposits that were collected by the SCA (two sample areas).[390] The material in the foundations had a span of the fifth to the seventh century, suggesting a *terminus post quem* for the construction of the floors in the seventh century. The surface deposits ranged in date from the Ptolemaic period (332–30 BCE) to the tenth or twelfth centuries.

WM.4.3.29

Located in the northernmost part of the zone, WM.4.3.29 contains the remains of a north–south running corridor with a granite threshold, indicating a northern access to the complex (pl. 4).[391] Other features of relevance to the discussion in Chapter 4 include two pipelines, one set in a casing at the current ground level (also found in WM.4.3.10, WM.4.3.7 and WM.4.24), one set into a thick layer of mud packing some 0.5 m above ground level—both led water from the north towards the south. The location of the second pipe immediately in front of the entrance suggests that it was inserted at a time when the zone's layout was no longer maintained. A continuation of this pipeline is found in WM.4.3.10.

WM.4.3.11

WM.4.3.11 forms an L-shaped room in the northwest part of the food production zone. The section measures 25 m NS × 13.4 m EW, but only the outer wall frame, patches of limestone flooring and five vats built from fired bricks remain *in situ* (pl. 4).[392] The room could be accessed through a doorway in the north wall and through a doorway in the south wall that led to WM.4.3.8. Remains of piers in both the north and the south end of the room reveal that it was once spanned by a roof. The outer wall contained four phases of architectural remodelling, which is consistent with developments described in relation to WM.4.3.6.

The vats are of two different types. One is rectangular in shape with a central slot and six limestone blocks placed within the vats (fig. 37). The vat is plastered, but not with a waterproof material, there are no remains of a drainage hole or a sump and there is nothing to indicate that the vat had been subjected to fire or heat. This type of vat is found in the north end of WM.4.3.11 (two vats) and measures on average 3.5 × 2.5 m.

Three versions of the second type of vat are found in the south end of WM.4.3.11. These are rectangular in shape and contain two chambers, the inner—a circular chamber with a low dome—is accessed from the outer octagonal chamber, through a low arch (0.75 m) (fig. 38). Both chambers are coated in a red plaster. On average, the second type of vat measured 3.2 × 2.2 m.

One vat of the first type was converted into the second type by constructing a second vat on top of the first. However, rather than representing two different phases of use as suggested by Grossmann, the vats may represent two different processes, perhaps associated with the production or storage of food.[393] While the vats are essential to the interpretation of the room's function, unfortunately it has not been possible to find suitable comparanda.

WM.4.3.10

WM.4.3.10 is located in the central part of the food production zone. It covers an area of 12 m NS × 9 m EW. The prominent feature is a square tank of fired bricks framed by limestone blocks and with a limestone floor (pl. 4).[394] The tank is flanked on its north and west sides by split limestone boulders, placed with the split side facing upwards. A channel, made

390 Pyke*, "White Monastery 2011: Pottery Report," 13–18.
391 Blanke*, "White Monastery Project 2012. Area Q," 23–24.
392 Blanke*, "White Monastery Project 2011. Area Q," 13–19; Grossmann et al., "Monastery of Apa Shenute," 199–205.
393 Grossmann et al., "Monastery of Apa Shenute," 199.
394 Blanke*, "White Monastery Project 2012. Area Q," 10–12; Grossmann et al., "Monastery of Apa Shenute."

Fig. 38. WM.4.3.11. Type two vat. View towards northwest (photograph by the author; © YMAP).

from fired bricks and set within a compacted mud packing, runs from WM.4.3.29 towards the tank, with three further pipes running from the tank towards the south. The tank measures 1.8 m NS × 1.7 m EW and is preserved to the depth of 0.45 m. It was drained from the southeast corner, above which a hole has been cut into the top of the tank to drain away excess water. Evenly spread holes in the limestone frame around the tank suggest that it was covered by a light—perhaps wooden—superstructure.

WM.4.3.10 developed over four phases, of which the tank belonged to the second (phase WM.4.3.10.ii). The final phase of use saw a reorganisation of the section, where the tank had gone out of use and a pipe was inserted into a mud-packed area in its northern end, some 0.8 m above the floor of the tank. Remains of this pipe are also found in WM.4.3.29.

WM.4.3.8

The southwest corner of the zone covers 11 m NS × 11 m EW (pl. 4). It could be accessed from the north (WM.4.3.11) and through the corridor (WM.4.2.4).[395] WM.4.3.8 is poorly understood and its main features will, therefore only be summarised. It consists of two rooms that were connected through a doorway. The eastern room is empty beyond a plastered, fired brick platform in the north end. The western room

395 Blanke*, "White Monastery Project 2012. Area Q."

contains a square limestone-paved basin in the southwest corner and flat-bottomed ceramic vessels are found in the south, east and west walls.

WM.4.3.7

WM.4.3.7 covers 11 m NS × 7 m EW and has been excavated to the level of natural sand and thus contains very few architectural features (pl. 4).[396] These features include a tank in the south end that consists of a plastered floor set within a fired brick frame. The casing for a pipe runs along the entire east stretch of the section and continues further north through WM.4.3.10 into WM.4.3.29. A second pipeline runs along the western half of the section. Both pipelines led water from the well area in the north towards south.

WM.4.3.12

WM.4.3.12 stretches the full length of the westernmost side of the food production area and thus covers 34 m NS × 9 m EW (pl. 4). It contains at least four rooms that could be accessed from the courtyard (WM.4.4.28). Three rooms were paved with plaster floors and one with limestones pavers. The rooms and their connection to the surrounding sections have not been studied in detail.

WM.4.3 — SUMMARY

The sections described above constitute a zone dedicated to food production and storage. The eastern half of the zone contains a production area with crushing basins and possibly also rooms for pressing and storage. The use of this area is further discussed in Chapter 4.2.2. Unfortunately, the processes which took place in the western half of the zone are not well-understood. The architectural stratigraphy suggests that the entire zone developed though a sequence of use, temporary abandonment and reuse. An early phase was identified in the northeast corner of the complex (WM.4.3.15), but otherwise, the earliest remains comprise the dark brown mud brick walls with cream-coloured mortar that have been found throughout the sections. It appears as though this phase defined the main design of the complex, which was maintained through most of the zone's usage. The mud brick walls were replaced by fired brick walls (in, for example, WM.4.3.6 and WM.4.3.11) or with fired brick veneers (in, for example, WM.4.3.13 and WM.4.3.15) throughout the zone. Only after an episode of abandonment and severe removal of reusable building materials was the integrity of the layout compromised. The ceramic evidence provides a *terminus post quem* in the sixth century, which suggests the complex housed three crushing basins and was at the height of its production capacity during or after the sixth century. This function was seemingly maintained throughout the use of the area, but at some point, the production was reduced to include just one crushing basin in full operation. This development could represent a reduction in the number of monastics or a change to the monastery's economic interactions with extramural communities. These points are further discussed in Chapters 3.9 and 4. The most recent development of the area is poorly understood, but it appears to reflect the usage also seen in WM.1, WM.2 and WM.5, which entailed remodelling of architecture to be used as domestic houses and to keep livestock.

3.5.4 *WM.4.4 — An open Square and a Building on its West Side*

Located to the west of the kitchen and food processing zones (WM.4.2 and WM.4.3), an open square served as an architectural focal point. The structures west of the square comprise a large building (WM.4.4.22), the western boundary wall and remains of several mud brick structures (WM.4.4.23-25) (pl. 3). In total, zone WM.4.4 covers 88 m NS × 58 m EW. Only the building and the square have been examined in detail.[397]

396 Blanke*, "White Monastery Project 2012. Area Q," 16–18.

397 Grossmann et al., "Excavation," 375–378; Grossmann et al., "Monastery of Apa Shenute," 172–175.

Fig. 39. WM.4.4.22. Steps giving access to large building. Note catchment pit. View towards west (photograph by the author; © YMAP).

WM.4.4.28

Located centrally in WM.4.4, a large rectangular square is found bounded by the food production zone (WM.4.3), the zone containing the well (WM.4.5) and the large building (WM.4.4.22) (pl. 4). The structure to the south of the square has been almost entirely removed, but a fired brick wall that runs east from the southeast corner of the building (WM.4.4.22) could mark the southern extent of the square. In its current state, it covers 39.3 m NS × 25 m EW and is paved in its western end by a thick plaster, which is laid on two courses of brick and a layer of gravel (see also WM.4.5.30 below). The eastern two-thirds have been dug out to the level of the gravel.

WM.4.4.22

Located on the western side of the square, WM.4.4.22 constitutes the best-preserved building on site, the monastic church excluded (pl. 4). The building takes up 22.8 m NS × 19.3 m EW and is built entirely of fired bricks, except for large limestone blocks that support the corners and doorways. The walls are coated with a thin white plaster and all floors are covered with an *opus signinum* plaster, except for the central corridors, which are paved with limestone slabs. Three doorways give access to the building: two located on the building's central east–west axis and a third on the north side. The main doorway faces the square and is accessed by three limestone steps (fig. 39). A catchment pit (1.05 m wide and 1.15 m deep) is located between the staircase and the doorway. Beam holes in the doorjambs show that all three entrances had doors that could be locked from the inside.

The north and east doorways give access to small entrance halls, which are separated from the rest of the building by another set of doors.[398] Both en-

398 Grossmann et al., "Excavation," 376.

trance halls include staircases that once led to an upper storey. The room by the north entrance contains a deep circular cistern (7 m deep and 2 m in diameter, total capacity of 87m^3) that was fed by a pipe that came through the north wall at floor level. From two central corridors, seven larger rooms (11–13.5 m × 3.7 m) and three smaller rooms (2.8 × 3.5 m) can be entered. The south corridor contains six square niches, which according to Grossmann were intended for oil lamps.[399] The coin hoard and mould found in relation to this building suggest that the building was already in use in the early seventh century.

Grossmann has made two suggestions for the building's function: a granary or a residential unit for some of the monastics of the White Monastery, but concluded that the latter was more probable.[400] He suggested that monks slept on mats that lined the walls with fourteen to sixteen men in each room.[401] This suggestion was based on comparisons with similar rooms in *coenobitic* monasteries previously examined by Grossmann (see Chapter 1.3.2). In Chapter 4.1.1, I argue for an alternative interpretation as the monastery's *diakonia*, which was the location of the main administration as well as a store for food.

WM.4.4.23–25

The three contiguous sections to the south and west of WM.4.4.22 contain few but similar architectural features and will, therefore, be described together (pl. 4). The main feature is the western monastic boundary wall, which has been uncovered over a stretch of 170 m when combined with the wall-section in WM.7. The wall is composed of two main phases, an original structure and a later reinforcement on its inner (east) side, bringing the thickness of the wall to 1.45 m. Other buildings in these sections include mud brick walls that form a series of rooms along the boundary wall as well as a couple of minor sections of fired brick walls and plaster floors to the south of WM.4.4.22. A group of circular features associated with burnt material in the southwest part of WM.4 were interpreted by the SCA as bread ovens (see Chapter 4.2.2).

WM.4.4 — SUMMARY

The highly eroded nature of the remains on the south and west side of the building in WM.4.4.22 means that it has not been possible to integrate the features into one coherent stratigraphic sequence. Based on construction technique and comparisons with WM.7 (see below), four main phases can be proposed. The architectural stratigraphy suggests that the boundary wall was part of the earliest building activity in the area. It is possible that the reinforcement to the wall was added relatively soon afterwards. The courtyard and the large building were constructed after the wall and, lastly, the many mud brick walls and features were built—probably over the course of several (now undetectable) episodes of construction.

3.5.5 *WM.4.5 — The Monastery's Main Well*

The monastery's main well is located in the northernmost part of WM.4 (pl. 4). The well is described in Chapter 4.1.2 as a component of my analysis of the monastic water supply and therefore these paragraphs contains only a brief outline. The well measures 6 m NS × 8 m EW. The current level of the water table is some 12.5 m below the top of the well. It is built from fired bricks and limestone ashlars and water was lifted from the well by two parallel *saqiya* gear drives. A staircase located on the eastern side of the well and perhaps intended for cleaning or maintenance gave access to the water level. From the bottom of the staircase, it can be observed that the lower part of the well contains two larger niches (fig. 40). Their function is not clear.

The section exposed through excavations to the south of the well revealed that it was built in a large foundation trench. The material within the founda-

399 Grossmann et al., "Excavation," 377.
400 Peter Grossmann, "Keep," in *The Coptic Encyclopedia*, ed. Aziz A. Atiya (New York: Macmillan Publishing Company, 1991), 1395; Grossmann et al., "Excavation," 377–378; Grossmann et al., "Monastery of Apa Shenute," 172–175.
401 Grossmann et al., "Monastery of Apa Shenute," 172.

tion trench consisted of gravel with a high quantity of pebble- to fist-sized stones. The total lack of material culture in this deposit would suggest that it was retrieved during the excavation of the foundation trench and, thereafter, used to fill the gap between the well and the hole. Two further observations have been made. Firstly, the technique employed in the construction of the well would imply that this particular part of the monastery was not in use at the time of the construction, as the surrounding area would have become unstable and existing adjacent buildings would be at risk of collapse. Secondly, the deposit found within the foundation trench was not found elsewhere on the monastic site, except for immediately south of the well underneath the brick foundation for the courtyard. This would suggest that the material was used to level the area for the construction of the courtyard and probably also for the adjacent building (WM.4.4.22). It is, therefore, possible that this part of the monastery was developed in one larger building programme but, unfortunately, there is no dateable material that can be associated with the constructions. The areas immediately north and south of the well contain several pipelines that run towards north and south and further to all parts of the site (see Chapter 4.1.2).

The wells at the Red Monastery and at Atripe are discussed in Chapters 5.1.2 and 5.2.2.

Fig. 40. WM.4.5.31. View of well from bottom of staircase (photograph by the author).

3.5.6 WM.4.6 — Structures to the East of the Well

The three sections that are located to the east of the well have not been studied in detail, but assessment work was undertaken during the topographical survey in 2012. The overall layout will be summarised and attention will be drawn to the most important features, some of which are further discussed in Chapter 4. The three sections cover 46.8 m NS × 50 m EW and are characterised by a cluster of pipelines that runs firstly south from the well and then turning east and then after 36 m split into branches leading north, east and southeast (pl. 3). At least four pipelines follow this course, of which three are encased in fired bricks and plaster, while a fourth runs within a large open channel. The technique applied in the construction of the former three would suggest a similar date, perhaps as part of the original water supply system. The channel could represent a change in function and possibly a later date. North of these pipes a series of at least four consecutive tanks is found. These were likely fed by a fifth pipeline, of which only little remains.

At the eastern extent of the pipelines, the channel turns north into a long, seemingly open channel, which may have served as a sedimentation tank in which impurities sank to the bottom, while the clean water continued further through the system. The remaining pipes split into branches leading east and southeast beyond the extent of the excavated area. Remains of fired brick and mud brick buildings are found throughout the area.

The two sections 26 and 27 are located immediately to the south of the extensive network of pipelines. The main features are yet another pipe and two tanks; one is a sedimentation tank, while the function of the other is less clear. Fragments of a pipeline are found running southeast from the well into the food processing area to connect to the pipeline found in WM.4.3.29, WM.4.3.10, WM.4.3.8 and WM.4.2.4.

3.5.7 WM.4.7 — Structures to the West of the Well

An extensive area to the west of the well (28 m NS × 43 m EW) has for our purposes been defined as a single section (pl. 3). Recording in this area was limited and focused on the water supply. Extensive pitting has obscured the layout, but a few rooms at the eastern end can be identified and it is clear that the section developed over several phases. The nature and internal relationship of these phases have not been examined, but comparisons with the stratigraphic development of other parts of WM.4 (especially the kitchen and food processing area) suggests that the structures in WM.4.7.30 represent one of the latest phases of the site's use. At least two pipelines ran from the north side of the well towards the west. After some ten metres, they split into several branches, leading west, southwest and south. Two pipes run from the south side of the well towards the south and then west. One feeds into a cistern, while the other continues in the direction of the building in WM.4.4.22. The westernmost part of the section is occupied by modern tombs, marked by a rise in the ground level of almost four metres.

3.5.8 WM.4 — Summary

The lack of stratified deposits and datable finds complicates any attempt to define a sequential development throughout WM.4. In most cases, the sections cannot be associated with any datable finds or such finds relate to one phase only out of several phases of use. However, some chronological indicators can be emphasised. The coin hoards found in the structure interpreted as a refectory (WM.4.1.16) and in the building on the west side of the square (WM.4.4.22) provide a *terminus ante quem* in the early seventh century for the construction of both buildings. Assuming that WM.4.1.16 is indeed a refectory, the adjacent kitchen would presumably have been in use in some form at this time.

Importantly, the architectural stratigraphy of the kitchen and food production zones can be traced from its earliest manifestation (in the form of the brown- and cream-coloured mud brick walls). No dateable remains can be tied to this early phase, but WM.4.3.13 contained finds (WM.4.3.13.iv) that suggest a *terminus post quem* in the seventh century, indicating that the building had already gone through several stages in its development. The development of the zone immediately to the west of the monastic church is likely to have begun around the time when the church was completed (WM.4.1). The architectural remains suggest that the area maintained its integrity at least until the point of the first period of abandonment and disuse, an event for which no dating evidence has been found.

The evidence from the western part of WM.4 ties the construction of the well, the courtyard and the building together, but unfortunately does not provide a date for their construction. The evidence from WM.7 (see below) ties the construction of the perimeter wall to the fifth century, thus predating the construction of this triad. The literary sources suggest that Shenoute constructed a well in the monastery, which has generally been assumed to be the large well in WM.4.5.31.[402] The archaeological data can neither confirm nor refute this claim.

Throughout WM.4, the composition of the ceramic evidence suggests that the height of the area's use took place in the seventh to eighth centuries, at which point all main buildings were in use. The architectural remains throughout WM.4 suggest two sequences of disuse, removal of building material and re-occupation, before its final abandonment. After the first sequence of disuse, mud brick walls were constructed throughout the area: they appear to have maintained the approximate layout of the preceding phase. The second episode of reuse was much more haphazard and seems to represent a

402 Emmel, "Shenoute's Place;" Grossmann et al., "Excavation," 379–380; Grossmann et al., "Monastery of Apa Shenute," 186–189.

more domestic purpose with low composite walls, which could have been intended for keeping livestock.

3.6 WM.5 — SOUTH OF THE WHITE MONASTERY CHURCH

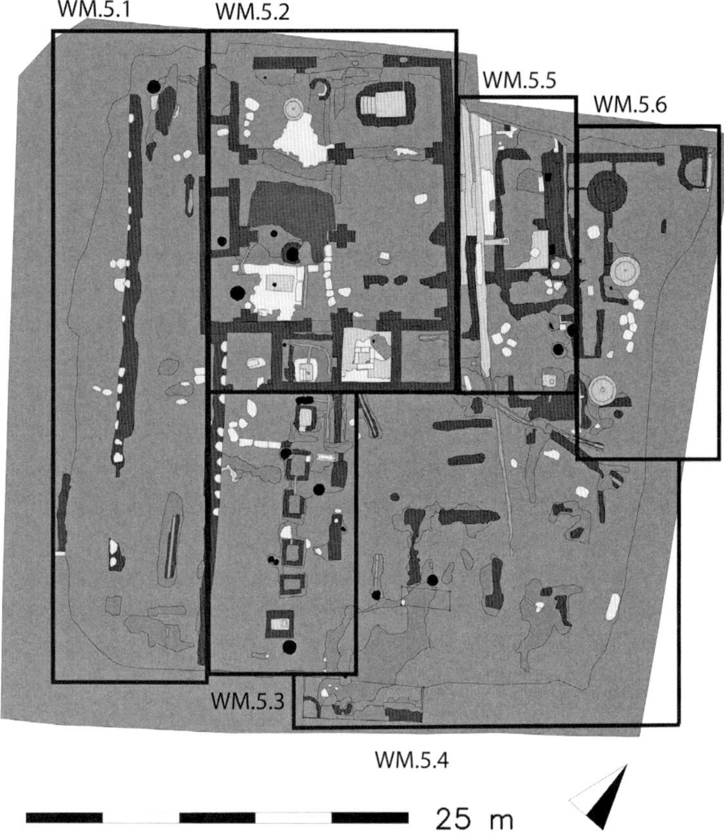

Fig. 41. WM.5 with zones (map by the author; © YMAP).

WM.5 has been the subject of work by three projects: excavations by the SCA in 1985–1999; a preliminary survey of the north and west parts by Grossmann and Brooks Hedstrom in 2002–2003; and a re-examination as a part of the White Monastery Project between 2008 and 2010.[403] WM.5 covers an area of 42 m NS × 45 m EW, which is characterised by a depression of some 6 m depth in the east end and 0.5 m in the west end (figs. 41 & 42). Located immediately to the south of the monastic church, WM.5 is by far the most exposed part of the archaeological site. Although the area is surrounded by a metal fence, the excavation forms a depression in the ground level in which windblown rubbish accumulates. Photographs from the archives of nineteenth-century travellers reveal some extensive changes to the monastic landscape in this area over the past one hundred and fifty years (fig. 43). Recent changes to the landscape were caused not only by the extensive excavations, but also as a result of preparing the surface for its modern use, which involved spreading out gravel and levelling the area with a bulldozer (also seen in WM.3 and WM.6). The following is an account of the main features of the six architectural zones and the internal stratigraphy of each, followed by a general chronology of WM.5. The six zones are:

- WM.5.1: the street and the west section;
- WM.5.2: the large building;
- WM.5.3: the tanks;
- WM.5.4: the southeast quadrant;
- WM.5.5: the four consecutive rooms;
- WM.5.6: the crushing basins.

3.6.1 *WM.5.1 — The Street and the West Section*

The western part of WM.5 is occupied by a north–south running thoroughfare, which continued beyond the extent of the excavated area. In its current state it is 40 m long and 5 m wide (fig. 44). In the

403 Grossmann et al., “Excavation,” 374–378; Grossmann et al., “Monastery of Apa Shenute,” 178–186. See also Louise Blanke*, “White Monastery Federation Project 2008. Area 3 Unit P. Report of Preliminary Work” (Yale Monastic Archaeology Project [South] interim report, 2008); Louise Blanke*, “White Monastery Project 2009. Archaeological Recording and Observations at Area 3 Unit P” (Yale Monastic Archaeology Project [South] interim report, 2009); Louise Blanke*, “White Monastery Federation Project 2010. Area 3 Unit P” (Yale Monastic Archaeology Project [South] interim report, 2010); Pyke*, “White Monastery 2008: Pottery Report;” Pyke*, “White Monastery 2010: Pottery Report;” Pyke*, “White Monastery 2011: Pottery Report.” See also Davis, “White Monastery,” 40–41.

Fig. 42. Overview of WM.5. View towards southwest (photograph by the author; © YMAP).

Fig. 43. Mounds of debris and discarded building material on the south side of the White Monastery church (photograph by Father Michel Jullien, reproduced with permission from College de la Sainte-Famillie, Faggalah, Cairo (nr. 521[1]). Courtesy of Cédric Meurice).

northernmost end of the street, a channel leads from below the large building to a ceramic storage vessel, the bottom of which had been removed, so it could function as a soak-away. This installation appears to have been a part of the earliest use of the large building (WM.5.2), thus predating the organisation of the adjoining area into a street. The original surface level is unknown, but the technique applied in the construction of the adjoining walls as well as a series of pipelines found in the southern and central part of the street would suggest an original surface level at 0.5 m above the current ground level.

The street is defined on its eastern side by a large building (WM.5.2) and the area with tanks (WM.5.3), while only a single fired brick wall defines the western extent of the street. This wall is preserved in two sections with a total length of 30 m. A series of flat limestone blocks were integrated into the construction of the wall, at intervals of 0.2 to 0.5 m. Each stone was positioned at the bottom of a shaft, which narrowed at the top to form a hollow square within the wall (fig. 45). Similar features are found across the street in the wall that defines the western extent of WM.5.3.

This layout led Grossmann to suggest that the two walls were toilet facilities that served the monastic community.[404] It is difficult to agree with this interpretation. The basic features associated with such facilities are missing. There was no drainage channel, a water supply to move the faecal matter, or soak-aways that could suggest that these architectural features were dry-latrines where the deposits were removed periodically through manual labour.[405] At the same time, the intensive and systematic use of the surrounding area would have prevented the process of deposit removal. Instead the channels should probably be interpreted as windows or ventilation shafts, which could supply the two buildings with fresh air and remove odours from the enclosed spaces.

Fig. 44. WM.5.1. Overview of street. View towards south (photograph by the author; © YMAP).

3.6.2 WM.5.2 — The Large Building

A large building (21 m NS × 17 m EW) is located east of the street in the northern part of WM.5 (fig. 46). The building developed through four phases. Phase WM.5.2.i comprised an open courtyard, flanked by four rooms on both the south and west sides. All rooms, apart from the southwest corner, were accessed from the courtyard. The courtyard itself was

404 Grossmann et al., "Excavation," 374–375.

405 General works on toilets include Barry Hobson, *Latrinae et Foricae: Toilets in the Roman World* (London: Duckworth, 2009); Gemma C.M. Jansen, Ann Olga Koloski-Ostrow, and Eric M. Moormann, *Roman Toilets: Their Archaeology and Cultural History* (Leuven: Peeters, 2011). See also Louise Blanke, "Washing the Masses, Washing the Self: An Architectural Study of the Central Bathhouse in Gerasa," *Syria* 92 (2005): 85–104; Louise Blanke, "Trois Latrines Publiques dans la Jérash de l'Antiquité tardive (Jordanie)," *Médiévales* 70 (2016): 43–58; Louise Blanke, Patrick D. Lorien, and Rune Rattenborg, "Changing Cityscapes in Central Jarash – Between Late Antiquity and the Abbasid Period," *Annual of the Department of Antiquities of Jordan* 54 (2010): 311–327 for the author's own excavation of a latrine in Jarash, Jordan.

Fig. 45. WM.5.1. Limestone and shafts in fired brick wall defining the east side of the street and interpreted by Grossmann as latrines. View towards west (photograph by the author; © YMAP).

Fig. 46. WM.5.2. Overview of building. View towards north (photograph by Gillian Pyke; © YMAP).

accessed via a small doorway in the east wall and possibly also a second through the north wall, but this part of the building was robbed out to the level of its foundation.

The rooms along the east side of the courtyard have been pitted out subsequent to abandonment below the foundation of the walls, leaving no indication of their original use. The rooms along the south wall are better preserved, although nothing remains in the far western room. The second room from the west contains a compacted mud subfloor with impressions of two pipelines that led through the room. One of these fed into a limestone tank with a plaster floor and two stone steps, which was drained through the wall and into the tank area (WM.5.3).

The third room from the west was composed of several layers of limestone paving with a small cistern in the centre. The cistern was coated with a red plaster and was equipped with an overflow drain in the south wall and an inlet in its north wall. Very little survives of the far eastern room, but it holds remains of three pipe inlets, located in the north, central and south part of the east wall. At least one of these pipes predates the construction of the building.

The courtyard contained several installations, which were associated with production. Among these were a rectangular tank surrounded by rough limestone paving with two adjoining pipelines (fig. 46) and a small oven of unknown type in the northern part of the building. Patches of a mud packed subfloor were preserved around both installations. Ceramic material associated with this deposit suggests a *terminus post quem* in the fifth century.[406] There are no architectural features to indicate that the courtyard was covered by a roof in this phase.

During the building's phase WM.5.2.ii, the courtyard was roofed and the floors were raised. Twelve piers were inserted into the courtyard—ten along the walls and two cross-shaped ones in the centre. The piers divided the courtyard into six equally-sized bays, each measuring 4.5 m NS × 6.4 m EW and spanned by vaults.[407] A staircase was fitted into the building's northwest room to give access to either a second storey or to the building's roof. Finally, a limestone floor was laid out at 0.4 m above the former floor level. Ceramic evidence retrieved from an excavation below the limestone floor offers a *terminus post quem* for the construction of the raised floor of around the seventh century.[408]

A large tank, located in the northeast part of the room, belongs to this phase (fig. 46). The tank, which measured 1.6 m NS × 1.9 m EW could be accessed via a staircase at its west end and was fed from the north through a narrow pipe, which served as a conduit for water from the well in the southwest corner of the church. The pipe is set in mortar with large sherds of the *Nebi Samwil*-type transport jar, arranged to make a flat surface.[409] The presence of these sherds gives a *terminus post quem* of the late eighth or early ninth centuries for the pipe and tank.

Later use of the building included minor repairs and modifications to the brick frame (phase WM.5.2.iii). Finally, a small granite crushing basin (exterior diameter 1.2 m) was moved to the limestone floor in the northwest part of the courtyard (phase WM.5.2.iv).

3.6.3 WM.5.3 — The Tanks

A zone containing six fired brick tanks, seven ceramic vessels and several pipelines is located to the south of the large building (WM.5.2) (fig. 47). The western wall of WM.5.3 is well-preserved, while only sections of the foundations of the east and south walls were preserved. The airshafts in the west wall suggest that the structure was once roofed. The area surrounding the tanks has been excavated or pitted far below the original floor level, but the technique applied in the construction of the walls suggests a surface level between 0.45 and 0.6 m above the current ground

406 Pyke*, "White Monastery 2010: Pottery Report," 5.
407 Grossmann et al., "Monastery of Apa Shenute," 178–186.
408 Pyke*, "White Monastery 2010: Pottery Report," 4.
409 Alison L. Gascoigne and Gillian Pyke, "*Nebi Samwil*-type Jars in Medieval Egypt: Characterisation of an Imported Ceramic Vessel," in *Under the Potter's Tree. Studies on Ancient Egypt Presented to Janine Bourriau on the Occasion of her 70th Birthday*, ed. David A. Aston, Bettina Bader, Carla Gallorini, Peter Nicholson and Sarah Buckingham (Leuven: Peeters, 2011), 417–431; Pyke 2010*, 10–19.

Fig. 47. WM.5.3. Overview of vats located south of the building. View towards north (photograph by the author; © YMAP).

level. It is likely that most tanks would have extended upwards by one or two additional courses at least.

Ceramic pipelines were preserved *in situ* between the three north tanks, meaning that fluids were moved directly from one tank to the next. A ceramic basin located at the northern end was fed by a pipe leading from the basin in the building's second room from the west. Water was also brought to the system from two other sources. One led from the main building (WM.5.2) through the same room as the above-mentioned pipeline and fed into the first and second tanks from the north. The second carried water through one of the airshafts in the western wall, which was then fed into the third or fourth tanks.

Seven ceramic emplacements were used with the tanks, but only three date to the primary use of the area. A flat-bottomed oval vessel was placed in the northernmost end of the row and fed directly from the tank within the building. A second vessel was incorporated into the row of tanks, while a ceramic emplacement at the end of the row of tanks served as a soak-away. A shallow sump at the bottom of the sixth tank suggests that the waste water was manually scooped into the soak-away. The size of the soak-away and its location on the edge of a building would indicate that only small quantities of waste water were discarded here, since large quantities would otherwise have threatened to cause damage to the structure.

3.6.4 WM.5.4 — The Southeast Quadrant

The southeast quadrant is characterised by a general lack of architectural remains, giving the false impression of an open area with few or no buildings. A closer examination of the remains revealed that this is not correct. The foundations of two mud brick walls in the northern end represent the earliest use of the quadrant. They run parallel to, and correspond in construction technique with, a mud brick wall found below the courtyard of WM.5.2.

The quadrant's most prominent features are a series of hard-packed anthropogenic Nile silt deposits, which served as floor foundations and remains of mud brick or fired brick foundation for walls. Other features include a few limestone floor pavers preserved in the southeast corner and a pipe that ran from the cistern in the building's third room towards a ceramic vessel set within the Nile silt. Another two ceramic vessels were found in the Nile silt—one was a part of the area's original use, while a transport vessel of the *Ballas* type was set into a cut in the Nile silt, suggesting a date between the ninth and the thirteenth century.[410]

3.6.5 WM.5.5 — The Four Consecutive Rooms

Four rooms, a hallway or alley and a cluster of north–south running pipelines were found immediately east of the large building in WM.5.2. The area covers 19 m NS × 7.8 m EW. The four rooms followed a development that was similar to the adjacent WM.5.2

410 William Yewdale Adams, *The Ceramic Industries of Medieval Nubia*. Memoirs of the UNESCO Archaeological Survey of Sudanese Nubia 1 (Lexington: University Press of Kentucky, 1986), 571–576; Pyke*, "White Monastery 2010: Pottery Report," 6.

where, at some point, plaster floors were replaced by raised limestone floors.

A plaster-lined channel that ran through the length of the eastern mud brick walls appears to post-date the remodelling of the rooms, and thus represents a later stage in the zone's development. The conduit was not equipped with a pipe, but led water from north to south in an open channel. The channel cuts a group of pipelines that led southeast from the passageway (see below) and, thereby, not only post-dated the original water supply, but were probably inserted at a time when the pipes no longer were in use. This situation corresponds to the development of WM.4.3.10 and WM.4.3.29. The final use of the rooms is clear from the northern edge of the excavation, where the profile reveals disuse, accumulated deposits and pitting from immediately above the level of the limestone floor.

The four rooms were separated from the building by a passageway that ran south from beyond the northern extent of the excavation. A plaster paving, laid upon several pipes encased in bricks and plaster, appears to derive from an early phase of use, while a limestone floor could be contemporary with the raised floors in WM.5.2 and in the four rooms. From this passageway access could be gained to the courtyard of WM.5.2 and possibly also to the four rooms (WM.5.5) and to buildings located in the southeast quadrant (WM.5.4).

At least four pipelines were encased below the passageway. These conduits supplied water from the north with branches feeding into the four rooms, the large building and further structures to the south. Two important features, defined as water inspection points, were located where the pipes entered the buildings (see Chapter 4.1.2). Immediately south of the building, the pipelines split into four branches—one led south towards the southeast quadrant, while the other three continued southeast before they split in three directions. A fourth, seemingly open branch looks as though it took waste water towards the east. The mud packing below the casing of one of these pipelines contained ceramic sherds suggesting a *terminus post quem* of the fifth century.

3.6.6 WM.5.6 — The Crushing Basins

The northeast corner of Area 5 contains three crushing basins and a semi-circular basin (fig. 42).

The semi-circular basin is located in the northeast corner and opens towards the east. It measures 1.83 m NS × 1.15 m EW and was built from fired bricks with a thick *opus signinum*-coated interior. The basin was entered via a limestone step, set between two small columns, of which only the granite bases remain. The basin was abutted by an *opus signinum* floor, suggesting that the surface was frequently exposed to water. There is no doubt that the basin belongs to a larger, still unexcavated structure, of which only a few traces have been exposed. The layout of the basin and the careful organisation of decorative columns at either side would suggest a different function from the adjoining industrial installations. The basin is similar in shape and size to basins found in bathhouses in Egypt.[411] Grossmann found the presence of such a structure strange within the monastic context and suggested that it could have pre-dated the monastic use of the site. He observed similarities in the design of the column bases with installations ascribed to the reign of Diocletian (r. 284–305) in the temple of the goddess Repyt in nearby Atripe.[412] Considering the location of the basin and comparing its construction technique with architectural remains across the site, this interpretation to me seems highly unlikely.

411 See Peter Grossmann, "Badeeinrichtungen in Ägyptischen Frühchristlichen Klöstern," in *Le Bain Collectif en Égypte,* ed. Marie-Francoise Boussa, Thibaud Fournet and Bérangère Redon (Cairo: Institut Français d'Archéologie Orientale, 2009) for bathhouses in Egypt. For bathing in a wider East Mediterranean context see Stephanie Hoss, *Baths and Bathing: The Culture of Bathing and the Baths and Thermae in Palestine from the Hasmoneans to the Moslem Conquest; with an Appendix on Jewish Ritual Baths (Miqva'ot)* (Oxford: Archaeopress, 2005); Inge Nielsen, *Thermae et Balnea: The Architecture and Cultural History of Roman Public Baths* (Aarhus: Aarhus University Press, 1993); Fikret Yegül, *Baths and Bathing in Classical Antiquity* (New York: Architectural History Foundation, 1992); Fikret Yegül, *Bathing in the Roman World* (Cambridge: Cambridge University Press, 2010).

412 Grossmann et al., "Monastery of Apa Shenute," 186.

While there is no dateable material that can be tied directly to the construction, the adjoining stratigraphic sequence would place it within the second or third phase of the general use of area WM.5.

At some point the basin went out of use and was filled by diagonally-laid fired bricks. The careful organisation of the bricks demonstrates that the building to which the basin belonged continued in use, though perhaps for a different purpose.

Remains of fired brick walls to the north, east and west frame the remains of a crushing basin built from fired brick (external diameter 2.66 m). Two granite crushing basins (external diameters 2 m) were later added to the zone after it had been subjected to extensive remodelling. The northern granite basin partly sat on top of a mud brick wall, but had shifted slightly off its foundation. The southern granite basin sits on a group of discarded architectural stone elements. One of these crushing basins is likely to originate from WM.4.3.9. This suggestion is based on the size of the crushing basins, their unstable foundations, and the size and layout of the foundation for the missing basin in the food production area.

The final discernible use of zone WM.5 involved a systematic robbing of building materials, followed by a phase where ceramic emplacements were inserted and low mud brick walls constructed. The nature of this phase is not clear, except that it is found throughout WM.5 and appears to utilize remains of existing architecture, while at the same time introducing new, often somewhat brittle, features made of mud brick.

3.6.7 WM.5 — General Stratigraphy

Combining the archaeological data from the six zones allows me to propose the following stratigraphic sequence through eight phases of use.

Phase WM.5.i is represented by mud brick walls found in the building (WM.5.2), the adjacent hallway or alley (WM.5.5) and in the southeast quadrant (WM.5.4). It is possible that pipes found in the building's south rooms along with the soak-away in the northern part of the street belong to this phase. Phase WM.5.ii saw the construction of the building in WM.5.2, which included an open courtyard and installations for activities that utilised both fire and water. The tanks to the south of the building form a part of this phase, and it is also possible that the basin in the northeast corner belongs to this phase. The dateable ceramics suggest that features belonging to phase WM.5.ii were constructed no earlier than the fifth century.

Phase WM.5.iii included the remodelling of the building, the passageway and the four rooms. The associated ceramic assemblage provided a *terminus post quem* of the seventh century. Phase WM.5.iv consisted of changes to the northern part of the building and probably also the construction of the brick crushing basin. After that, WM.5 saw its first episode of disuse and removal of building materials.

During phase WM.5.v, walls were repaired and the granite crushing basins were moved to WM.5.2 and to WM.5.6. Ceramic vessels were incorporated into the architecture throughout WM.5, but particularly in WM.5.3, WM.5.4 and WM.5.6. In this phase, WM.5 maintained its architectural integrity although the structures were used for new purposes.

In phase WM.5.vi, the area was finally abandoned with a gradual deposition of rubble layers and sand caused by both human deposition and natural accumulation. Material remains from this phase suggest a date in the second half of the Ottoman period. The deposition was followed by extensive pitting. A surface that overlays the rubble and contains several post-holes constitutes phase WM.5.vii, while the modern monastic use of the area can be defined as phase WM.5.viii.

WM.5 — FINDS

The majority of the finds relevant to the development of specific parts of WM.5 have been addressed above. This section provides a brief overview of material remains that cannot be contextualised in archaeological deposits, but may yield information on the use and development of the area as a whole. The main material component is ceramic, of which two groups will be briefly addressed.[413] One group consists of a corpus collected during the surface cleanings carried out by

413 Pyke*, "White Monastery 2009: Pottery Report;" Pyke*, "White Monastery 2010: Pottery Report;" Pyke*, "White Monastery 2011: Pottery Report."

the WMP, while the other is an assemblage left behind by the SCA in the courtyard of the building. The origin of the latter is not clear. The specialist study of the assemblages is currently in progress and the observations described below are therefore preliminary.

Both assemblages contain a date range from Late Antiquity to the modern period.[414] From the surface assemblage, several water pipes are of particular importance as they can help us understand the area's internal organisation. They apparently belong to the early flourishing of the monastery. Otherwise, the surface material contains similar wares and dates as found throughout WM.5 with some later items, including Ottoman tobacco pipes and fragments of soft-paste porcelain produced in Europe.

The assemblage collected by the SCA contains an important range in both dates and wares.[415] Sherds from the Late Antique period include imports from Aswan and Tunisia, and glaze wares of the ninth to eleventh centuries were also found. Furthermore, the presence of Ottoman tobacco pipes of various dates demonstrates activity on the site through the sixteenth to the late nineteenth centuries, while handmade domestic vessels with geometric motifs represent the last two hundred years.

3.6.9 WM.5 — Summary

In summary, the archaeological remains from WM.5 bear witness to the prolonged history of the monastery with several phases of use, disuse and re-use. WM.5 appears to have been in use from the early years of the monastery, although the nature of this early use is poorly understood. The industrial nature of the installations found in the first and second phases could be associated with the construction of the church. If this assumption is correct, the construction of the building in WM.5.2 would have taken place after the church was built. The tanks (WM.5.3) found to the south of the building could have been associated with dyeing of textiles (see Chapter 5.2.2), while the basin in the northeast corner suggests quite a different use for this part of the site, perhaps that of bathing. Following a period of abandonment, WM.5 seems to have reverted to industrial purposes, in particular the production of oil, as can be seen from the three granite crushing basins introduced to the area.

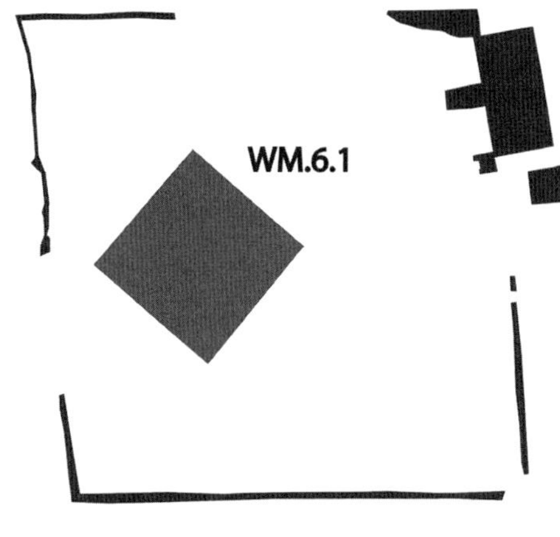

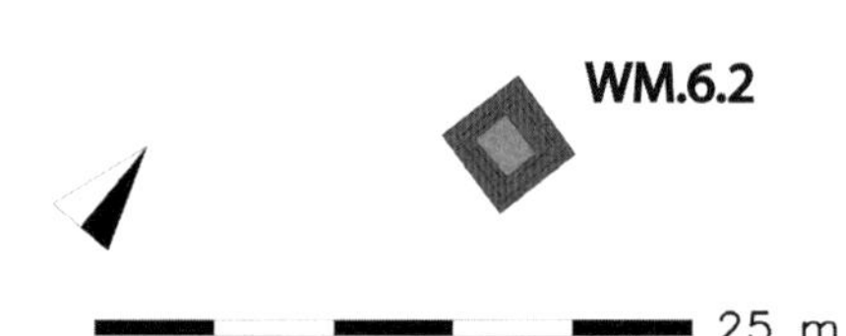

Fig. 48. WM.6 (map by Dawn McCormack and the author; © YMAP).

The general appearance of WM.5 today would suggest an open area with freestanding architectural remains. A detailed examination of the site, with a particular focus on the southeast quadrant, has demonstrated that this was not the case. On the contrary, WM.5 should be conceived as a densely constructed environment with movement between buildings arranged through highly structured streets and passageways.

3.7 WM.6 — THE SOUTHEAST CORNER OF THE MONASTERY

As a part of the first season of the White Monastery Project, two soundings were excavated in the monastery's far southeastern corner (fig. 48). The first, a 4 × 4 m square, was placed near the southeast corner

414 Pyke*, "White Monastery 2010: Pottery Report," 27–32.
415 Pyke*, "White Monastery 2009: Pottery Report," 14–21.

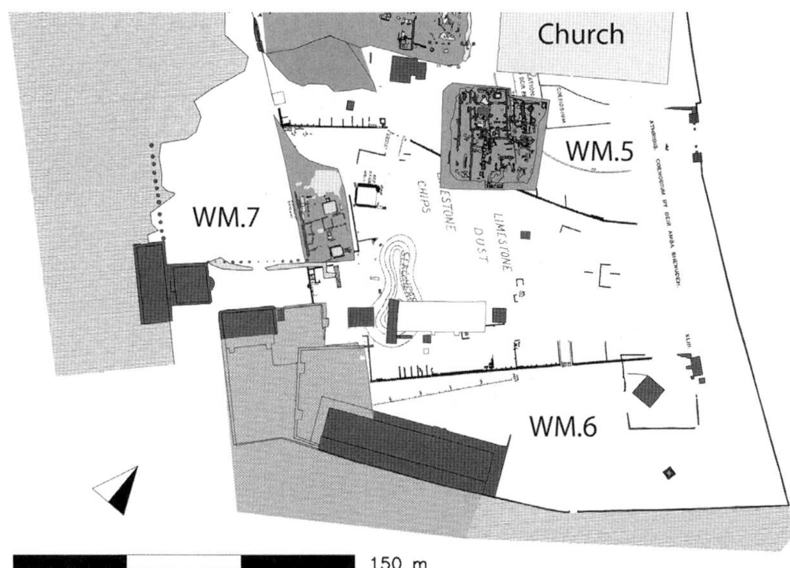

Fig. 49. Map of southern part of the White Monastery archaeological site. Petrie's plan with overlay of the WMP survey map (© YMAP).

of the modern enclosure wall; the second sounding, a trench measuring 1.5 × 10 m, was located within the precinct of a clinic that pre-dates the use of the modern monastery.[416] Petrie's and Ward's excavations in 1907 exposed a section of the perimeter wall immediately north of this area, suggesting that the two soundings were located outside the walls of the ancient monastery (fig. 49). Excavations in this area were expected to yield information on extramural activities as well as the spatial expansion and contraction of the monastery complex over time.

3.7.1 *WM.6.1 and WM.6.2*

The sounding in WM.6.1 was abandoned when the monastic community pointed out that the area in which it was located was believed to contain recent burials, associated with the adjacent clinic. The partially executed excavation uncovered modern finds and eroded mud bricks that could have either originated from buildings or from the tombs which were said to be located there.

The sounding in WM.6.2 was excavated to the level of natural sand. The sounding contained a rubbish deposit, mostly comprising pottery. Bulldozing of this area, in preparation of construction activities for the modern use of the monastic grounds meant that the dump was filled with a mixture of modern glass, plastic and paper. It is worth noting that the garbage dump was located on a prepared surface of gravel with a mud coating, which was placed directly on natural sand with no indications of other uses.

WM.6 — FINDS

The initial analysis of the pottery from the rubbish dump suggested a Late Antique date.[417] Unfortunately, the ceramic assemblage could not be accessed again after its procurement and was therefore not studied in detail. Other finds include unidentified pieces of metal, mostly iron, animal bones, glass and plaster fragments.

3.7.2 *WM.6 — Summary*

Three important points can be made from the test trenches in WM.6. Firstly, a modern clinic with a surrounding cemetery served the local community (and possibly the inhabitants of the monastic church and the village of Nag al-Deir) before the modern use of the site. Secondly, there are no indications that this area was at any time used by the ancient monastic community for purposes that required architectural construction, i.e., there are no indications that this area was located within the monastic walls. Thirdly, the presence of large quantities of Late Antique pottery and very few remains from later periods would suggest that the midden in WM.6.2 was in use until the seventh or eighth century, whereafter the monastics' garbage was deposited elsewhere. This could have resulted from a reduction in the size

416 Louise Blanke*, "Square Summary. Area 1, square B & C, Area 3, square E & F" (White Monastery Project interim report, 2005), 9–11.

417 Gillian Pyke, personal communication with author, 2005, reproduced in Blanke*, "Area 1, square B & C, Area 3, square E & F," 11.

of the monastic complex, which prompted the transfer of the dump to a more convenient location (see Chapter 4.1.1). This development corresponds with both the history of the monastery (see Chapter 2) and the material remains from other parts of the site in, for example, WM.1.1 and WM.5.

3.8 WM.7 — THE SOUTHWEST CORNER OF THE MONASTERY

WM.7, measuring 40 m NS × 21.5 m EW, is located in the southwest corner of the ancient monastic site. It was excavated by the SCA over two seasons in 1998 and 2003,[418] and recorded by the White Monastery Project during a single season in the winter of 2006–2007 (fig. 50).[419]

The most prominent feature is the monastic boundary wall, which spans the entire west section of the excavated area, but several other prominent structures—both buildings and individual features—are also found. A part of WM.7 was excavated by Petrie and Ward,[420] but it is not clear whether this excavation was visible when the SCA commenced their work. In the following text, the stratigraphy and relevant finds associated with the structures will be described, followed by a summary of the development of WM.7 as a whole, which includes a comparison with the results in Petrie's report. Area WM.7 has been divided into seven zones. These are:

- WM.7.1: A rectangular room and an adjacent burial;
- WM.7.2: A structure with two small compartments;
- WM.7.3: A mud brick structure with two rooms;
- WM.7.4: A subterranean room;
- WM.7.5: A small structure consisting of a mud brick wall and a plastered floor;
- WM.7.6: A section of the enclosure wall with abutting mud brick structures – south end;
- WM.7.7: A section of the enclosure wall with abutting mud brick structures – north end.

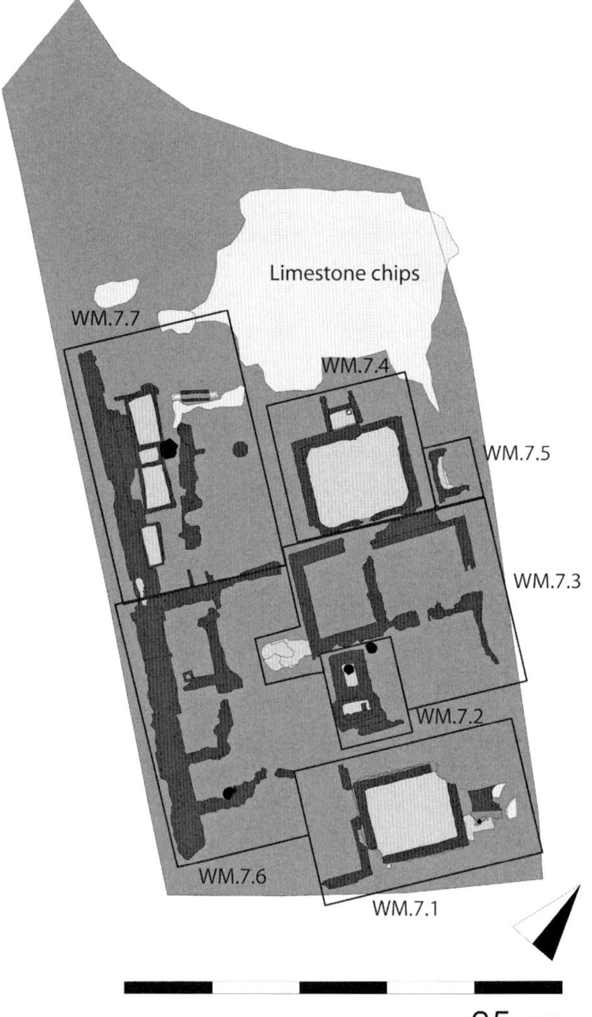

Fig. 50. WM.7 with zones (map by Dawn McCormack and the author; © YMAP).

Several of these zones contain only scant archaeological data. Therefore, they will be dealt with below according to their location in the eastern part of WM.7 (WM.7.1–WM.7.5) or the western part of WM.7 (WM.7.6–7.7).

3.8.1 WM.7.1–WM.7.5 — The Eastern Part

WM.7.1 is located in the southeast corner of WM.7 and developed over three main phases (fig. 51).

418 Pyke*, "Supreme Council," 2.

419 The primary archaeological reports are Louise Blanke*, "Final Report of Area 3 Unit M. December 2006 – January 2007" (White Monastery Project interim report, 2007); Pyke*, "White Monastery Pottery Report 2007," 1–3. Results have been published in Davis, "White Monastery," 39–40.

420 Petrie, *Athribis*.

Fig. 51. WM.7.1. Overview of single-room structure. View towards south-southwest (photograph by the author; © YMAP).

Phase WM.7.1.i consisted of a single room (4.9 m NS × 5.8 m EW) built from fired brick walls with a mortar coating on the exterior face and a white plaster facing on the interior. The interior surface was an *opus siginum* plaster floor, laid on a foundation of two courses of fired bricks. Nothing remains of the entrance and the surrounding surface level is unknown. The eastern exterior side of the building was excavated, revealing a foundation trench, which contained ceramic material and two coins providing a *terminus post quem* for the construction of the building in the fifth century.

Phase WM.7.1.ii included two sections of a mud brick wall constructed along the western side of the building, which was contemporary with an area of limestone paving abutting the eastern side of the building. Here a burial (phase WM.7.1.iii) had been dug into the limestone paving, thus representing the most recent use of the area. Ceramic material from the burial's superstructure contained material of a seventh or eighth century date.

WM.7.2 (4.6 m NS × 2.8 m EW) is located just north of WM.7.1 and was developed over two phases. It consists of a rectangular fired brick building containing two small rooms (phase WM.7.2.i). The construction technique and building material would suggest that WM.7.2 was contemporary with WM.7.1. The brick floor and the interior and exterior wall faces were covered in a rough mortar with no indication of a finer plaster coating. Phase WM.7.2.ii includes two ceramic emplacements, located in the north room and at the exterior northeast corner, and a mud brick wall, located on the south side of the structure. This mud brick wall is contemporary with and probably formed part of a building with the mud brick walls from WM.7.1.ii.

Fig. 52. WM.7.4. Overview of sunken storeroom. Note vaulting in far-left corner. View towards south (photograph by the author; © YMAP).

Fig. 53. WM.7.6. Overview of zone. View towards southwest (photograph by the author; © YMAP).

WM.7.3 (5.8 m NS × 10.3 m EW) contains two phases. The earlier phase, WM.7.3.i, was a rectangular building made from mud bricks. Phase WM.7.3.ii consisted of a partition wall—dividing the structure into two rooms—and a reinforcement of a fire-damaged area in the northeast part of the building. The fire appears to have been local, only affecting the eastern half of WM.7.3 and the southeast corner of WM.7.4. Nothing remains of the surface level from either phase and no ceramic evidence can be confidently associated with the building's construction or use.

WM.7.4 is a single-phased building, located in the northeast corner of WM.7 (fig. 52). It consists of a rectangular room, built from mud brick walls with a plastered floor (7.3 m NS × 6.5 m EW). The lower parts of vaulting preserved in the interior corners reveal that the room was once covered by a vault or dome. Remains of windows or ventilation shafts are found in the centre of the east and west walls. The floor is located 1 m below the current ground level, creating excellent conditions for cool storage. A minor fire-damaged area in the northwest corner could have resulted from the use of an oil lamp, while fire damage in the southeast corner is connected with damage to the adjacent WM.7.3. A sondage in the northeast corner of WM.7.4 recovered a small assemblage of ceramic sherds, dating from the fifth to the seventh century, thus suggesting a *terminus post quem* for the construction of the building in the seventh or eighth centuries. The room was accessed from the north via a few steps or a short ladder leading from a small enclosure framed by two single-row mud brick walls. The floor of the entrance area is covered in plaster with a square depression formed by four fired bricks inserted immediately north of the room. Given the purpose of storage, the walls and depression most likely served to prevent wind-blown deposits from entering the room.

WM.7.5 is located immediately east of WM.7.4 and appears to be the remains of a tank-like feature (2.7 m NS × 0.9 m EW). It was constructed with a mud brick base and a frame that lines a thick layer of plaster. Only the westernmost part is preserved and no dateable material was associated with the structure.

3.8.2 WM.7.6–WM.7.7 — The Western Part

The western half of WM.7 comprises a section of the monastic boundary wall and a series of interconnected structures that abut the wall. The boundary wall was built in two phases (see Chapter 3.5.4 above). The early version of the wall was severely damaged by fire; the second phase was constructed to reinforce the first, possibly as a direct result of the fire damage. WM.7.6 and WM.7.7, respectively, represent the southern and northern part of the wall and its adjoining features.

WM.7.6 covers 15.8 m NS × 8.9 m EW and contains three rooms that abut and thus post-date the boundary wall (fig. 53). The rooms were built from mud brick walls with a compacted mud floor with a high component of organic inclusions. The surface was laid out on a layer of seemingly unintentionally fired bricks, possibly deriving from the damaged boundary wall or from associated architectural remains. Ceramic material found within this layer suggests a sixth to seventh century date for the construction of the floor.

Located immediately north of WM.7.6, WM.7.7 covers 14.5 m NS × 9.8 m EW and contains three sunken rooms, a tank and a staircase that gave access to areas beyond the monastic enclosure wall. WM.7.7 developed over five phases—the boundary wall representing phase WM.7.7.i. The cutting of limestone blocks in an area northeast of the structure has left a distinct layer of limestone chips and powder (phase WM.7.7.ii). This stratigraphic relation suggests that the production area post-dated the construction of the boundary wall and the devastating conflagration, but pre-dated the reinforcement of the wall. The size of the deposit would suggest that a large production of limestone blocks took place over the course of a relatively limited period of time. Petrie identified the deposit and suggested that the chippings marked the former site of a church, which had been dismantled and its stones removed (see Chapter 2.6). The archaeological remains, however, do not support this interpretation. Instead, it would seem that the limestone blocks were shaped in this location for use elsewhere—possibly to be used in the construction of the monastic church.

The reinforcement to the boundary wall (phase WM.7.7.iii) also included constructing a doorway and a plastered staircase in the boundary wall—a feature which is also marked on Petrie's plan (fig. 10)—along with the construction of a series of three rooms located to the north of the staircase. These rooms consisted of at least two storeys: a basement some 1.3 m below the current surface level, accessed through the north room, and a ground floor of which only fragments of the floor have survived. Ceramic material associated with this room provided a Late Antique date.[421]

During phase WM.7.7.iv, the basement was refurbished. A storage vessel was inserted into the central room, but possibly accessed from the ground floor, and a wall in the north room was altered to contain a niche. This phase was brought to an end by a localised fire, which destroyed the ground floor, but only left marks on the basement. The final phase (phase WM.7.7.v) included a new ground-level floor and walls—all done with reused fire-damaged bricks.

3.8.3 WM.7 — General Stratigraphy

Combining the architectural phasing from WM.7.1–WM.7.7 on a basis of shared stratigraphy, construction technique, material and finds suggests the following sequence.

- WM.7.i: the boundary wall was constructed along with a compacted mud surface. No further evidence can securely be tied to this phase, which came to an abrupt end caused by an episode of conflagration.
- WM.7.ii: the northern end was used for cutting limestone blocks. The lack of naturally accumulated material between this deposit and the mud surface would suggest that the transformation of the area took place almost immediately after the fire. If the blocks were cut for the monastic church, this phase took place in the early fifth century.
- WM.7.iii: the boundary wall was refurbished and the rooms in WM.7.1, WM.7.2 and WM.7.7 were built. The ceramic finds suggests a *terminus post quem* of the fifth century for this phase.
- WM.7.iv: the rooms in WM.7.6 were built.
- WM.7.v: the ceramic evidence from WM.7.3 and WM.7.4 provides an Early Medieval date for these two zones.
- WM.7.vi: the basement in WM.7.7 was reorganised, a storage jar was inserted and a niche was built in the north room. The evidence of smaller local fires from WM.7.3, WM.7.4 and WM.7.7 possibly concluded this phase.
- WM.7.vii: the final phase involves the refurbishment of WM.7.7 with a new ground floor and possibly also the partition wall in WM.7.3 as well as the reinforcement of its northeast wall. The use of fire damaged bricks in WM.7.7 and mud bricks in WM.7.3 would, however, suggest two separate events. The use of fire damaged bricks for the superstructure in WM.7.7 suggests a minor construction, that probably was not supported by a roof—the bricks would have been fragile and would not have been able to carry the weight of a roofing structure. The supportive wall in WM.7.3, however, was clearly built as an integrated part of a standing building to avoid (further?) collapse. Also, the use of mud brick as the principal building material suggests a different access to material or rather a different willingness to supply adequate building material.

WM.7 — FINDS

The ceramic material from WM.7 was mainly collected for dating purposes, which means that only a minor assemblage was retrieved.[422] The dates represented by the material range from the fifth to the eighth centuries with some modern material—possibly resulting from the long exposure of the area. The assemblage consisted of fine, coarse and transport wares, but the material holds no clues to the use of the area.

421 Pyke*, "White Monastery Pottery Report 2007," 1–3.

422 Pyke*, "White Monastery Pottery Report 2007," 1.

Phases	Period	WM.1.1	WM.1.2	WM.2	WM.3	WM.4	WM.5	WM.6	WM.7	Description
WM.i	5th–7th		WM.1.2.i	WM.2.i		*	WM.5.i	WM.6.2	WM.7.i WM.7.ii	Mud brick architecture
WM.ii	5th–7th	WM.1.1.i WM.1.1.ii	WM.1.2.ii	WM.2.ii		**	WM.5.ii WM.5.iii	WM.6.2	WM.7.iii WM.7.iv	Fired brick buildings
WM.iii	7th–9th	WM.1.1.iii		WM.2.iii		***	WM.5.iv		WM.7.v	Repairs or extensions to existing buildings – no evidence for substantial building activity?
WM.iv	10th–14th			WM.2.iv?		WM.4.2.4.iv? WM.4.2.3.iv WM.4.3.6.iv WM.4.3.13	WM.5.v		WM.7.vi WM.7.vii?	Repairs to buildings with mud brick walls – ceramic vessels incorporated into architectural design
WM.v	15th–19th	WM.1.1.iv?		WM.2.iv?		WM.4.3.6.v?	WM.5.vi WM.5.vii?			Site used for dumping, pitting, and perhaps some domestic usage
WM.vi	20th–21st	WM.1.1.iv? WM.1.1.v		WM.2.v	WM.3.i–iii		WM.5.vii? WM.5.viii	WM.6.1		Modern use related to livestock and domestic use

* WM.4.1.17, WM.4.2.4.i, WM.4.2.3 i, WM.4.3.6.i, WM.4.3.9, WM.4.3.14, WM.4.3.13, WM.4.3.15, WM.4.3.29, WM.4.3.11, WM.4.3.10, WM.4.3.8, WM.4.3.7, WM.4.3.12
** WM.4.1.16, WM.4.4.22, WM.4.1.18, WM.4.1.19, WM.4.1.20? WM.4.2.4.ii, WM.4.2.3.ii, WM.4.2.2, WM.4.2.1, WM.4.3.6.ii, WM.4.3.9, WM.4.3.14, WM.4.3.13, WM.4.3.15, WM.4.3.29, WM.4.3.11, WM.4.3.10, WM.4.3.8, WM.4.3.7, WM.4.3.12, WM.4.4.28, WM.4.4.22, WM.4.5, WM.4.6
*** WM.4.1.20? WM.4.2.4.iii?, WM.4.2.3.iii?, WM.4.2.2, WM.4.2.1, WM.4.3.6.iii, WM.4.3.9, WM.4.3.14, WM.4.3.13, WM.4.3.15, WM.4.3.29, WM.4.3.11, WM.4.3.10, WM.4.3.8, WM.4.3.7, WM.4.3.12, WM.4.4.28, WM.4.4.22, WM.4.6
Unknown: WM.4.4.23–25, WM.4.6, WM.4.7

Table 4. Phasing of the White Monastery archaeological site.

3.8.4 WM.7 — Summary

The excavation of WM.7 by Petrie and Ward and later by the SCA has, unfortunately, removed all deposits that could inform not only about the use of the area but also about its disuse. This means that remains of all portable architectural structures as well as natural build-ups and rubbish deposits, essential in the interpretation of the use of an area, have been removed. What can be extracted from WM.7, however, is a sense of development of the site, which corresponds to observations made in WM.2, WM.4 and WM.5. The architectural remains from the earliest use comprise mud brick architecture; the next substantial phase saw the construction of fired brick architecture with plaster floors, while mud bricks were continuously used for specific purposes, such as the reinforcement of the boundary wall. Buildings from the eighth century onwards were constructed in mud brick, while later undated phases displayed a reuse of building material, suggesting a continuous use of the area, but a lack of economic resources.

In his brief report on the White Monastery, Petrie referred to the 'southwest area' (WM.7). He mentioned a series of walls and rooms abutting the boundary wall and referred specifically to the basement in WM.7.7, with no further description of local features. He focused his attention on another subterranean room, which was located further north and accessed by a staircase and through a corridor from the east. Unfortunately, nothing remains of this structure.

3.9 A CHRONOLOGY OF THE WHITE MONASTERY

Any attempt to define sequential development across the White Monastery encounters difficulties caused by the lack of stratigraphic continuity and datable finds. It is, however, possible to detect general trends in the development of the monastery through the architectural stratigraphy of the areas, zones, and sections. Table 4 presents a simplified overview of this development, where the construction and use of zones and sections have been gathered into six phases that relate to the entire site.

During its early use (WM.i), the White Monastery comprised structures of mud brick as found in

WM.2, WM.4–5 and WM.7. In some cases, the plan of the early buildings could not be reconstructed, but in the eastern part of WM.4, it looks as though the layout of the structures in the food production area was established in phase WM.i and maintained throughout the majority of the monastery's use.

Fired bricks and lime-based mortars replaced the use of mud brick architecture as the materials of choice in the second phase of use (WM.ii). This phase has been identified in all parts of the site except from WM.3. More expensive materials requiring skilled labour were also found in the floor surfaces, which were coated with *opus signinum* plaster or paved with limestone. The buildings belonging to the first two phases (WM.i and WM.ii) were most likely constructed between the fifth and the seventh centuries. This was also the period when the monastery was at its largest extent.

Thereafter, repairs and some additions to the built environment took place from the seventh to the ninth century. Buildings were added to WM.7 (WM.7.3–4) and new building phases were detected in WM.4 and WM.5. During this phase, the monastery began to shrink in size. The midden deposit in WM.6.2 was abandoned and a new area for garbage was taken into use in WM.1.1. It is not possible to estimate if these two events were directly related, or WM.1.1 became the principal dumping ground for the monastic community, or just one of several areas used for garbage disposal.

It looks as though repairs were made to structures in WM.2, WM.4, WM.5 and WM.7 between the tenth and the fourteenth century, but there is also evidence within the archaeological remains that many of these repairs followed a phase of temporary abandonment during which building materials had been removed to be used elsewhere. It is possible that the repairs and reuse of the site corresponded with the extensive restructuring made to the monastic church during the thirteenth century (see Chapter 2.3). Until the reuse has been properly dated, this point must remain speculative.

The following two phases (WM.iv and WM.v) are by far the most elusive. The use of the site and the nature of the architectural remains are not easily determinable. During phase WM.v the site was used for disposing rubbish—probably by the community living inside the nave of the church—as a source of building materials and perhaps also with some domestic usage associated with the village inside the church.

The final phase (WM.vi) took place during the twentieth and twenty-first centuries and consisted of the modern use of the site, which has been summarised in Chapter 2.4 and in Chapter 3.1.

The development of the built environment and its changing use of building materials is an important marker of the monastery's economic vitality. The use of fired bricks with lime-based mortars and *opus signinum* or limestone floors suggest a monastery with a financial surplus as well as access to raw materials, either through production on landholdings owned by the monastery or through a local market. The reuse of building materials in composite walls and floors towards the end of the history of the site suggests not only that such financial surplus was no longer present, but also that disused building materials were in abundance—most likely within the derelict monastic landscape itself.

Grossmann suggested that the damage caused by conflagration in WM.1.2 resulted from the Persian invasion of Egypt around 619.[423] He saw this event as linked to at least one of the coin hoards that dates to the early seventh century and to observations made within the monastic church. He suggested that the roof over the nave collapsed as a result of severe fire damage, which he observed on the stonework. I find this suggestion speculative and do not see correlations with the actual archaeological remains. There are no sources—archaeological or textual—supporting a collapse of the roof of the nave in the early seventh century. On the contrary, I suggested—tentatively—in Chapter 2 that the church roof collapsed in the thirteenth century during which the remaining part of the church also suffered substantial damage. The fire damage observed by Grossmann could have resulted from the raids in the late eighteenth and nineteenth centuries as reported by Denon and Curzon.

423 Grossmann et al., "Monastery of Apa Shenute," 203.

Regarding damage caused to the areas outside the church, only WM.1 and WM.7 show evidence of fire damage: the stratigraphy of WM.7 suggests that here, the conflagration took place before the church was built and thus several hundred years before the Persian invasion. Therefore, there are no indications of a devastating site-wide event of burning in the early seventh century. On the contrary, the event in WM.1 appears to be local and was more likely the consequence of a knocked over oil lamp than of marauding intruders.

Finally, it should be emphasised that although the contents of the two coin hoards are of an early seventh century date, this does not mean that the hoards were deposited in the early seventh century, but could suggest that this was the time when the monastery accumulated its wealth. It is, of course, remarkable, that this enormous wealth was not reclaimed, and it is worth considering why that was the case. The coin finds are further investigated in Chapter 4.2.4.

The main source for the Persian invasion is the *History of the Patriarchs*, which reports on the exploitation of Egypt through tax revenue and of Persian atrocities, including massacres of monks and destruction of monasteries.[424] This source, however, is problematic, as pointed out by James Howard-Johnston:

> With little or no comparative material to hand, George [the author] was at the mercy of his sources. It was impossible for him to counter the propaganda infused into the account of the Persian invasion in 619 which reached him nearly a hundred years later.[425]

Limited evidence from papyri and ostraca shows that the concern of the imminent arrival of the Persian army was genuine, when, for example, a woman wrote to a person at the Monastery of Epiphanius in Thebes asking for 'instruction in the matter of the Persians, for they will be coming south.'[426]

The archaeological remains suggest that the heyday of the White Monastery lasted up to the seventh or eighth century, with continuous building activities on a reduced scale into the ninth century. There could be several reasons why the monastery shrunk in size, but it is noteworthy how the chronological development corresponds with what is known of socio-political events and attitudes towards the monasteries in the Early Medieval period, where, for example the land tax (*kharaj*) and poll tax (*jizyah*) gradually increased during the Umayyad period.[427]

The *History of the Patriarchs* records that the poll-tax was imposed on monks under al-Asbagh (c. 704), who 'under the guise of overseeing the collection of taxes throughout Egypt, began to crack down on monasticism.'[428] Of al-Asbagh's successor, 'Abd Allah ibn 'Abd al-Malik, the History records that no one was permitted a burial before their poll tax had been collected.[429] Al-Qasim ibn Ubaydallah (r. 734–741), the financial director of Egypt during the reign of Hisham, was described as a lover of luxury who found new ways of extorting money from the church.[430] The story of his visit to the White Monastery should be seen within this context. During the Abbasid period the heavy taxation continued. The dissatisfaction among the Christian population led to no less than thirteen revolts between 767 and 832.

The caliph 'Umar (r. 717–720) encouraged conversion to Islam under a promise of exemption from

424 Howard-Johnston, *Witnesses*, 317.

425 Howard-Johnston, *Witnesses*, 320. See also Stephen J. Davis, *The Early Coptic Papacy. The Egyptian Church and Its Leadership in Late Antiquity* (Cairo & New York: The American University in Cairo Press, 2004), 112–115.

426 Ruth Altheim-Stiehl, "The Sassanians in Egypt – Some Evidence of Historical Interest." *Bulletin de la Société d'Archéologie Copte* 31 (1992): 93.

427 Swanson, *Coptic Papacy*, 4–25. For Egypt under Umayyad rule in general see Hugh Kennedy, "Egypt as a Province in the Islamic Caliphate, 641–868," in *The Cambridge History of Egypt*, ed. Carl F. Petry (Cambridge: Cambridge University Press, 1998), 62–85. For Copts under Umayyad rule see Geoffrey R.D. King, "Islam, Iconoclasm, and the Declaration of Doctrine," *Bulletin of the School of Oriental and African Studies* 48.2 (1985): 267–277; Terry G. Wilfong, "The non-Muslim Communities: Christian Communities," in *The Cambridge History of Egypt*, ed. Carl F. Petry (Cambridge: Cambridge University Press, 1998), 175–197.

428 Howard-Johnston, *Witnesses*, 322.

429 Swanson, *Coptic Papacy*, 18.

430 Swanson, *Coptic Papacy*, 19.

the poll tax, a trend that continued throughout the Umayyad period and into the reign of the Abbasids. Consequently, the number of Christians in Egypt gradually decreased.[431] The taxation (both land tax and poll tax) and conversion would inevitably gradually have weakened the monasteries and consequently led to a reduction in their landholdings and building activity. It is tempting to read the development of the White Monastery into this context.

The thirteenth century saw a large part of the monastic churches restored and equipped with the decorative programme still visible today.[432] This period is perceived by modern scholars as a Coptic golden age or renaissance,[433] brought forth by generally peaceful and prosperous times, where sharing of ideas, texts and artistic styles between Egypt and neighbouring regions became possible.[434] At the same time, a class of Coptic notables with the capacity to lavish patronage on artists and scholars existed.[435] It is possible that these developments corresponded with the White Monastery's archaeological phase WM.iv, during which buildings in WM.2, WM.4 and WM.5 were either repaired or remodelled for different usage, although the lack of dateable material means that this suggestion remains speculative.

There is hardly any evidence that points to a relationship (religious or economic) between the White Monastery and the monasteries in Akhmim (see Chapter 1.2). The material remains associated with the monasteries in and near Akhmim are minimal and it is therefore not possible to comment on their development or economic circumstances. It is significant that several monasteries were founded in the thirteenth century around the time when both the White and Red Monasteries saw extensive architectural refurbishment (see also Chapter 5).

Swanson describes how anti-Christian rioting broke out in the middle of the fourteenth century, that churches and monasteries were destroyed and Christian civil servants were dismissed or compelled to convert to Islam. In 1321, anti-Christian riots led to the destruction of sixty churches throughout Egypt.[436] There is no indication that these events were associated with the abandonment of the main part of the White Monastery, but in the 15th century, al-Maqrizi described the site as being in ruins with only the church standing.[437]

The current preservation of the archaeological remains does not allow us to evaluate the full effects of the earthquake in the thirteenth century. However, an event that brought structural damage to the sturdiest building on site—the church—certainly would have damaged the surrounding settlement.

Finally, it is important to consider what effect the Black Death and the following cycles of plague had on the White Monastery. Stuart J. Borsch and Michael Dols have convincingly suggested that as much as 40% of Egypt's population perished between 1347 and 1517 with almost equal effect on urban and rural populations.[438] Al-Maqrizi noted that during the first outbreak in 1347–1350, the daily death toll in Cairo reached 7000 people at its highest, while most cities in Upper Egypt were almost obliterated.[439] This depopulation had a deep and long-term

431 Swanson, *Coptic Papacy*, 19–31.

432 Swanson, Coptic Papacy, 83. See also Elizabeth S. Bolman, "A Medieval Flourishing at the White Monastery Federation. Material Culture," in *The Red Monastery Church*, ed. Elizabeth S. Bolman (New Haven and London: Yale University Press, 2016), 203–215

433 Adel Y. Sidarus, "The Copto-Arabic Renaissance in the Middle Ages: Characteristics and Socio-Political Context," *Coptica* 1 (2002): 141–160. See also Elizabeth S. Bolman, *Monastic Visions: Wall Paintings in the Monastery of St. Anthony at the Red Sea* (New Haven & London: American Research Center in Egypt/Yale University Press, 2002); Davis, *Coptic Christology*.

434 Swanson, *Coptic Papacy*, 83. See also Bolman, *Monastic Visions*, and Sidarus, "The Copto-Arabic Renaissance" for developments in art (Bolman) and literature (Sidarus).

435 Swanson, *Coptic Papacy*, 83–84.

436 Swanson, *Coptic Papacy*, 102.

437 Wüstenfeld, *Macrizi*, 96.

438 Stuart J. Borsch, *Black Death in Egypt and England: A Comparative Study* (Austin: University of Texas Press, 2005), 24–54; Stuart J. Borsch, "Plague Depopulation and Irrigation Decay in Medieval Egypt," *The Medieval Globe* 1 (2014): 134; Michael Dols, "The General Mortality of the Black Death in the Mamluk Empire," in *The Islamic Middle East, 700–1900: Studies in Social and Economic History*, ed. Abraham Udovitch (Princeton: Darwin Press, 1981), 404–411.

439 Borsch, "Plague Depopulation," 125 does not see these numbers as exaggerated.

impact on Egypt's economy and led in some areas to a total collapse of Egypt's economic infrastructure.[440] Borsch has demonstrated how the extensive decline in the labour force meant that Egypt's irrigation system was not maintained, thus leading to failed crops, famine, as well as destruction of settlements caused by floods. This situation must have influenced the production output and economic vitality of the White Monastery.

As such, it is not possible to ascribe the decline and eventual abandonment of the White Monastery to a single event, but it should probably be considered the consequence of several factors of both socio-political and natural background.

APPENDIX – AREAS, ZONES, AND SECTIONS AT THE WHITE MONASTERY

Site Code	Area	Zone	Section	Description
WM	1			WM.1 lies in the northernmost part of the White Monastery. The area is subdivided into two zones. Total size: 78 m NS × 54 m EW.
WM	1	1		Several units excavated by the White Monastery Project in 2005–2006. The architectural remains consist of a fired brick building, later replaced with mud brick walls, with limestone floors and subfloor deposits, several middens of different dates, and mud pens for small animals. Total size: 20 m NS × 27 m EW.
WM	1	2		Northernmost SCA excavation. Contains remains of a large, centrally located mud brick building with plaster floors, and a smaller, less-preserved square structure in the southeast corner of the excavation. WM.1.2 also contains a pottery kiln and several waterproof tanks for manufacture processes. Size of building: 16.5 m NS × 18m EW. Total size: 58 m NS × 54 m EW.
WM	2			WM.2 is the tri-conch funerary chapel, which lies on the northwest fringe of the ancient monastery, on the edge of the modern cemetery. The area is subdivided into two zones. Total size: 35 m NS × 21 m EW.
WM	2	1		The northern part of the church complex, consisting of the church itself, four additional tombs that abut the church and a later square mud brick structure. Size of church: 11 m NS × 20.5 m EW. Total size: 19 m NS × 21 m EW.
WM	2	2		The southern part of the church complex, consisting of an open pillared hall and additional mud brick buildings to the east. A later domestic building occupies the southernmost part of the zone. Size of hall: 6.7 m NS × 16.7 m EW. Size of domestic structure: 8 m NS × 11 m EW. Total size: 15 m NS × 20 m EW.
WM	3			WM.3 lies immediate to the north of the main church. The area is not subdivided into zones. Total size: 20 m NS × 15 m EW.
WM	4			WM.4 lies immediately to the west of the church. The area is subdivided into seven zones, which are further divided into 32 sections. Total size: 115 m NS × 120 m EW.
WM	4	1		WM.4.1 consists of a north–south running thoroughfare and the architectural remains that lie between the thoroughfare and the main church. The zone contains five sections: 16–20. Total size: 70 m NS × 26 m EW.
WM	4	1	16	WM.4.1.16 consists of a large open hall in which the ceiling was supported by pillars. The floor is made from limestone slabs and a basin occupied the southeast corner of the hall. The structure is interpreted as a refectory. Total size: 45 m NS × 20 m EW.
WM	4	1	17	A thoroughfare, which runs between WM.4.1 and WM.4.2–3. Size: 75 m NS × 5 m EW.

440 Borsch, "Plague Depopulation," 125.

Site Code	Area	Zone	Section	Description
WM	4	1	18	A poorly-preserved structure, which consists of a north–south running hallway, which gave access to rectangular rooms on either side. A staircase in the southeast corner gave access to a second storey. The structure is interpreted as a storage hall or as a dormitory.15.8 m NS × 26 m EW.
WM	4	1	19	Two connected underground rooms, accessed by a sloping ramp. Interpreted as cooling rooms. 6.5 m NS × 4.6 m EW.
WM	4	1	20	A rectangular mud brick room and the remains of a plastered tank. 12.8 m NS × 5 m EW.
WM	4	2		WM.4.2 consists of structures in the southernmost part of WM.4, located immediately east of WM.4.1. The zone is interpreted as part of the monastic kitchen. The zone contains five sections: 1–5. Total size: 28 m NS × 32 m EW.
WM	4	2	1	A square room with a centrally placed cistern, remains of a plastered tank and three ceramic vessels inserted into the architectural layout. Size: 10.5 m NS × 6.5 m EW.
WM	4	2	2	Remains of plastered floors, fired brick walls and mud brick walls. Preservation is very poor. 5.5 m NS × 15.6 m EW.
WM	4	2	3	A long hall with plastered storage bins along the north wall as well as ceramic storage vessels inserted in this wall. Remains of eight bread ovens line the south side of the south wall. 7 m NS × 32 m EW.
WM	4	2	4	A long hallway, whose principal function was to allow communication between WM.4.2 (the kitchen) and WM.4.3 (the zone for food production and storage); it also gives access to the thoroughfare (WM.4.1.17) and the courtyard (WM.4.4.28). 5 m NS × 32 m EW.
WM	4	2	5	Remains of a plastered tank and a floor. 7 m NS × 7 m EW.
WM	4	3		WM.4.3 is centrally located in WM.4, north of WM.4.2 and east of WM.4.1. It contains buildings that are associated with the production and storage of food. The zone contains eleven sections: 6–15, 29. Total size: 37.7 m NS × 34 m EW.
WM	4	3	6	A room with a limestone paved floor and six roof supporting pillars. 10.8 m NS × 12.6 m EW.
WM	4	3	7	This section is almost empty. It contains remains of two pipelines, a pillar and a plastered tank. Size: 11 m NS × 7 m EW.
WM	4	3	8	Two rooms. The eastern is almost empty with only remains of a floor surface, the western is rectangular in shape, with a limestone-paved tank in the south end and several ceramic vessels inserted into the walls. Size: 11 m NS × 11 m EW.
WM	4	3	9	Two square rooms, once covered by domes. A crushing basin sits in the centre of the western room, a base for a crushing basin is found in the eastern room. 5.9 m NS × 14 m EW.
WM	4	3	10	The most prominent structure is a low plastered tank, which is lined by cut limestone boulders on the north and west sides. Section also contains the remains of two later pipelines. 12 m NS × 9 m EW.
WM	4	3	11	A room containing five vats of two different types. 25 m NS × 13.4 m EW.
WM	4	3	12	Four plastered rooms that line the western edge of the food production zone. 34 m NS × 3.1 m EW
WM	4	3	13	A room with several limestone-paved floors placed on top of each other. The room is interpreted as a pressing room for olive oil. 12.7 m NS × 6.5 m EW.
WM	4	3	14	This section contains a crushing basin, remains of four plastered tanks and a cistern. 12.7 m NS × 8.1 m EW.
WM	4	3	15	Five or six rooms that could be accessed from the thoroughfare (WM.4.1.17) and possibly also from section WM.4.3.14 or WM.4.3.29. The room is interpreted as a storage facility. 9 m NS × 13.5 m EW.

Site Code	Area	Zone	Section	Description
WM	4	3	29	A hallway with a doorway that gave access from the north to the food processing zone. 14.5 m NS × 4.5 m EW.
WM	4	4		WM.4.4 consists of the southwest section of WM.4. It contains a large open courtyard, a large well-preserved building, sections of the western boundary wall and remains of mud brick structures. The zone contains five sections: 22–25, 28. Total size: 88 m NS × 58 m EW.
WM	4	4	22	A large building with two hallways from which seven long rectangular rooms and three smaller rooms could be reached. Two staircases gave access to an upper storey. Three entrances: in the north, east and west walls. The west entrance opened onto the courtyard (WM.4.4.28). Size: 22.8 m NS × 19.3 m EW.
WM	4	4	23	A wall running south from WM.4.4.22, remains of a plaster floor and scattered remains of mud brick architecture. Size: 15.6 m NS × 20.8 m EW.
WM	4	4	24	A section of the western enclosure wall and the abutting mud brick structures. Size: 32 m NS × 14.5 m EW.
WM	4	4	25	A section of the western enclosure wall and features interpreted by the SCA as bread ovens. 56 m NS × 26 m EW.
WM	4	4	28	A large courtyard paved with plaster on a fired brick subfloor. 39.3 m NS × 25 m EW.
WM	4	5		WM.4.5 contains a well and the immediately adjacent architectural features related to the water supply. The zone contains one section: 31. Size: 28 m NS × 11 m EW.
WM	4	5	31	A well and features related to the water supply. Size: 28 m NS × 11 m EW.
WM	4	6		WM.4.6 consist of the northeastern part of WM.4. It contains architectural features associated with the water supply system as well as remains of a few mud brick buildings. The zone contains three sections: 26, 27, 32. Totalsize: 46.8 m NS × 50 m EW.
WM	4	6	26	This section contains a plastered tank, pipes and a room with a plastered floor, which may have been built as an extension to the zone for food production (WM.4.3). Size: 13.4 m NS × 13.7 m EW.
WM	4	6	27	A plastered tank and a mud-packed subfloor. Size: 11.5 m NS × 7.5 m EW.
WM	4	6	32	A large section, which contains pipes and tanks associated with the water supply, remains of mud brick structures and the entrance to a staircase, which gave access to the bottom of the well. Size: 34.8 m NS × 47 m EW.
WM	4	7		WM.4.7 consists of the northwestern part of WM.4. It contains poorly-preserved structures of mud brick, fired brick, and also features associated with the monastery's water supply. The zone contains one section: 30. Total size: 28 m NS × 43 m EW.
WM	4	7	30	This section contains poorly-preserved structures of mud brick, fired brick, and also features associated with the monastery's water supply. Size: 28 m NS × 43 m EW.
WM	5			Area 5 lies immediately to the south of the main church. The area is subdivided into six zones. Total size: 42 m NS × 45 m EW.
WM	5	1		A north–south running thoroughfare and parts of a structure, which is to the west of the excavated area. Remains that are associated with the monastic water supply are found in the northern and southern ends of the zone. Total size: 40 m NS × 9 m EW. Width of thoroughfare: 5 m.
WM	5	2		A large building, which consists of a pillared hall lined by rooms to the south and west. A stair case in the northwest corner gave access to a second storey. Plastered tanks are found in the northern end of the hall and in the central south rooms. Several structures remains in the hall from an earlier phase where the hall was not covered by a roof. A small crushing basin is found in the northern end of the hall. Size: 21 m NS × 17 m EW.

Site Code	Area	Zone	Section	Description
WM	5	3		A room with six consecutive plastered tanks that are connected by pipes. Size: 17.7 m NS × 7 m EW.
WM	5	4		The southeast quadrant of area WM.5. It contains wall fragments, Nile silt subfloors, pipelines and ceramic vessels that were included in the architectural layout, but the preservation is too poor to suggest the zone's original layout. Size: 21 m NS × 18.6 m EW.
WM	5	5		Four consecutive rooms built from mud brick walls and plastered floors. Size: 19 m NS × 7.8 m EW.
WM	5	6		The northeast corner of WM.5. The main features are a semi-circular basin and three crushing basins. Size: 20.5 m NS × 9.5 m EW.
WM	6			Area 6 lies in the southeast corner of the monastery. The area is subdivided into two zones. Total size: not applicable.
WM	6	1		A trench intended for excavation. No results. Size: 10 × 10 m.
WM	6	2		An excavated trench. Contains parts of a pottery dump. Size: 4 m NS × 4 m EW.
WM	7			Area 7 lies in the southwest corner of the ancient monastery. The area is subdivided into seven zones. Total size: 40 m NS × 21.5 m EW.
WM	7	1		A rectangular room with fired brick walls and a plaster floor. East of this a limestone paved surface adjacent to which was found a burial. West of room are remains of a mud brick building. Total size: 6.4 m NS × 11.8 m EW.
WM	7	2		A structure with two small compartments. Size: 4.6 m NS × 2.8 m EW.
WM	7	3		A mud brick built structure with two rooms. Total size: 9.2 m NS × 12.8 m EW. Size of two rooms: 5.8 m NS × 10.3 m EW.
WM	7	4		A subterranean room built from mud brick walls with a plaster floor. Entered via movable steps from the north wall. The room was covered by a dome. Size: 7.3 m NS × 6.5 m EW.
WM	7	5		Easternmost remains of structure consisting only of a mud brick wall and a plastered floor. Size: 2.7 m NS × 0.9 m EW.
WM	7	6		A section of the western enclosure wall and abutting mud brick architecture. Size: 15.8 m NS × 8.9 m EW.
WM	7	7		A section of the western enclosure wall and abutting mud brick architecture. The zone contains three subterranean rooms, a human-sized storage vessel and a staircase, which gave access to the desert to the west of WM.7. Size: 14.5 m NS × 9.8 m EW.

Chapter 4

SETTLEMENT, ECONOMY, AND DAILY LIFE AT THE WHITE MONASTERY

This chapter is broadly concerned with testing the extent to which the range of different textual and archaeological sources can be used to address the fundamental question of the scale of the architectural, human and economic environment, which made up the monastic community.

The first part of my analysis focuses on the monastic settlement, its size, infrastructure and diachronic development with particular attention paid to the monastic water supply. The economic circumstances of life in the White Monastery are pursued through an investigation into the production profile and the consumption of goods within the community, while the economic impact of the pilgrimage industry—affecting religious centres in Egypt from the fifth century onwards—also is considered. The purpose of the analysis is to bring the archaeological evidence to bear on the question of what daily life was like at the White Monastery at different stages of its history. Each section summarises the relevant textual evidence followed by a discussion of the archaeological remains and, where appropriate, the information presented by written sources is challenged. The archaeological evidence discussed is mostly pertinent to the heyday of the White Monastery between the fifth and the seventh centuries, while later developments are discussed in brief. Throughout the chapter, references are made to similar developments at the Red Monastery and Atripe. The two sites are discussed in full in Chapter 5.

4.1 SETTLEMENT

4.1.1 Internal Organisation

Shenoute's writings do not contain any detailed descriptions of the layout of the White Monastery, but by carefully sifting through his canons, Layton has identified the following elements in the site's built environment in the fifth century: a wall that surrounded the monastery, with a single gate controlled by a gate-keeper; shared cells for the monks in buildings referred to as 'houses', which may have been associated with a particular craft or workshop, a refectory, which served as the venue for a daily meal and a kitchen that was located next to the refectory; an infirmary for sick monks with its own kitchen and geriatric wards for elderly monks; a building referred to as the *diakonia*, which was the location of the main monastic administration as well as a storage place for food; a library; a store for records; and the monastic church.[441] Further references attest to streets, a bakery and a communal latrine. The latter is evident from a rule that states that only elderly monks were allowed chamber pots in their cells.[442] A structure, which Shenoute calls a *nipterion*, has been interpreted by Emmel as a washing area and by Lopez as a latrine.[443] Finally, Layton notes

441 Layton, "Rules," 47–50.
442 Layton, "Rules," 57.
443 Emmel, "Shenoute's Place," 31; Lopez, *Shenoute*, 47.

that other structures, such as a laundry and perhaps also bathing facilities, would have been found within the monastery's walls, but were not mentioned in Shenoute's writings.[444]

Later sources on the monastic built environment are scarce and limited to three sets: the hagiographic *Life of Shenoute*, Abu al-Makarim's *The Churches and Monasteries of Egypt and some Neighbouring Countries* and pre-modern travellers' accounts (evaluated in Chapter 2). The travellers' accounts mostly refer to the state of the main church from the seventeenth century onwards and will not be repeated here. The *Life of Shenoute* mentions bakeries, a grain mill, a bread store, vegetable gardens, orchards and fields—the fields were most likely located on extra-mural landholdings.[445] Finally, the thirteenth century author Abu al-Makarim notes a keep, an enclosure wall and an intra-mural garden.[446]

CALCULATING THE SIZE OF THE WHITE MONASTERY

The enclosure wall referred to by Shenoute has only partly been identified in the archaeological record. Petrie and the SCA uncovered sections of the southern and western walls and through examinations of WM.6 and WM.7, the White Monastery Project documented that the fullest extent of the monastery was reached at some point between the fifth and the seventh century (phase WM.ii). Although the archaeological record does not contain reliable evidence for the enclosure towards the north and east, several factors can assist in determining the full size of the monastery. The northern boundary is hinted at in the results of the geophysical survey combined with the archaeological surface finds. Immediately north of WM.1, the ceramic surface scatter drops drastically in quantity over the course of just ten to twenty metres, after which the surface consists of clean desert sand. The results of the magnetometric examination (pl. 5) confirm this observation. While the exact position of the circuit wall cannot be determined, these two indicators suggest its approximate location.

The eastern section of the enclosure wall is also missing from the archaeological record, but there is good evidence for its location. Five metres east of the church, a steep slope causes the ground level to drop about 6.5 m from the bare desert plateau to the modern cultivated area. There is enough evidence to suggest that the eastern extent of the ancient monastery was located in this area. This reconstruction draws in part on photographic evidence that predates the construction of the Aswan High Dam in the 1960s. The photo shows the inundation of the Nile reaching the plateau almost all the way to the church, thereby placing the monastery on the edge of a lake for six to eight weeks every year.[447] Pococke and Granger observed this phenomenon when they visited the monastery towards the end of the inundation in the mid-eighteenth century,[448] and William Wilcocks described it in detail as a part of his survey of modern Egyptian irrigation.[449] Assuming, as Mark Lehner did in a significant study published in 2000, that the pre-modern hydraulic situation also applied to antiquity,[450] it would not have been feasible for any part of the monastic built environment to be located at the bottom of the slope. This suggestion is further supported by a fourteenth-century description of the monastery's setting by Ibn Fadl Allah al-Umari, who visited Upper Egypt around 1330 as secretary for the Mamluk sultan al-Nasir Muhammad Ibn Qalawun. He described how the White Monastery was located opposite a lake, which was created by a channel from the Nile and that a road ran between the monastery and the lake.[451]

444 Layton, "Rules," 47–50.
445 Besa, *Life*, 48–51, 53, 81–82.
446 Abu Salih the Armenian, *The Churches & Monasteries*, 237.
447 Mark Lehner, "Fractal House of Pharaoh: Ancient Egypt as a Complex Adaptive System, a Trial Formulation," in *Dynamics in Human and Primate Societies. Agent-based Modeling of Social and Spatial Processes*, ed. Timothy Kohler and George Gumerman (Oxford: Oxford University Press, 2000), 298.
448 Granger, *Relation du Voyage*, 92–93; Pococke, *A Description of the East*, 79.
449 William Wilcocks, *Egyptian Irrigation* (London: Spon Ltd, 1889).
450 Lehner, "Fractal."
451 Swanson "Eclipsed History," 200.

By combining these observations, the size of the intra-mural monastic site can be calculated as an impressive 77,500 m^2. Of that figure, 20,175 m^2, or 26%, of the ancient monastery has been excavated and another 2,700 m^2 or 3.5% is constituted by the main church.

In comparison, the seventh-century complex of the Monastery of Balaʿizah measured about 15,000 m^2, while the excavated part of the seventh-century Monastery of St Jeremias at Saqqara took up some 31,500 m^2. The sixth-century Monastery of St Catherine in Sinai covered 5600 m^2, and finally the tenth-century Deir Anba Hadra in Aswan took up 15,000 m^2. Only the extensive complex of the Monastery of Apa Apollo at Bawit dwarfs the White Monastery. At Bawit, the plan of the monastery, which was produced through a combination of excavation and geophysical survey, covers an area of 366,000 m^2. However, it is unclear whether Bawit was actually two neighbouring monasteries—a male congregation to the north and a female congregation to the south—or if the settlement partly consisted of a group of hermitages.[452] In any case, the White Monastery was among the largest walled monasteries of Late Antique Egypt.

According to the written sources, the monastic estate of the White Monastery reached far beyond the settlement's core. These extra-mural landholdings amounted to 50 km^2 in the fifth century according to Leipoldt and one *feddan* (around 4200 m^2) in the fifteenth century (see Chapter 2.3) and would mainly have been used for agriculture and for processing agricultural products.[453] This agrarian economy is important for a full understanding of the daily running of the White Monastery and its place within Late Antique society. Unfortunately, the present evidence is too scarce (and missing entirely from the archaeological record) to allow such discussion and I have decided to exclude these extra-mural landholdings from major consideration in this book. Importantly, a sixth-century documentary papyrus mentions a certain Aurelius Phoibammon, who would lease land from various landowners. Among these were five monastic and ecclesiastical institutions that owned land in the region of Aphrodito (some 30 km north of Akmim). One of these was the White Monastery.[454]

Land use in the immediate vicinity of the settlement included the monastic graveyard and areas for disposal of rubbish. Only limited evidence exists for the location of the graveyard, but in Late Antiquity it could have been located at the northwestern edge of the monastic complex near the triconch funerary chapel (WM.2). From the eighth century, it appears to have extended to include WM.7 (the southwest part of the monastery) with further expansions to the north side of the main church (WM.3) at the time when the settlement was confined to the church (see Chapters 2.4 & 3.4). A similar development is seen in the spread of the rubbish disposal, where extra-mural disposal in WM.6 (the southeast part of the monastery) appears to be the norm up to the seventh or eighth century, in WM.1 (the northernmost part of the monastery) from the ninth century and in WM.5 (the area immediately south of the church) during the latest developments of the settlement (pl. 6).

INTRA-MURAL ORGANISATION: STREETS AND BUILDINGS

In 2003, Brenningmeyer and McNally analysed the White Monastery's built environment by correlating a preliminary map published in 1991 by Mohammed and Grossmann with QUICKBIRD satellite imagery.[455] The study argued that even the church (described as the most important building) derived some of its meaning from its context and for this reason all settlement activity should be studied as a whole—including all buildings and the spaces between them.[456] Applying Bill Hillier and Julienne

452 Bagnall and Rathbone, *Egypt*, 177.

453 Layton mentions fields, vegetable gardens, palm groves, fruit orchards and farm animals as well as storage for agricultural equipment and irrigation systems (see Layton, "Rules," 51–52). See also Leipoldt, *Schenute*, 95–96.

454 James G. Keenan, "Aurelius Phoibammon. Son of Tridelphus: A Byzantine Egyptian Land Entrepreneur," *Bulletin of the American Society of Papyrologists* 17.3–4 (1980): 151.

455 Brenningmeyer and McNally, "White Monastery;" Mohammed and Grossmann, "Dayr Anba Shinuda."

456 Brenningmeyer and McNally, "White Monastery," 25–26.

Hanson's Space Syntax Analysis,[457] they examined the layout of exterior spaces, focussing on points of interaction and areas of isolation. This analysis was based on the basic principle that axial spaces allow movement from one place to another, thus allowing integration, while convex spaces can provide a shared identity to surrounding buildings and to those who use them, while at the same time isolating that group of structures from other parts of the built environment.[458] By these means, the built environment can both facilitate movement in and between buildings as well as isolation or social interaction.[459] Unfortunately, Brenningmeyer and McNally's incomplete data set and their lack of access to the physical remains meant that their study did not reflect the actual situation on the ground. For this reason, I will not summarise their results but will instead build upon their ideas by examining the monastic access routes and public areas that are available for study. I use the term 'public' for areas that appears to have been accessible to most members of the monastic community.

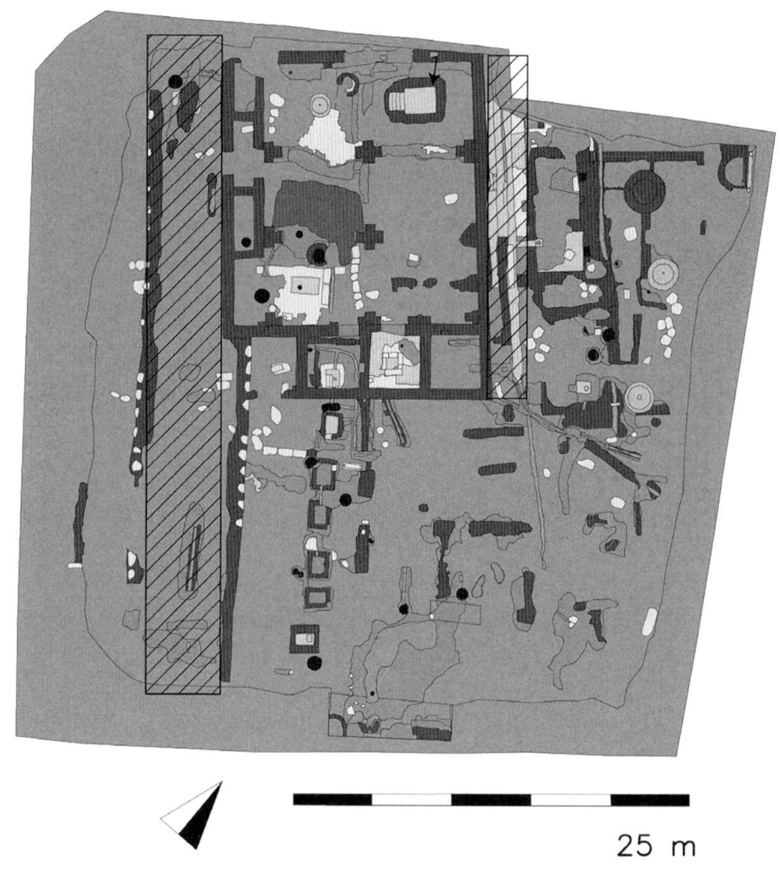

Fig. 54. Location of thoroughfares in WM.5 (diagonal lines) (map by Dawn McCormack and the author; © YMAP).

Streets and access routes have been identified in WM.4 (the area to the west of the church) and WM.5, but the poor preservation of the remaining five areas does not allow for comments to be made on their internal organisation. The public areas in WM.4 and WM.5 remained integral throughout the use of the monastery—at least until its first period of abandonment (phase WM.iv). A thoroughfare (5 m wide) ran through the western part of WM.5 and provided access from the main church to the southern part of the monastery (fig. 54). The width of the street suggests that it was among the main thoroughfares and was intended to facilitate the passage of a large number of people. A paved passage (2.3 m wide) led from the northeast end of WM.5 to a doorway to the courtyard in the southern part of the area. The narrow passage gives the impression of a more secluded space, not used for general movement through the monastery, but perhaps for monastics with a specific purpose. Following Hillier and Hanson's suggestion on the function of convex spaces (see above), it is possible that the buildings surrounding the courtyard in the southern part of WM.5 once served associated purposes, although that information has now been lost.

Only one street can securely be identified in WM.4 (WM 4.1.17). It separated the food production zone

457 Bill Hillier and Julienne Hanson, *The Social Logic of Space* (Cambridge: Cambridge University Press, 1984).

458 Brenningmeyer and McNally, "White Monastery," 27.

459 Aravecchia, "Hermitages and Spatial Analysis," 29; See also Nicola Aravecchia, Christians of the Western Desert in Late Antiquity: The Fourth-Century Church Complex of Ain el-Gedida, Upper Egypt (unpublished PhD, University of Minnesota, 2009), 186–216.

Fig. 55. Map showing thoroughfares, access routes and open courtyards in WM.4 (diagonal lines) (map by Dawn McCormack and the author; © YMAP).

and the kitchen from the refectory and the buildings towards north (fig. 55). The width of the street (5.5–6 m), combined with its location, leaves no doubt that it was utilised as one of the monastery's main thoroughfares. It continues south into unexcavated territory and towards the north, with the architectural remains suggesting that it intersected with either an east–west running street or a small open square. The archaeological evidence supporting this interpretation is as follows: a doorway in the north end of the food production area (in WM.4.3.29) and the layout of the pipes in WM.4.6.32 (see Chapter 4.2.2). From the food production area, two doors opened onto the main thoroughfare. A narrow doorway in the north end gives access to WM.4.3.15 and a large doorway gives access to the hallway (WM.4.2.4). The former appears to have been utilised by a limited number of monastics and should perhaps be seen as a service entrance, while the hallway could be perceived as a public area serving not only as an access point to the facilities within the enclosure, but also as a shortcut for monastics travelling from one part of WM.4 to another.

The carefully paved square (WM.4.4.28) gives the impression of an important space with a high level of activity. The courtyard could be reached through doorways in WM.4.2.4, through WM.4.6.26 (north of the food enclosure) and through WM.4.5.31, where a doorway separated the courtyard from activities near the well. The south part of the square and the associated buildings have disappeared entirely from the archaeological record. Constructed at the same time as the square, the large building in WM.4.4.22 flanks the entire east side. The (at least) two-storey building with a large central access point would have imposed itself visually on the courtyard and it would appear as though this area in part was laid out to create such impression. Considering that convex spaces create a shared identity for the surrounding buildings, the utilitarian functions of the well area (north) and food enclosure (east) can perhaps throw light on the use of the large building on the east side of the square. It is difficult to agree with Grossmann's suggestion that it functioned as a dormitory.[460] On the contrary, taking all factors into consideration—the prominent position, the central location, the monumental layout, the solid construction and the functions of the surrounding buildings—it probably served an important administrative purpose, which may also have involved storage. Shenoute's description of the *diakonia* springs to mind.[461]

460 Grossmann et al., "Excavation," 376–378; Grossmann et al., "Monastery of Apa Shenoute," 172–175.

461 Layton, "Rules," 48.

Several factors suggest that the main church was set in the centre of a convex space—perhaps an open square, which was lined by buildings on its west, south and probably also north sides, but not on the east side, where the enclosure wall would have stood. It is clear from the position of doorways (two in each wall, except the east) that the building was freestanding and that at some point during its early history it allowed direct passage to adjacent buildings without the necessity of circumambulation. The west doors sat across from the refectory and the south doors sat across from the pillared hall and basin in WM.5.6. I will discuss the use and internal relationships of these buildings in Chapter 4.3.

The area to the south of the church that was cleared and planned by Petrie and Ward does not appear to have contained any remains of streets or alleys.[462] Two gates were, however, uncovered—one or both may have served as the main point(s) of entry into the monastic complex, but could also have been secondary access points connecting the monastery with nearby fields. There is not much that can be said about the gates based on their plan, but it should be noted that at five and seven metres they were both wide enough to allow several camels to pass each other at the monastic entrance, presumably to allow both the pick-up and delivery of goods. The doorway in the west wall, which was excavated by Petrie and re-examined by the WMP (see Chapter 3.8.2), could have provided access from the monastery to the mountains.

Fig. 56. Western end of well in WM.4.5.31. Showing transverse arch for *saqiya* fitting. View towards south (photograph by the author; © YMAP).

4.1.2 The Supply, Distribution and Disposal of Water

Water was essential for many aspects of daily life such as food preparation, basic hygiene, animal husbandry and many types of craft production.[463] In Late Antiquity these included, but were not limited to, the production of pottery, textiles, oil and wine,[464] and in the process of constructing and maintaining the monastic built environment, water was used for the making of materials such as bricks, mortar, plaster and paint.

Sizeable communities such as that of the White Monastery, therefore, needed a substantial and sustainable water supply, which required adequate organizational infrastructure, not only with regard to planning and construction, but also regarding maintenance, supervision and repairs.[465] Maintaining

462 Petrie, *Athribis*, 13–15.

463 A shorter account of the White Monastery's water supply has been published in Louise Blanke, "Life on the Desert's Edge: The Water Supply of a Late Antique Monastery in Egypt," in *Water of Life*, ed. John Kuhlmann Madsen, Nils Overgaard Andersen, and Ingolf Thuesen (Copenhagen: Orbis, 2016).

464 Andrew Wilson, "Industrial Use of Water," in *Handbook of Ancient Water Technology*, ed. Örjan Wikander (Leiden, Boston, Köln: Brill, 2000), 127.

465 Gemma C.M. Jansen, "Urban Water Transport and Distribution," in *Handbook of Ancient Water Technology*, ed. Örjan Wikander (Leiden, Boston, Köln: Brill, 2000), 103.

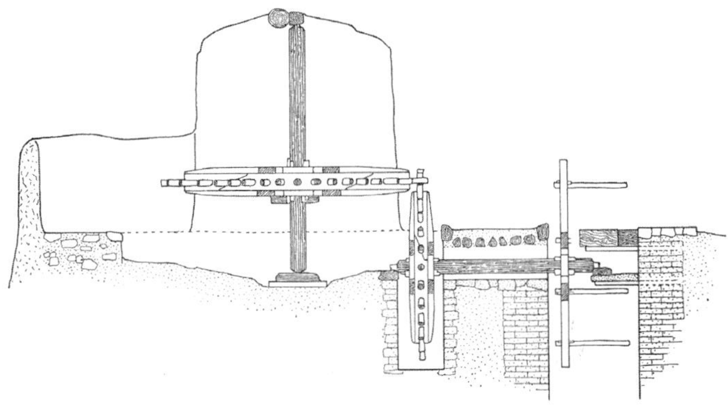

Fig. 57. Section view of *saqiya* gear drive with installation for pot garland or bucket chain (Ménassa and Laferrière, *La Saqia*, fig. 25; © IFAO).

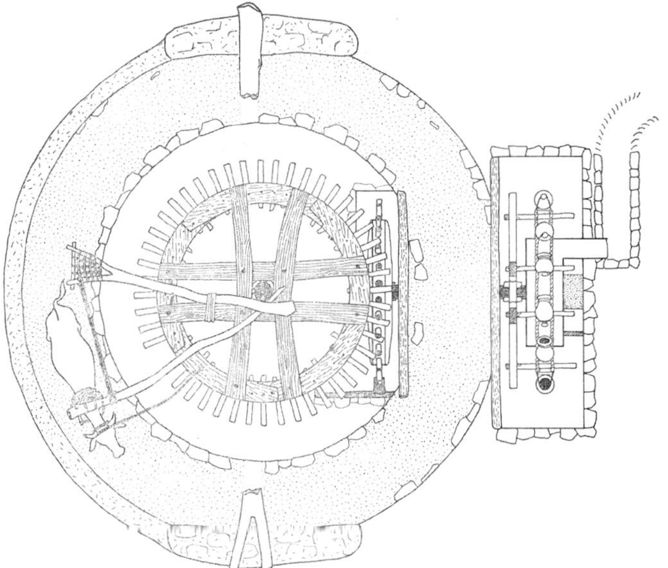

Fig. 58. View from above of ox driven *saqiya* gear drive with pot garland (Ménassa and Laferrière, *La Saqia*, fig. 24; © IFAO).

a steady water supply posed a particular challenge in the hot and dry desert setting of the monastery and specific means were required to preserve the precious commodity. The archaeological remains presented in Chapter 3 do indeed show that features related to the use or storage of water were prominent on the site. In the following sections, the different components of the monastic water supply and their impact on the built environment are discussed.

THE WELL IN WM.4.5.31

The main sources of water at the White Monastery are the two large wells, located in the northern part of WM.4 and in the south-west corner of the church itself (pl. 7). The latter is dealt with in a separate section below. The best-preserved part of the water system is found in the immediate surroundings of the well in WM.4. This well is rectangular in shape, measuring about 6 × 8 m, and the current water level is about 12.5 m below the surface, as observed by Grossman.[466] It has not been possible to examine the full depth of the well. It is constructed of fired bricks with dressed limestone blocks placed towards the bottom. The northern part of the structure is located directly on bedrock, which was cut to reach the full depth of the well (fig. 40).

The layout of the well shows that it was built to support two parallel water-lifting devices: one on the east side and one on the west side. Two transverse arches and characteristic circular wear marks on the interior walls would suggest that a *saqiya* gear drive combined with a pot garland was used to haul water from the east and west ends (fig. 56).[467] A *saqiya* consists of two large wooden gearwheels engaged at a right angle.[468] Operated by an ox, donkey or other draught animal, the gearwheels would drive a vertical wheel, located on the top of the well, on to which ropes with pots or buckets were attached (figs. 57 & 58).[469] When the wheel turned, the containers would dip into the water source directly below.[470]

466 Grossman et al., "Monastery of Apa Shenute," 186.

467 John P. Oleson, "Water-Lifting," in *Handbook of Ancient Water Technology*, ed. Örjan Wikander (Leiden, Boston, Köln: Brill, 2000), 261.

468 Trevor Hodge, "Collection of Water," in *Handbook of Ancient Water Technology*, ed. Örjan Wikander (Leiden, Boston, Köln: Brill, 2000), 33.

469 Myrto Malouta and Andrew Wilson, "Mechanical Irrigation: Water-Lifting Devices in the Archaeological Evidence and in the Egyptian Papyri," in *The Roman Agricultural Economy: Organisation, Investment and Production*, ed. Alan Bowman and Andrew Wilson (Oxford: Oxford University Press, 2013), 288.

470 John P. Oleson, *Greek and Roman Mechanical Water-Lifting Devices: The History of a Technology* (Toron-

At the White Monastery, none of the elements associated with the actual lifting of the water has survived, but the presence of *saqiya* pots found in WM.1 confirms the interpretation made from the architectural remains. *Saqiya* pots are easily recognisable, as they typically have a broad mouth, no handles, but a narrowing at the neck and a protruding knob on the base to allow them to be tied on to the pot garland in two places. The strain on the pot was primarily in its lower part, meaning that the lower body could break off and fall into the well.[471]

Until the introduction of the modern motorised pump, the *saqiya* was by far the most effective way of lifting water to land higher than a local water source.[472] Its introduction to Egypt in the Ptolemaic period allowed large-scale perennial irrigation resulting in twice-annual harvest in addition to the Nile-fed winter crops.[473]

The lifted water would be emptied from the pots into a channel and then be further distributed through pipelines by a gravity-fed system to the parts of the monastery where it was needed. Examinations throughout the monastic site reveal that the water system consisted of five individual components: 1) conduits; that is, the architectural structures used to move water between different locations; 2) distribution and inspection boxes; 3) sedimentation tanks for settling of particles and temporary storage of water; 4) plastered water containers (i.e., tanks or cisterns); and 5) soak-aways for drainage.

THE CONDUITS

The main element in the water supply system consisted of ceramic pipes used as conduit systems. They are found in all parts of the White Monastery, from single pipes preserved *in situ* to long stretches of pipelines, as well as abundant fragments. The individual pipes are of a thick tapered type, most of which are 0.17 m wide and about 0.60 m long, slightly conical in shape and joined by inserting the narrow end of one pipe into the wide end of the next and then fixing the connection with mortar.[474] The best-preserved sections of the water conduits are located immediately east and west of the well. Four pipelines run a stretch of more than 50 m along the length of a fired brick wall, after which they turn north, northwest and south. Pipelines are, however, located in all central parts of the site and are particularly predominant in WM.4 and WM.5, while no remains of pipes have been found along the edge of the monastery, WM.1.1, WM.2, WM.3, WM.6 and WM.7. This distribution confirms the proposition, established in Chapter 3, that the monastic industrial production was focussed in the areas immediately south and west of the church. Three examples of lead pipes were found in the monastery, one within the church (see section below) and two in the food processing area in WM.4.4.13 and WM.4.4.14. The choice of material in these specific locations is peculiar and it has not been possible to find comparanda that might clarify these choices. In the Roman world, lead was preferred to ceramics, but in the Near East, where lead sources were less abundant, lead pipes were only occasionally used.[475]

A recurring problem relating specifically to the pipes has been identified. Pipes throughout the monastery, but especially near the well in WM.4, show evidence of mineral encrustation and clogging from sedimentation. In some cases the build-up was so great that it left only a few centimetres at the top for water to flow. The pipelines to the east of the well were blocked to the point that they were unusable, which may explain the presence of

to, Buffalo, London: University of Toronto Press, 1984), 358.

471 Etan Ayalon, "Typology and Chronology of Water-wheel (*Saqiya*) Pottery Pots from Israel," *Israel Exploration Journal* 50 (2000): 220–221.

472 Ayalon, "Water-wheel Pottery," 216.

473 Larry W. Mays, "Water Technology in Ancient Egypt," in *Ancient Water Technologies*, ed. Larry W. Mays (London & New York: Springer, 2010), 62.

474 Jansen, "Urban Water Transport and Distribution," 108–109.

475 Zena Kamash, "An Exploration of the Relationship between Shifting Power, Changing Behaviour and New Water Technologies in the Roman Near East," *Water History* 4 (2011): 84–85.

Fig. 59. Two distribution boxes in WM.4.7.30. View towards south-southeast (photograph by the author; © YMAP).

several adjacent pipelines—one replacing the other. This clogging varies with the rate of water flow—a fast flow needs minimal maintenance because it would be self-scouring.[476] The fact that such extensive clogging took place indicates that the water flow was relatively gentle and that the necessary periodic cleaning did not take place, at least not towards the end of the lifetime of these sections of the conduit system. Vats found throughout the monastery could very well have served as sedimentation vats, allowing impurities to sink to the bottom before the water was directed to its point of use. This process was required to use the water for various processes such as pottery manufacturing, the making of a number of building materials, as well as cooking. A series of interconnected vats found immediately east of the well could very well have served this purpose.

The location and organisation of the pipes indicates how parts of the monastery were used. Pipelines are commonly located between buildings, below streets, alleys or elsewhere where easy access could be gained for repairs.[477] The pipelines that run along the line of the building east (WM.4.4.32) of the well can, therefore be interpreted as lying below a thoroughfare or passageway (pl. 8). A similar arrangement can be found in WM.5 immediately south of the monastic church between the church and WM.5.4 and below the surface level of the street in the western part of the same area. Within buildings, pipelines would commonly be placed in walls or below floors, meaning that the many pipes that are visible in the archaeology remains today would not have been visible to the ancient monastics.

Distribution boxes were installed as a means for cleaning the pipes and for managing the water flow. These boxes consist of a plastered brick construction in which several pipelines would meet (fig. 59). They

476 J. Patrick Greene, *Medieval Monasteries* (Leicester, London & New York: Leicester University Press, 1992), 121.
477 Jansen, "Water Transport," 108.

were open at the top, so the water distribution could be manipulated by, for example, closing off one pipeline and thereby increasing the pressure in another.[478] The pipeline could be closed by using a ball of cloth or string as still seen today. Three distribution boxes were identified and only in close proximity to the well in WM.4 (pl. 7).

A second type of box is the inspection box. This type consists of just an inlet and an outlet, and is found at the White Monastery immediately before a pipe enters a building. The inspection box served the primary purpose of allowing a workman to check if the water was running and thereby isolate potential problems in the system. The pipe could then be shut off when repair or cleaning were necessary. Seven inspection boxes are found distributed between WM.1, WM.4 and WM.5 (pl. 7).

WATER STORAGE AND DISPOSAL

The fourth component of the water system is water storage in the form of the plastered tanks and cisterns that are found in WM.1.2, WM.4 and WM.5. The dispersal of water containers indicates that water was transported to where it was needed and stored there.[479] This suggests that water was lifted from the wells episodically rather than continuously and distributed throughout the site for storage and local use. Establishing the exact nature of this use in each location is problematic because of the general state of preservation and the lack of portable architecture or associated material culture. Although minor cisterns are found throughout the site, only one substantial structure for water storage has been excavated. A cylinder-shaped cistern (7 m deep and 2 m in diameter, total capacity of 87 m^3) is located in the large building in WM.4.4.22, supplied by a pipe, which leads directly from the well 30 m away.

An element of almost equal importance to the supply of water is its disposal. Andrew Wilson defined four orders of drainage.[480] The first order drains from a tank or basin within a building, the second order combines drainage from several installations into one main drain that exits the building, the third order collects waste water from several buildings and the fourth order brings these together to remove the waste from the settlement. Only three examples of water drainage have been found at the White Monastery, two in WM.5 and one in WM.4 (pl. 7), all belonging to the first order. These three soakaways each consist of a large, deep ceramic vessel of which the base has been removed. In WM.5, the lower part of the vessel contained a layer of ceramic sherds, allowing the water to drain while the build-up of silt could easily be removed. All three soakaways were placed immediately outside of the buildings that they served, possibly to avoid unpleasant smells and facilitate the efficient removal of built-up materials, as well as to avoid undermining the buildings. Based on this archaeological evidence, it would seem that the disposal of water was locally organised, at least in this part of the monastery, where there is no evidence for a larger system of drainage channels. Considering the complexity of the water supply and the quantity of water consumed on the site, it is likely that more sophisticated drainage systems were in use elsewhere on site.

The lack of identified drainage systems could also result from a lack of clear distinction between pipes used for drainage and pipes used for clean water. To date, the difference in the pipes' diameter (from 0.09–0.22 m) has been ascribed to chronological variants rather than usage, although it seems plausible to offer an alternative suggestion: that the narrow pipes were always used for water supply, while the wider pipes on some occasions could be interpreted as drains. This suggestion is based on the location of the larger pipes on the site and would imply that the pipe below the street in WM.5 and the wide pipe (0.22 m) in the southern end of the kitchen in WM.4.1.2, were used for drainage.

478 Jansen, "Water Transport," 109.

479 Hodge, "Collection of Water," 21.

480 Andrew Wilson, "Drainage and Sanitation," in *Handbook of Ancient Water Technology*, ed. Örjan Wikander (Leiden, Boston, Köln: Brill, 2000), 152.

Fig. 60. Sluice gate in channel in WM.5.4. View towards south (photograph by the author; © YMAP).

THE WELL IN THE CHURCH AND THE LATER WATER SUPPLY SYSTEM

The water system associated with the well in the southwest corner of the main church is less clearly discernible, but the well is broadly similar in layout and organisation to that found at the neighbouring Red Monastery (see Chapter 5.1.2). It has not been possible to fully record this well, as a metal lid with only a small hatched opening currently covers the well. It has been possible to establish that the well is circular in shape, which suggests that it was sunk rather than constructed with the use of a scaffold. Such well-sinking technique allows the well to be built while the shaft is dug, thus sinking the well section by section until a suitable level is reached. This technique does not require major stabilisation of the surrounding areas and it could tentatively be suggested that the well was constructed after the completion of the church.[481] The remains of two transverse arches span the centre of the structure, meaning that this well also was operated by a *saqiya* gear drive. It is, unfortunately, not possible to date the construction of the well based on its stylistic qualities, but from the description of travellers, we know that this well served as the main supplier for the community living inside the church. Vansleb mentions that the water rises and falls with the Nile, is sweet (as opposed to brackish/salty), and the monks informed him that it was forty cubits (about 20 m) deep.[482] It is worth considering if the collapse of this corner of the church in the early 19th century was related to the location of the well here (fig. 6).

Within the church, a pipe led from the well to the south church wall and a basin to the east of the well would likely have served to hold water lifted from the well. It is not possible to associate any exterior pipelines with this well, although judging by their positions it seems that at least some of the pipelines found in WM.5 would have been fed by the well.

In both WM.4 and WM.5, open channels constitute a later incarnation of the water supply system. Channels that clearly postdate the original use of WM.4 are found in WM.4.3.10 and WM.4.4.28, as well as in WM.5.4. These could be associated with a reorganisation of the water supply after the seventh or eighth century. A sluice gate set in the channel in WM.5.4 (fig. 60) could relate to the specific purpose of the channel, but could also result from the continuous problem of silted-up drains.[483] Unfortunately, the water system of the later monastic use is only very partially preserved and therefore poorly understood. It is clear, however, that the system was less sophisticated, presumably only consisting of a few main channels that directed water to where it was needed, rather than the myriads of intersecting conduits that characterised the earlier system.

481 See Trevor Hodge, "Wells," in *Handbook of Ancient Water Technology*, ed. Örjan Wikander (Leiden, Boston, Köln: Brill, 2000), 29–34 for construction of wells.

482 It is not clear if the forty cubits refer to the full depth of the well or the depth from the surface to the water level (Vansleb, *Egypt*, 225).

483 Greene, *Medieval Monasteries*, 121.

QUANTIFYING THE MONASTIC WATER SUPPLY

The quantification of the use of the *saqiya* gear drives and their associated pot garlands is not easy, given the problem of accurate data collection, but nevertheless worthwhile since it allows us to estimate an approximate water provision within the site. The variables include the following: the number of pots on the garland can only roughly be estimated, the individual pot size can vary and the type of draught animal used, as well as the height of the lift can all influence the quantity of water drawn from the well.[484] At the same time, the output would not have been 100 percent efficient and factors such as water spillage and friction drag, when the pots scoop up the water, must be taken into account.[485] Although somewhat speculative, it is possible to make an approximate calculation of the output of the wells in the White Monastery. The minimum lift required was 12.5 m, meaning that the pot garland must have been about 30 m long to allow for passage over the wheel at the top and dipping into the water at the bottom. If there was one pot per metre, the pot garland would have carried a total of 30 pots. The size of the *saqiya* pots is somewhat more complicated, as no complete vessels have been found on site. Comparing the diameter of the rim (0.23 m) with typologies made by John P. Oleson and Etan Ayalon, as well as modern Egyptian ethnographic comparanda suggests a capacity of about 6 litres, bringing the total capacity of the pot garland to 180 litres and the weight of 15 pots (the number of pots filled with water at any given time) to 90 kg.[486] It is not necessary to consider the weight of the actual pots in the equation, as the even distribution means that for each pot on its way up, one would be on its way down. It is assumed that the *saqiya* was driven by one draught animal providing an effective output of 1 hp or 736 W. The energy required to lift 6 litres 13.5 m (adding 1 m to reach the top of the drive wheel) is

z (lift in m) × weight (kg) × gravitational acceleration (9.82 m/second^2) = E (joule)
meaning: 13.5 m × 6 kg × 9.82 = 795 J

Assuming an efficiency of 60% (of the 1 hp/736 J/s) resulting from a loss to friction from water and gearing, 442 J/s is available for lifting the water. Therefore, (442 J/s / 795 J) × 6 litres = 3.33 litres per second or 795 J / 442 J/s = 1.8 seconds per pot. However, the result of 3.33 litres per second or 199.8 litres per minute does not take spillage into account and it is possible that the effective output was just 50 percent, thus bringing the discharge to 1.66 litres per second, 99.9 litres per minute and 5994 litres per hour (ca. 6 m^3). At this rate, the *saqiya* could fill the cistern in WM.4.4.22 in about 14.5 hours.[487]

These numbers are consistent with observations made by Willcocks and Julien Barois and calculations made by the Food and Agriculture Organization of the United Nations, which suggests a discharge of 6–8 m^3 per hour for water lifted to a height of 12.5 m.[488]

One more factor must be taken into consideration when quantifying the capacity of the wells at the White Monastery. The well recovery rate is the rate at which water runs into the well from the rock fissures and openings while water is lifted.[489] The well recovery rate is measured over a 24-hour period and should ideally be considered for different times

484 Ayalon, "Water-wheel Pottery," 218–219; John P. Oleson, *Greek and Roman Mechanical Water-Lifting Devices: The History of a Technology* (Toronto, Buffalo, London: University of Toronto Press, 1984), 364–366.

485 http://www.fao.org/docrep/010/ah810e/AH810E05.htm

486 Ayalon, "Water-wheel Pottery;" Laïla Ménassa and Pierre-Henry Laferrière, *La Sāqia. Technique et vocabulaire de la roue à eau Égyptienne* (Cairo: Institut Français d'Archéologie Orientale, 1974); Oleson, *Devices*, 367. See also Jane Faiers, "A Corpus of Late Roman Pottery from Kom el-Nana," in *Late Roman Pottery at Amarna and related Studies*, ed. Jane Faiers (London: Egypt Exploration Society, 2005), 149; Winlock, Crum and Evelyn-White, *Monastery*, 64, A–F.

487 Calculations were made with the help of Mogens Blanke.

488 Julien Barois, *Irrigation in Egypt* (Washington, DC: Government Printing Office, 1889); Wilcocks, *Irrigation*, 240; http://www.fao.org/docrep/010/ah810e/AH810E05.htm

489 https://inspectapedia.com/water/Well_Flow_Rate.php

of the year. It has not been possible to recover exact data pertaining to the Sohag desert fringe, but some general numbers can be assumed.[490] According to the *American Free Encyclopedia of Building & Environmental Inspection, Testing, Diagnosis, Repair*,[491] a small well suitable for residential use should have a well recovery rate of 5 gallons per minute (1 gal = 4.55 litres), while 10 gallons per min (45.5 litres) is considered a high well recovery rate for residential use. Applying the latter figure of 45.5 litres per minute or 2730 litres per hour, the well's recovery rate would be 45.5 percent of the lifting capacity of each *saqiya*. Assuming the accuracy of these features, this means that one *saqiya* could lift water from the well in WM.4 for 10.8 hours per day (10 hours to avoid total depletion) and two *saqiyas* could be in use for a total of 5 hours a day. Thereby, the total amount of water that could be drawn from each well per day was approximately 60 m^3. If the two wells were in use at the same time, the number would be 120 m^3.

The Arabic *Life of Shenoute* reports that during the saint's lifetime, the monasteries under his rule grew to contain 2200 monks and 1800 nuns.[492] If, for example, two thirds of the monks resided at the White Monastery, the wells would have supplied water to 1450 monastics. The World Health Organisation (WHO) estimates that 7.5 litres per person per day will meet the requirements of most people under most conditions, but stresses that about 20 litres are required when basic personal and food hygiene is taken into considerations.[493] A population of 1450 at the White Monastery would, therefore, require 29,000 litres or 29 m^3 water per day, which, according to the above calculations would constitute 48% of the maximum daily capacity of one well.[494] Beyond the needs of the monastics, water was also required for the industries documented in the archaeological record. I will return to this point below.

The writings of Shenoute record that more than 20,000 people sought refuge from the Blemmyes over a period of three months in the fifth century. In a detailed account, Shenoute lists the many expenses relating to the upkeep of this large group of people and even recalls that 'the small spring was wonderful, for *had He* (God) *not blessed it*, it would not have been enough for them to drink water.'[495] However, accommodating a group of people that size would require the impossible amount of 429,000 litres or 429 m^3 per day (3.6 times more than the wells' maximum capacity). Storing such an amount of water poses an obvious problem and cannot be affirmed through the capacity of the cisterns found in the archaeological record. Considering that all industry was stopped during the three-month period, the White Monastery could supply a maximum of 6000 people including the monastics (using both wells), while the Red Monastery and the convent in Atripe could each supply a maximum of 3000 people—once again including the monasteries' own population. It is not possible to quantify to what extent the three month long annual flooding affected the monastery's water supply, but if the refugee crises took place during the inundation, it is likely that the available water could have supported a higher number than my calculations suggest.

In terms of cost, a *saqiya* was an expensive installation, as made clear through lists of prices mentioned in papyri.[496] The seventh-century Papyrus Baden 95 from Hermopolis mentions the cost of 12 *solidi* (4.5 gr of gold each) for a water-lifting device

490 Several PhD theses on the hydrology of the Sohag region have been completed from Sohag University (see bibliography in Ayman A. Ahmed and Mohamed H. Ali, "Hydrochemical Evolution and Variation of Groundwater and its Environmental impact at Sohag, Egypt," *Arab Journal of Geoscience* 4 [2011]), unfortunately, none of these addresses the desert fringe environment (Ayman Abdelhameed Ahmed, personal communication with author, 2014).

491 https://inspectapedia.com/water/Well_Flow_Rate.php

492 Amélineau, *Monuments*, 331; confirmed by Leipoldt (Leipoldt, *Schenute*, 93–94).

493 http://www.who.int/water_sanitation_health/emergencies/qa/emergencies_qa5/en/

494 Breton Connelly & Wilson suggested 10 litres per person per day for their calculations for the monastery on the island of Geronisos (Joan Breton Connelly and Andrew I. Wilson, "Hellenistic and Byzantine Cisterns on Geronisos Island. Report of the Department of Antiquities, Cyprus [2002]: 288). If applied to the White Monastery, the 1450 monastics would require 14,500 litres per day or 24% of the maximum daily capacity of one well.

495 Lopez, *Shenoute*, 57–58.

496 Oleson, "Water-Lifting," 385.

that has been interpreted as a *saqiya*. In comparison, the late sixth-century Papyrus London 1724 lists the price of a spacious and good-quality house in Syene (modern Aswan) as 10 *solidi*.[497] In addition to the gear-drive and its installation came maintenance and the cost of draught animals and their upkeep. The *saqiya* was possibly, however, the least costly element of the water supply at the White Monastery. The extensive wells, the advanced system of pipes, tanks and drainage must have been a major item in the monastic budget, but is, unfortunately, impossible to quantify due to the many different factors involved such as materials, labour and maintenance.

WATER MANAGEMENT AT THE WHITE MONASTERY

What does this archaeological evidence tell us about water management at the White Monastery? In terms of architectural organization, the water supply was clearly an integral part of the design of the monastic space and of the construction of individual buildings. This demonstrates a planning strategy as well as significant economic investment into the monastic built environment.

In terms of administration, water management was a multi-tier process. The first tier, lifting the water from the well, required a central organization that could administer a strategy for the allocation of the water and its distribution. The second tier involved organization at each cistern or workstation to manage specific local distribution and use. The archaeological record does not reveal how formally either tier was structured, or if they formed part of a systematic control of the use of water within the monastery. It is relevant to ask if each area was allocated a certain amount of water per day, or if the water could be lifted according to when it was needed. In both scenarios an overseer, who was specifically responsible for maintaining the water system, would have been required. The gradual build-up of silt in the pipelines would suggest that at some point around the seventh century this system did not work. The complete blocking of the pipelines by accumulated silt indicates a gradual decline in the effectiveness of the pipes due to a lack of maintenance rather than an abrupt abandonment of the water system.

The specific architecture of water management at the White Monastery shows that the water supply was based on a long tradition of plumbing that is found in the Hellenistic period (332–30 BCE) across the Eastern Mediterranean and hardly changed until the Medieval period.[498] The water system of the White Monastery is, however, rare in that all elements of the system are preserved, whereas contemporary sites most often contain only a few of these elements.

4.2 ECONOMY: PRODUCTION AND CONSUMPTION AT THE WHITE MONASTERY

A traditional view of monastic economy is found in the literary sources where it is suggested that artisanal craftsmanship such as weaving, rope-making and basketry were the main sources of income for the monasteries.[499] Wipszycka has challenged this view in several studies in which she combines documentary sources with a survey of the archaeological remains.[500] According to Wipszycka, the documentary sources reveal that the main income for monasteries was based on the production of cash-crops for sale in local markets, while some monasteries also specialised in specific products.[501] The Monasteries in Wadi Sarga and Bawit, and St Jeremias in Saqqara, for example, produced large quantities of wine, while St Jeremias also was the centre for a large-scale ceramic production, including amphorae that most likely were utilised to transport the wine.[502] Unfortunately, there are hardly any documentary sources pertinent to the White Monastery, which means that informa-

497 Allan C. Johnson and Louis C. West, *Byzantine Egypt: Economic Studies* (Amsterdam: Adolf M. Hakkert, 1967), 189–199.

498 Jansen, "Water Transport," 119; Kamash, "New Water Technologies;" Wilson, "Drainage," 178.

499 Lopez, *Shenoute*, repeats this position.

500 Ewa Wipszycka, *Les Ressources et les Activités Économiques des Églises en Égypte du IVe au VIIIe Siècle* (Bruxelles: Foundation Égyptologique Reine Élisabeth, 1972); Wipszycka, "Resources."

501 Wipszycka, "Resources," 172.

502 Wipszycka, "Resources," 200.

tion about its economy derives from circumstantial references and from the archaeological remains.

Substantial parts of the archaeological remains of the White Monastery consist of vats or tanks that in many cases are connected to pipes. Found together, these features are, according to Wilson, a primary indicator that one is dealing with an area used for manufacturing.[503] The written sources contain some information on monastic production but, as before, the main source of information is found in Shenoute's writings, while later texts are negligible.

Layton has extracted the categories of jobs mentioned in passing in Shenoute's writings. Presented in alphabetic order these include: 'baker, bell ringer, catechizer, chanter, cook, construction worker, copyist of manuscripts, craft worker, deacon, *diakonia* worker, *diakonia* cleaner, doctor, field hand, food server, fruit picker, fuel gatherer, gatehouse server, grinder and miller, guardian of keys and locked objects, harvester, infirmary cleaner, kitchen cleaner, livestock herder, nurse, pall bearer, priest, refectory cleaner, rope maker, supervisor of children, transportation worker, waiter.'[504] Layton suggests that anyone who joined the monastery would be asked to renounce the exercise of any skills he had in civilian life, take on an assigned job, and learn how to weave (baskets were made by the male congregation and cloth from wool and flax was woven by the female monastics at Atripe). Failure to perform a specially assigned job meant that the monastic concerned would go back to the weaving.[505]

The list informs us about several important aspects of life in the White Monastery in the fifth century: it brings us closer to the daily life of the monastics and the facilities that were available for their use. Of particular importance for this part of the chapter is that it lists activities that relate to food and craft production intended for intra-mural consumption or as a way to generate income or use for barter. The jobs specifically associated with food production are baker, cook, field hand, fruit picker, grinder and miller, harvester and livestock herder. Jobs associated with craft production are copyist of manuscripts, rope maker and the somewhat opaque term 'craft worker'. The transportation worker can be associated with both production and consumption through the ability to supply the monastery with raw materials or finished products, as well as moving produce out of the monastery for distribution on a market. In concurrence with the built environment discussed above, the organisation of labour suggests a well-regulated settlement.

In the text that follows, an examination of the archaeological remains of monastic production and consumption will be undertaken, starting with the evidence for the industrial use of water, then food and craft production, followed by an examination of the monastic consumption of material goods. Production is here defined as the process of combining raw materials in order to make something for consumption. Consumption, on the other hand is defined as 'a material social practice involving the utilization of objects [and food], as opposed to their production or distribution'.[506]

4.2.1 Water Usage in Production

The quantitative study of the water supply in Chapter 4.1 established that the daily maximum capacity of the two wells was 120 m^3. A proportion of this water would have been used for industrial manufacturing. It is also possible, though unlikely, that these wells supplied water to the orchards on the desert fringe that are mentioned in Shenoute's writings, in the *Life of Shenoute* and by Abu al-Makarim.[507] Olive trees and vines, for example, require perennial water supply and cannot grow in areas of natural inundation. The water needs for olive trees are continuous and sensitive and the ideal Egyptian context is, therefore, an irrigated desert margin environment, where the

503 Wilson, "Use," 148.
504 Layton, "Rules," 56-57.
505 Layton, "Rules," 56-57.
506 Michael Dietler, "Consumption," in *The Oxford Handbook of Material Culture Studies*, edited by Mary C. Beaudry and Dan Hicks (Oxford: Oxford University Press, 2010). Available online: http://www.oxfordhandbooks.com/view/10.1093/oxfordhb/9780199218714.001.0001/oxfordhb-9780199218714-e-8, 1.
507 Abu Salih the Armenian, *Churches & Monasteries*, 237; Besa, *Life*, 53; Layton, "Social Structure," 33.

trees would be planted in specially dug pits in order to create the right soil conditions and maintain water in the root area.[508]

Estimations of how much water a plantation would require vary considerably according to the observer and to the specific type of crop. The largest field that can be attributed to a single irrigation device is a plot of 2.37 ha at Oxyrhynchus,[509] while observations from Nubia suggests a much lower number ranging from about 0.5 ha to 1.25 ha.[510] A low average would seem to be that one *saqiya* could water about 1.25 ha, or 12,500 m^2. It seems unlikely that water from the two wells within the monastic complex would have been directed towards such plantations, as this would require extensive pipelines beyond the enclosure walls and would cause a serious strain on the monastery's water supply. It is more probable that wells were dug where they were needed for the specific purpose of supplying the orchards. Other types of agriculture would have taken place in the inundated agricultural zone east of the monastic complex.

A number of craft activities required water. Among these were manufacturing processes such as pottery production, cloth manufacture and the preparation of materials for the construction industry. I will here mention a few that are attested in the archaeological record or referred to in the written sources.

Pottery production requires considerable quantities of water for the preparation of the clay. Clay is aged by spreading it out to dry after which unwanted inclusions are removed and the clay is levigated in a pit or vat of water. The clay is left to dry in drying beds or in shallow pits, where the water evaporates until the clay achieves sufficient plasticity for working. Water is used in lower quantities during the process of adding materials to change the properties of the clay and in the actual throwing process. Finally, water is needed for surface treatment of the completed pottery where, for example, slips could be applied.[511] A single pottery kiln was excavated by the SCA on the edge of WM.1.2 next to several vats with pipes for both supply and drainage of water (see Chapter 3.2.2). It is possible that some of these vats could have been used in stages of the pottery production.

The building industry was even more demanding in its requirement for water. At the White Monastery water would have been needed for both fired bricks and mud bricks, for mortars, plasters and for paint. The preparation of lime mortar and plaster, for example, involved the slaking of lime in water-filled pits.[512] Considering the size of the monastic estate, it seems plausible to suggest that production of bricks and mud bricks took place on the monastic lands, with subsequent transport to the monastery. Evidence for the shaping of limestone blocks is found in the northern part of WM.7 and the amount of chips makes it seem very likely that this part of the monastery was used to prepare the blocks used in the construction of the church. An installation immediately south of the church, excavated in the courtyard of the large building (WM.5.2) and seemingly predating its construction, looks as though it could have been used for the slaking of lime, which suggests that a workshop was located immediately adjacent to the place where the plaster would have been used.

Water was used in large quantities for textiles. The flax industry, which was important throughout the Pharaonic period but dominated Egypt's agricultural production from the ninth century onwards, also required large quantities of water, as the flax was soaked in water, in a process called retting, for up to two and a half weeks to loosen the fibres.[513] Woollen cloth was prepared through the process of fulling, in

508 Christopher J. Eyre, "The Water Regime for Orchards and Plantations in Pharaonic Egypt," *Journal of Egyptian Archaeology* 80 (1994): 57–60.

509 Oleson, *Devices*, 368.

510 Ruffini, *Medieval Nubia*, 80–81.

511 Wilson, "Use," 128–133. See also Dorothea Arnold and Janine Bourriau, *An Introduction to Ancient Egyptian Pottery* (Mainz am Rhein: Philipp von Zabern, 1993), 11–14.

512 Wilson, "Use," 133–134.

513 Barry J. Kemp and Gillian Vogelsang-Eastwood, *The Ancient Textile Industry at Amarna* (London: Egypt Exploration Society, 2001), 28. See also Gladys Frantz-Murphy, "A New Interpretation of the Economic History of Medieval Egypt. The Role of the Textile Industry," *Journal of the Economic and Social History of the Orient* 24.3 (1981): 274–297. Experimental studies by Kemp suggest that retting was not a necessary part of preparing the flax, as the linen fibre could be separated by beating the flax stalks with a mallet in a process described as de-cor-

which the cloth was trampled in tubs containing an alkaline solution of water, earth and urine. This process served to remove animal fats and grease. The process required several small tubs for trampling the cloth and several larger vats for rinsing it afterwards, often followed by dyeing.[514] Tanneries also required large quantities of water for the production of leather goods.

A final note should be made on the use of water in relation to food production. The daily running of the monastic kitchen(s) required water for processes such as boiling, washing and cleaning. Only two types of food processing can be securely recognised in the White Monastery's archaeological record. These are bread-making and the production of oil, perhaps from olives. Water is sometimes used to soak the olives for a second pressing and is an essential ingredient in the making of bread.

4.2.2 *Food production*

Food consumption in a monastery was subject to strict rules about what, how and when to eat, and Shenoute indeed expressed extensive concerns about food and the regulation of its distribution within the community. He explicitly mentions foods that were permitted in the diet of all members of the community, while also mentioning foods that were either forbidden or restricted to the consumption of sick, elderly or very young monastics. The permitted foodstuffs were herbaceous vegetables (served raw, cooked or salted), the gourd family (e.g., cucumbers and pumpkins), beans, lentils, bread (both newly-baked and soaked, dried bread), sweet fruit, vinegar, various pickles and olives.[515] Forbidden foodstuffs included milk and a number of cheeses, eggs, wine, meat and dried-smoked fish, baked fish and brined anchovies.[516] We are made aware that many of the permitted foods were produced in the monastery or on the nearby landholdings, with Shenoute indirectly mentioning the production of flour, olive oil and salted food as well as produce from vegetable gardens, orchards and fields that, among other crops, grew barley as fodder for the monastery's stock animals. Wheat, on the other hand, was listed among products that were purchased and brought to the monastery to be milled into flour.[517]

The archaeological study of the production and consumption of food in the White Monastery is limited by the fact that neither archaeobotanical samples from deposits on the site nor the bone material have been studied. The available indicators of food production consist exclusively of architectural remains and thus any study is limited to processes that would leave substantial traces in the archaeological record: oil and bread.

OLIVE OIL

The *Life of Pachomius* tells of a philosopher who arrived at a new Pachomian monastery in the city of Panopolis (modern Akhmim) and teased the monks by asking 'who would ever bring olives from elsewhere to sell them in Panopolis?'[518] Although this analogy referred to the wisdom brought by the monks to Panopolis—a city that was already imbued with a rich intellectual life—it also tells us that olives were grown in abundance. Indeed, the archaeological evidence suggests that olives were also processed at the White Monastery.

In antiquity, olives were used for a myriad of purposes. Pickled, olives could be eaten as a light snack or as a component in a larger meal. Olive oil was a standard ingredient in perfume, body-care and medical products, lighting, cooking and for a variety of industrial processes, and the pulp left behind from the pressing could be used for fodder or fuel.[519] For these reasons, olive oil was among the most

tification. This is a more labour efficient process compared to retting but produces fibre of an inferior quality (Kemp and Vogelsang-Eastwood, *Amarna*, 30).

514 Miko Flohr, *The World of the Fullo: Work, Economy, and Society in Roman Italy* (Oxford: Oxford University Press, 2013), 98–121.

515 Layton, "Social Structure," 44–45.

516 Layton, "Social Structure," 38; Layton, "Rules," 57.

517 Layton, "Social Structure," 33.

518 Philip Rousseau, *Pachomius. The Making of a Community in Fourth-Century Egypt* (Berkeley, Los Angeles & London: University of California Press, 1985), 164.

519 Marie-Claire Amouretti, *Le Pain et l'Huile dans la Grèce Antique: de l'Araire au Moulin* (Paris: Belles Lettres,

traded and used commodities in the ancient world and Marie-Claire Amouretti has proposed that the consumption of oil in Greece may have been as high as 20 litres per person per year.[520] In a monastic context this number would presumably have been much lower as oil for personal grooming was less common, but oil would still have been essential for cooking and lighting. To give an example of the quantities needed, one litre of oil would provide 250–300 hours of light.[521] This means that if each of the suggested 4000 monastics (1450 in the White Monastery) lit a single lamp for just one hour per day, this would amount to 4870–5830 litres of oil per year (or 1765–2115 litres for the White Monastery). On top of this, the writing of Shenoute confirmed that at least in the fifth century, oil was used in large quantities in food preparation, and in the seventh century it was also an important component in religious activities, such as anointment after the baptism.[522]

The production of olive oil consists of three stages that follow the initial picking and transportation to the place of processing.[523] Firstly, the olives are crushed. This would be done by using a stone roller or a mortar and pestle in small-scale production, while larger productions would employ a rotary olive crusher. Unlike the roller and the mortar and pestle, the crusher is an unmoveable architectural feature, often incorporated in the structural design of the olive processing facilities. It consists of a round vertical crushing stone (an edge runner), which rotates around a circular crushing basin in order to produce a uniform, broken-down pulp of skin, flesh and pit fragments.[524] The edge runner would normally be set on an axle that turned on a pivot, which was fixed in a socket in the centre of the basin (fig. 61), but many different variations of this arrangement exist.[525] The edge runner would be moved manually or by using a draught animal.

The second stage involved the pressing of the olive pulp. The easiest way would be to apply pressure by placing weights on a board and lay it directly on the pulp—such a process would not leave any obvious traces in the archaeological record. Commonly used in larger productions were the more sophisticated lever press and the direct screw or wedge press. The lever press would consist of a beam, which was set into the wall in one end and held down by weights in the other. Halfway between the two ends, the oil would move from a pressing bed into a collection tank. The lever press would be an integrated part of the architectural plan and would therefore leave traces behind in the archaeological record. The screw press on the other hand, could consist entirely of moveable components and thus be untraceable in the architectural remains. In its basic form, the screw or wedge press consists of a pressing bed with two mortises supporting a frame, which would hold the screw or wedge in place.[526] This type of press would normally have a smaller pressing bed than the lever press and thus produce smaller quantities of oil

1986), 181–183; David J. Mattingly, "Oil for Export? A Comparison of Libyan, Spanish and Tunisian Olive Oil Production in the Roman Empire," *Journal of Roman Archaeology* 1 (1988): 33; David J. Mattingly, "Olea Mediterranea?" *Journal of Roman Archaeology* 1 (1988): 159. Alternative oil sources commonly used in Egypt were castor, sesame, safflower and radish. In Ptolemaic Egypt, castor oil was preferred for lighting and radish oil was preferred for cooking (Brent D. Sandy, *The Production and Use of Vegetable Oils in Ptolemaic Egypt*. Bulletin of the American Society of Papyrologists, Supplement 6 [Atlanta: Scholars Press, 1989], 3).

520 Amouretti, *Le Pain et l'Huile*, 190.

521 Amouretti, *Le Pain et l'Huile*, 190.

522 See Timbie "Liturgical Procession," 439 for anointment with oil in the White Monastery church.

523 Rafi Frankel, "Introduction," in *Oil and Wine Presses in Israel from the Hellenistic, Roman and Byzantine Periods*, ed. Etan Ayalon, Rafi Frankel, and Amos Kloner (Oxford: Archaeopress, 2009), 3–8. See also Lin Foxhall, *Olive Cultivation in Ancient Greece* (Oxford: Oxford University Press, 2007), 131–217.

524 Brun identified eight different modes of crushing olives, paraphrased in Mattingly, "Olea Mediterranea?" 154.

525 See Etan Ayalon, Rafi Frankel and Amos Kloner, *Oil and Wine Presses in Israel from the Hellenistic, Roman and Byzantine Periods* (Oxford: Archaeopress, 2009).

526 Neither process will be described here in detail, see instead Brun's typology (Jean-Pierre Brun, *L'Oléiculture Antique en Provence: Les Huileries du Département du Var* [Paris: Éditions du Centre National de la Recherche Scientifique, 1986]). See also Mattingly, "Madness and Measurement;" Mattingly, "Olea Mediterranea?."

Fig. 61. Crushing basins in WM.4.3.9 and WM.4.3.14. View towards southeast (photograph by the author; © YMAP).

during each pressing. In both pressing methods, the olive pulp would be placed in sacks or baskets, which were stacked in layers on the press bed. This second stage in the production is the most time-consuming and would take between 24 and 48 hours.[527] Neither a crushing basin nor a press is necessary to make oil and most households would have used methods that leave virtually no archaeological traces. The involvement of a press is, according to David Mattingly, generally an indicator of a higher form of social or economic organisation.[528]

In the third and final stage, the oil was separated from the watery lees (olives consists of about 20% oil, 40% waste and 40% watery lees).[529] The simplest method involved skimming the floating oil off by using a ladle. Another solution was to separate the oil using either an over- or underflow decanter. In the former option, the oil would run into a second receptacle through an outlet at the top, whereas an underflow decantation would allow the lees to escape through an outlet at the bottom. In the archaeological record, the decantation technique would be recognisable through two interconnected vats, whereas the skimming technique would require just a single vat with a drain.

Olive presses were most often placed on or near the estate that produced the crops as the finished product is lighter and thereby cheaper to transport than the olives themselves. The presence of no less than six crushing basins at the White Monastery

527 Mattingly, "Madness and Measurement."
528 Mattingly, "Olea Mediterranea?" 157.
529 Frankel, "Introduction," 8.

would suggest that olives were grown on the nearby monastic landholdings and that they formed an integral part of the monastic food production and perhaps also its economic revenue. Two granite basins are located *in situ* in WM.4 adjacent to the foundation of a third basin (WM.4.3.9 and WM.4.3.14, figs. 32 & 33). WM.5 contains three granite basins and one basin constructed from fired bricks (WM.5.6, fig. 42). In the archaeological phasing discussed in Chapter 3.6 and Chapter 3.9, I proposed that the crushing basins in WM.4 were installed in the first main phase of the monastery's use (WM.ii, fifth to seventh centuries). The insertion of crushing basins in WM.5, on the other hand, was a later development that followed a period of temporary abandonment of most parts of the monastic site (WM.iv, at some point between the tenth and the fourteenth centuries).

Brooks Hedstrom and Bolman described the crushing basins as *trapeta*—stone vats, each of which would have held two rotating crushing stones.[530] A closer analysis of the installations suggests that this description is not correct and neither is the suggestion that the two crushing basins in WM.4.3.9 could have been used as grain mills. A grain mill is an altogether different construction with two horizontal grinding stones set above a collection tank.

Centrally placed in the eastern half of the food production area (WM.4), the crushing basins can give us information about activities that took place in the empty rooms around them. This suggestion is based on the assumption that the production of olive oil required not only the three steps described above, but also storage for the different components employed in the production. These components were the untreated olives, brought in from the orchards during the harvest season, a storage area for the empty containers for the oil and storage space for the containers filled with oil.

The archaeological evidence lends itself to a couple of suggestions. It is useful to look at the routes of access to this part of the enclosure (fig. 24). The current layout of the building shows that the crushing basins could be accessed from WM.4.3.15 and from WM.4.3.6. The archaeological remains leave no room for doorways connecting the eastern part of the enclosure to the exit towards the north (WM.4.3.29). WM.4.3.13 and WM.4.3.15 appear to be associated with the production of oil. WM.4.3.15 with its many small rooms would be ideal for storage of large quantities of products and materials and the doorway onto the thoroughfare (WM.4.1.17) would allow the delivery and removal of goods without having to transport them through the entire complex. WM.4.3.13 seems ideal for the pressing of the oil with its thick floors that could have supported the weight of a press. Nothing remains of the actual press installation, but it is possible (although speculative) that the vat in the southwest corner of the room was associated with the pressing. The construction of the walls is unlikely to have been able to support a lever press and therefore it seems more likely that moveable screw or wedge presses were employed. Finally, it is also possible that the tanks in WM.4.3.14 were used in relation to the pressing, but this remains speculative. It is unclear whether WM.4.3.6 was associated with the production of oil or served another purpose.

The lack of olive presses means that it is not possible to quantify the oil production, but nonetheless, the number of crushing basins is noteworthy. Assuming that all six basins at some point were in use at the same time, the oil production would have been of large proportions. One basin could easily serve several presses and it is not possible to conclude whether they had other uses.[531] However, even if this was the case, the number of basins is still remarkable and brings to mind the Roman-period

530 Brooks Hedstrom and Bolman, "White Monastery," 339.

531 Oils produced in Ptolemaic and Roman Egypt are listed by Margaret Serpico and Raymond White, "Oil, fat and wax," in *Ancient Egyptian Materials and Technology*, ed. Paul T. Nicholson and Ian Shaw (Cambridge: Cambridge University Press, 2009), 390. The list includes balanos, moringa, castor, colocynth, almond, lettuce, linseed, olive, radish, safflower, sesame and malabathrum (cinnamon). From the eighth century onwards, the crushing basins could also have been used to produce sugar (Jon H. Galloway, "The Mediterranean Sugar Industry," *Geographical Review* 67.2 [1977]: 177–178). Without residue analysis it is not possible to conclude on potential other uses for the crushing basins.

oil factories in North Africa.[532] Although the White Monastery production would have been smaller in scale, it would appear that the level of production was sufficient to supply a market beyond the needs of the monastics.

It is significant that the production of olive oil was perceived as an activity that generated revenue in Late Antique ecclesiastical society. The Coptic patriarch Benjamin I (r. 623–662) invested funds in the restoration of monasteries with a special view to the infrastructure of economic production.[533] In addition, the patriarch Yusab (r. 831–849) 'stressed the development of income-generating projects for the church, including both pilgrimage sites and productive enterprises (vineyards and mills and oil-presses).'[534]

BREAD

According to Shenoute's writings, bread was a primary component of the monastic diet. Bread was served at every meal and was the only food source that the monastics were allowed to keep in their cell.[535] In the archaeological record of the White Monastery, bread production can be identified by the presence of two structures. A single millstone from a grain mill is located south of WM.4. The millstone was excavated by the SCA and moved to this location, which means that its point of origin is unknown. Unlike the facilities for the production of olive oil, grain mills were not necessarily placed on or near the fields that produced the crops. Grain keeps better than flour and would normally be ground close to the point of consumption. Therefore, the distribution of grain mills says more about consumption than it does about production.[536]

WM.4.2.3 contains the remains of eight ovens that further testify to the production of bread (each c. 1.15 m in diameter). Only the lower parts of the ovens are preserved and it is therefore not possible to reconstruct the superstructure (fig. 29). From the remains, however, it seems clear that the ovens were brick built with an internal clay lining. Alison McQuitty has identified four general types of ovens used to bake bread in the Near East. These are the *tannur*, the *tabun*, the *saj* and the *waqdiah*.[537] The ovens differ in layout and construction material but are constructed on a similar principle, where the fire is fed through a central opening at the top and the bread is baked on the interior walls. Only the *saj* and the *waqdiah* contain separate compartments for bread and fire. The average time taken to bake a loaf of bread in this manner is just one to three minutes.[538] Five additional ovens were excavated by the SCA in the southwest corner of WM.4.4.25. These ovens and their adjacent architecture are, however, eroded to a point where they cannot be associated with a specific phase of use.

The five vats in WM.4.3.11 were possibly associated with food production and perhaps even with bread production. The three vats defined in Chapter 3 as type 2 resemble small grain silos, with an internal dispensary,[539] but the lack of comparative material means that it has not been possible to confirm this suggestion.

Returning to Shenoute's writings, he states in a rule that bread was baked just once every year in the White Monastery and distributed to the three con-

532 Mattingly, "Madness and Measurement;" Mattingly, "Oil for Export?;" Mattingly, "Olea Mediterranea?."

533 Swanson, *Coptic Papacy*, 6, 11.

534 Swanson, *Coptic Papacy*, 30.

535 Layton, "Rules," 48.

536 Malouta and Wilson, "Mechanical Irrigation," 273.

537 Alison McQuitty, "An Ethnographic and Archaeological Study of Clay Ovens in Jordan," *Annual of the Department of Antiquities of Jordan* 28 (1984): 259–267. See also David D.E. Depraetere, "A Comparative Study on the Construction and the Use of the Domestic Bread Oven in Egypt during the Graeco-Roman and Late Antique/Early Byzantine Period," *Mitteilungen des Deutschen Archäologischen Instituts Abteilung Kairo* 58 (2002): 119–156 for a study of the Egyptian remains. Depraetere concludes that the *tannur* oven is the closest comparison to the bread ovens found in the Egyptian archaeological record.

538 Depraetere, "Domestic Bread Oven," 138–141; Delwen Samuel, "Their Staff of Life: Initial Investigations on Ancient Egyptian Bread Baking," in *Amarna Reports V*, ed. Barry Kemp (London: Egypt Exploration Society 1989), 255.

539 Ignacio Arce, personal communication with author, 2014.

gregations, then stored until rendered hard and dry and soaked before being eaten.[540] Layton does not qualify Shenoute's statement, but it is important to consider whether it refers to an actual practice, to an ideal or to a specific type of bread consumed, for example, in relation to religious practices rather than as the principal source of bread. If the reference is to daily bread consumption, the amount of bread would be an enormous strain on the storage capacity for grain, flour and fuel for the ovens, but also for the baked bread. If, for example, 500 monastics each would consume two loaves of bread per day, that would require a year's supply of 365,000 loaves to be baked and stored in the monastery.[541] If the number of monastics were 4000 (Arabic *Life of Shenoute*), this number would rise to an unrealistic 2.92 million loaves of bread. If each oven could bake ten loaves of bread at the same time and each loaf took five minutes to bake (including the time spent inserting the dough and removing the baked bread), it would take ten ovens two weeks to bake 365,000 loaves if they worked 24 hours per day. If ten ovens were to bake 2.92 million loaves, it would take 103 days working 24 hours per day.

Considering this calculation in terms of weight, Wipszycka suggested that a standard-sized bread loaf would weigh around 150 gr, which means that one monastic would require about 10 kg of bread per month and 120 kg per year.[542] 500 monastics would consume 60,000 kg of bread and for 4000 monastics, 480,000 kg would be required.

OTHER TYPES OF FOOD PRODUCTION

Other types of food commonly found in the Mediterranean production and diet, such as wine and *garum*, are not evident in the White Monastery's archaeological record.[543] This could be related to the fact that they, according to Shenoute, were not permitted as food in the community, although wine was required for the Eucharist and was included in the special diet for the sick.[544] Sugar production, which was introduced to the Egyptian agricultural scene as a luxury item in the eighth century, is not present in the archaeological record either.[545] Some of these goods may have been produced on the monastic landholdings, but this remains speculative. The intra-mural production appears to have been limited to products that were consumed in the community. It is possible that, for example, oil from olives and other plants was produced in surplus and sold for revenue, but otherwise the archaeological remains would suggest that agricultural production intended for sale (if any) took place on the monastic landholdings or in yet unexcavated parts of the ancient site. It is not possible to comment any further on the production or consumption of food without examinations of the bone material and the botanical samples. Such ex-

540 'As for the siblings in the other congregation and those who are in the village, whatever they are to receive in the way of bread shall be provided yearly, and they shall get them at the time of baking. And they shall not be left lacking what they need. Nor again shall they get too much. So whatever is left over after bread has stopped being made shall be eaten. And they shall not bring any back to this [congregation]. Rather, if they fall short they shall get some from this [congregation]. It is better for them to fall short of these provisions and have more delivered to them, than for some to be brought back to this [congregation] when they have a surplus over there.' Layton, *Canons*, rule nr 381.

541 See the discussion on bread in Wipszycka, "Resources," 186–190.

542 Wipszycka, "Resources," 244.

543 See for example Frankel, "Introduction," 3–8; Wim Van Neer and David D.E. Depraetere, "Pickled Fish from the Egyptian Nile: Osteological Evidence from a Byzantine (Coptic) context at Shanhur," *Revue de Paléobiologie* 10 (2005): 159–170; Van Neer et al., "The Roman Trade in Salted Nilotic Fish Products: Some Examples from Egypt," *Documenta Archaeobiologiae* 4 (2006): 173–188; Van Neer et al., "Salted Fish Products from the Coptic Monastery at Bawit, Egypt. Evidence from the Bones and Text," in *The Role of Fish in Ancient Time*, ed. Heidemarie Hüster Plogmann (Rahden: Verlag Marie Leidorf, 2007), 147–159.

544 Brooks Hedstrom and Bolman, "White Monastery," 350.

545 Marie-Louise von Wartburg, "Design and Technology of the Medieval Refineries of the Sugar Cane in Cyprus. A Case Study in Industrial Archaeology," in *Paisajes del Azúcar. Actas del Quinto Seminario Internacional Sobre la Cana de Azúcar*, ed. Antonio Malpica (Granada: Disputaciòn Provincial de Granada, 1995), 81–116.

aminations have proven highly valuable at, e.g., the monastery at Kom al-Nana (Amarna), where Smith's study of the archaeobotanical remains from the seventh century illustrated that the foodstuffs available were far more varied than the textual sources would allow us to believe.[546]

4.2.3 Craft Production, Trade and the Monastic Built Environment

Shenoute's writings report on the trade in monastic products such as linen, rope, baskets, sacks and books, which were sold or traded in return for raw products such as grain or wool.[547] Linen was supposedly woven from flax in the convent, while the remaining items were produced in the two male congregations.[548] Of this short list, only the production of textiles would have left traces behind in the archaeological record. There are, to my knowledge, no written sources of later date reporting on production or trade at the White Monastery.

Only a few features that can be associated with craft production have been preserved in the archaeological record. These limited remains consist of a pottery kiln in WM.1.2 and a group of vats in WM.5. The pottery kiln is constructed as a single round firing chamber with a rectangular firing channel (fig. 13). The kiln was excavated by the SCA. Ash and wasters that could help identify the ceramic manufacture and its date, if encountered, were not retained. The presence of only a single kiln could result from the limited excavation in this area, but could also suggest that the production was of a small scale and only intended for monastic consumption.

The function of the six vats located in WM.5.3 has not been resolved, but their organisation, where one vat drained into the next, could imply that processes associated with fulling or dyeing occurred here (dyeing is briefly discussed in relation to the convent in Atripe in Chapter 5.2).

Although book manufacturing is not visible among the architectural remains, there is ample archaeological and textual evidence that confirm its presence at the White Monastery. From the early textual sources Shenoute lists 'copyist of manuscripts' as a monastic occupation and refers to books as an object of revenue or barter in return for raw materials.[549] Kuhn has suggested that during the leadership of Shenoute's successor Besa, a *scriptorium* came into being at the White Monastery.[550] The archaeological evidence consists of dated colophons from the monastic library that suggest that books were copied as late as the sixteenth century (see Chapter 2.3). Excavations in 2011 and 2012 by the Yale Monastic Archaeological Project (South) of three cavities in the floor of a room in the main church revealed the second-floor space as one possible location for the storage of manuscripts. Located off the stairwell in the northeastern part of the church, the so-called Candle Room yielded more than 1200 tiny fragments of text during the course of excavation. The composition of fragments suggests to Davis that this room was used for a time as a storage space of manuscripts. The Candle Room thereby constitutes just one of several rooms that would have made up the monastic library at different stages in the history of the monastery.[551]

In Late Antiquity, the book or codex consisted of sheets of parchment or papyri, written on both sides and stitched together at one end. From the fourth century onwards, the codex replaced the scroll as the most popular way of storing written works.

Chrysi Kotsifou has examined the monastic production of books in two articles in which she argues that from the fourth to the seventh century, the majority of books were produced in monasteries.[552] The

546 Smith, *Archaeobotanical Investigations*; Harlow and Smith, "Fasting and Feasting." Mennat Allah Al-Dorry has conducted a similar study for the monastic site of John the Little in Wadi Natrun for her PhD, submitted to the Universit of Münster in 2015. See also Włodzimierz Godlewski and Jarosław Zieliński, "Naqlun (Nekloni). Excavations in 2008–2009," *Polish Archaeology in the Mediterranean* XXI (2012): 193–211 for preliminary studies from Naqlun.

547 Layton, "Rules," 49.

548 Layton, "Rules," 66.

549 Layton, "Rules," 49, 56–57.

550 Kuhn, "Besa's Christianity," 48.

551 Davis et al., "Left Behind," 80–83.

552 Kotsifou, "Books and Book Production."

process of manufacturing a book required several steps; the first was the production of the papyri or parchment.[553] Thereafter, the manuscript was copied onto the sheets, which could be stitched together either before or after the writing process. According to Kotsifou, punctuation was done in a separate process after the text had been copied.[554] Illustration was added at a further stage and, once completed, the book was bound. The latter two stages vastly increased the cost of the book and were often omitted.[555]

Book production was a highly labour-intensive process, which involved expensive materials such as parchment. Based on papyrological evidence, Roger S. Bagnall has suggested that in the sixth century, a full Bible could vary in price between 3 and 16 *solidi*, depending on the material, binding and whether it was illustrated.[556] In the same study, Bagnall calculates the annual income of a contemporary bishop in a rural seat as between 40–50 *solidi* per year, thus demonstrating that very few people could afford to buy books.[557] The non-monastic consumers of codices could be ecclesiastical institutions, but also wealthy individuals. As such, the book manufacturing could be a highly profitable business for the monasteries.[558]

The built environment must be included in the discussion of production and consumption at the White Monastery. By examining the quality and quantity of materials used, the state of maintenance and the architectural complexity in different periods, the built environment becomes an index of the monastery's economic vitality.

The building materials used in the primary phases (WM.ii–iii, ca. fifth to seventh/eighth century) included limestone blocks and pavers, fired bricks, mud bricks, mortar, plaster and paint. It is possible that wood was also needed for some constructions, but if so, it has not been preserved in the archaeological record. The limestone would have been either quarried in the mountains to the west before being transported to the monastery for further dressing (in WM.7), or would have been transported from nearby sites such as Atripe.[559] Either way, the process would require skilled labour for the retrieval of the blocks, their transportation, redressing and for their later use in the well and the main Church.

The limestone pavers found in WM.1.1, WM.2, WM.4.2.4, WM.4.3.8, WM.4.3.13, WM.4.3.15 and WM.4.4.22 and in WM.5 would similarly have been reused from another site or cut new. The marks on both sides of the stones reveal that they were cut with a stone saw, which could either be mechanical or manual. The granite edge runners, crushing basins and millstone found in WM.4 and WM.5 would have imposed an expensive demand on the monastery's budget if cut from new. The nearest source of red granite is found in the Red Sea littoral some 180 km away and would, therefore, entail considerable costs in terms of transportation to the monastery. According to the Roman author Cato (234–149 BCE), the cost of transporting a millstone 40 km was 11% of its value, rising to 39% for 120 km.[560] It is possible that the six crushing basins not only served the monastic community, but also aided extra-mural communities in processing their agricultural produce.

No remains of brick manufacturing have been found on the monastery's ground and it is possible that bricks were produced closer to the Nile, where the required raw material would have been found in abundance. According to Barry Kemp, the best-suited material is cultivated topsoil, which through regular turning would have been mixed with sand and organic materials. Otherwise, the bricks were composed from a combination of clay, silt, sand and sometimes also organic materials such as straw to achieve the right combination of hardness and

553 Kotsifou, "Bookbinding," 220.
554 Kotsifou, "Books and Book Production," 60.
555 Kotsifou, "Books and Book Production;" Kotsifou, "Bookbinding."
556 Roger S. Bagnall, *Early Christian Books in Egypt* (Princeton & Oxford, Princeton University Press, 2009), 60.
557 Bagnall, *Early Christian Books*, 65.
558 See Kotsifou, "Books and Book Production" for a discussion of layman commissioning books from monastic *scriptoria*.
559 Klotz, "Triphis;" Klotz, "Nectanebo."
560 Marcus Porcius Cato, *On Agriculture*, trans H.B. As, (Cambridge, Mass: Harvard University Press, 1935), 41.

Group	Total number	Dates	Coin value	Find spot	Current location
1a	220	First half of seventh century	Gold solidi	A on fig. 3.17	Coptic Museum, Cairo
1b	180	Mid seventh century	Gold semisses	A on fig. 3.17	Coptic Museum, Cairo
2	420	Unknown, but some mid sixth century	Gold – composition unknown	B on fig. 3.17	Islamic Museum, Cairo
3	1185	Unknown	Copper	WM.4?	SCA store room

Table 5. Coins found by the SCA at the White Monastery.

elasticity.[561] The choice of using fired bricks in phase WM.ii (fifth to seventh centuries) of the monastery's development would have added further expenses to costs of fuel.

The mortar, plaster and paint would most likely have been mixed on site when needed, but its production would not leave many traces behind, as the construction of new buildings most often would involve *ad hoc* installations, which were removed when the building was completed. The transition from lime-based mortars and plasters in the earlier phases of the monastic site (WM.ii–iii, fifth to ninth centuries) to mud-based materials for both walls and floors is significant. The use of high-quality lime-based plasters required skilled labour, a large amount of fuel for slaking the lime and a central organisation with financial means that could purchase the materials needed. The mud-based floors, mortars and plasters, on the other hand, were faster, easier and cheaper to construct as the basic materials were readily available and did not require skilled labour.

The last phase of the pre-modern use of the monastic site was constructed exclusively from re-used materials (WM.v, WM.vi, as seen in WM.2, WM.4.2.4, WM.4.3.6, WM.4.3.13, WM.5 and WM.7). These materials were taken from ruined buildings within the monastic compound and used indiscriminately for unimposing structures of low quality and resilience. Such use reflects an economically poorer community.

4.2.4 Coins found at the White Monastery

The coins found at the White Monastery offer an important insight into the economic conditions of the monastic community. Although coins were recovered in abundance from the excavations carried out by the SCA, they remain largely unpublished. Only a few coins were retrieved during the more recent examinations carried out by the WMP. Two of these were found in the spoil heaps of the SCA's excavation of WM.2. They date to the Umayyad period and were briefly described in Chapter 3.3.1.
The coins retrieved by the SCA include (see also table 5):

- Group 1a: 220 gold *solidi* that date to the reigns of Phocas (r. 602–610) and Heraclius (r. 610–641);
- Group 1b: 180 gold *semisses* of Constans II (r. 641–668);
- Group 2: 420 gold coins (unspecified), some coins dating to the reign of Justinian I (r. 527–565);
- Group 3: 1185 single finds of copper coins, presumably found throughout WM.4.

The coins were not published by the SCA, but Cécile Morrisson briefly reported on the findings of hoards Group 1a and 1b to the international numismatic community.[562] Gawdat Gabra published a slightly more detailed account in relation to the transfer of the same hoards to the Coptic Museum in Cairo.[563]

561 Barry Kemp, "Soil (Including Mud-brick Architecture)," in *Ancient Egyptian Materials and Technology*, ed. Paul T. Nicholson and Ian Shaw (Cambridge: Cambridge University Press, 2000), 78–104.

562 Cécile Morrisson, "No title," *International Numismatic Newsletter* 17 (1990).

563 Gawdat Gabra, "Die Münzschätze aus dem Shenute-Kloster bei Sohag," in *Ägypten–Münster: Kulturwissenschaftliche Studien zu Ägypten, dem Vorderen Orient und verwandten Gebieten*, ed. Anke I. Blöbaum, Jochem Kahl, and Simon D. Schweitzer (Wiesbaden: Harrassowitz, 2003), 125–128.

Most recently, Noeske published an overview of the gold coins, again with an emphasis on hoards Group 1a and 1b.[564] Noeske reported that the find spots of the three hoards (Group 1a, 1b, and 2) were somewhat uncertain. Group 1a and Group 1b were found two weeks apart, but were located in close proximity to the building interpreted as the *diakonia* (fig. 11, a; WM.4.4.22), according to a member of the SCA. Group 2 was found below a limestone paver in the southern end of the refectory (fig.11, b; WM.4.1.16).[565] All three hoards were found in ceramic vessels placed in cavities below floors or in walls.

The location of the Group 2 hoard would suggest that either the refectory had gone out of use at the time of its deposition, or that the hoard was hidden in a building that was utilised every day by most members of the community. Groups 1a and 1b were found immediately south of the *diakonia* within a building that has been removed to the level of natural sand. It is therefore not possible to evaluate the use or state of this building at the time of the hoards' deposition.

Grossmann and Noeske have raised an important question concerning the deposition of the hoards and their lack of retrieval. Were the hoards a part of the monastery's treasury or were they put aside for safekeeping during an emergency or a time when the monastery was under threat?[566] Group 1a contains coins with dates immediately prior to the Persian conquest of Egypt in 619.[567] This led Grossmann and Noeske to suggest that this hoard was indeed deposited in the face of emerging danger.[568] Hoard Group 1b contained coins that post-dated the Arab conquest, while the content of Group 2 is uncertain. Among the coins were *solidi* from the reign of Justinian I, but the quantity of these coins as well as the composition of the remaining coins are unknown. Unfortunately, Group 2 has not been accessible for scholarly examination since it was relocated to the Islamic Museum in Cairo.[569]

A comparable example was found in a large residential house in the city of Bet Shean (Scythopolis) in modern Israel. Here, 751 *solidi* ranging in date from Phocas to Constantine IV (r. 602–685) were found in a ceramic vessel below a floor paver in the corner of a room.[570] The coins were interpreted as an emergency hoard that was buried within the first fifteen years of Caliph Abd al-Malik's rule (r. 685–705). Gabriela Bijovsky presented two possible explanations for the hoard. During the first eight years of Abd al-Malik's rule, an annual tribute of 365,000 *solidi* was paid to the Byzantine emperor, who demanded the coins paid in the Byzantine mint. The hoard was therefore buried for fear of confiscation. According to the second explanation, the coins were buried around the time of Abd al-Malik's coin reform in 696/697. Until this point, Byzantine *solidi* were in circulation, but at the time of the reform, severe sanctions were introduced regarding the use of Byzantine coinage, which was recalled to the mint in order to be remelted.[571] It is worth considering if a similar motivation should be seen as the reason for the deposition of the hoards at the White Monastery.

A few copper *dodekanummi* struck in neighbouring Akhmim (Panopolis) are ascribed to Benjamin I (r. 623–662), the Coptic patriarch who was exiled to Upper Egypt during the Byzantine pro-Chalcedonian rule that followed the Persian incursion.[572] On the obverse, the coins show two facing busts with a cross between them. On the reverse, they show the

564 Grossmann et al., "Monastery of Apa Shenute," 209–219.

565 Grossmann et al., "Monastery of Apa Shenute," 215.

566 Grossmann and Noeske prefer the latter explanation (Grossmann et al., "Monastery of Apa Shenute," 210–219).

567 Noeske evaluated the coins of Heraclius (r. 610–641) to date to within the first ten years of his reign (Grossmann et al., "Monastery of Apa Shenute," 218).

568 Noeske refers to other coin hoards that could have been hidden as a response to the Persian conquest. These three hoards containing gold *solidi* were found in Saqqara, Alexandria and Minshat Abu Omar, while hoards with copper coins were retrieved from Alexandria and Antinoe. See Hans-Christoph Noeske, *Münzfunde aus Ägypten I. Die Münzfunde des ägyptischen Pilgerzentrums Abu Mina und die Vergleichsfunde aus den Dioecesen Aegyptus und Oriens vom 4.–8. Jh. n. Chr.* (Berlin: Gebr. Mann Verlag, 2000), 210–251, 359.

569 Grossmann et al., "Monastery of Apa Shenute," 217.

570 Gabriela Bijovsky, "A Hoard of Byzantine *Solidi* from Bet She'an in the Umayyad Period," *Revue Numismatique* 158 (2002): 161–227.

571 Bijovsky, "Byzantine *Solidi*," 182–185.

572 Swanson, *Coptic Papacy*, 1-6.

letters A and Ω, also with a cross between them, as well as the letters ΠAN, which have been interpreted as an abbreviation of the city of Panopolis (Akhmim).[573] Noeske emphasised that, legally, a patriarch was at no time allowed to issue coins, and could not suggest specific circumstances under which such coins could have been struck.

A pottery mould for the production of coin imitations was found near the *diakonia*.[574] According to Noeske, several examples have been found in Egypt, where they were used to make copper coins in response to shortage of small change on the market.[575] That the imitations appear to have been made in the monastery could suggest that the White Monastery held a significant economic status in the local region. By comparison, two coin dies of bronze (obverse and reverse) were found in the Monastery of Naqlun concealed in a niche and wrapped in straw in the corner of a room in an area defined as sector S.3.[576] The dies were provisionally dated to the Abbasid period.

Concealed parcels of gold coins are not uncommon in monastic contexts, but in most cases, they are found in smaller groups of no more than 20 *solidi*.[577] In Naqlun, for example, 18 intact gold *dinars* and 62 cut pieces were found in a small ceramic vessel in the rubble of a building that burned and collapsed in the tenth century.[578] Most *dinars* were of the Abbasid Caliph Muqtadir (r. 908–932). In comparison, the hoard sizes at the White Monastery are remarkable. They reveal a scale of wealth that emphasises the economic importance of the White Monastery (whatever the reasons for their burial might have been). Altogether, finds such as these from Naqlun and the White Monastery emphasise that more work is required on the monetary role of monasteries in the Late Antique and Early Medieval periods.

Finally, the 1185 single finds of copper coins are also significant. Noeske remarks that the number is unusually high, but he could not get access to this collection.[579] This is unfortunate, as physical or temporal clusters could prove a valuable archaeological source for interpreting the use of the White Monastery as well as its economic history. In general, the coin finds at the site represent evidence of great potential value, but they are so poorly published that little can be deduced from them at present.

4.3 VISITORS TO THE WHITE MONASTERY

This part of Chapter 4 discusses evidence for a different type of monastic interaction with the surrounding world—not through trade, as touched upon in the previous sections, but through visitation or pilgrimage.[580] Before describing the material pertinent to the White Monastery, it is necessary to briefly define the term pilgrimage and contextualise the phenomenon in Late Antique Egypt.

According to Georgia Frank, 'Early Christian Pilgrimage involved a journey to a place in order to gain access to sacred power, whether manifested in living persons, demarcated spaces, or specific objects.'[581] Movement towards and within the sacred sites was an important aspect of pilgrimage, but neither distance nor the duration of the pilgrimage was significant for the potency of the visit.[582]

In Late Antiquity, the cult of the saints engulfed Egypt in a dense network of churches and shrines.

573 Grossmann et al., "Monastery of Apa Shenute," 217–218.
574 Grossmann et al. "Monastery of Apa Shenute," figs. 45–46.
575 Grossmann et al., "Monastery of Apa Shenute," 211–215.
576 Włodzimierz Godlewski, "Naqlun (Nekloni) Preliminary Report, 2005," *Polish Archaeology in the Mediterranean* XVII (2007):" 199.
577 Grossmann et al., "Monastery of Apa Shenute," 216; Noeske, *Münzfunde*, 87–89.
578 Godlewski and Zielinski, "Naqlun," 203.
579 Grossmann et al., "Monastery of Apa Shenute," 117.
580 This part of the chapter has been expanded for publication in Louise Blanke, "The Allure of the Saint: Late Antique Pilgrimage to the Monastery of St Shenoute," in *Excavating Pilgrimage. Archaeological Approaches to Sacred Travel and Movement in the Ancient World*, ed. Troels M. Kristensen and Wieke Friese (Routledge, 2017), 203–223.
581 Georgia Frank, "Pilgrimage," in *The Oxford Handbook of Early Christian Studies*, ed. Susan A. Harvey and David G. Hunter (Oxford: Oxford University Press, 2008), 826.
582 Frank, "Pilgrimage," 826. For other definitions of pilgrimage see for example Jas Elsner and Ian Rutherford, "Introduction," in *Pilgrimage in Graeco-Roman & Early Christian Antiquity. Seeing the Gods*, ed. Jas Elsner and Ian Rutherford (Oxford: Oxford University Press, 2005), 1–40; Frankfurter, *Religion*, 18.

Egypt was a part of the biblical lands, through its association with biblical heroes such as Moses and Joseph, and from the fifth century onwards, towns and villages began to associate themselves with the story of the flight of the Holy Family.[583] At the same time, hagiographic writings and travelogues spread the word about holy men and women with great spiritual powers who lived alone in the desert, and of shrines of martyrs where one could seek healing or redemption from sins.[584]

This new Egyptian landscape attracted pilgrims to worship at shrines and participate in the religious feasts that celebrated the saints and martyrs.[585] To begin with, these cults were based in towns and cities, but from the sixth century onwards, monasteries gradually became the most important sites in the sacred landscape of Egypt.[586] The monasteries obtained the relics of established cults and promoted their own by, for example, changing their names to honour the patron saint. This process has been described by Arietta Papaconstantinou as the 'monasticization of the cult of the saints'.[587] While pilgrimage to Sinai, Alexandria and sites in the Nile Delta such as Abu Mena and the shrine of SS Cyrus and John in Menouthis boomed and achieved great international fame,[588] most of the cults in the monasteries of the Upper Egyptian Nile Valley remained local, with a catchment area that was limited to nearby towns and villages. For this reason, travellers' accounts that describe the built environment and the activities that took place at the monasteries are rare and written sources mainly consist of liturgical calendars or hagiographic texts. That pilgrimage remained important well into the Early Medieval period is clear from the continuously developing tradition of the Holy Family's flight to Egypt and from the statements of the Alexandrian Patriarch Yusab I (r. 831–849), who encouraged the construction of pilgrimage sites as an income-generating activity for the church.[589] The following pages review the textual and archaeological sources, which provide evidence that pilgrims also found their way to the White Monastery.

An early reference to pilgrimage is found in Shenoute's own writings, in which he expressed his disgust at the Christian obsession with the hunt for the bones of martyrs. He condemned the practice of placing martyrs' bones in churches and chapels and raged against the worship that took place at these shrines. In his view, this form of worship was surely the work of demons, as it included singing, feasting and drinking to a point that led to fornication and even to murder.[590] Despite Shenoute's strong opposition towards martyr veneration, the rhetorical character of these objections could indicate a concern with practices that were already taking place, if not at the White Monastery, then at least at nearby locations.[591]

583 See for example Stephen J. Davis, "A Hermeneutic of the Land: Biblical Interpretation in the Holy Family Tradition," in *Coptic Studies on the Threshold of a New Millennium. Proceedings of the Seventh International Congress of Coptic Studies*, edited by Mat Immerzeel and Jacques van der Vliet (Leuven: Peeters, 2004), 329–336; Davis, *Coptic Christology*, 126–149; Gabra et al., *Be thou there: the Holy Family's Journey in Egypt* (Cairo: American University in Cairo Press 2001).

584 For travellers' accounts see for example Bruria Bitton-Ashkelony, *Encountering the Sacred: the Debate on Christian Pilgrimage in Late Antiquity* (Berkeley & London: University of California Press, 2005), 1–29; Georgia Frank, "Miracles, Monks and Monuments: The *Historia Monachorum in Aegypto* as Pilgrims' Tales," in *Pilgrimage and Holy Space in Late Antique Egypt*, ed. David Frankfurter (Leiden: Brill, 1998), 483–506; Georgia Frank, *The Memory of the Eyes: Pilgrims to Living Saints in Christian Late Antiquity* (Berkeley: University of California Press, 2000); John Wilkinson, *Jerusalem Pilgrimage* (London: Hakluyt Society, 1988).

585 Roger S. Bagnall, "Introduction," in *Egypt in the Byzantine World, 300–700*, ed. Roger S. Bagnall, (New York: Cambridge University Press, 2007), 13–14.

586 Papaconstantinou, "Cult."

587 Papaconstantinou, "Cult," 358.

588 See for example Peter Grossmann, "The Pilgrimage Center of Abu Mina," in *Pilgrimage and Holy Space in Late Antique Egypt*, ed. David Frankfurter (Leiden: Brill, 1998), 281–302 ; Dominic Montserrat, "Pilgrimage to the Shrine of SS Cyrus and John at Menouthis in Late Antiquity," in *Pilgrimage and Holy Space in Late Antique Egypt*, ed. David Frankfurter, 257–280.

589 Gabra et al., *Be thou there*; Swanson, *Coptic Papacy*, 30.

590 Timbie, "Liturgical Procession," 415. See Bitton-Ashkelony, *Christian Pilgrimage* for attitudes towards pilgrimage in the fourth and fifth centuries.

591 For a discussion of similar use of rhetoric in Shenoute's writing, see for example Caroline T. Schroeder, "Prophecy and Porneia in Shenoute's Letters: The Rhetoric of

Based on other writings by Shenoute, Layton has argued that under Shenoute's leadership, visitors were confined to the gatehouse where they could remain for as long as three days, during which time a monk would engage them in conversation.[592]

There are various indications that the White Monastery had entered the Egyptian pilgrimage industry by the sixth or seventh century. Although it does not constitute evidence for pilgrimage on its own, it is important to note a reference to the Monastery of St Shenoute in a papyrus of 567, which reveals that Shenoute had by then become the monastery's patron saint.[593]

At the time when the *Life of Shenoute* was compiled, visitors appear to have played an important role in the life of the monastery. The *Life*, for example, describes visits to the White Monastery by Christians who lived beyond the walls of the monastic federation. According to Heike Behlmer, these visitors were mostly from towns and villages in the immediate vicinity of the monastery, who came for mass and prayer.[594] Other visitors included ecclesiastics or monks from nearby monasteries, people who were looking for relief in difficult economic situations, or consolation for emotional or spiritual anguish.[595] Although Shenoute is the protagonist of these accounts, they do not reflect the historical reality of the fifth century, but should be seen as reflections of life in the monastery at the time of their composition, compilation and liturgical performance.

The *Life* quotes Shenoute as saying that 'He who cannot visit Jerusalem in order to prostrate himself before the cross on which Jesus the Messiah has died should come to offer in this church together with all the angels, and I shall pray for the sins they have committed previously, and whoever hears me, his sins shall not be held against him, even including the dead buried in this mountain, because I shall intercede with the Lord on their behalf.'[596] In this quote, Shenoute offers a free pass to heaven for people who worship in the church or are buried in the monastic grounds, providing a powerful attraction for local pilgrims.

Another passage informs us that a local monastic leader named Martyrius came to visit Shenoute at least twice and, during those visits, declared him a prophet.[597] Martyrius was the leader of an important Pachomian monastery near Panopolis in Shenoute's lifetime and later a venerated saint himself. Davis describes a similar saintly encounter between Shenoute and Macarius in the hagiographical work known as *The Virtues of St Macarius* as 'an act of hagiographical appropriation and "co-opetition"—a combination of friendly cooperation and pious competition'.[598] Davis sees the exchange as a way to capitalize on another saint's reputation. In the case of Martyrius, his visit in the *Life* was both a blessing to Shenoute's congregation while also acting as a witness to Shenoute's saintly powers. The passage can therefore be read as an endorsement of Shenoute by a celebrated monastic leader or as a passage in which the famous leader rendered Shenoute more holy than himself and thus constructed a local hierarchy of saints where Shenoute stood at the top.

It is not just the *Life* that reports on the growing influence of Shenoute the saint. Further evidence for pilgrimage to the White Monastery is found in papyri, originally kept in the monastic library, which contain a liturgical calendar dating to the eighth century. The papyri mention a number of saints whose feast days were commemorated in the White Monastery.[599]

Sexuality in a Late Antique Egyptian Monastery," *Journal of Near Eastern Studies* 65.2 (2006): 81–97.

592 Layton, "Rules," 57, 65.

593 Zereteli and Jernstedt, *Papyri*, vol 3, 48.

594 Heike Behlmer, "Visitors to Shenoute's Monastery," in *Pilgrimage and Holy Space in Late Antique Egypt*, ed. David Frankfurter (Leiden, Boston, Köln: Brill, 1998), 341–343.

595 Behlmer, "Visitors."

596 Behlmer, "Visitors," 367.

597 Behlmer, "Visitors," 354, 356–357.

598 Davis, "Shenoute," 14.

599 Leslie S. B. MacCoull, "Chant in Coptic Pilgrimage," in *Pilgrimage and Holy Space in Late Antique Egypt*, ed. David Frankfurter (Brill: Leiden, Boston, Köln, 1998), 403–415; Ugo Zanetti, "Un Index Liturgique du Monastère Blanc," in *Christianisme d'Égypte: Hommages à René-Georges Coquin*, ed. Jean-Marc Rosenstiehl (Paris: Peeters, 1994), 55–75.

The calendar reveals a busy schedule with a total of 51 listed feast days, with the most important being the celebration of Shenoute on the 1st of July. A papyrus records a hymn with the title *On the Prophet Apa Shenoute* that may have been sung on this occasion. The hymn compares Shenoute to Moses and recalls how 'He (Shenoute) laid the foundation of the church; All men upon earth, when they come to your monastery, marvel at that stone, for there is no mark on it.'[600] The text of the hymn suggests that the church at least on certain days was accessible to visitors.

Another important example of visitors' activity is a second liturgical text that dates to the fifteenth or sixteenth century, but accounts for a rite that, according to Janet Timbie, took place until the twelfth century.[601] The translated title of the text is *The Rite for the Feast of the Desert of Apa Shenoute*.[602] It describes a ritual procession performed by the people of Panopolis to several sites in and around the White Monastery. The focal points of the procession were two churches. The first, located near or outside the monastic enclosure walls, was dedicated to the Virgin Mary—the *Etrigamou*—and has been interpreted as containing the bodily remains of Shenoute.[603] According to *The Rite*, the processions of pilgrims would enter the church and listen to a series of biblical readings followed by the reading of a sermon by Shenoute. Thereafter, the pilgrims would proceed to the place of the 'sea of Apa Shenoute', interpreted by Timbie and Davis as a repository for Shenoute's relics located below the altar of the church.[604] Finally, the pilgrims exited the church and circumambulated the building.[605] Although there are no descriptive indicators in the *Rite* that can be matched to the archaeological remains, it is possible that this structure was identical with the funerary chapel (WM.2).[606] The recent association of the tomb of the funerary chapel with Shenoute raises the possibility of this identification. The other church mentioned in *The Rite* has been identified as the main church of the White Monastery.[607]

Even a brief survey of the written sources such as this suggests that visitation became an integral part of life in the White Monastery. Unfortunately, the written sources do not refer to facilities within the monastic built environment that could have served the visitors' physical needs during their stay. Nor do the texts provide information on the number of visitors, the length of their visit or to what extent the monastics engaged with their visitors. Not all such questions can be answered by looking at the physical remains, but when viewed through the lens of pilgrimage, archaeology does yield information on some of the activities that could have taken place.[608]

A closer look at the sanctuary of the monastery's main church reveals several features that can be associated with visitors to the monastery. The triconch sanctuary is dedicated to St George (north), St Shenoute (east) and to the Virgin Mary (south) (fig. 62, 1–3). *The Rite for the Feast of the Desert of Apa Shenoute* mentions that as a part of the procession, an icon of St George was venerated in this space, as was the receptacle that contained his relics.[609] According

600 Karl H. Kuhn, and William J. Tait, *Thirteen Coptic Acrostic Hymns from Manuscripts M574 of the Pierpont Morgan Library* (Oxford: Griffith Institute, Ashmolean Museum, 1996), 137–145.

601 It is not clear on what evidence Timbie bases this date (Timbie, "Liturgical Procession," 418).

602 See also Davis, *Coptic Christology*, 114–125; Grossmann, "Schenute."

603 Timbie, "Liturgical Procession," 432; Davis, *Coptic Christology*, 117

604 Davis, *Coptic Christology*, 117; Timbie, "Liturgical Procession," 432.

605 Davis, *Coptic Christology*, 117.

606 Bolman et al., "Shenoute;" Bolman et al. "Tomb of St. Shenoute?." Stephen J. Davis is currently collaborating with Mary Farag and Daniel Schriever on producing an edition and translation of *The Rite* and as part of that publication, Davis will further explore its possible association with the tomb chapel.

607 Davis, *Coptic Christology*, 118.

608 Most commonly, pilgrimage is detected in the archaeological record through pilgrims' tokens such as medallions or *ampullae* for oil or holy water. See for example Jesper Bild, "Sacred Movement to Labrauda—An Archaeological Perspective." *HEROM. Journal on Hellenistic and Roman Material Culture* 1 (2012): 157–196; Heather Hunter-Crawley, "Pilgrimage made portable: A sensory Archaeology of the Monza-Bobbio Ampullae," *HEROM. Journal on Hellenistic and Roman Material Culture* 1 (2012): 135–156.

609 Davis, *Coptic Christology*, 118; Timbie, "Liturgical Procession," 439.

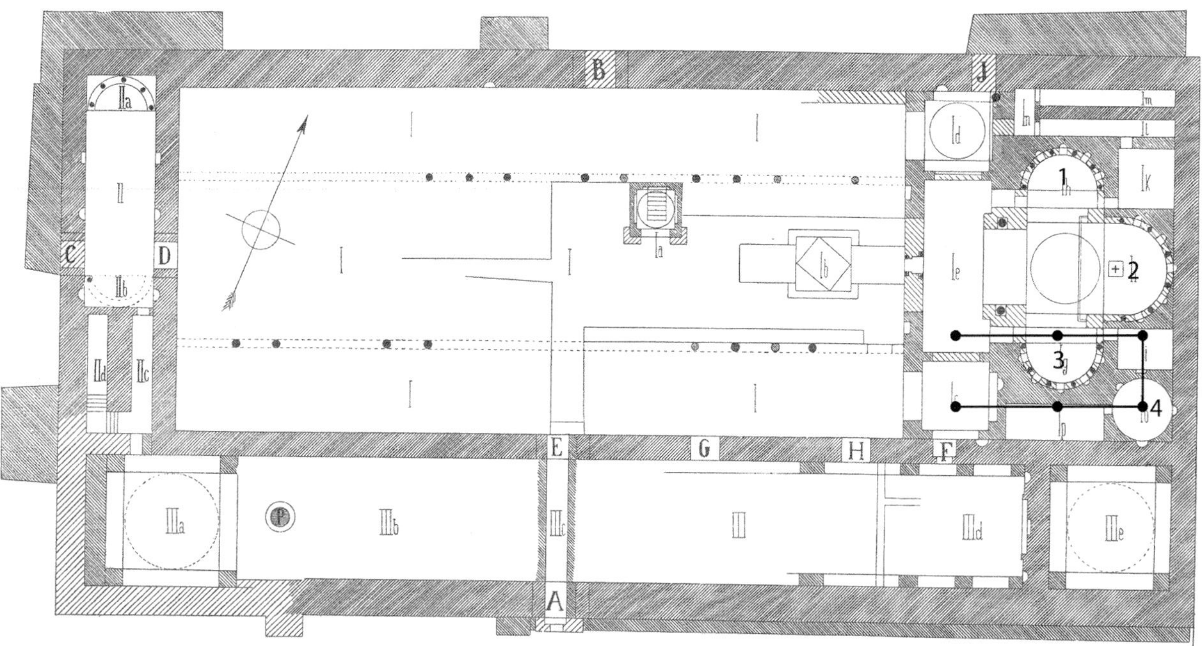

Fig. 62. Plan of church. 1. Dedicated to St George. 2. Dedicated to St Shenoute. 3. Dedicated to the Virgin Mary. 4. Baptistery. Route showing possible movement into and through baptistery and adjacent room (modified from De Bock, *Matériaux*, fig. 60).

to the *Rite*, oil from the shrine was used to cure diseases and to remit the sins of those who were anointed with it.[610] The account does not state whether the oil received its healing qualities from its proximity to the shrine or was in physical contact with the relics, as was the case in, for example, churches in the north Syrian Limestone Massif.[611] There, relics were kept in limestone reliquaries, with holes drilled at the top that allowed oil to pass through the interior cavity and escape through holes at the bottom after it had been in contact with the relics.[612] It is not indicated in the text whether the oil was used on site or collected in containers and carried by the visitors to their homes.

Both textual and archaeological evidence suggests a further association with relics at the White Monastery church. From the north conch (dedicated to St George), a doorway gives access to the northern *pastophorium*. From here, a subterranean crypt can be entered through a niche in the wall. The crypt consists of a vaulted room with a cavity in the south wall currently containing the bones of at least two individuals. Gaining access to the tiny crypt is both difficult and uncomfortable, as it requires moving through a narrow sloping passage into the subterranean room. As such, the architectural layout implies that the crypt was not intended for regular visits. Instead, placing these bones in a location almost immediately below the altar seems to have served other purposes: to venerate commemorated individuals by the central location of their relics and to imbue the church with blessings via the presence of these individuals. Ann Marie Yasin argues that the association of altars with relics became increasingly important during Late Antiquity.[613] This development culminated at the second council of Niceae (787), which decreed that all altars should contain the physical remains of a saint. However, it is not clear how far this edict affected the anti-Chalcedonian community in Christian Egypt.

It is not known whose remains were buried in such a prominent position below the altar in the main church of the White Monastery—whether it was monastic leaders, benefactors, saints or martyrs.

610 Timbie, "Liturgical Procession," 439.
611 Yasin, *Saints*, 164–171.
612 Yasin, *Saints*, 164–171.
613 Yasin, *Saints*, 154.

An entry in the *History of the Patriarchs of Alexandria* that deals with the later part of the eleventh century mentions that the White Monastery was host to the remains of two apostles: Bartholomew and Simon the Zealot.[614] Although it is not possible to link this or the account of the healing oil at the shrine of St George to the physical remains of the church, it is important to note that the textual sources state—and the archaeological evidence suggests—that relics were kept and venerated in this church, but the nature of the veneration remains unknown.

The configuration of the rooms in the south part of the church signifies a different set of rituals. Located at the church's southeast end, the baptistery was accessed from the southern part of the sanctuary and from the south aisle of the nave (fig. 62, 4). It consists of a single circular room, which centres on an immersion tank with a staircase in its west and east ends (internal dimensions are 1.62 × 1.93 m, with additional 1.10 × 0.94 m for the staircase).

The design and decoration of rooms used for baptism was, according to Robin M. Jensen, purpose-built to reflect and inform the ritual that took place within.[615] Adult baptism entailed a series of physical actions including 'undressing, anointing, dunking, and re-garbing the body'.[616] The architectural layout was designed to direct the pattern of movement through the ritual actions, to conceal the ritual from being observed or overheard by non-participants and to shield the modesty of the naked neophytes.

The architectural arrangement, which includes a room to either side of the baptistery, resembles the layout of the baptistery in the Great Basilica at the pilgrimage site of Abu Mena.[617] Grossmann suggested a ritual sequence corresponding to the Coptic rite of baptism and reflected in the architectural layout, in which the first room, which was accessed from an exterior space, was used for undressing before the neophytes proceeded to be baptised. After the immersion, the neophytes were anointed with oil in the adjacent room, redressed and then admitted into the church interior to participate in the service. At the White Monastery, it is possible to imagine a similar scenario where the rooms to the north and west of the baptistery were used for undressing, anointing and redressing. The newly baptised may have proceeded directly to the south part of the triconch (dedicated to the Virgin Mary), although it is possible that the use of this entry was limited to the clergy.

Since a sizeable part of the church architecture was taken up by these rooms, it is reasonable to ask who was baptised in the church of the White Monastery: did the baptistery serve non-monastics, was it reserved for new initiates into the monastic community or could it have been used by both? Shenoute's writings make no reference to the baptism of newcomers, but the *Life of Pachomius* recounts a story involving a sick monk, who had yet to be baptised. From the story, we learn that only ordained priests could perform the rite of baptism and that *catechumens* from the entire *koinonia* would gather at Easter to be baptised at Pbow—the Pachomians' leading monastery.[618] It is possible that the baptistery in the church at the White Monastery served a similar purpose in the monastery's formative years. None of the other churches in the federation (the churches in the Red Monastery and in the monastic complex in the village of Atripe) contained a baptistery and the title 'priest' (who could administer the baptism) figures within the list of jobs mentioned by Shenoute.[619]

614 Coquin and Maurice Martin, "Dayr Anba Shinudah," 764.

615 Robin M. Jensen, "Archaeology of Christian Initiation," in *A Companion to the Archaeology of Religion in the Ancient World*, ed. Rubina Raja and Jörg Rüpke (Oxford: Wiley Blackwell, 2015), 253–267.

616 Jensen, "Christian Initiation," 259.

617 Grossmann, "Abu Mina," 283.

618 The story is discussed in Hugo Lundhaug, "Baptism in the Monasteries of Upper Egypt. The Pachomian Corpus and the Writings of Shenoute," in *Ablution, Initiation, and Baptism: Late Antiquity, Early Judaism, and Early Christianity*, ed. David Hellholm, Tor Vegge, Øyvind Norderval and Christer Hellholm (Berlin: Walter de Gruyter, 2011), 1347–1380, who also recounts other references to baptism in Shenoute's writings and in texts associated with Pachomius.

619 Layton, "Rules," 56–57.

Baptism was certainly integral to pilgrimage at sites such as Abu Mena and Qalʿat Simʿan (Syria), but such connection remains speculative at the White Monastery. Baptism, however, is an integral part of modern pilgrimage practice and is especially important for the annual feast days, although today baptism of infants has become standard. During the often-week-long feasts, parents bring their children to be baptized in the auspicious presence of the saint.[620]

Viewing the organistion of the built environment through the lens of visitation, it is possible to suggest that not only was the church accessible to travellers, but that pilgrimage at some point became an integral part of the monastery's life and economy and, therefore, the practice was physically facilitated within the complex. The archaeological remains do not allow us to identify buildings that conclusively can be associated with the practice of pilgrimage. The facilities needed would be related to sustenance, accommodation and hygiene. The kitchen and refectory (WM.4.2 and WM.4.1.16) supplied the permanent monastic residents, but could also have produced food for the transient visitors.

Interpreting the semi-circular basin in WM.5.6 within the framework of pilgrimage would suggest that it functioned as a part of a small bathhouse for visitors. Examples of monastic bathhouses are found in Palestine in, for example, the monastery of St Hilarion and in the Judean monastery of St Martyrius, but they are generally a rare occurrence.[621] The bathhouses at both sites were located by the entrance in areas that have been interpreted as used by visitors to the monasteries. Grossmann identified two public bathhouses within the ecclesiastical area in Abu Mena and suggested that the neophytes would bathe before they were baptised.[622] Suggesting a similar practice at the White Monastery, the location of the basin would allow an almost direct passage from the bathing facility into the church via its south entrance.[623]

The presence of extra-mural facilities, analogous to the guesthouse found at Balaʿizah, has not been confirmed at the White Monastery due to the modern occupation of the areas surrounding the ancient monastery. It is perfectly possible that all activities concerning visitors not pertinent to the church remained beyond the enclosure walls.

4.4 SUMMARY

A careful examination of the archaeological remains has allowed us to supplement and contextualise the information obtained from the texts and deepen our understanding of the monastery's economic circumstances and daily life. The organisation of the built environment, its infrastructure and the materials used allows for a reconstruction of the White Monastery as densely populated and prosperous, as a dynamic centre of industry and crafts. At 77,500 m^2, it was among the largest monastic establishments of Late Antique Egypt, comprising a well-organised built environment with a complex infrastructure that was renewed and maintained well into the Islamic period. The archaeological evidence suggests that it was a self-sufficient community capable of not only meeting its own daily needs, but also accumulating monetary wealth and land as well as undertaking major building projects and maintaining an intricate built environment. Although donations from local patrons were required for major building projects such as the White Monastery church, there are no indications in either archaeology or text suggesting that donations were needed for the daily running of the monastery. This situation may, however, have changed over the centuries. The increased taxation of monasteries from the eighth century onwards and the White Monastery's gradual loss of landholdings likely resulted in a dependency on local Coptic donors. The monastery was no longer capable of upholding a high material output through production and instead increasingly focused on an economy built on spiritual services, as is the case today.

620 Viaud, *Pèlerinages*, 76.

621 René Elter and Ayman Hassoune, "Le Complexe du Bain du Monastère de Saint Hilarion à Umm el-ʿAmr: Première Synthèse Architecturale," *Syria* 85 (2008): 129–144; Hirschfeld, *Judean Desert Monasteries*, 44.

622 Grossmann, "Abu Mina," 292.

623 For discussions of baths at pilgrimage sites in Egypt, see several articles in Boussac et al., *Le Bain Collectif*.

Chapter 5

THE RED MONASTERY AND ATRIPE

The White Monastery's early history is intimately tied to two other monastic communities: a congregation to the north that is commonly referred to as the Red Monastery and a community of female monastics in the village of Atripe to the south (pl. 1). Together they formed a federation of which the White Monastery was the leading partner.[624] A recently published manuscript known as the Naples fragment suggests that a man named Pshoi founded a male *coenobium* (the Red Monastery) around the middle of the fourth century and submitted it to the supreme rule of Pcol—the founder and first leader of the White Monastery.[625] The origin of the female congregation is somewhat obscure, but since Shenoute does not mention its foundation, it was likely an early development that was fully established by the time of Shenoute's ascension to monastic leadership.[626]

Our principal source of information for the internal organisation of the federation is the *Canons* and *Discourses* of Shenoute. These writings provide a unique insight into the lives of both male and female monastics: they portray the ideal ascetic behaviour in a *coenobitic* community, but also reveal resistance to Shenoute's leadership and monastic rules. From the *Canons*, Layton has extracted more than 500 rules, which applied to the three communities, with certain modifications that were appropriate to context, such as those pertaining to the female congregation at Atripe.[627] The rules suggest that the communities were fairly independent: each was built on a strict monastic hierarchy that was headed by a mother superior or a father superior who was responsible for the daily management of their congregations.[628] All three superiors were under the leadership of a supreme father, who was based at the White Monastery, although he could reside in solitude in the nearby mountains, as was the case with Shenoute.

Certain economic and religious aspects of monastic life pertaining to the federation were organised from the White Monastery. Aspiring (male) monastics would begin their tenure there. Only after swearing an oath and transferring legal title of their possessions to the *diakonia* were they assigned to a specific monastery. The new monks would then either be assigned to the Red Monastery or remain where they were. The induction process for aspiring nuns was probably somewhat different; it is unlikely that women would have been allowed to stay in the main monastery—the White Monastery—at any point during their monastic lives.

The White Monastery exerted some degree of control over food rations for the federation. The question of the annual production of bread at the White Monastery and its shipment to the smaller communities has already been discussed in Chap-

624 Layton, *Canons*.
625 Emmel & Layton, "Pshoi;" Layton, *Canons*, 14–18.
626 Layton, *Canons*, 22.
627 Layton, *Canons*, 51.
628 Layton, "Rules," 11.

ter 4.2.2, where the conclusion was reached that this practice was not viable given the size of the settlements. However, vinegar (for mixing with water and drinking) and wine for the Eucharist were, according to the Canons, stored here and distributed to the smaller communities based on their needs.[629]

The White Monastery may also have presided over aspects of the communities' religious life, such as baptism (suggested in Chapter 4.3), as well as specific feast days and other liturgical practices. The monasteries' medieval history suggests that this was the case, but we do not know when these practices began.[630]

A far greater quantity of material evidence survives from the White Monastery than from either of the two smaller settlements. For the other two foundations, there are far fewer indications in the archaeological record of their shape and structure, and only a few architectural traces of features related to economic activities survive. Consequently, the interpretation of their material remains will inevitably be coloured by what is known from the archaeology and textual record of the larger community. However, in spite of the paucity of the material remains, a close study of what survives tends to confirm the economic interdependence suggested by Shenoute's writings.

A biography of the White Monastery is not complete without including a study of the monasteries on which it relied for certain essential resources and to which it provided in return a measure of administrative control, labour and food. The physical layout of the two smaller complexes is examined below using the same categories of settlement, economy and daily life to allow for comparison between all three sites. The aim is to establish the degree of interdependence between the three communities and determine to what degree they functioned as a cluster of discrete but mutually supportive settlement units.

5.1 THE RED MONASTERY

The Red Monastery, also known as the monastery of St Pshoi, lies on the fringe of the cultivated zone, three km to the north of the White Monastery. It takes its name from a fired brick church, which is the only part of the ancient community that has survived as a standing structure. Otherwise, the site contains only scarce archaeological remains and is dominated by buildings belonging to the modern monastery, an encroaching village and a cemetery that lies between the ancient site and the desert (fig. 63). The modern monastery is modest in size and, until a recent expansion towards the west, its wall enclosed an area of just 30,400 m^2. This area included the monastery's ancient church as well as modern buildings such as a guesthouse, a kitchen and a refectory. The main church lies in the southeast corner of the enclosure and the archaeological remains of the ancient monastery are found to the north of the church.

The Naples fragment suggests that the monastery was founded by the fourth-century ascetic Pshoi.[631] He was a contemporary of Pcol, the founder of the White Monastery, and the leader of a group of loosely organised ascetics who lived together in the desert. When the group grew to a sizeable number, Pshoi founded a *coenobium* and submitted it to the supreme rule of Pcol at the White Monastery.[632]

Shenoute referred to the Red Monastery as the 'little congregation to the north', but did not provide much specific information about the community beyond rules that applied to all three congregations.[633] The lack of sources is not confined to the early history of the site, but extends to later Coptic and Arabic texts.[634] A manuscript from the eleventh century mentions a monk from the monastery of St Pshoi, and a monk named Mercurius left his name

629 Layton, Canons, 13.

630 Ugo Zanetti and Stephen J. Davis, "Liturgy and Ritual Practice in the Shenoutean Federation," in *The Red Monastery Church. Beauty and Asceticism in Upper Egypt*, ed. Elizabeth S. Bolman, 27-35 (New Haven and London: Yale University Press, 2016).

631 Emmel & Layton, "Pshoi," 13; Layton, *Canons*, 14–18.

632 Emmel & Layton, "Pshoi," 13.

633 Paul Dilley, "Dipinti in Late Antiquity and Shenoute's Monastic Federation: Text and Image in the Paintings of the Red Monastery," *Zeitschrift für Papyrologie und Epigraphik* 165 (2008): 111; Timm, *Das Christlich-Koptische Ägypten*, 639–640.

634 Nicholas Warner, "Architectural Survey," in *The Red Monastery Church*, ed. Elizabeth S. Bolman, 49.

Fig. 63. Site plan of the Red Monastery showing location of church in relation to the archaeological remains and the modern monastery. Key: 1. Church; 2. Keep; 3. Well; 4. Structures related to the ancient monastery; 5. Modern church (drawing by Nicholas Warner; Warner, "Architectural Survey," fig. 6.2; © ARCE).

in five inscriptions in the church between 1300 and 1322.[635] Abu al-Makarim does not mention the monastery, and although Al-Maqrizi refers to it by both its names, the Monastery of St Pshoi and the Red Monastery, he provides no further details.[636] Swanson suggests that the paucity of sources relates in part to the Red Monastery being concealed behind the more famous White Monastery, which would be used as a shared reference to both. The story of the Armenian Bahram, for example, recounts how he

635 Swanson "Eclipsed History," 194. See also Réne-Georges Coquin, Peter Grossmann, and Hans-Georg Severin, "Dayr Anba Bishoi," in *The Coptic Encyclopedia*, ed. Aziz S. Atiya (New York, Oxford, Singapore, Sydney: Maxwell Macmillan International, 1991), 736; Timm, *Das Christlich-Koptische Ägypten*, 639–640.

636 Abu Salih the Armenian, *The Churches & Monasteries*, 235–240; Wüstenfeld, Macrizi, 96.

retired to the 'White Monasteries' (*al-diyarat al-bid*) (see also Chapter 2.3).[637]

From the seventeenth century onwards, European travellers began to make their way to the monastery. The accounts left by the most influential of these have been summarised by Nicholas Warner and Cédric Meurice.[638] These include Vansleb, Pococke, Denon, Wilkinson, De Bock, Clarke, Monneret de Villard and Creswell. Of these accounts, only Clarke's described the area that surrounded the church. When he visited the site in the early twentieth century, he saw the remains of a fired brick perimeter wall, preserved to the north, west and south sides of the church. Within this enclosure, he observed a considerable scatter of brick debris that formed a rectangular space around the church.[639] At this point in its history, the Red Monastery church had been transformed into a village.

Conservation of the church began in 1909, when the Comité removed the houses in the nave and, among other projects, consolidated the walls and constructed a protective roof over the nave.[640] Further conservation was carried out in the 1980s and 1990s by the SCA.[641]

In 2002, the church became the focus of renewed attention when the Red Monastery Conservation Project began.[642] Directed by Bolman, the project conserved and consolidated all remains of the church's lavish decoration programme found in the sanctuary and in surrounding rooms.[643] The conservators identified four consecutive layers of plaster, each with their set of figural and non-figural motifs. From stylistic comparisons, Bolman dated the fourth and final layer to the seventh century with additions in adjoining rooms added between the tenth and thirteenth centuries.[644] An impressive edited volume concluding this work was published in 2016.[645]

The area to the north of the church—the focus of this section—was excavated by the Sohag department of the SCA for Coptic and Islamic Antiquities in 1996, 2002–2003 and 2009, but the results from these excavations have not been published. The descriptions of the archaeological remains below are based on a survey carried out in 2012 under the auspice of the Red Monastery Conservation Project and with funding from the Danish Institute in Damascus.[646]

5.1.1 *The Archaeological Remains*

The modern use of the Red Monastery has seen the construction of several buildings as well as the levelling of surfaces by the use of bulldozers. This means that access to the archaeological remains is limited to an area to the north of the church that roughly measures 115 × 110 m. Of this area, about 50% has

637 Swanson "Eclipsed History," 194.

638 Nicholas Warner and Cédric Meurice, "'A Strange Jumble of Roman Detail.' Western Explorers and Antiquarians at the Red Monastery, 1673–1926," in *The Red Monastery Church*, ed. Elizabeth S. Bolman, 231–241.

639 Clarke, *Christian Antiquities*, 161.

640 Nicholas Warner and Cédric Meurice, "The Comité. Conserving the Red Monastery Church in the Early Twentieth Century," in *The Red Monastery Church*, ed. Elizabeth S. Bolman, 243–259.

641 Warner and Meurice, "Comité," 258–259.

642 Luigi De Cesaris, Alberto Sucato, and Emiliano Ricchi, "Wall Painting Conservation at the Red Monastery Church," in *The Red Monastery Church*, ed. Elizabeth S. Bolman, 261–279.

643 See for example Elizabeth S. Bolman, "Late Antique Aesthetics, Chromophonia and the Red Monastery, Sohag, Egypt," *Eastern Christian Art* 3 (2006): 1–24, Elizabeth S. Bolman, "The Red Monastery Conservation Project, 2006 and 2007 Campaigns. Contributing to the Corpus of Late Antique Art," in *Christianity and Monasticism in Upper Egypt*, ed. Gawdat Gabra and Hany N. Takla (Cairo: American University in Cairo Press, 2008); Elizabeth S. Bolman, "Reflections on the Red Monastery Project, 2000-2008," *Bulletin of the American Research Center in Egypt* 194 (2009): 9–13; Bolman, "The White Monastery;" Elizabeth S. Bolman, *The Red Monastery Church: Beauty and Asceticism in Upper Egypt* (New Haven and London: Yale University Press, 2016).

644 Bolman, "Red Monastery," 313; Elizabeth S. Bolman, "Introduction," in *The Red Monastery Church*, ed. Elizabeth S. Bolma, xxviii; Bolman, "Medieval Flourishing."

645 Bolman, *The Red Monastery Church*.

646 Louise Blanke*, "Red Monastery Survey. Preliminary Report on the Mapping of the Archaeological Remains, Spring 2011" (Red Monastery Project interim report, 2011); Gillian Pyke*, "Red Monastery 2011: Architectural Observations and Pottery Report" (Red Monastery Project interim report, 2011).

Fig. 64. Overview of Red Monastery archaeological church. View towards east (photograph by the author).

Site Code	Area	Zone	Description
RM	1		RM.1 comprises the southwest part of the archaeological area. Size: 40 m NS × 40 m EW.
RM	1	1	The well and the tanks and pipes immediately to the east of the well. All features are associated with the monastery's water supply. Size of well: 5.5 m diameter. Total size: 20 m NS × 40 m EW.
RM	1	2	A structure to the south of the well. This zone consists of two rooms built from fired bricks with *opus signinum* floors. Size: 11 m NS × 4.5 m EW.
RM	1	3	A large room or courtyard to the south of the well area. Size: 14.7 m NS × 13.3 m EW.
RM	2		RM.2 comprises the central part of the archaeological area. Size 23 m NS × 63 m EW.
RM	2	1	The westernmost part of RM.2. This zone contains a rectangular tank built from fired bricks with an *opus signinum* interior and several patches of Nile silt floor deposits. Size of tank: 2.15 m NS × 7 m EW. Total size: 26.5 m NS × 19 m EW.
RM	2	2	The central part of RM.2. This zone contains a rectangular fired brick building with an *opus signinum* floor and a paved area to the east of the building. Size of building: 9.8 m NS × 17.4 m EW. Total size: 11.7 m NS × 22.8 m EW.
RM	2	3	The easternmost part of RM.2. This zone contains of several pipelines and a cistern placed centrally in a small room. Total size: 12 m NS × 17 m EW.
RM	3		RM.3 comprises the northern part of the archaeological area. Size: 39 m NS × 42 m EW.
RM	3	1	Northwest part of archaeological site. This zone contains a wall built from limestone in the northern end and several Nile silt deposits. Size: 30 m NS × 17 m EW:
RM	3	2	Northeast part of site. This zone comprises the remains of a food producing area. It contains several fragmented walls, floor foundations and twenty-nine ceramic vessels incorporated into the built environment. Size: 37 m NS × 25 m EW.

Table 6. Areas and zones at the Red Monastery.

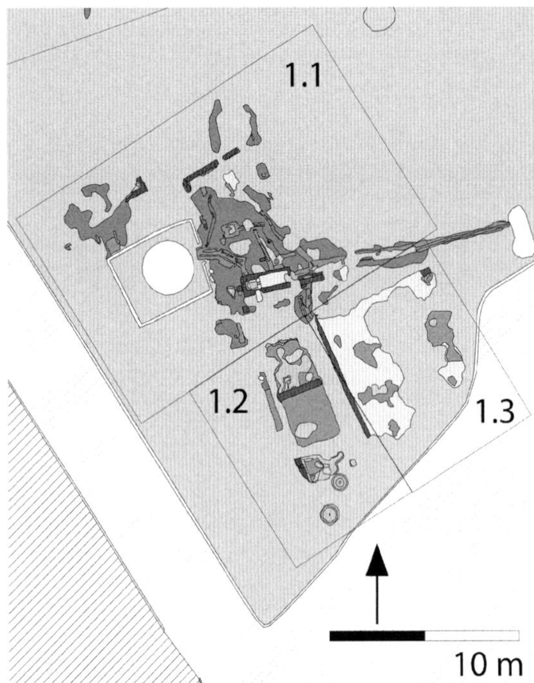

Fig. 65. RM.1.1–3 (map by the author).

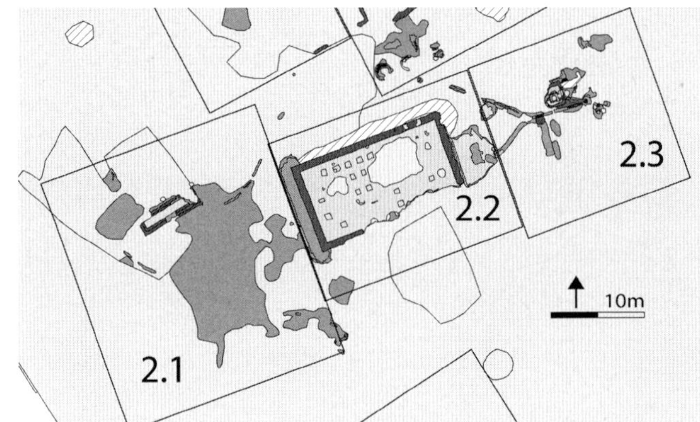

Fig. 66. RM.2.1–3 (map by the author).

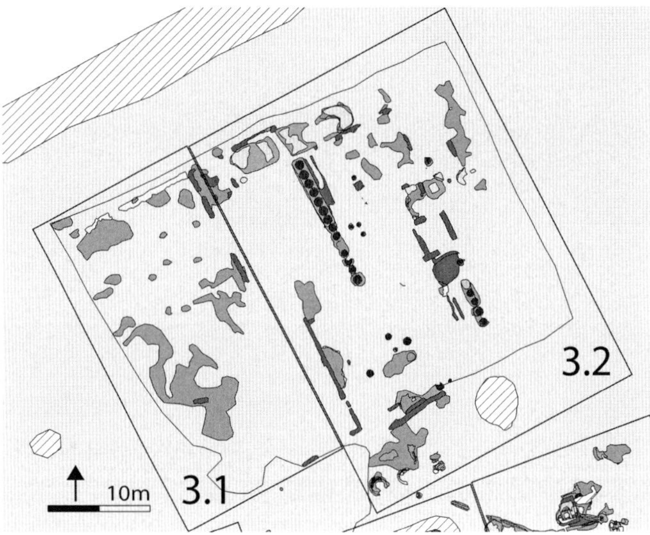

Fig. 67. RM.3.1–2 (map by the author).

been excavated by the SCA (fig. 64). To adequately discuss the archaeological remains, I have divided the excavations into areas (RM.1–RM.3), with further subdivisions into sections (pl. 9, figs. 65–67 & table 6). RM.1.1 contains a circular well, pipes and several features associated with the monastic water supply. Two structures are found to the south of the well. RM.1.2 contains several rooms with fired brick walls and a plastered floor, while all that remains of RM.1.3 is part of a paved courtyard that is framed to the west by a fired brick wall (fig. 68). Further south, two granite crushing basins sit on the edge of the excavated area (fig. 69). These features are not *in situ*, but were presumably brought here by the SCA during their excavations or by the monks as a part of the modern monastic refurbishment.

RM.2.1 contains Nile silt foundations, a single rectangular vat built from fired bricks and plastered with *opus signinum* as well as remains of two pipelines—one leads north from the well (RM.1.1) and the other leads towards the east. RM.2.2 contains the best-preserved building on site, apart from the main church. It measures 9.8 m NS × 17.7 m EW and consists of a single rectangular room, framed by fired brick walls (fig. 70). It is built on a foundation of fired bricks and mortar and the floor is coated in a thick plaster. A long step or bench lines the western exterior end of the building, while the eastern end is abutted by a paved floor. It is not clear if this paved area formed an additional room or should be considered as an exterior space. The interior plaster floor carries the impression of at least fifteen equally-sized squares, each measuring 0.5 × 0.5 m. (fig. 66).

A pipeline runs south of RM.2.2 towards the east where it splits into two directions. One leads further east to a cistern in RM.2.3 and the other leads northwest to RM.3. RM.2.3 contains three ceramic vessels that were included in the architectural de-

Fig. 68. RM.1.3. Overview of structure. View towards south-southeast (photograph by the author).

Fig. 69. RM.1.1. Note two crushing basins. View towards southwest (photograph by the author).

Fig. 70. RM.2.2. Overview of structure. Note paving in front of photo. View towards east-northeast (photograph by Gillian Pyke).

sign, and a cistern, which is set into a small square room with an entrance in the east wall. In its current state, the cistern is filled with modern garbage and fired bricks that have been thrown in from the surface. It was, therefore, not possible to record its full dimensions.

RM.3 features several smaller isolated areas of Nile silt foundations (RM.3.1); a total of nineteen ceramic vessels, set in two rows in a frame of fired bricks and lime-based mortar; a cistern and three ovens with clay floors and brick linings (RM.3.2). Another ten ceramic vessels are set in the ground or incorporated into the architecture in RM.3.2. Fragmented wall sections reveal that RM.3 contained at least fourteen rooms (pl. 10) and remains of plaster floors in the northern and eastern part of RM.3.2 give an impression of the height of the original floor, some 0.40 m above the current ground level. RM.3.1 also contains the foundation of a wall that was built exclusively from roughly cut limestone boulders (fig. 71). The thickness of the wall—0.65 m, compared to the 0.3 m of most other walls in the settlement—would suggest that it was built to support either more weight or greater height. It was therefore tentatively suggested during the survey season that this foundation could constitute the remains of the monastery's northern boundary wall.

CERAMICS

The survey project did not include excavation, therefore the finds available for study were limited to ceramic material found on the surface or incorporated into the architectural design as intact vessels or

Fig. 71. RM.3.1. Suggested location of boundary wall indicated by dotted line. View towards south (photograph by the author).

individual sherds. The ceramic assemblage has been preliminarily studied by Pyke. The surface finds belonged to two groups. One was collected by the SCA during their excavation in 2009 and left in a distinct group on the surface; the other was systematically sampled from the surface scatter found throughout the archaeological areas (RM.1–RM.3).

The ceramic vessels that were incorporated into the architectural design were concentrated in RM.3.2 where twenty-nine vessels were identified. All were associated with storage. The nineteen vessels that were set in two rows all belong to the same type. None are preserved to their full height and the maximum preserved diameter is 0.94 m. Six further intact vessels were found incorporated into the architectural design—three near the cistern in RM.2.3 and three within a few metres of the well in RM.1.1. All six were associated with the monastery's water supply.

Ceramic sherds were used as fill in wall mortars and floor foundations in the structures in RM.1.2, RM.1.3 and RM.2.2. According to Pyke, these sherds were almost exclusively locally-produced types that provide a *terminus post quem* for the construction of the structures in the fifth century.[647] A large storage vessel (height 0.90 m and diameter 0.75 m) was moved by the SCA from the area to the east of RM.1 to the site guard's house (fig. 72).

Pyke noted that the quantity of ceramic material in the Red Monastery's archaeological area was low compared to the surface scatter in the White Monastery.[648] Only a few sherds were found on the

647 Pyke*, "Red Monastery."

648 Pyke*, "Red Monastery," 22.

surface and the most common types were fragments of pipes associated with the water supply and locally-produced transport amphora. The contents of the SCA collection and the surface scatter were very similar. The predominant vessel type was the early form of the Late Roman Amphora type 7, but other types of amphora were also found, although in smaller quantities. Fine wares were not particularly well-represented, but a few sherds of goblets, plates and bowls of Aswan production were found. One of these, a silt bowl dating to between the fifth and the seventh century, carried a post-firing inscription, which may tentatively be read as identifying the owner as one Apa Thomas.

Pyke concluded that the ceramic material was clustered in four main temporal stages: the fifth to the seventh centuries (the vast majority of the material belongs to this period), the eight-century, the thirteenth century (a small quantity of material) and a small representation of modern material.[649]

Fig. 72. Storage vessel found in eastern part of excavated area (precise location unknown) (photograph by Gillian Pyke).

THE CHURCH

The architectural layout of the Red Monastery church has been examined in detail by Warner, as a part of the Red Monastery Conservation Project.[650] The appearance of the building is that of a smaller version of the White Monastery church.[651] It measures 43 m EW × 23 m NS and the walls stand to a height of 11 m. It is constructed from fired brick walls with limestone quoins, a cavetto cornice and a doorway in the north and south walls (fig. 73). As it appears today, the church interior consists of a limestone-built triconch sanctuary with adjacent side rooms, a basilica-style nave, a long hall to the south, but no western narthex as otherwise found in the White Monastery. A modern well in the southwest corner of the nave was perhaps modified from an older water source.[652] The modern version, however, measures just 1.2 m in diameter, allowing only a low discharge.

The construction of the church has been dated to the late fifth to mid-sixth-century,[653] but the structure bears witness to extensive change (fig. 74).[654] Warner has suggested that only the limestone doorways and the sanctuary were part of the original building.[655] The architectural design, which employed pointed arches in the fenestration in the exterior walls, indicates a late replacement of the original walls with the current fired brick version. These architectural features are, according to Warner, not attested in Egypt before the late eighth century and therefore

649 Pyke*, "Red Monastery."
650 Warner, "Architectural Survey."
651 Bolman, "Late Antique Aesthetics," 3.
652 Warner, "Architectural Survey," 57–58.
653 Severin suggests a construction date between 525 and 550 (Hans-Georg Severin, "On the Architectural Decoration and Dating of the Church of Dayr Anba Bishuy ("Red Monastery") near Suhag in Upper Egypt," *Dumbarton Oaks Papers* 62 (2008): 75–112), while Grossmann believes the church was built in the second half of the fifth century (Grossmann, *Christliche Architektur*, 536–539).
654 Warner, "Architectural Survey."
655 Warner, "Architectural Survey."

Fig. 73. Overview of Red Monastery church. View towards southeast (photograph by the author).

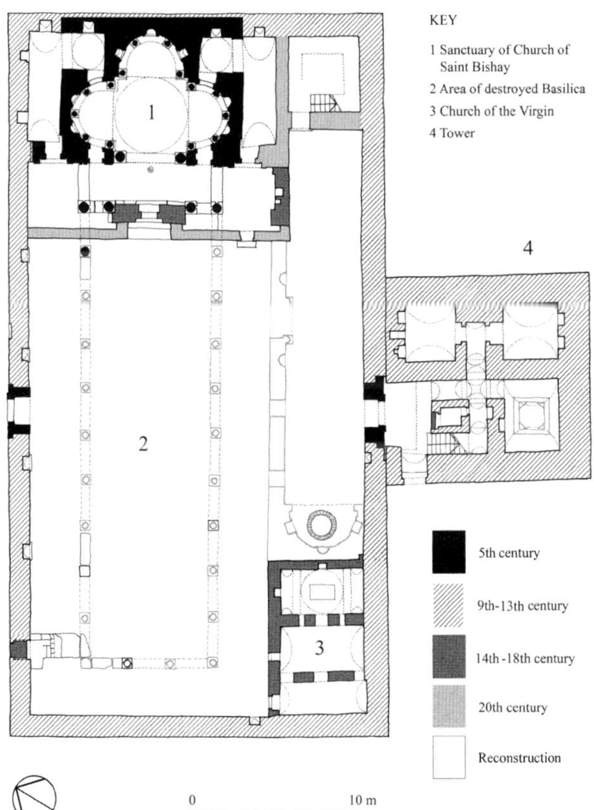

Fig. 74. Reconstructed plan of Red Monastery church with suggested dating (drawing by Nicholas Warner; Warner, "Architectural Survey," fig. 6.1; © ARCE).

provide a *terminus post quem* for the construction of the walls.[656] Furthermore, architectural similarities with the fired brick modifications in the White Monastery church have prompted Warner to suggest that the two brick phases were built contemporaneously, possibly following a major earthquake in the middle of the thirteenth century, which is attested in an inscription in the White Monastery church.[657]

A two-storey tower or keep abuts the south entrance to the church, but the architectural design as well as the choice of material together suggest that it was constructed around the same time as the church's brick walls.[658]

CHRONOLOGY

The poor preservation of the site and the limited range of material evidence mean that it is not possible to schematise the site's development, but some observations can be noted. It is evident from the archaeological remains that the Red Monastery underwent several phases of use, modification and disuse.

656 Warner, "Architectural Survey," 49–50.
657 Grossmann et al., "Monastery of Apa Shenute," 169; Warner and Meurice, "Strange Jumble."
658 Warner, "Architectural Survey," 54–55.

Examples of these are found in RM.1.2 and RM.1.3, where several layers of flooring are found consecutively on top of each other. Some of these layers are separated by new foundations of fired brick. Elsewhere on site, walls were cut or modified and the distribution of ceramic vessels in the northern part of RM.3 shows two distinct phases. One phase features the two rows of ceramic vessels, the other, later phase displays a more scattered pattern of ceramic installations, seemingly following a different architectural configuration from the original design.

The date of the ceramic sherds embedded in the mortar of the earliest phase of the structures in RM.1.2, RM.1.3 and RM.2.2 is consistent with the flourishing period of the formative years of the monastic federation. Importantly, they do not date to the time of Pshoi, the founder of the Red Monastery, but can, at the earliest, be ascribed to the time when Shenoute was the federation's leader. Therefore, the archaeological evidence would suggest that the Red Monastery underwent a transformation similar to that at the White Monastery, where the monastic built environment was enlarged and perhaps fundamentally altered. It can be assumed that this development was associated with rising economic prosperity in the wake of a growing community, which in turn required an increased number of monastic buildings.

The seventh-century date for the final decorative programme in the sanctuary of the church cannot be fitted precisely to the development of the archaeological site. The paintings, however, testify to a continuously prosperous community, which once again fits well with the development of the archaeological site of the White Monastery.

There is no dateable material that can be directly assigned to the mud brick walls or the Nile silt floor-foundation, but the stratigraphic relations seem to mirror the development at the White Monastery. At the White Monastery, structures built between the fifth and the seventh centuries were constructed from the more expensive fired brick and lime-based mortar with lime-based plaster floors, while later buildings employed less costly materials, such as Nile silt floor foundations and mud bricks. Similar to that at the White Monastery, the integrity of the layout of all areas was maintained until the point of abandonment, after which the Red Monastery was heavily pitted in search of fertiliser and re-useable building material.

The ceramic evidence suggests continuous activity on the site into the thirteenth century, which is mirrored by renewed activities in the church nave.[659] This visual programme roughly corresponds in date with the time of the refurbishing of the nave of the White Monastery church (Chapter 2.3).

5.1.2 Settlement, Economy and Daily Life

The textual sources do not provide any information about the layout of the Red Monastery, nor do we learn much about the organisation of the congregation's daily life. We know, however, that the monastic rules of the White Monastery, recorded by Shenoute, also applied to the Red Monastery. Emmel and Layton have extracted a few pieces of information from which we learn of both the hierarchy and the interdependency of the monastic communities.[660] We learn that Shenoute on his own initiative assigned new monks to both the White and the Red Monastery, that monks from the White Monastery would assist in manual labour at the Red Monastery and that both monasteries were represented at funerals of monks and nuns from the federation.[661]

According to Emmel and Layton, the Red Monastery was to some extent economically dependent on the White Monastery.[662] Shenoute, for example, regulated how many beasts of burden the northern monastery could own (one camel and three donkeys), while certain goods such as wine and vinegar were delivered to the congregation from the White Monastery.

INTERNAL ORGANISATION

The archaeological indicators for the size of the Red Monastery are scarce and somewhat speculative. The

659 Bolman, "Medieval Flourishing."
660 Emmel & Layton, "Pshoi."
661 Emmel & Layton, "Pshoi," 13.
662 Emmel & Layton, "Pshoi," 13.

Fig. 75. Suggested size of Red Monastery (map by the author).

physical remains are limited to the suggested portion of the boundary wall in RM.3.1, while a few other indicators suggest where the enclosure wall could have stood. The modern use of the monastery and the encroaching village mean that all physical remains of the west and south walls have disappeared. It is possible, however, to suggest an approximate location for the monastery's eastern extent. Similar to the White Monastery, the Red Monastery was limited towards the east by the annual inundation. It is, therefore, possible to suggest that the eastern extent of the Red Monastery would have been located at about the same height above sea level as the wall of the White Monastery (about 65.5 m). This height is reached some 50 m east of the Red Monastery church and would suggest a maximum extent of the monastery in this direction.

The plan produced by Clarke is another source of information, but overlaying Clarke's plan onto the survey map places his perimeter wall in the middle of the archaeological site. This problem could result from Clarke having observed a brick wall, which has now entirely disappeared from the monastic landscape, but more likely, Clarke did not note the correct scale on his map. Assuming, however, that the relative distance between the church and the outer wall is correct, it is possible to adjust Clarke's map to align it with the northern boundary wall. This would mean the size of the monastery was about 280 m NS × 170 m EW (fig. 75) or 47,600 m^2, of which the church occupied about 2%. It is possible that the Red Monastery church was placed at the edge of the settlement to allow the building to be seen from afar—as in the White Monastery. In that case, the total size of the monastery could have been about 42,000 m^2.

The sporadic preservation of the archaeological material means that it is not possible to discuss the location of thoroughfares, alleys or even access points to buildings. Several features, however, provide some indication of the layout of the monastic space. Firstly, the spread of Nile silt sub-floor deposits in all excavated areas suggests a densely built environment, as do the sporadic wall sections found especially in RM.3.2. By extending the existing wall lines and marking the location of walls along the lines of the edges of floor deposits, it is possible to reconstruct fourteen rooms. The northern end of RM.3.2 is flanked by at least four smaller rooms (pl. 10, a–d), which could have been used for storage, the eastern end contains at least five rooms (pl. 10, h–l).

One of these rooms (j) contains a cistern. The central and southern part appears to consist of larger rooms (f, g, m, n), while (e) could be a corridor separating RM.3.1 from RM.3.2. The storage units, cistern and three ovens in RM.3.2 resemble the functions found in the kitchen at the White Monastery (WM.4.2).

The location of pipelines might be another indicator of access routes, indoor and outdoor spaces. Pipelines would commonly be located between buildings, below streets, alleys or elsewhere where easy access could be gained for repairs.[663] This was demonstrated to be the case at the White Monastery (see Chapter 4.1.2) and also fits well with the layout of the Red Monastery. The pipelines in RM.2.2 and RM.2.3 circumvent the structure in RM.2, suggesting that it was partly freestanding rather than attached to adjoining rooms or structures. Similarly, numerous pipelines (at least eleven) in RM.1.1 suggest that the area to the east of the well was not enclosed within a building, but open and exclusively dedicated to the manipulation of the water supply. A pipeline runs along the north side of RM.1.3, which could indicate either a continuation of the open area, or a thoroughfare that ran along the north side of RM.1.3.

In general, RM.1–RM.3 feature architectural remains that can be associated with food production and water supply. Pipelines and other water-related features are found in RM.1 and RM.2, while features associated with food storage or production are found in all three areas. Most of these have already been mentioned above, but it is worth emphasising the structures in RM.2.2. The impressions of 15 small squares that are not set far apart (0.7 m) seem too small to have been stools or desks. Their spread resembles the ceramic *pilae* found in a hypocaust or the wooden posts sometimes found in Roman granaries in northern Europe, where they were used to support a raised floor.[664] This construction type was intended to protect the stored grain from damp and overheating. Although the Egyptian climate is warmer and dryer than its Northern European counterpart, this room may nevertheless have been used for storage of materials raised from the ground. At the White Monastery, deep rectangular pits flanked the storage rooms (WM 4.1.18 & WM.4.4.22) and possibly served to keep out vermin. Such features have not been preserved in the archaeological remains of the Red Monastery and the raised floor could, therefore, be an alternative solution to keep the rodents at bay.

THE WATER SUPPLY

The primary water supply for the Red Monastery was the well in RM.1.1. This well is circular in shape and measures 5.5 m in diameter. It is constructed from fired bricks and is equipped with decorative niches similar to those found within the sanctuary of the Red Monastery church (fig. 76). The well appears to have been constructed using a well-sinking technique. The architectural organisation shows that water was lifted by a pot garland attached to a single *saqiya* gear drive through a central opening lined with two transverse arches. The water was lifted into a channel from where it was distributed via gravity-fed ceramic pipes towards north, south and east. A different system was used here compared to the White Monastery. Sluice gates between areas of vats located immediately east of the well were used to control the water flow and perhaps also to build water pressure to flush the pipes (fig. 77). At the same time, the vats worked as sedimentation tanks to remove impurities from the water before it was distributed to different parts of the monastery. No distribution tanks and only one inspection tank have been identified and just two small cisterns were found on site (in RM.2.3 and in RM.3.2, room j). Both cisterns were filled with modern debris to a point where it was not possible to calculate their capacity. Nothing remains of the monastery's drainage system.

The distance from the ground level to the water table was about the same as at the White Monastery, which means that a single *saqiya* gear drive with an attached bucket chain could lift about 6 m^3 per hour. The cisterns identified in the archaeology could only hold small quantities of water and it is therefore very likely that further water containers were scattered through the monastery and specifically associated

663 Jansen, "Water Transport," 108.

664 Geoffrey Rickman, *Roman Granaries and Store Buildings* (Cambridge: Cambridge University Press, 1971), 232.

Fig. 76. RM.1.1. Red Monastery well. Note internal niche and remains of transverse arches. View towards west (photograph by the author).

Fig. 77. RM.1.1. Sluice gate separating two tanks immediately east of the well. Note impression of pipeline feeding the tank in foreground. View towards east (photograph by the author).

with activity areas. As such, a system comprising several small cisterns according to a localised water management plan would be expected. It is not possible to link the well inside the church to the early history of the site and there are no remains of pipelines leading from the church, as is the case at the White Monastery. The size of the well (1.2 m diameter) suggests that it was built as a source for smaller households and their livestock and not to supply a larger congregation.

PRODUCTION AND CONSUMPTION

The archaeological remains contain features associated with production of oil, flour and bread, but there are no indications that craft production took place in this part of the site. The architectural features associated with food production consist of the two crushing basins, located just south of RM.1 (fig. 69), three ovens located in RM.3.2 and the upper part of a millstone from a grain mill found leaning against the west wall of the nave in the church. Of these features, only the ovens are *in situ*. It is, therefore, not possible to suggest in which part of the monastery the milling and crushing took place, but given the organisation of the exposed part of the site, it seems likely that these processes could have taken place near the proposed kitchen area (RM.3.2).

Flour can be produced on a small scale by using a hand mill, which consists of two stones set on top of each other. The lower stone has a central wooden pivot on which the upper stone rotates. Grain is fed through a central hole in the upper stone and a wooden handle is used to grind the flour. The flour spills from the sides of the hand mill into a collection bowl. Larger mills work on the same principle, the grain being fed through a hopper and a draught animal being used to turn two horizontal cog-wheels that rotate the lower millstone. Given the scale of production at the Red Monastery, it is more likely that flour was produced exclusively in a larger mill. The ovens belong to a later phase of use of RM.3.2 and were not a part of the original layout of the kitchens. Their presence, along with the millstone in the church, shows that the Red Monastery's assumed dependency on the White Monastery for bread did not last into the later phases of the use of the site.

The archaeological evidence for use of material culture at the Red Monastery is limited to two types, namely ceramic sherds and building materials. Both can provide evidence for the longevity of the monastic settlement and its use, while the changing choice of building materials yields information on the settlement's economic vitality.

The ceramic material is somewhat limited and its content has already been summarised above. The general lack of fine wares is worth noting. This situation could have resulted from the nature of the excavated area, but could also suggest that these types of ceramic vessels were less commonly used in the monastery, perhaps suggesting a more modest household or a poorer settlement compared to the White Monastery. While the latter would have been the recipient of gifts from patrons and visitors, it is possible that the Red Monastery did not receive the same type of economic attention.

The building materials used on site include fired bricks, mud bricks, lime-based mortars and plasters, mud-based mortars, limestone and paint. Finally, grey granite was used for the two crushing basins found just south of RM.1 and the millstone located within the church nave. If one considers the consumption of materials as an index of the monastery's economic vitality, some trends and developments become apparent. During the early use of the monastery (the fifth to the seventh/eighth centuries), the monastery's buildings consisted of fired bricks and lime-based mortar walls with plaster floors. These materials are found in RM.1.1–3, RM.2.3 and RM.3.2 (fig. 78). The construction of the church towards the end of the fifth century included a sanctuary and doorways of dressed limestone. From the fifth to the eighth century, the sanctuary saw four full programmes of decoration, which would suggest a period defined by economic prosperity and perhaps also benefaction from the local community. The source of the limestone is unknown. The stone could either have been retrieved from another building and re-dressed or quarried from the mountains, but at the Red Monastery, the distance from the site to the quarries in the cliff face is much greater (3–5 km) than at the White Monastery.

The following centuries saw an increase in the use of less expensive materials and it appears as though mud bricks and mud-based mortars became the most used material for construction activities in the monastery (seen in RM.2.1, RM.2.3 and RM.3.1–2).

After a devastating event—presumably the earthquake in the thirteenth century—the outer walls of the main church were completely rebuilt with fired bricks and lime-based mortar.[665] The construction work would have required a substantial investment in materials as well as in skilled labour. In Warner's words 'building a brick wall more than a meter (three feet) thick at its base and eleven metres (thirty-six feet) high with an external taper and a vertical inner face is not an operation to be entrusted to any but the most skilled of masons.'[666] Such investment in the Red Monastery church shows not only that it was still in use in the thirteenth century, but also that it was considered important to the local Christian community. The ceramic evidence shows that some activity took place on site during this time, but it is not possible to draw conclusions on the nature of this activity.

665 Warner, "Architectural Survey," 77.
666 Warner, "Architectural Survey," 53.

Fig. 78. Overview of Red Monastery archaeological site, emphasis on suggested oldest buildings on site (map by the author).

5.1.3 Synthesis

The archaeological evidence from the Red Monastery is scarce, sporadic and not easily combined to form a coherent synthesis. It has been established above that the archaeological remains comprise architectural elements associated with the supply and distribution of water and with food production and storage. The use of the area to the north of the church seems to have been consistent until it was abandoned (possibly before the thirteenth century). Several factors demonstrate that this was a much smaller monastic community than the White Monastery. The indicators are the size of the church (945 m^2), the proposed enclosure (42,000–47,600 m^2) and the simpler and more easily manageable water supply system. Therefore, the analysis of the archaeological remains is consistent with Shenoute's reference to the 'little congregation to the north.'[667]

A water system that is slightly different from the one at the White Monastery is found immediately to the east of the well, in which sluice gates between areas of tanks were used to control the water flow (fig. 77). This situation could result from better preservation in this part of the Red Monastery compared to the White Monastery, but could also be a response to specific local conditions. This system offers the same amount of control as that found at the White Monastery, but was managed immediately next to the well rather than through a series of distribution boxes spread out further in the monastic site. It seems unlikely that the water supply to the entire Red Monastery was controlled immediately adjacent to the well, but the organisation does suggest a simpler system, adjusted to the specific needs of the monastic community and perhaps managed more centrally.

The archaeological remains suggest that the Red Monastery, throughout its history, had fewer resources than its southern counterpart. It is worth questioning the economic relationship between the two communities and also whether the monastic federation, which was begun under Shenoute's leadership, continued throughout Late Antiquity and into the Islamic period. Unfortunately, this is impossible to answer from the archaeological and textual sources that are currently available. The veneration of Shenoute, Besa and Pshoi in the final phase of the decoration programme in the sanctuary of the Red Monastery would suggest that in the eighth century, the community still associated itself with the Shenoutean monastic tradition.[668] Furthermore, the stylistic similarities of the brick-work (dating to the thirteenth century) would suggest a central organization of the construction work and perhaps also of its funding. At the White Monastery, this construction phase can perhaps be associated with the Armenian presence (see Chapter 2.3), but no such records exist for the Red Monastery.

In terms of economic dependency, the writings of Shenoute suggest a division of labour where, for example, bread was baked at the White Monastery and distributed to the Red Monastery and to Atripe. Flax was woven into linen and dyed at Atripe and there is textual evidence for the manufacture of woollen clothing here, and at both the Red and the White Monasteries the monks produced rope and baskets.[669] As such, the craft production at the three monasteries may have been specialised and complementary. It is not clear if each monastery was responsible for producing its own revenue (and keeping its own budget) or whether this was centrally organised at the White Monastery. Layton deduced from Shenoute's writings that a prospective monk would meet the leader of the congregation at the White Monastery's gatehouse; after a trial period he would officially transfer his possessions in writing to the monastery's *diakonia* and not until this point was he assigned to either the Red or White Monastery.[670] This would suggest that only the White Monastery contained a *diakonia*—the monastic administration that in the fifth century apparently had control of all three monasteries.

It is not clear whether the Red Monastery participated in the pilgrimage industry, which seems to have been important for the White Monastery's economy, at least from the seventh or eighth century

667 Dilley, "Dipinti," 111.
668 Dilley, "Dipinti," 111.
669 Layton, "Rules," 56–57.
670 Layton, "Rules," 60.

onwards. There are no hymns, liturgical calendars or rites pertinent to the Red Monastery, but the size of the church (945 m^2) suggests that it could have been used by a wider congregation.[671] Emmel and Layton mention a reference to a controversy concerning lay participation in the monastic Eucharist service, suggesting that this was indeed the case during the first centuries of the monastery's history.[672] The *Synaxarion* records that when Pshoi died, Shenoute oversaw his funeral and placed the corpse in the Red Monastery. Finally, this association with the saint could suggest that the Red Monastery took part in the 'monasticization of the cult of the saints' described by Papaconstantinou,[673] although there are no remains in the archaeological record that can be associated with pilgrimage.

On a final note, the keep that was constructed at the same time as the new church enclosure wall could suggest a continuous use of the church and perhaps also the monastery into the thirteenth century. As stated already, no keep has been found at the White Monastery, although the church itself may have served such purpose.

5.2 A MONASTERY IN THE VILLAGE OF ATRIPE

The archaeological site of Atripe is located three km south of the White Monastery on the fringe of the desert between the cultivated land and the mountains. Here is to be found the remains of the third monastic congregation in Shenoute's federation—a convent for female monastics. The convent was founded in an existing settlement, which dates from the later part of the Ptolemaic period (around 150 BCE).[674] The town was a cult centre for the Egyptian goddess Repyt and at least two temples were dedicated to her worship. One of these—commonly referred to as the temple of Ptolemy XII—served as the centre of the monastic complex.[675]

Our knowledge of the convent comes from texts found in the White Monastery library and from archaeological exploration, but these sources are so scarce that for most part, the history of the site is unknown. The written sources include the rules extracted from Shenoute's canons by Layton and fragments of letters that are attributed to Shenoute and Besa. In thirteen letters, Shenoute addresses the women of the convent. Some were intended for the entire congregation, while others were directed at named individuals.[676] Their content provides detailed insights into specific aspects of monastic life, but is not informative on the general organisation of the congregation. Instead, the letters address situations of insubordination or transgression, such as theft of food and sexual misconduct,[677] and deal with complaints of inedible food or uneven distribution by the refectory workers.[678] We also learn of certain services carried out by members of the White Monastery for the nuns. Accordingly, the White Monastery provided certain types of food, builders for construction work, spiritual education, a messenger service, a funeral service and twenty-four-hour guarding of the gate to the convent.[679] The letters were perceived as a part of the church father's teachings and thus copied through the centuries, but none of the women's letters were preserved.[680]

After the fifth century, only few written sources can be associated with the convent. Rafed El-Sayed suggests that it was still in use towards the end of the eighth century, but evidence from later periods is negligible.[681] This is in part because most Arab au-

671 Warner, "Architectural Survey," 49.
672 Emmel & Layton, "Pshoi."
673 Papaconstantinou, "Cult," 358.
674 El-Sayed, El-Masry and Altmann, *Athribis*, 10, 212–214.
675 El-Sayed, El-Masry and Altmann, *Athribis*, 10.
676 These letters have been analysed and published by Krawiec: Rebecca Krawiec, "Space, Distance and Gender: Authority and the Separation of Communities in the White Monastery," *Bulletin of the American Society of Papyrologists* 35 (1998): 45–63; Krawiec, "Shenoute & Women;" Krawiec, "Female Elder."
677 Layton, "Rules," 72.
678 Krawiec, "Shenoute & Women," 31–50.
679 Layton, *Canons*, 22.
680 Krawiec, "Shenoute & Women," 5; Kuhn, "Monastic life."
681 El-Sayed, El-Masry and Altmann, *Athribis*, 29. See Timm for an overview of the written sources (Timm, *Das Christlich-Koptische Ägypten*, 601–634).

thors and European travellers focussed on Akhmim and the White Monastery.[682]

Four archaeological missions have explored the site. The first was led by Petrie in 1906/07 and it was during this project that Petrie engaged Ward at the White Monastery.[683] In the process of excavating the temple of Ptolemy XII, Petrie uncovered parts of a church, located in the converted pronaos and a dye-shop within one of the rooms of the temple.

The second archaeological mission was carried out by the Sohag department of the SCA over fourteen seasons between 1981 and 1998.[684] The project's main objective was to continue the examination of the Pharaonic structures, but later remains located nearby the main temple were also uncovered and mapped.[685] These included the monastic church, which was fully excavated, as well as a refectory located east of the temple and a manufacturing area to the north of the temple.[686]

The third archaeological mission is the on-going collaboration between Tübingen University and the Sohag department of the SCA, which was initiated in 2003. This project continues to focus on the Pharaonic structures, but has included an examination of the Late Antique and Early Medieval remains.[687] In 2016, Yale University joined Tübingen in a collaborative effort to record the full history of the site, with Yale focusing on the Late Antique remains.[688] So far, the project has comprised excavation, digital recording of standing structures and epigraphic analysis. The discussions below are based on the published results from these four projects. All interpretations of the material, however, are my own.

682 El-Sayed, El-Masry and Altmann, *Athribis*, 36.
683 Petrie, *Athribis*.
684 Published in El-Farag, Kaplony-Heckel and Kuhlmann, "Athribis;" El-Masry, "Athribis."
685 El-Masry, "Athribis," 207.
686 El-Masry, "Athribis."
687 So far, the archaeological examinations have been published in El-Sayed, El-Masry and Altmann, *Athribis*.
688 Stephen J. Davis and Gillian Pyke*, "Preliminary Report on the Yale Monastic Archaeology Project Excavations at Atripe, Sohag. February-March 2016" (Athribis interim report, 2016).
689 El-Sayed, El-Masry and Altmann, *Athribis*, 92.

5.2.1 The Archaeological Remains

The archaeological site of Atripe covers 160,000 m^2 (only a small percentage has been excavated), but the original extent was larger as cultivation and modern housing have taken over the eastern perimeter.[689] The site consists of three main areas: a temple precinct, which occupies the northwest quarter of the site; a town area to the east of the temple; and a necropolis of rock-cut tombs located in the cliff face to the west of the temple (pl. 11).[690] The monastery represents the fourth phase in the long history of the site and was, according to the excavators, in use from the beginning of the fourth century, continuing at least into the seventh century. It was presumably abandoned between the tenth and the thirteenth century.[691] Although the date of the current spatial configuration of the archaeological remains is uncertain, the stratigraphic evidence suggests that the structures maintained their architectural integrity throughout their usage and that repairs and modifications did not fundamentally alter the existing plan. Based on the published reports and plans, I have divided the remains of the monastery into eight areas (AT.1–AT.8) (fig. 79 & table 7). In brief, they consist of:

- a group of buildings to the north of the temple of Ptolemy XII. The most prominent are a dye-shop and a well (AT.1). Size: 50 m NS × 20 m EW;
- a pillared hall with twelve bays (AT.2). Size: 13 m NS × 10 m EW;
- a structure with a central hallway, an entrance in the south wall and five rooms on both sides of the central hallway (AT.3). Size: 30 m NS × 15 m EW;
- a row of four consecutive rooms that once were a part of a larger structure (AT.4). Size: 12 m NW × 20 m EW;
- a refectory with circular seating arrangements (AT.5). Size: 50 m NS × 10 m EW;

690 Although the necropolis is of Pharaonic date, evidence of Late Antique use is found through an undated wall painting depicting St. Thecla, among other (See Davis, *Saint Thecla*, 173).
691 El-Sayed, El-Masry and Altmann, *Athribis*, 212–215.

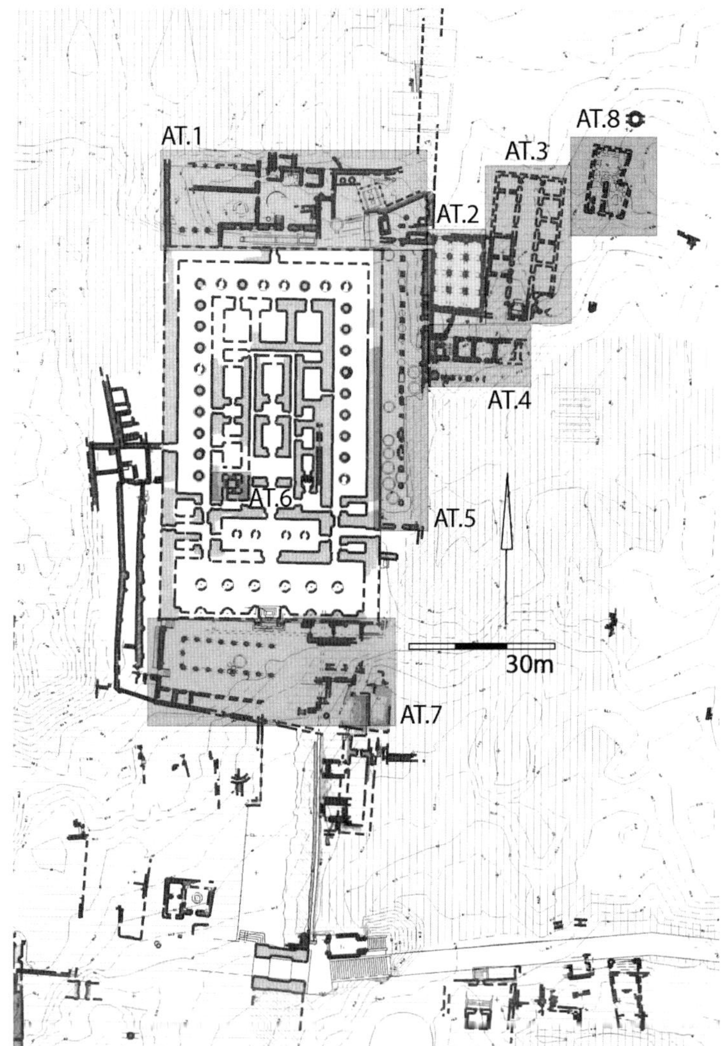

Fig. 79. Map detail of convent with eight area divisions (AT.1-8) (modified from El-Sayed & El-Masry, Athribis, plate IV. Reproduced with permission by Christian Leitz and Universität Tübingen).

- a dye-shop located inside the remains of the temple (AT.6) Size: 5 m NS × 5 m EW;
- a church in the temple's pronaos (AT.7) Size: 20 m NS × 40 m EW;
- a dye-shop (AT.8). Size: 12 m NS × 8 m EW.

These remains are described in the reports published by W.M.F. Petrie, Rifaat El-Farag, Rafed El-Sayed and Yahia El-Masry and their descriptions will not be repeated here.[692] Instead, the remains are discussed thematically below.

5.2.2 *Settlement, Economy and Daily Life*

It is not possible to reconstruct the physical layout of the convent based on the letters of Shenoute and Besa, but presumably the congregation contained all the necessary buildings to function as an independent *coenobitic* monastery.[693] A few tidbits of circumstantial references, however, alert us to the presence of specific buildings. We learn that the convent was located in a village, that it had a gatehouse where initiates lived and where male monastics were stationed as guards and that these men received their daily meals from the White Monastery to protect the women's privacy.[694] The women ate communally in a refectory and lived in houses under the leadership of a senior nun. Food was kept in a storeroom.[695] Although scarce, this information is important for the discussion that follows.

INTERNAL ORGANISATION

It is not possible to determine the size of the convent, as remains of neither the external wall nor the gatehouse have been found. Shenoute referred to the convent as located within the village of Atripe,[696] which means that the size of the archaeological site (160.000 m^2) does not inform us about the monastery's physical extent, but only on the extent of the village. There are, however, other factors that can be used to suggest the convent's maximum capacity. The most important factor is the size of the refectory (AT.5), which, unlike the facility in the White Monastery, contains remains of seating.

692 El-Farag, Kaplony-Heckel and Kuhlmann, "Athribis;" El-Masry, "Athribis;" Petrie, *Athribis*; El-Sayed, El-Masry and Altmann, *Athribis*.
693 El-Sayed, El-Masry and Altmann, *Athribis*, 27.
694 Krawiec, "Shenoute & Women," 43; Kuhn, "Monastic Life," 179; Layton, "Social Structure," 34.
695 Krawiec, "Shenoute & Women," 35–36, 47.
696 El-Sayed, El-Masry and Altmann, *Athribis*, 25.

Site Code	Area	Description
AT	1	Area located immediately north of the temple of Ptolemy XII. The Area contains the architectural remains of several structures, hereunder a tannery and a well. Size: 50 m NS × 20 m EW.
AT	2	A building with twelve square bays, divided between three aisles. Size: 13 m NS × 10 m EW.
AT	3	A building that consists of a central hallway with five rooms on either side. A staircase leads to an upper floor. The building was entered from the south. Size: 30 m NS × 15 m EW.
AT	4	A row of four consecutive rooms that once were part of a larger structure. Size: 12 m NW × 20 m EW.
AT	5	A refectory located immediately east of the temple. It contains the remains of ten circular benches. Size: 50 m NS × 10 m EW.
AT	6	A tannery located inside the remains of the temple. Size: 5 m NS × 5 m EW.
AT	7	The remains of a church located in the temple's pronaos. Size: 20 m NS × 40 m EW.
AT	8	A tannery marking the northeast extent of the excavation of the monastic complex. Size 12 m NS × 8 m EW.

Table 7. Areas at Atripe.

From Shenoute's writing we know that all female monastics would share a meal once per day in the refectory.[697] Assuming that the convent contained only one refectory and that this refectory was spacious enough to seat all nuns, it is possible to suggest a maximum capacity for the monastery. The refectory is about 50 m long and almost 10 m wide. Several pillars are evenly spread through the centre of the room, suggesting that it was once roofed and, according to El-Sayed and El-Masry, covered by vaulting.[698] The refectory contains the remains of 10 circular benches, found in both the north and south end of the room as well as in both aisles (fig. 80). The distribution of the benches suggests that they once filled the entire room. Assuming that they were of equal size and distribution, the room could have contained a maximum of 35–40 benches. The internal diameter of each bench is 2.8 m, which means that the internal rim of each bench is 8.8 m (diameter × π). Several benches, however, do not form complete circles and therefore the internal rim is averaged at 7.6 m. The width of a modern chair is about 0.50 m, but allowing slightly more distance between the monastics, I have allocated 0.95 m per person (allowing 45 cm between each monastic). This distance corresponds with a Pachomian rule that dictates that monastics at all times should keep a distance of one cubit—the distance between the elbow and the tip of the middle finger, or about 45 cm.[699] According to these calculations, the total number of people that could be seated in the refectory would be 280 with 35 benches and 320 with 40 benches.

According to the Arabic *Life of Shenoute* the convent housed as many as 1800 female monastics during Shenoute's rule. However, the spatial layout of the complex could never have housed such large numbers of inhabitants. As for the refectory, the size of the room would have to be multiplied by six to accommodate a population of this size. This seems most unlikely and, as noted in Chapter 4, one must conclude that the numbers provided by the Arabic *Life* should be considered as a rhetorical exaggeration.

On a final note, it is interesting to compare the size of the convent's refectory with the structure interpreted for the same use in the White Monastery (WM.4.1.16). Here, the remains of the structure take

697 Bentley Layton, "The Monastic Rules of Shenoute," in *Monastic Estates in Late Antique and Early Islamic Egypt. Ostraca, Papyri, and Essays in Memory of Sarah Clackson*, ed. Anne Boud'hors, James Clackson, Catherine Louis, and Petra M. Sijpesteijn (Cincinnati, Ohio: The American Society of Papyrologists, 2009), 171. See also Krawiec, "Shenoute & Women," 35–36.

698 El-Sayed, El-Masry, Altmann, *Athribis*, 108.

699 Layton, "Monastic Rules," 172; Louis T. Lefort, *Œuvres de S. Pachome et de ses Disciples* (Louvain: Imprimerie Orientaliste, 1956), 31.

Fig. 80. AT.5. Preserved circular benches in refectory. View towards north (photograph by Gillian Pyke; © YMAP).

up some 40 m NS × 20 m EW, or 800 m^2. Following the suggested people-to-space ratio at Atripe (500 m^2/ 320 persons = 1.56 m^2 per person), the available space at the White Monastery would allow c. 510 monastics to be seated at the same time. From Shenoute's writings we know, however, that sick and elderly monks were fed in separate refectories, which suggests that the total population of the White Monastery could have been as many as 600 monastics. Although no remains of the seating arrangements have been found in the refectory of the White Monastery, the maximum people-to-space ratio would be approximately the same regardless of the type of benches used.

By comparison, Wipszycka suggested based on the *Epistula Ammonis* that each of the Pachomian monasteries housed 200–300 monastics, except for the leading partner of the federation in Pbow, which held twice that number.[700] The refectory in the tenth-century Deir Anba Hadra is preserved with eight circular benches similar to those found at Atripe, although smaller in size and set further apart. The layout of the refectory at Deir Anba Hadra suggests that another two benches would have been present. An average internal diameter of 1.8 m of each bench means that 81 monastics could have been seated there if each person was allocated 0.90 m. However, the nineteen preserved shared cells with room for six or seven in each cell suggest that the monastery's maximum capacity was closer to 120 monastics and it is not unlikely that meals were taken in shifts. As such, it is important to keep

700 Ewa Wipszycka, *Moines et Communautés Monastiques en Égypte*. The Journal of Juristic Papyrology, Supplement XI (Warsaw: The Raphael Taubenschlag Foundation, 2009), 419–421.

in mind that monastics living in monasteries outside the White Monastery federation would have kept to different sets of rules and did not necessarily share a meal at a fixed daily time, as was customary according to Shenoute.

The excavated part of the Atripe convent takes up about 6,200 m², but it is important to emphasise that no enclosure wall has been found and there are as-yet-unexcavated areas. This area includes the temple of Ptolemy XII, although the focus of past excavators on the Pharaonic remains means that only few structures that can be associated with the convent have been identified (AT.6).[701] No thoroughfares or other remains indicate how one could move from one part of the monastery to another. It is very likely that movement was dictated by the layout of the reused temple and its adjacent facilities. The organisation of the monastic structures was not only facilitated but also restricted by the temple. According to the excavators, the temple itself was reused for activities associated with household (kitchen facilities) and economic activities, as attested by installations for production that were built into the rooms and passageways.[702] Of these, only a single dye-shop (AT.6) is found in published plans and photos. A second dye-shop was located immediately to the north of the temple in AT.1 and both are discussed below.

The eastern part of the complex contains a structure that consisted of a long hall with rooms on either side (AT.3). Immediately to the west of this structure lies a twelve-bay pillared hall (AT.2). This building was partly excavated during Yale University's work in 2016–2018, but so far it has not been possible to establish how the building was used. El-Sayed and El-Masry suggested that AT.3 served as a dormitory, a hospital or a geriatric ward, but the building's form could also suggest that it was used for storage.[703] The organisation of AT.2 and AT.3 immediately adjacent to each other is significant. Although it is not possible to determine the use of this area, it is important to note that a very similar organisation was found in recent excavations of the Monastery of St Moses in Abydos, some 50 km to the south of Sohag (fig. 81). Here, a building of similar proportions and organisation has been interpreted as a dormitory. It is set immediately adjacent to a pillared hall, which appears to have served industrial purposes.[704] Similar spatial organisations are also found in the ninth-century monastery of Deir al-Fakhuri (Monastery of the Potter) near Esna and in a monastery at Ansina.[705] At Deir al-Fakhuri, at least ten rooms line a long hall, and a staircase in the northwest corner leads to a second storey. Each room is equipped with several niches and the four-pillared hall abutts the southeast wall. The two areas were built as a single integrated architectural unit. At Ansina, a long hall with just five rooms is lined by a pillared hall to the south.[706] At both sites the pillared hall has been interpreted as a refectory and the long hall with adjoining rooms as dormitories. Such interpretation is currently not supported by the results from Atripe.

THE WATER SUPPLY

The convent's main water source was a well that is located in AT.1. The well is preserved with the superstructure in place, which means that only a single transverse opening is visible on the surface. This organisation suggests that a *saqiya* gear drive was used to haul water from the well. The location of the well suggests that it was constructed as a part of the re-organisation of the temple for the use as a monastery. El-Sayed states that the level of the site is between 75 and 95 m above sea level, the latter presumably being the elevation of the necropolis in the cliffs.[707] At the White Monastery, the well is located 69.5 m above sea level and the water is lifted 13.5 m. This means that in Atripe, water must have been lifted 19 m to reach the surface. Repeating the calculations used to quantify the water supply at the

701 Petrie describes how the temple of Ptolemy XII was covered with about twenty feet of debris.

702 El-Sayed, El-Masry, Altmann, *Athribis*, 108, 215.

703 El-Sayed, El-Masry, Altmann, *Athribis*, 109.

704 The results from the excavation are still unpublished, but access to the site was provided by the project's director Ayman Mohammed Damarany in 2011.

705 Coquin and Maurice Martin, "Dayr al-Fakhuri."

706 Wipszycka, *Moines*, 151–155.

707 El-Sayed, El-Masry, Altmann, *Athribis*, 68.

Fig. 81. Overview of the Monastery of St Moses, Abydos. View towards west (reproduced with permission by Ayman Mohammed Damarany)

White Monastery, the discharge would be 1.2 litres per second, 72 litres per minute and 4,320 litres per hour (4.32 m^3). A total of 280 monastics would require 5,600 litres of water per day plus additional water for industries, which means that the *saqiya* would have been in use at least two hours per day. It is not possible to quantify the water needed for the industries, as their extent is not known, but it seems reasonable to suggest that the monastery would require a daily discharge of 9,000–11,000 litres. Such a quantity of water could be stored in one or more smaller cisterns, possibly near the area where it was needed, but so far no cisterns have been identified.

El-Sayed and El-Masry describe the area around the well as containing many water installations, but do not specify what these installations consist of or how they were internally connected.[708] Ceramic pipes are visible in published photos and it can be assumed that they were the main component in the water conduits. Facilities related to the transport of water or to its use were found in the dye-shops in AT.1 and AT.6, a room in the western part of AT.4. Water may also have been used in the refectory for drinking and for washing before meals. Therefore, it seems that most activities that would have required water were located in relative proximity to each other and to the well. Distribution and inspection boxes are not mentioned in the publications and neither are features associated with drainage.

708 El-Sayed, El-Masry, Altmann, *Athribis*, 110.

PRODUCTION AND CONSUMPTION

Several passages in Shenoute's letters refer to the manufacture of clothes by the women in the convent. From one such passage, we learn that Shenoute ordered a cloak from the convent with specifications on both colour and materials and in another passage he complained that the women would not allow him and other monks to enter the monastery to have their measurements taken—a situation that resulted in cloaks that did not fit.[709] He emphasised towards the end of this letter that the material interdependency between the monasteries for food and clothing were meant to unite them, not to bring them apart.[710]

The excavation of the monastery has yielded the remains of three dyeing workshops, which have been identified securely from their architectural properties. These include the presence of several consecutive vats. One is located in a room within the temple proper (AT.6; fig. 79), the second is found immediately north of the temple (AT.1) and the third is found in the far northeastern part of the monastic settlement (AT.8). Only the latter has been described in some detail in publications.[711]

The process of dyeing required the following: a sufficient water source and drainage system; adequate storage for both consumables (textiles or yarn, dyes, adhesives and materials used for cleansing) and finished items; vats for washing and dyeing the fabric; and ovens for heating the water.[712]

El-Sayed and El-Masry suggested that the entire complex to the north of the temple should be understood as associated with dyeing and described the structures as elaborate installations that included dyeing vats, washing basins and water heating tanks that were interconnected by a sophisticated system of water conduits.[713] Unfortunately, they do not provide any details of the number of basins or their size. Petrie described the third dye-shop (AT.8) in further detail.[714] From his description, the dye-shop was a freestanding building with two entrances in the south wall. The eastern door led to a room with a large well, a small cistern and a bench with three vats. The western room contained only a small basin and a staircase leading to an upper storey. From this room, one could access the inner room, which contained sixteen vats in a raised bench. These vats were, according to Petrie, deeply stained with colour—most with dark blue indigo, but some with a red colour.

The vats in AT.1 are organised in a long row, which was lined with ceramic vessels that were built into the architectural design. The tanks are rectangular and placed in a row, which means that they resemble sedimentation tanks rather than the dye-shop found in AT.8. The limited amount of published material means, however, that it is not possible to question the excavator's interpretation.

A plan of the third dye-shop, found in AT.6, was published by El-Masry.[715] According to the plan, it consists of two rooms, the south room containing five vats and a single ceramic installation. The north room contains two vats and six ceramic installations.

Although the excavations have provided ample evidence for fabric dyeing, no evidence for weaving has so far been found. In Late Antique Egypt, the most common loom for large-scale weaving was upright-standing and made from wood. In the archaeological record, looms are identified through the distinctive marks they leave on the architecture. Most often these marks consist of a loompit in the floor along with evenly distributed holes in walls and ceiling to hold the loom in place. Loompits were found in, for example, the Monastery of Epiphanius (7), in the North Tomb settlement at Amarna (7), in Gournet Murrai in Western Thebes (4), in Deir al-Bachit (4) and also in several Theban Tombs (TT29, TT89, TT95 and TT1152).[716]

709 Krawiec, "Shenoute & Women," 46.
710 Krawiec, "Shenoute & Women," 46.
711 El-Sayed, El-Masry, Altmann, *Athribis*, 110; Petrie, *Athribis*, 11.
712 Heather J. Hopkins, "Using Experimental Archaeology to Answer the Unanswerable: A Case Study Using Roman Dyeing," in *Experiments with Past Materials*, ed. George Children and Dragos Gheorghiu. BAR International Series 2302 (Oxford: BAR, 2011), 82.
713 El-Sayed, El-Masry, Altmann, *Athribis*, 110.
714 Petrie, *Athribis*, 11.
715 El-Masry, "Athribis," fig. 4.
716 Joanna Sigl, "Pits with Cross-Bars – Investigations on Loom Remains from Coptic Egypt," in *Studia Aegypti-*

Other types of production are testified by the remains of the lower part of a grain mill which was found near the church.[717] The lack of context means that it is not possible to determine whether this installation was a part of the monastic compound or whether it belonged to the later use of the area by the adjacent village. Excavations of the ancient village have revealed grain mills, bread ovens and a dovecote, but it is not possible to say whether these structures were contemporary with the convent or what relationship existed between the two settlements.[718]

There are no remains in the published archaeological record that suggest that olive oil was produced in the convent. Given the evidence for production in the White and Red Monasteries, it is possible that the production of oil was part of the interdependency that was mentioned in Shenoute's letter.

The range of building materials used in the convent is similar to that found at the White and Red Monasteries. Limestone was used for the construction of the church, fired bricks, lime-based mortars and plasters, ceramic vessels and pipes were found throughout the architectural remains and also mud bricks and mud-based mortars were in use. The internal chronology of the archaeology is not discussed in any of the published reports and it is therefore not possible to examine evidence of development or decline through the material used. Considering the development of the White and Red Monasteries, it is likely that expensive materials and craftsmanship were employed in the early history of the site, while less expensive materials were utilised towards its end.

After the abandonment of the convent, some of the buildings were converted for other uses. An oven was built in the church nave and the temple proper was used as a dumping ground for household waste from the adjacent village.[719] El-Sayed and El-Masry have suggested that the collapse of the temple could be associated with the earthquake in 1240, which damaged the two other congregations. The construction of the oven in the church suggests that at this time the convent had already been abandoned.[720]

5.2.3 *Synthesis*

The archaeological remains as well as the letters of Shenoute reveal an important exchange of goods between the three monastic congregations. While it is unclear what contribution was made by the Red Monastery, the convent in Atripe appears to have been the sole supplier of garments to the monastic federation. In turn, monks from the other congregations stood guard by the gates of the convent to protect the women from intruders, but also to regulate the women's contact with the outside world.

Only a few buildings that can be associated with the monastery are preserved in the archaeological record. These reveal a built environment that was organised around the settlement's core activities: prayer, meals and work, but the use of the space was restricted by existing structures, such as the temple. This could explain why the three dye-shops (AT.1, AT.6 and AT.8) were spread over the northern part of the settlement rather than gathered in one part of the site. An alternative explanation could be a chronological development in which the community gradually required more dye-shops, either because the demand of the three congregations increased or because the produce through sale to a larger market became integral to the convent economic foundation.

5.3 SUMMARY

The archaeological and textual evidence from the White Monastery federation suggests an internal economic dependency, where the production of goods as well as labour was shared between the

aca XVIII. Proceedings of the Fourth Central European Conference of Young Egyptologists, ed. Kata Endreffy and András Gulyás (Budapest: NKTH, 2007), 357–372; Joanna Sigl, "Weaving Copts in Amarna: Further Studies on Coptic Loompits in the Northern Tombs of Tell el-Amarna," *Studien zur Altägyptischen Kultur* 40 (2011): 357–386.

717 Gilian Pyke, personal communication with author, 2014.

718 El-Sayed, El-Masry, Altmann, *Athribis*, 115–120.

719 Petrie, *Athribis*, 5.

720 El-Sayed, El-Masry, Altmann, *Athribis*, 215.

three congregations. The written evidence suggests that the White Monastery took the lead in supplying the other monasteries with bread and labour as well as housing the main economic administration for the entire federation. At the same time the White Monastery received goods, e.g., in the form of textiles, from the convent in Atripe. The monasteries' later development shows continuous ties between the Red and the White Monastery, as indicated by the Red Monastery church's final visual programme and more directly through the similar building styles of the modifications made to both monastic churches in the thirteenth century. The archaeological remains of all three monasteries suggest a period of continuous economic stability into the Early Medieval period, after which the White Monastery in particular, but also the Red Monastery to some extent, went through a prolonged period of fluctuating economic prosperity and decline—trending toward the latter in later centuries. The fate of the convent in Atripe is more obscure, as the published archaeological material holds very little evidence that can suggest how this congregation developed beyond the seventh century.

The study of the refectory of Atripe is important as it demonstrates that the convent's architectural design supported a maximum of c. 320 nuns and more likely less than 300. A comparison with the size of the refectory in the White Monastery allows for an estimation of the population of the White Monastery—a topic for which the only source hitherto was the Arabic *Life of Shenoute*.[721] Sources that indicate the size of the population of the Red Monastery are few. Shenoute referred to it as the 'little congregation to the north,'[722] which means that it must have been somewhat smaller than the White Monastery. The archaeological evidence suggests that the Red Monastery in its heyday in the fifth to seventh century was slight less than half the size of the White Monastery and the church was just about one third of the equivalent in the bigger monastery. Somewhat speculatively, this might suggest that the Red Monastery's population also was about half the size—i.e., less than 300.

The physical remains provide data that can be used to estimate the number of inhabitants, but a nuanced picture considering gender and age cannot be reconstructed from the archaeological record as it currently exists. Rules concerning the elderly and children in the canons of Shenoute inform us that both groups were integral to the monastic demography, but evidence for their physical presence has yet to be recognised in the remains.[723] Yale University's examination of the inscriptions at the women's monastery is providing new evidence in these areas. The analysis is still in progress and the results will be published by Davis in due time. It is important to underline the potentially gendered production profile: oil was pressed and grain was milled in the male congregations, while fabric was produced and dyed by the women.

The economic foundations of the monasteries were agricultural in nature, but neither the textual nor archaeological sources hold much data that can inform us about the crops that were grown or other manufacturing processes. The evidence for olives (for oil produced in the White and Red Monasteries) and flax and wool (for textiles produced in the convent) suggests that these were produced not only for consumption, but perhaps also for further sale in a local market. The written evidence suggests that basketry was among the products made by the monks in the federation, but as Wipszycka has demonstrated, these goods were never a main source of income for any monastic community.[724] Lastly, the monastic *scriptorium*, mentioned only in written sources but documented through the immense quantity of manuscripts found at the White Monastery, was very likely another important source of income.[725]

721 Amélineau, *Monuments*, 331; Leipoldt, *Schenute*, 93–94.
722 Dilley, "Dipinti," 111.
723 Layton, *Canons*, 67.
724 Wipszycka, "Resources," 173.
725 Kotsifou, "Books and Book Production."

CONCLUSION

At its peak, the White Monastery federation was a hive of industry and a massive production machine, both densely populated and prosperous. It was a vibrant community engaged with extra-mural religious and non-religious communities through intellectual, spiritual and economic exchange. It was an important landowner and a powerhouse in the local economy. It was a spiritual beacon imbued with the presence of some of Christendom's most famous saints, and it was home to a number of ordinary and extraordinary men and women, who lived, worked, prayed and died within its walls. This book is an attempt to write its biography, to reconstruct its *longue durée*—from the fifth century until the present day—through archaeological and textual sources and to assess its place within the world of Late Antiquity. The main focus has been on the federation's heyday between the fifth and the eighth centuries.

Several thematic questions were raised at the beginning of this study and examined in the preceding chapters. These questions addressed the relationship between the archaeological and textual sources pertinent to the White Monastery, the development of the federation after Shenoute's death, economic interdependency within the federation and the federation's economic relationship with the extra-mural world. The following pages reiterate my main conclusions and suggest a few pathways for future research into Egypt's monastic past.

ARCHAEOLOGY AND TEXT

The archaeology and texts offer two complementary sources through which it becomes possible to reconstruct parts of the layout, use and development of the White Monastery federation. Each source offers information that cannot be obtained through a study of the other. The textual sources dealt with in this book are, in most cases, directly associated with the White Monastery and particularly with the monastery's third leader, Shenoute, who produced a large corpus of writing that offers a unique insight into monastic life in the fourth and fifth centuries. Another textual source is the *Life of Shenoute*, a hagiographic text that was compiled and amended throughout Late Antiquity and the Medieval period. Although the *Life* served to promote Shenoute as a saint rather than provide 'accurate' information about the White Monastery, it contains circumstantial evidence associated with the economy and the built environment of the highest importance. Information obtained through papyri, inscriptions, ostraca and typika has also been included.

Each of these sources has provided valuable data for my analysis of the White Monastery. Such information includes references in Shenoute's writings, which Layton has usefully extracted. Layton compiled a list of buildings within the monastery mentioned by Shenoute, a list of jobs that the monastics performed and a list of food that the monastics consumed; he also identified personal hierarchies within the organisation of the monastery and accounted for the organisation of the monastics' daily routines. The *Life of Shenoute* contains many miraculous stories relating to the production of bread. From this source, as well as from Shenoute's writings, we learn that wheat was not grown on the monastic landholdings, but was bought as grain and milled at the White Monastery, after which it was made into bread. Other stories mention vegetable gardens within the monastery's walls and orchards and fields on nearby monastic landholdings. From the textual evidence we also learn that at some point, perhaps as early as the fifth or sixth century, the White Monastery became a pilgrimage site.

Later sources, such as the *History of the Patriarchs of Alexandria* and reports in Arabic by travellers and historians including Abu al-Makarim, Yaqut and al-Maqrizi, provide us with tidbits of information about the monastery's development into the fifteenth century. This information is often brief and uncontextualised, but is nonetheless useful in reconstructing the monastery's development.

My examination of the archaeological remains of the White Monastery federation means that some information gained from textual sources has been re-evaluated and rejected. Such rejections are particularly relevant in relation to the hagiographical texts that provide unrealistic numbers of monastics who were supposed to be living in the three monasteries. The Arabic version of the *Life* claims that towards the end of Shenoute's leadership, the White Monastery federation contained no less than 2200 monks and 1800 nuns. This number has been questioned by several earlier scholars, but a careful study of the archaeological remains has enabled me to suggest an alternative.

Since the White Monastery was the larger of the two male congregations, I based my calculations on the hypothesis that two-thirds of the monks mentioned in the Arabic *Life* (in other words, 1450 out of 2200) would have been located here. My examination of the water supply at the White Monastery suggests that the wells would not have provided enough water to maintain such large numbers along with industries and garden plots (Chapter 4.1.2). There are several uncertainties connected with the quantification of the water supply. Most importantly, it is unclear if the two wells were both in use at the time of Shenoute: I have speculated that the well inside the church may have been a later addition to the monastery. Additionally, I have assumed a water recovery rate of almost 50 litres per min. It is possible that this rate could have been lower and it would certainly have fluctuated with the inundation of the Nile. For these reasons, I do not see it as feasible that the White Monastery's water supply could have supported 1450 monks.

An important finding from the excavations of the convent in Atripe is a refectory with ten circular benches preserved *in situ*. The distribution of benches in a rectangular room that measures 50 × 10 m suggests that the entire room was at one point used as a refectory. The size of the benches suggests that the room once contained 35–40 such benches. In Chapter 5.2.2, I calculated the total capacity of the refectory to have been between 280 and 320 monastics. Following Shenoute's rules, elderly and sick monastics would take their meals elsewhere, but I have assumed that under some circumstances the refectory would have housed the entire monastic population. This means that the seating arrangements provide a number for the maximum capacity of monastics based at the convent in Atripe.

Comparing the refectory in Atripe with the size of the building that has been identified as the refectory at the White Monastery would imply a maximum capacity of c. 500 to 600 monks for the latter complex (see calculations in Chapter 5.2.2). According to this calculation, the maximum number of monastics would be about half of that stated in the Arabic *Life of Shenoute*. However, 500 to 600 monks is still a high number compared to other monasteries. A papyrus reports that 600 monks were based at the Pachomian monastery in Pbow in the fourth century, while Wipszycka's calculations suggest that the remaining Pachomian monasteries each housed 200 to 300 monastics. In comparison, the monastery of Naqlun housed some 120 monks and 200 servants, while Deir Anba Hadra in Aswan could have housed up to 120 monastics.[726] Comparing the physical size

726 Wipszycka, *Moines*, 419.

of the White Monastery (c. 77.500 m^2) to other Egyptian monasteries suggests that it was among the largest known walled monastic communities in Late Antique Egypt, surpassed only by Bawit (c. 366.000 m^2).

It is not only the *Life* that produced information that should be reconsidered in the light of the archaeological remains. Shenoute's writings also provide some questionable claims. One such claim is that bread was produced only once per year at the White Monastery and then delivered to the two other congregations. This claim has been challenged in Chapter 4.2.2. If the White Monastery contained between 500 and 600 monks and each monk consumed two loaves of bread every day, the monastery would require between 365,000 and 438,000 loaves of bread every year. It would take ten ovens sixteen days to bake 438,000 loaves if they worked 24 hours per day. This calculation does not include the bread that would have been provided to the Red Monastery and Atripe. Additionally, the practice of annual bread making would have made considerable demands on the monastic capacity to purchase grain and to store grain, flour and bread, as well as to operate mills for grinding the grain into flour. Perhaps Shenoute's reference was to a type of bread used only for specific liturgical purposes, while the bread consumed on a daily basis was baked more frequently.

Finally, Shenoute's account of 20,000 refugees being housed and fed at the White Monastery during a three-month crisis is not plausible. Neither the size of the monastery nor its water supply could sustain such a large group of people, although I have emphasised that it is not currently possible to reconstruct the effects of the inundation on the monastery's water holdings. Based on the number of births and deaths mentioned by Shenoute, Lopez has suggested that the actual group of refugees amounted to just 5000 people,[727] but even this number seems too high for the water supply. It seems more plausible that the large group of people was based in nearby villages or perhaps even tented camps, where they could have received food and medical care from the monastery. Considering that the White Monastery's landholdings amounted to 50 km^2, the refugees could, for example, have been maintained in villages on the extra-mural landholdings.

It is clearly necessary to consider the purpose for which the textual sources were produced. Since these texts cannot be considered within the genre of documentary sources such as receipts or accounts, they should be approached with the highest caution. This has long been acknowledged to be the case for the hagiographic sources, as their principal aim was to promote a saint by demonstrating his or her piety, ascetic practice and miraculous deeds. More interesting are the exaggerations found in Shenoute's own writings. Is it possible that aspects of Shenoute's original writings included exaggerations to serve particular rhetorical purposes, or were the numbers embellished during the process of their transmission through the centuries? It is beyond the scope of this book to examine the purpose and reception of these accounts, but it seems essential to consider such factors in order to fully assess the value of these texts.

THE WHITE MONASTERY AFTER SHENOUTE

The detailed analysis of the textual evidence pertinent to the White Monastery in Chapter 2 and the archaeological remains in Chapter 3 suggests that the site may have been in continuous use from its foundation in the fourth century until today—not necessarily as a monastery, but at least as a church and Christian village. Scraps of information from papyri, inscriptions and the *History of the Patriarchs* produce an unbroken, although not very informative, history of the monastery into the fifteenth century; thereafter the continuous use of the White Monastery church can be traced through travellers' accounts, among others, until the present day.

The archaeological evidence shows that the monastery reached its largest size at some point between the fifth and the seventh century, at which point it covered an area of c. 77,500 m^2 (see Chapter 4.1.1). The earliest remains of the monastery reveal that most buildings were constructed from mud brick bonded with a mud mortar. During the monastery's heyday new buildings were constructed of

727 Lopez, *Shenoute*, 58–60.

high-quality fired bricks with lime mortar and *opus signinum* or limestone paved floors, while pre-existing structures in, for example, WM.4 were replaced by buildings of fired brick. The evidence of extensive building activity with expensive materials is a good indicator of the monastery's economic vitality as well as for its importance for contemporary society. It is very likely that parts of the monastery were constructed with the help of donors, as was the case of the White Monastery church (see Chapter 1.1.3), but at least part of the funds to build and maintain a large monastery with a complex water supply must have come from the monastery itself.

The further development of the monastery bears clear evidence of cycles of gradual decline, during which the monastery shrank in size and gradually utilised cheaper building material (see Chapters 3.9 and 4.1.1). In the last phase of the use of the monastic grounds, the community living inside the protective walls of the church harvested building material from within the site itself for use in minor structures, such as livestock shelters.

There is not one simple explanation as to why the White Monastery declined in wealth and size. Instead, many interlinked socio-economic factors were at play (these are discussed in Chapter 3.9). Grossmann saw a buried coin hoard from the early seventh century along with fire damage to parts of the archaeological site as an indication of damage caused by the invading Sasanians around 619. Although it is possible that the coin hoard was hidden in fear of the invading Persians, the physical damage to the site cannot be linked with marauding invaders (see discussion in Chapter 3.9). The decline of the White Monastery was more likely associated with the continuous pressure put upon the Christian community in the Early Medieval period. During the Umayyad and Abbasid periods, both the land tax (*kharaj*) and the poll tax (*jizyah*) heavily affected Egypt's monasteries. At first, monks were exempted from the poll tax, but this changed around 705 when all Christians (including monks) were charged with an annual tax of 1 *dinar* (roughly equivalent to 1 *solidus*).[728]

728 Wipszycka, "Resources," 250.

Attitudes towards private ownership among the monastics varied between monasteries (see Chapter 1.1.3). At the White Monastery, at least under Shenoute, monks were forbidden to own private property and if that remained the case into the Islamic period it therefore would have been the monastery that was expected to pay the poll tax for the monks. At the White Monastery this would mean an annual expense of up to 600 *dinars*, assuming the same number of monks, on top of which the monastery would probably have been liable to pay a land tax. Such large sums would have to come from somewhere else and it is possible that the cessation in building activity at the White Monastery in part was a response to this new financial situation. The effects of the tax situation is seen in documentary papyri from the smaller Monastery of Bala'izah (15,000 m^2), which had to pay more than 88 *dinars* in a single year. Al-Asbagh, the official who was responsible for the introduction of the poll tax on monks, also forbade monasteries to recruit new novices and thus limited the number of monastics. This policy continued until 717.

The gradual decrease in Egypt's Christian population due to conversion—in order to avoid the poll tax, among other factors—would have influenced the monasteries. Fewer Christians meant less monastic influence on contemporary society, which in turn would have affected the patronage of the monasteries and their income. It is possible that the increased focus on pilgrimage in the Early Medieval period was developed to maintain influence and revenue for the churches and monasteries. The Coptic Patriarch Yusab I (r. 831–849), for example, actively encouraged the construction of pilgrimage shines as an income-generating activity for the church.

The *History of the Patriarchs of Alexandria* suggests that the Abbasid civil war in the middle of the ninth century affected the White Monastery, although it does not state how. The Ayyubid and Ghuzz incursion in Egypt in the twelfth century also got close to the monastery as we know from manuscript colophons that supply evidence of the theft of manuscripts from the library specifically related to this incursion. It is worth considering what effect this event (and other violent events) had on the White Monastery.

The extensive alterations to the church in the thirteenth century suggest that at this point the White Monastery was still in use and at least retained sufficient status to attract Christian donors. The alterations were made in response to damage caused by an earthquake, which possibly took place almost twenty years earlier in 1240. Warner's interpretation of the rebuilding of the Red Monastery church as a part of the same process is appealing as it suggests that the Red Monastery was seriously damaged during the earthquake, but that funds were available either through patronage or from the monastery's own holdings. Simultaneous repair work in both complexes might suggest a continued association between the two monasteries. Importantly, the last leader of the White Monastery whose name figures in textual sources was the abbot John (thirteenth century): he was responsible for the repairs to the White Monastery. His title was *archimandrite*, which could mean that he was the leader of more than one monastery and, thereby, possibly also responsible for refurbishing the Red Monastery.

The Black Death in the fourteenth century and the cyclical sweeps of plague that followed were devastating to Egypt and its monasteries, although the details of their impact in the case of the White Monastery are unknown. A century later, the Arabic author, al-Maqrizi, describes all but the church of the White Monastery as being in ruins.

An inscription inside the church from the sixteenth century suggests activity on the site, and from the seventeenth century European travellers reached the White Monastery and recorded the presence of monks on site. At some point, perhaps as late as the early nineteenth century, the church was transformed into a village—a situation that persisted until the removal of the houses in 1985 and the following re-inauguration of the monastery in the 1990s.

THE ECONOMY OF THE WHITE MONASTERY FEDERATION

Stories found in hagiographic literature, such as the *Sayings of the Desert Fathers*, paints a picture of monastics who lived alone in poverty and occupied themselves with the production of rope and baskets, crafting these objects and materials primarily for the meditative purposes and only secondarily with the aim of generating income.[729] In this way, the hagiographies explained the saints' survival by means of divine intervention through miracles worked as a reward for pious behaviour. Although these stories are not directly linked to the White Monastery, they have influenced the scholarly view on monasticism to such an extent that basketry and rope-making traditionally have been seen as the principal form of income for these communities. This idea has been reproduced in recent scholarship, for example by Lopez, who argued that the sole reason for the wealth of the White Monastery was donation from wealthy patrons.[730] Shenoute does indeed mention weaving as a basic occupation for monks and notes that ropes and baskets were among the objects traded at the market, but he also lists other jobs that were carried out within the monastery.

From textual evidence, we know that at the time of Shenoute, the White Monastery possessed extra-mural landholdings that amounted to 50 km^2. This land was probably accumulated through a combination of donation, which is well attested in relation to the Pachomian monasteries, and transfer of property from monastics joining the community. The funding of the White Monastery church by Caesarius, son of Candidianus, testifies to this practice, as does a sixth-century testament that records the donation of landed property and livestock to the White Monastery.

Other types of income are attested at the White Monastery through textual and archaeological evidence. Shenoute's writings report on trade in monastic products such as linen, rope, baskets, sacks and books, which were sold or traded in return for raw materials such as grain or wool. Linen production is confirmed by several dye-shops found in the remains of the convent at Atripe, and book production is confirmed at the White Monastery through the content of colophons and evidence for an extensive library. Books were sold at great expense, while lin-

729 S. Benedicta Ward, *The Sayings of the Desert Fathers* (Kalamazoo: Cistercian Publications, 1975).
730 Lopez, *Shenoute*, 63.

en could be produced in several qualities, the finer quality being a material of high value. The evidence from colophons from the White Monastery library reveals that books were produced into the fifteenth or sixteenth centuries.

The archaeological remains reveal that bread was produced at all three monasteries, although the dates of the millstones are uncertain and production was most likely for consumption by the monastics. Oil was also produced at the White Monastery, where no fewer than six crushing basins have been found. Although a large part of the oil would have been consumed within the three monasteries, it is possible that some was produced for sale or barter in the local markets.

Other monasteries contain further evidence for revenue-generating activities, such as the North Tomb settlement at Amarna where many loom-pits were found and the monastery of St Jeremias at Saqqara, which contained a factory of eight kilns for the production of different types of ceramics.

It is very important to take into consideration the spiritual aspect of monastic production as well. Through the monastics' ascetic practice and perceived proximity to God, products produced and blessed within the monastery would hold a value that cannot be quantified through studies of the products themselves or the mode of their production. Funerals, baptisms, blessings and prayers should be perceived as a commodity, which resulted in indirect payment through donations from the community.

From the sixth century onwards, monasteries, among other significant Christian institutions, began to associate themselves with patron saints and also housed relics. The White Monastery certainly appears to have participated in the pilgrimage industry: in the twelfth century, for example, the *History of the Patriarchs* reports that the remains of two apostles were kept at the White Monastery. Most pilgrimage was local, but the presence of figures important to the biblical tradition, such as the apostles Bartholomew and Simon the Zealot, could suggest that pilgrims from farther away would make the journey to the monastery.

It is clear that the three monasteries within the White Monastery federation complemented each other in their production. Textual sources suggest that the *diakonia* at the White Monastery was responsible to some extent for the administration of the three monasteries. The leader of the White Monastery decided where new recruits should be based and it was supposedly also from here that bread was distributed to the federation. There is, however, evidence for the production of bread at all three monasteries, which suggests that either Shenoute's recommendation was not followed or the smaller monasteries developed more autonomy after his death.

Documentary evidence from the monastery of Apa Apollo at Bawit reveals that there monastics could own their cells and also have small landholdings that could be leased to a third party or farmed by the monks themselves. There is no evidence that a similar practice was observed in the White Monastery. On the contrary, both the Pachomian and Shenoutian rules dictated total poverty among the individual monks, while the monastery gradually accumulated its wealth. The more than 700 gold coins found in hoards within the monastery surely testify to this prosperity.

FUTURE PERSPECTIVES

The archaeological study of Egyptian monasticism is still in its infancy and there are several trajectories that require further exploration. Building on the results of this book, a few of these research pathways are outlined below.

It is important to consider the role of monasteries as benefactors and caretakers of refugees and the poor within a long-term historical perspective. In the Pharaonic period, the temples were powerful landowners and distributors of grain and food in times of crisis. In the transition from pagan to Christian Egypt, this role was partly taken over by the Church. If we want to understand more fully the role of monasteries in Egypt it is not sufficient simply to compare them to other monastic communities in, for example, the Levant or Europe. It is necessary to pursue a local diachronic perspective where the society within which the monasteries developed is taken into consideration. Such study should compare archaeological examinations of the facilities within temple compounds from the Pharaonic period with the organisation of monasteries, as well as examine landholdings and extra-mural facilities through textual records. It is noteworthy that Egyptian monasteries were much larger than their Levantine equivalents in both the size of their communities as well as the extent of landholdings, and it is possible that this difference can be best approached through the *longue durée*.

Further studies are required on the relationship between monasteries, towns, villages and the great estates of Egypt, such as that of the Apion family. How were monastic landholdings geographically distributed compared to the great estates? And can monastic land ownership and production be compared in scale to that of the private landowners? Such studies would require extensive mapping based on the archaeological and textual sources regarding property.

In relation to the White Monastery, the next step is to examine the large group of finds, which includes but is not limited to bones, textile, rope and other organic materials and samples, glass and objects of various materials. Studies of these find groups hold the potential to provide important information about diet and the objects that were used in the daily life at the monastery. The coins retrieved by the SCA certainly require further study—both the coin hoards and the single copper finds. This material holds the potential to transform our understanding of the economic history of the White Monastery.

The next step for the study of the federation is to further the survey, recording and excavation at Atripe, which was initiated in 2016 by Yale University and is directed by Stephen Davis. The excavations that have been carried out so far suggest that the well-preserved site holds an immense potential for our understanding of several important aspects of early Egyptian monasticism. The physical circumstances of female monastic life have, so far, mainly been studied through texts. Through further work at Atripe, we can begin to address questions of how the life of these women differed from that of the men. The settlement's *longue durée* will help us address the development of the federation, while the monastic complex's location within a village offers an important insight into local connectivity and into the community's spiritual and economic exchange with its non-monastic context.

Finally, the convent's reuse of a Ptolemaic temple offers a fuller insight into Christian responses to the pagan past. Many Christian monasteries and villages developed in and around the pre-existing pagan temples. Past scholarly bias towards the Pharaonic remains meant that clearance strategies were employed to free the monumental structures from their later reuse. Therefore, we know very little about the nature of these architectural reuses. Textual records, travellers' accounts, early photographs and sometimes remains of decoration or architectural modification reveal that the temples in Karnak, Philae, Abydos, Dendera and Deir al-Bahari (to mention a few) were reused and modified by Copts. Although we cannot assume that Atripe's development mirrored that of other sites, the material remains offer a rare insight into this aspect of the monastic relationship to Egypt's past.

BIBLIOGRAPHY

Abu Salih the Armenian. *The Churches & Monasteries of Egypt and Some Neighbouring Countries*, translated by B.T.A. Evetts. Oxford: The Clarendon Press, 1895.

Adams, William Yewdale. *The Ceramic Industries of Medieval Nubia*. Memoirs of the UNESCO Archaeological Survey of Sudanese Nubia 1. Lexington, Kentucky: University Press of Kentucky, 1986.

—. "Beja Tribes." In *The Coptic Encyclopedia*, edited by Aziz. S. Atiya, 373–374. New York: Macmillan Publishing Company, 1991.

Ahmed, Ayman A., and Ali, Mohamed H. "Hydrochemical Evolution and Variation of Groundwater and its Environmental impact at Sohag, Egypt." *Arab Journal of Geoscience* 4 (2011): 339–352.

Altheim-Stiehl, Ruth. "The Sassanians in Egypt - Some Evidence of Historical Interest." *Bulletin de la Société d'Archéologie Copte* 31 (1992): 87–96.

Ambraseys, Nicholas. *Earthquakes in the Mediterranean and Middle East: A Multidisciplinary Study of Seismicity up to 1900*. Cambridge: Cambridge University Press, 2009.

Amélineau, Emile. *Monuments pour servir à l'histoire de l'Égypte chrétienne*. Paris: Ernest Leroux, 1888–1895.

—. *Œuvres de Shenoudi: Texte Copte et Traduction Francaise*. 2 vols. Paris: Ernest Leroux, 1907–1914.

Amouretti, Marie-Claire. *Le Pain et l'Huile dans la Grèce Antique: de l'Araire au Moulin*. Paris: Belles Lettres, 1986.

Andrén, Anders. *Between Artifacts and Texts: Historical Archaeology in Global Perspective*. New York: Plenum Press, 1998.

Anonymous. "Royal Scottish Museum." *Museums Journal* 6.4 (1906): 154.

—. *Archaeological Site Manual*. London: Museum of London Archaeological Service, 1994.

El-Antony, Maximous. "Prologue. The Renaissance of the Red Monastery." In *The Red Monastery Church: Beauty and Asceticism in Upper Egypt*, edited by Elizabeth S. Bolman, xvii–xx. New Haven and London: Yale University Press, 2016.

Aravecchia, Nicola. "Hermitages and Spatial Analysis: Use of Space at the Kellia." In *Shaping Community: The Art and Archaeology of Monasticism*, edited by Sheila McNally, 29–38. Oxford: Archaeopress, 2001.

—. *Christians of the Western Desert in Late Antiquity: The Fourth-Century Church Complex of Ain el-Gedida, Upper Egypt*. PhD diss., University of Minnesota, 2009.

Arnold, Dorothea, and Janine Bourriau. *An Introduction to Ancient Egyptian Pottery*. Mainz am Rhein: Verlag Philipp von Zabern, 1993.

Athanasius of Alexandria. *The Life of Antony. The Coptic Life and the Greek Life*, translated by Tim Vivian. Kalamazoo, Michigan: Cistercian Publications, 2003.

Ayalon, Etan. "Typology and Chronology of Water-Wheel (Saqiya) Pottery Pots from Israel." *Israel Exploration Journal* 50 (2000): 216–226.

Ayalon, Etan, Rafi Frankel, and Amos Kloner. *Oil and Wine Presses in Israel from the Hellenistic, Roman and Byzantine Periods*. BAR International Series 1972. Oxford: Archaeopress, 2009.

Bagnall, Roger S. "Monks and Property: Rhetoric, Law, and Patronage in the Apophtegmata Patrum and the Papyri." *Greek, Roman, and Byzantine Studies* 42 (2001), 7–24.

—. "Public Administration and the Documentation of Roman Panopolis." In *Perspectives on Panopolis. An Egyptian Town from Alexander the Great to the Arab Conquest*, edited by A. Egberts, Brian Paul Muhs, Joep Van der Vliet, 1–12. Leiden, Boston & Köln: Brill, 2002.

—. "Introduction." In *Egypt in the Byzantine World 300–700*, edited by Roger S. Bagnall, 1–20. New York: Cambridge University Press, 2007.

—. *Early Christian Books in Egypt*. Princeton & Oxford: Princeton University Press, 2009.

Bagnall, Roger S., and Dominic W. Rathbone. *Egypt. From Alexander to the Copts*. London: The British Museum Press, 2004.

Barois, Julien. *Irrigation in Egypt*. Washington, DC: Government Printing Office, 1889.

Behlmer, Heike. "Visitors to Shenoute's Monastery." In *Pilgrimage and Holy Space in Late Antique Egypt*, edited by David Frankfurter, 341–372. Leiden, Boston, Köln: Brill, 1998.

—. "Do not believe every word like the fool…! Rhetorical Strategies in Shenoute, Canon 6." In *Christianity and Monasticism in Upper Egypt*, edited by Gawdat Gabra and Hany N. Takla, 1–12. Cairo & New York: The American University in Cairo Press, 2008.

Bell, Harold I. *Greek Papyri in the British Museum,* Vol. 4. London: The British Museum, 1910.

Besa Abbot of Athribe. *The Life of Shenoute*, translated by David N. Bell. Kalamazoo, Michigan: Cistercian Publications, 1983.

Bierbrier, Morris L. *Who was who in Egyptology.* 4th revised edition. London: The Egypt Exploration Society, 2012.

Bijovsky, Gabriela. "A Hoard of Byzantine Solidi from Bet She'an in the Umayyad Period." *Revue Numismatique* 158 (2002): 161–227.

Bild, Jesper. "Sacred Movement to Labrauda – An Archaeological Perspective." *HEROM. Journal on Hellenistic and Roman Material Culture* 1 (2012): 157–196.

Bitton-Ashkelony, Bruria. *Encountering the Sacred: The Debate on Christian Pilgrimage in Late Antiquity*. Berkeley & London: University of California Press, 2005.

Blanke, Louise. "Washing the Masses, Washing the Self: An Architectural Study of the Central Bathhouse in Gerasa." *Syria* 92 (2015): 85–104.

—. "Life on the Desert's Edge: The Water Supply of a Late Antique Monastery in Egypt." In *Water of Life*, edited by John Kuhlmann Madsen, Nils Overgaard Andersen, and Ingolf Thuesen. Copenhagen: Orbis, 2016.

—. "Trois Latrines Publiques dans la Jérash de l'Antiquité tardive (Jordanie)." *Médiévales* 70 (2016): 43–58.

—. "The Allure of the Saint: Late Antique Pilgrimage to the Monastery of St Shenoute." In *Excavating Pilgrimage. Archaeological Approaches to Sacred Travel and Movement in the Ancient World*, edited by Troels M. Kristensen and Wieke Friese, 203–223. Abingdon: Routledge, 2017.

Blanke, Louise, Patrick D. Lorien, and Rune Rattenborg. "Changing Cityscapes in Central Jarash – Between Late Antiquity and the Abbasid Period." *Annual of the Department of Antiquities of Jordan* 54 (2010): 311–327.

Bolman, Elizabeth S. *Monastic Visions: Wall Paintings in the Monastery of St. Anthony at the Red Sea.* New Haven & London: American Research Center in Egypt/Yale University Press, 2002.

—. "Late Antique Aesthetics, Chromophonia and the Red Monastery, Sohag, Egypt." *Eastern Christian Art* 3 (2006): 1–24.

—. "The Red Monastery Conservation Project, 2006 and 2007 Campaigns. Contributing to the Corpus of Late Antique Art." In *Christianity and Monasticism in Upper Egypt*, edited by Gawdat Gabra and Hany N. Takla, 305–317. Cairo: American University in Cairo Press, 2008.

—. "Reflections on the Red Monastery Project: 2000–2008." *Bulletin of the American Research Center in Egypt* 194 (2009): 9–13.

—. "The White Monastery Federation and the Angelic Life." In *Byzantium and Islam. Age of Transition, 7th–9th Century*, edited by Helen C. Evans and Brandie Ratliff, 75–77. New Haven & London: Yale University Press, 2012.

—. *The Red Monastery Church: Beauty and Asceticism in Upper Egypt.* New Haven and London: Yale University Press, 2016.

—. "Introduction." In *The Red Monastery Church: Beauty and Asceticism in Upper Egypt*, edited by Elizabeth S. Bolman, xxi–xxxvi. New Haven and London: Yale University Press, 2016.

—. "A Medieval Flourishing at the White Monastery Federation. Material Culture." In *The Red Monastery Church: Beauty and Asceticism in Upper Egypt*, edited by Elizabeth S. Bolman, 203–215. New Haven and London: Yale University Press, 2016.

Bolman, Elizabeth S., Louise Blanke, Darlene L. Brooks Hedstrom, Mohammed Khalifa, Cédric Meurice, Saad Mohammed, Gillian Pyke, and Peter Sheehan. "Late Antique and Medieval Painted Decoration at the White Monastery (Dayr al-Abiad), Sohag." *Bulletin of the American Research Center in Cairo* 192 (2007): 5–11.

Bolman, Elizabeth S., Stephen J. Davis and Gillian Pyke. "Shenoute and a Recently Discovered Tomb Chapel at the White Monastery." *Journal of Early Christian Studies* 18.3 (2010): 453–462.

Bolman, Elizabeth S., Stephen J. Davis, Luigi De Cesaris, Father Maximous Al-Anthony, Gillian Pyke, Emilliano Ricchi, Alberto Sucato, and Nicholas Warner. "Tomb of St. Shenoute? More Results from the White Monastery (Dayr Anba Shenouda), Sohag." *Bulletin of the American Research Center in Egypt* 198 (2011): 31–38.

Borsch, Stuart J. *Black Death in Egypt and England: A Comparative Study.* Austin: University of Texas Press, 2005.

—. "Plague Depopulation and Irrigation Decay in Medieval Egypt." *The Medieval Globe* 1 (2014): 125–156.

Boud'hors, Anne. *Le Canon 8 de Chénouté: d'après le Manuscrit IFAO Copte 2 et les Fragments Complémentaires.* Cairo: Institut Français d'Archéologie Orientale, 2013.

Boud'hors, Anne, James Clackson, Catherine Louis, and Petra M. Sijpesteijn. *Monastic Estates in Late Antique and Early Islamic Egypt. Ostraca, Papyri, and Essays in Memory of Sarah Clackson.* Cincinnati, Ohio: The American Society of Papyrologists, 2009.

Boussac, Marie-Françoise, Thibaud Fournet, and Bérangère Redon. *Le Bain Collectif en Égypte.* Cairo: Institute Francais d'Archéologie Orientale, 2009.

Brenningmeyer, Todd, and Sheila McNally. "Analysis of Space at the White Monastery: Short Report on Methods and Techniques." In *Living for Eternity: The White Monastery and its Neighborhood. Proceedings of a Symposium at the University of Minnesota, Minneapolis, March 6–9. 2003*, edited by Philip Sellew (2009): 25–38, http://egypt.umn.edu/Egypt/1-pb%20pdfs/Bren.pdf

Breton Connelly, Joan, and Andrew I. Wilson. "Hellenistic and Byzantine Cisterns on Geronisos Island." *Report of the Department of Antiquities, Cyprus* (2002): 269–292.

Bridel, Philippe. *Le Site Monastique Copte des Kellia: Sources Historiques et Explorations Archéologiques: Actes du Colloque de Genève, 13 au 15 août 1984*. Geneva: Mission Suisse d'Archéologie Copte de l'Université de Genève, 1986.

Brooks Hedstrom, Darlene L. *"Your Cell will teach you all Things:" The Relationship between Monastic Practice and the Architectural Design of the Cell in Coptic Monasticism, 400–1000*. PhD diss., Miami University, 2001.

—. "An Archaeological Mission for the White Monastery." *Coptica* 4 (2005): 1–26.

—. "Divine Architects: Designing the Monastic Dwelling Place." In *Egypt in the Byzantine World 300–700*, edited by Roger S. Bagnall, 368–389. Cambridge: Cambridge University Press, 2007.

—. "The Geography of the Monastic Cell in Early Egyptian Monastic Literature." *Church History* 78.4 (2009): 756–791.

—. *The Monastic Landscape of Late Antique Egypt: An Archaeological Reconstruction*. Cambridge: Cambridge University Press, 2017.

Brooks Hedstrom, Darlene L., and Elizabeth S. Bolman. "The White Monastery Federation Project: Survey and Mapping at the Monastery of Apa Shenoute (Dayr al-Anba Shinuda), Sohag, 2005–2007." *Dumbarton Oaks Papers* 65/66 (2012): 333–364.

Brooks Hedstrom, Darlene L., Stephen J. Davis, Tomasz Herbich, Salima Ikram, Dawn Mccormack, Marie-Dominique Nenna, Gillian Pyke. "New Archaeology at Ancient Scetis: Surveys and Initial Excavations at the Monastery of St. John the Little in Wadi al-Natrun. Yale Monastic Archaeology Project." *Dumbarton Oaks Papers* 64 (2010): 217–227.

Brun, Jean-Pierre. *L'Oléiculture Antique en Provence: Les Huileries du Département du Var*. Paris: Éditions du Centre National de la Recherche Scientifique, 1986.

Burton-Christie, Douglas. *The Word in the Desert: Scripture and the Quest for Holiness in Early Christian Monasticism*. New York: Oxford University Press, 1993.

Cameron, Alan. "Poets and Pagans in Byzantine Egypt." In *Egypt in the Byzantine World 300–700*, edited by Roger S. Bagnall, 21–46. Cambridge: Cambridge University Press, 2007.

Canard, Marius. "Un vizir chrétien à l'époque fatimide, l'arménien Bahram." *Annales de l'Institut d'études orientales de la Faculté des lettres d'Alger* 12 (1954): 84–113.

—. "Notes sur les Arméniens à l'époque fatimide." *Annales de l'Institut d'études orientales de la Faculté des lettres d'Alger* 13 (1955): 143–157.

Casselberry, Samuel E. "Further Refinement of Formulae for Determining Population from Floor Area." *World Archaeology* 6.1 (1974): 117–122.

Cato, Marcus Porcius. *On Agriculture*, translated by H.B. As. Cambridge, Mass: Harvard University Press, 1935.

Chitty, Derwas J. *The Desert a City*. London & Oxford: Mowbrays, 1966.

Clackson, Sarah J. It is *Our Father who Writes: Orders from the Monastery of Apollo at Bawit*. Cincinnati, Ohio: American Society of Papyrologists, 2008.

Clarke, Somers. *Christian Antiquities in the Nile Valley. A Contribution towards the Study of the Ancient Churches*. Oxford: Clarendon Press, 1912.

Colin, Gérard. *La Version Éthiopienne de la Vie de Schenoudi*. Corpus Scriptorum Christianorum Orientalium 444, 445. Leuven: Peeters, 1982.

Conti Rossini, Carlo. "Aethiopica III." *Rivista degli Studi Orientali* 9 (1923): 461–462.

Coquin, Réne-Georges. "Le Synaxaire des Coptes: Un nouveau témoin de la recension de Haute Egypte." *Analecta Bollandiana* 96 (1978): 351–365.

—. "Akhmim." In *The Coptic Encyclopedia*, edited by Aziz S. Atiya, 78. New York, Oxford, Singapore, Sydney: Maxwell Macmillan International, 1991.

—. "Zenobios." In *The Coptic Encyclopedia*, edited by Aziz S. Atiya, 2371–2373. New York, Oxford, Singapore, Sydney: Maxwell Macmillan International, 1991.

Coquin, Réne-Georges, Peter Grossmann, and S.J. Maurice Martin. "Dayr Al-Sab'at Jibal." In *The Coptic Encyclopedia*, edited by Aziz S. Atiya, 732–733. New York, Oxford, Singapore, Sydney: Maxwell Macmillan International, 1991.

—. "Dayr Sitt Dimyanah." In *The Coptic Encyclopedia*, edited by Aziz S. Atiya, 870–871. New York, Oxford, Singapore, Sydney: Maxwell Macmillan International, 1991.

Coquin, Réne-Georges, Peter Grossmann, and Hans-Georg Severin. "Dayr Anba Bishoi." In *The Coptic Encyclopedia*, edited by Aziz S. Atiya, 736–740. New York, Oxford, Singapore, Sydney: Maxwell Macmillan International, 1991.

Coquin, Réne-Georges, and S.J. Maurice Martin. "Dayr Anba Shinudah. History." In *The Coptic Encyclopedia*, edited by Aziz S. Atiya, 761–766. New York, Oxford, Singapore, Sydney: Maxwell Macmillan International, 1991.

—. "Dayr al-Fakhuri." In *The Coptic Encyclopedia*, edited by Aziz S. Atiya, 802–805. New York, Oxford, Singapore, Sydney: Maxwell Macmillan International: 1991.

Coquin, Réne-Georges, S.J. Maurice Martin, and Sheila McNally. "Dayr anba Bakhum." In The Coptic Encyclopedia, edited by Aziz S. Atiya, 730-731. New York, Oxford, Singapore, Sydney: Maxwell Macmillan International, 1991.

—. "Dayr Anba Bisadah." In *The Coptic Encyclopedia*, edited by Aziz S. Atiya, 732–733. New York, Oxford, Singapore, Sydney: Maxwell Macmillan International, 1991.

—. "Dayr al-Malak Mikha'il." In *The Coptic Encyclopedia*, edited by Aziz S. Atiya, 823. New York, Oxford, Singapore, Sydney: Maxwell Macmillan International, 1991.

—. "Dayr Mar Jirjis al-Hadidi." In *The Coptic Encyclopedia*, edited by Aziz S. Atiya, 831–832. New York, Oxford, Singapore, Sydney: Maxwell Macmillan International, 1991.

—. "Dayr al-Shuhada." In *The Coptic Encyclopedia*, edited by Aziz S. Atiya, 865–866. New York, Oxford, Singapore, Sydney: Maxwell Macmillan International, 1991.

Cribiore, Raffaella. "Higher Education in Early Byzantine Egypt: Rhetoric, Latin, and the Law." In *Egypt in the Byzantine World 300–700*, edited by Roger S. Bagnall, 47–66. New York: Cambridge University Press, 2007.

Crislip, Andrew. *From Monastery to Hospital: Christian Monasticism and the Transformation of Health Care in Late Antiquity*. Ann Arbor: University of Michigan Press, 2005.

—. "Care for the Sick in Shenoute's Monasteries." In *Christianity and Monasticism in Upper Egypt*, edited by Gawdat Gabra and Hany N. Takla, 21–30. Cairo & New York: The American University in Cairo Press, 2008.
—. *Thorns in the Flesh: Illness and Sanctity in Late Antique Christianity*. Philadelphia: University of Pennsylvania Press, 2013.
—. "The Red Monastery in Early Byzantine Egypt." In *The Red Monastery Church. Beauty and Asceticism in Upper Egypt*, edited by Elizabeth S. Bolman, 3–6. New Haven and London: Yale University Press, 2016.

Crum, Walter E. "Inscription from Shenoute's Monastery." *Journal of Theological Studies* 5 (1904): 552–569.
—. *Catalogue of the Coptic Manuscripts in the British Museum*. London: British Museum, 1905.

Curtis, Robert I. *Garum and Salsamenta: Production and Commerce in Materia Medica*. Leiden: Brill, 1991.

Curzon, Robert. *Visits to Monasteries in the Levant*. London: Arthur Barker, 1955.

Dadoyan, Seta B. "Bahrām." In *Encyclopedia of Islam*, edited by Gudrun Krämer, Denis Matringe, John Nawas, and Everett Rowson. Brill Online, 2013.
—. *The Armenians in the Medieval Islamic World. Paradigms of Interaction. Seventh to Fourteenth Centuries*. 2 vols. New Brunswick & London: Transaction Publishers, 2011–2013.

Davis, Stephen J. *The Cult of Saint Thecla: A Tradition of Women's Piety in Late Antiquity*. Oxford: Oxford University Press, 2001.
—. *The Early Coptic Papacy. The Egyptian Church and Its Leadership in Late Antiquity*. Cairo & New York: The American University in Cairo Press, 2004.
—. "A Hermeneutic of the Land: Biblical Interpretation in the Holy Family Tradition." In *Coptic Studies on the Threshold of a New Millennium. Proceedings of the Seventh International Congress of Coptic Studies*, edited by Mat Immerzeel and Jacques van der Vliet, 329–336. Leuven: Peeters, 2004.
—. *Coptic Christology in Practice: Incarnation and Divine Participation in Late Antique and Medieval Egypt*. Oxford: Oxford University Press, 2008.
—. "Jerome's 'Life of Saint Paul' and the Promotion of Egyptian Monasticism in the West." In *The Cave Church at the Monastery of St. Paul*, edited by William Lyster, 25–41. New Haven: Yale University Press/ American Research Centre in Egypt, 2008.
—. "Archaeology at the White Monastery, 2005–2010." *Coptica* 9 (2010): 25–58.
—. "Shenoute in Scetis: New Archaeological Evidence for the Cult of a Monastic Saint in Early Medieval Wadi al-Natrun." *Coptica* 14 (2015): 1–19.
—. "Curriculum Vitae et Memoriae: The Life of Saint Onophrius and Local Practices of Monastic Commemoration." In *From Gnostics to Monastics: Studies in Coptic and Early Christianity*, edited by David Brakke, Stephen J. Davis and Stephen Emmel, 383–391. Leuven: Peeters, 2018.

Davis, Stephen J., Darlene L. Brooks Hedstrom, Tomasz Herbich, Gillian Pyke, and Dawn McCormack. "Yale Monastic Archaeology Project: John the Little. Season 1 (June 7–27, 2006)." *Mishkah: The Egyptian Journal of Islamic Archaeology* 3 (2009): 47–52.
—. "Yale Monastic Archaeological Project. Pherme (Qusur Higayla and Qusur 'Erayma). Season 1 (May 29–June 8, 2006)." *Mishkah: The Egyptian Journal of Islamic Archaeology* 3 (2009): 53–57.

Davis, Stephen J., Darlene L. Brooks Hedstrom, Dawn McCormack, and Gillian Pyke. "Yale Monastic Archaeology Project: John the Little, Season 2 (May 14–June 16, 2007)." *Mishkah: The Egyptian Journal of Islamic Archaeology* 3 (2009): 59–64.

Davis, Stephen J., Gillian Pyke, Elizabeth Davidson, Mary Farag, and Daniel Schriever. "Left Behind: A Recent Discovery of Manuscripts Fragments in the White Monastery Church." *Journal of Coptic Studies* 16 (2014): 69–87.

De Cesaris, Luigi, Alberto Sucato, and Emiliano Ricchi. "Wall Painting Conservation at the Red Monastery Church." In *The Red Monastery Church. Beauty and Asceticism in Upper Egypt*, edited by Elizabeth S. Bolman, 261–279. New Haven and London: Yale University Press, 2016.

De Bock, Vladimir G. *Matériaux pour servir à l'archéologie de l'Égypte chrétienne*. St. Petersburg: Tip. E. Tile Preemn, 1901.

Debono, Fernand. "La Basilique et le Monastère de St. Pacôme (Fouilles de l'Institut Pontifical d'Archéologie Chretienne, à Faou-el-qibli, Haute-Egypte – Janvier 1968)." *Le Bulletin de l'Institut Français d'Archéologie Orientale* 70 (1971): 191–220.

Deerr, Noël. *The History of Sugar*. London: Chapman and Hall, 1949.

Deferrari, Roy J. *Early Christian Biographies; Lives of: St. Cyprian, by Pontius; St. Ambrose, by Paulinus; St. Augustine, by Possidius; St. Anthony, by St. Athanasius; St. Paul the first hermit, St. Hilarion, and Malchus, by St. Jerome; St. Epiphanius, by Ennodius*. Washington: Catholic University of America, 1964.

Dekker, Renate. "An Updated Plan of the Church at Dayr Qubbat al-Hawa." In *Christianity and Monasticism in Aswan and Nubia*, edited by Gawdat Gabra and Hany N. Takla, 117–136. Cairo & New York: The American University in Cairo Press, 2013.

Denon, Vivant. *Travels in Upper and Lower Egypt, in Company with several Divisions of the French Army during the Campaigns of General Bonaparte in that Country*, translated by Arthur Aikin. London: Longman and Rees, 1803.

Depauw, Mark. "The Late Funerary Material from Akhmim." In *Perspectives on Panopolis. An Egyptian Town from Alexander the Great to the Arab Conquest*, edited by A. Egberts, Brian Paul Muhs, Joep Van der Vliet, 71–81. Leiden, Boston & Köln: Brill, 2002.

Depraetere, David D.E. "A Comparative Study on the Construction and the Use of the Domestic Bread Oven in Egypt during the Graeco-Roman and Late Antique/Early Byzantine Period." *Mitteilungen des Deutschen Archäologischen Instituts Abteilung Kairo* 58 (2002): 119–156.

Descœudres, Georges. "Wohntürme in Klöstern und Ermitagen Ägyptens." In *Themelia: Spätantike und Koptologische Studien Peter Grossmann zum 65. Geburtstag*, edited by Martin Krause and Sofia Schate, 69–79. Wiesbaden: Ludwig Reichert Verlag, 1998.

Dey, Hendrik. "Building Worlds Apart. Walls and the Construction of Communal Monasticism from Augustine through Benedict." *Antiquité Tardive* 11 (2004): 357–371.

Dietler, Michael. "Consumption." In *The Oxford Handbook of Material Culture Studies*, edited by Mary C. Beaudry and Dan Hicks. Oxford: Oxford University Press, 2010. Available online: http://www.oxfordhandbooks.com/view/10.1093/oxfordhb/9780199218714.001.0001/oxfordhb-9780199218714-e-8

Dilley, Paul. "Dipinti in Late Antiquity and Shenoute's Monastic Federation: Text and Image in the Paintings of the Red Monastery." *Zeitschrift für Papyrologie und Epigraphik* 165 (2008): 111–128.

Dols, Michael. "The General Mortality of the Black Death in the Mamluk Empire." In *The Islamic Middle East, 700–1900: Studies in Social and Economic History*, edited by Abraham Udovitch, 404–411. Princeton: Darwin Press, 1981.

Dunn, Marylin. *The Emergence of Monasticism. From the Desert Fathers to the Early Middle Ages*. Oxford: Blackwell Publishers, 2001.

Dzierzbicka, Dorota. "Wine Consumption and Usage in Egypt's Monastic Communities (6th–8th Century)." In *Aegyptus et Nubia Christiana. The Włodzimierz Godlewski Jubilee Volume on the Occasion of his 70th Birthday*, ed. Adam Łajtar, Artur Obłuski, and Iwona Zych, 99–112, Warsaw: Polish Centre of Mediterranean Archaeology, 2016.

Elderen, Bastiaan van. "The Second Season of the Nag Hammadi Excavation." *American Research Center in Egypt Newsletter* 99/100 (1977): 36–54.

—. "The Nag Hammadi Excavation." *Biblical Archaeologist* 42 (1979): 299–331.

Elm, Susanna. *Virgins of God: The Making of Asceticism in Late Antiquity*. Oxford: Clarendon Press, 1994.

Elsner, Jas, and Ian Rutherford. "Introduction." In *Pilgrimage in Graeco-Roman & Early Christian Antiquity. Seeing the Gods*, edited by Jas Elsner and Ian Rutherford, 1–40. Oxford: Oxford University Press, 2005.

Elter, René, and Ayman Hassoune. "Le Complexe du Bain du Monastère de Saint Hilarion à Umm el-'Amr: Première Synthèse Architecturale." *Syria* 85 (2008): 129–144.

Emmel, Stephen. "Shenoute the Monk: The Early Monastic Career of Shenoute the Archimandrite." In *Il Monachesimo tra editià e aperture: Atti del Simposio "Testi e temi nella Tradizione del monachesimo Cristiano" per il 50 anniversario dell'Instituto Monastico di Sant'Anselmo. Roma, 28 maggio–1 giugno 2002*, edited by Maciej Bielawski and Daniel Hombergen, 151–174. Rome: Centro Studi Sant' Anselmo, 2004.

—. *Shenoute's Literary Corpus*, 2 vols. Leuven: Peeters, 2004.

—. "The Library of the Monastery of the Archangel Michael at Phantoou (al-Hamuli)." In *Christianity and Monasticism in the Fayoum Oasis*, edited by Gawdat Gabra, 63–70. Cairo & New York: The American University in Cairo Press, 2005.

—. "Shenoute's Place in the History of Monasticism." In *Christianity and Monasticism in Upper Egypt*, edited by Gawdat Gabra and Hany N. Takla, 31–46. Cairo & New York: The American University in Cairo Press, 2008.

Emmel, Stephen, and Bentley Layton. "Pshoi and the Early History of the Red Monastery." In *The Red Monastery Church: Beauty and Asceticism in Upper Egypt*, edited by Elizabeth S. Bolman, 11–15. New Haven: Yale University Press, 2016.

Endsjø, Dag Ø. *Primordial Landscapes, Incorruptible Bodies. Desert Asceticism and the Christian Appropriation of Greek Ideas on Geography, Bodies and Immortality*. New York: Peter Lang, 2008.

Evelyn-White, Hugh G., and Walter Hauser. *The Monasteries of the Wadi 'N Natrun*. New York: The Metropolitan Museum of Art Egyptian Expedition, 1926–1933.

Evers, Hans-Gerard, and Rolf Romero. "Rotes und Weisses Kloster bei Sohag, Probleme der Rekonstruktion." In *Christentum am Nil*, edited by Klaus Wessel, 175–194. Recklinghausen: A. Bongers, 1964.

Eyre, Christopher J. "The Water Regime for Orchards and Plantations in Pharaonic Egypt." *Journal of Egyptian Archaeology* 80 (1994): 57–80.

Faiers, Jane. "A Corpus of Late Roman Pottery from Kom el-Nana." In *Late Roman Pottery at Amarna and Related Studies*, edited by Jane Faiers, 57–181. London: Egypt Exploration Society, 2005.

El-Farag, Rifaat, Ursula Kaplony-Heckel, and Klaus P. Kuhlmann. "Recent Archaeological Explorations at Athribis." *Mitteilungen des Deutschen Archäologischen Instituts Abteilung Kairo* 41 (1986): 1–8.

Finneran, Niall. *The Archaeology of Christianity in Africa*. Stroud, Glouscestershire: Tempus Publishing, 2002.

Flohr, Miko. *The World of the Fullo: Work, Economy, and Society in Roman Italy*. Oxford: Oxford University Press, 2013.

Fluck, Cäcilia. "Akhmim as a Source of Textiles." In *Christianity and Monasticism in Upper Egypt*, edited by Gawdat Gabra and Hany Takla, 211–223. Cairo: American University of Cairo Press, 2008.

Forrer, Robert. *Über Steinzeit-Hockergräber zu Achmim, Naqada etc. in Oberägypten und über Europäische Parallelfunde*. Achmim-Studien I. Strassburg: von E. Birkhäuser, 1891.

Foxhall, Lin. *Olive Cultivation in Ancient Greece*. Oxford: Oxford University Press, 2007.

Frank, Georgia. "Miracles, Monks and Monuments: The *Historia Monachorum in Aegypto* as Pilgrims' Tales." In *Pilgrimage and Holy Space in Late Antique Egypt*, edited by David Frankfurter, 483–506. Leiden: Brill, 1998.

—. *The Memory of the Eyes: Pilgrims to Living Saints in Christian Late Antiquity*. Berkeley: University of California Press, 2000.

—. "Pilgrimage." In *The Oxford Handbook of Early Christian Studies*, edited by Susan A. Harvey and David G. Hunter, 826–841. Oxford: Oxford University Press, 2008.

Frankel, Rafi. "Introduction." In *Oil and Wine Presses in Israel from the Hellenistic, Roman and Byzantine Periods*, edited by Etan Ayalon, Rafi Frankel, and Amos Kloner, 1–19. BAR International Series 1972. Oxford: Archaeopress, 2009.

Frankfurter, David. *Religion in Roman Egypt. Assimilation and Resistance*. Princeton: Princeton University Press, 1998.

Frantz-Murphy, Gladys. "A New Interpretation of the Economic History of Medieval Egypt. The Role of the Textile Industry." *Journal of the Economic and Social History of the Orient* 24.3 (1981): 274–297.

Gabra, Gawdat. *Coptic Monasteries: Egypt's Monastic Art and Architecture*. Cairo: American University in Cairo Press, 2002.

—. "Die Münzschätze aus dem Shenute-Kloster bei Sohag." In *Ägypten-Münster: Kulturwissenschaftliche Studien zu Ägypten, dem Vorderen Orient und verwandten Gebieten; Donum natalicium viro doctissimo Erharto Graefe sexagenario ab amicis collegis discipulis ex aedibus Schlaunstrasse 2/Rosenstrasse 9 oblatum*, edited by Anke I. Blöbaum, Jochem Kahl, and Simon D. Schweitzer, 125–128. Wiesbaden: Harrassowitz, 2003.

Gabra, Gawdat, William Lyster, Cornelis Hulsman, Stephen J. Davis, and Norbert Schiller. *Be thou there: The Holy Family's Journey in Egypt*. Cairo: American University in Cairo Press 2001.

Gabra, Gawdat, and Hany N. Takla. *Christianity and Monasticism in Upper Egypt: Volume 1, Akhmim and Sohag*. Cairo: American University in Cairo Press, 2008.

Galloway, Jon H. "The Mediterranean Sugar Industry." *Geographical Review* 67.2 (1977): 177–194.

Gascoigne, Alison L. and Gillian Pyke. "Nebi Samwil-type Jars in Medieval Egypt: Characterisation of an Imported Ceramic Vessel." In *Under the Potter's Tree. Studies on Ancient Egypt Presented to Janine Bourriau on the Occasion of her 70th Birthday*, edited by David A. Aston, Bettina Bader, Carla Gallorini, Peter Nicholson and Sarah Buckingham, 417–431. Leuven: Uitgeverij Peeters en Depertement Oosterse Studies, 2011.

Gascou, Jean. "Monasteries, Economic Activities of." In *The Coptic Encyclopedia*, edited by Aziz S. Atiya, 1639–1645. New York: Macmillan Publishing Company, 1991.

Godlewski, Włodzimierz. *Le Monastère de St. Phoibammon*. Warsaw: PWN, 1986.

—. "Naqlun (Nekloni) Preliminary Report, 2005." *Polish Archaeology in the Mediterranean* XVII (2007): 195–205.

—. "Monastic Life in Makuria." In *Christianity and Monasticism in Aswan and Nubia*, edited by Gawdat Gabra and Hany N. Takla, 157–173. Cairo & New York: The American University in Cairo Press, 2013.

Godlewski, Włodzimierz, and Jarosław Zieliński. "Naqlun (Nekloni). Excavations in 2008–2009." *Polish Archaeology in the Mediterranean* XXI (2012): 193–211.

Goehring, James E. "New Frontiers in Pachomian Studies." In *The Roots of Egyptian Christianity*, edited by Birger A. Pearson and James E. Goehring, 236–257. Philadelphia: Fortress Press, 1986.

—. "Through a Glass Darkly: Diverse Images of the Apotaktikoi(ai) of Early Egyptian Monasticism." *Semeia* 58 (1992): 25–45.

—. "The Encroaching Desert: Literary Production and Ascetic Space in Early Christian Egypt." *Journal of Early Christian Studies* 5 (1993): 61–84.

—. "Melitian Monastic Organization: A Challenge to Pachomian Originality." *Studia Patristica* 25 (1993): 388–395.

—. "Withdrawing from the Desert: Pachomius and the Development of Village Monasticism in Upper Egypt." *The Harvard Theological Review* 89.3 (1996): 267–285.

—. *Ascetics, Society and the Desert: Studies in Egyptian Monasticism*. Harrisburg, Pennsylvania: Trinity Press International, 1999.

—. "The Dark Side of Landscape: Ideology and Power in the Christian Myth of the Desert." *Journal of Medieval and Early Modern Studies* 33.3 (2003): 437–451.

—. "2005 NAPS Presidential Address: Remembering Abraham of Farshut: History, Hagiography, and the Fate of the Pachomian Tradition." *Journal of Early Christian Studies* 14.1 (2006): 1–26.

—. "Monasticism in Byzantine Egypt: Continuity and Memory." In *Egypt in the Byzantine World 300–700*, edited by Roger S. Bagnall, 390–407. Cambridge: Cambridge University Press, 2007.

—. "Pachomius and the White Monastery." In *Christianity and Monasticism in Upper Egypt*, edited by Gawdat Gabra and Hany N. Takla, 47–58. Cairo & New York: The American University in Cairo Press, 2008.

Granger, Claude. *Relation du Voyage fait en Egypte par le sieur Granger en l'année 1730. Oú l'on voit ce qu'il y a de plus remarquable, particulièrement sur l'Histoire naturelle*. Paris: Jacques Vincent, 1745.

Greene, J. Patrick. *Medieval Monasteries*. Leicester, London & New York: Leicester University Press, 1992.

Grossmann, Peter. "The Basilica of Pachomius." *Biblical Archaeologist* 42 (1979): 232–236.

—. *Kirche und spätantike Hausanlagen im Chnumtempelhof: Beschreibung und Typologische Untersuchung*. Mainz am Rhein: von Zabern, 1980.

—. *Mittelalterliche Langhauskuppelkirchen und verwandte Typen in Oberägypten: Eine Studie zum mittelalterlichen Kirchenbau in Ägypten*. Glückstadt: J.J. Augustin, 1982.

—. *Abu Mina. I, Die Gruftkirche und die Gruft*. Mainz am Rhein: von Zabern, 1989.

—. "Keep." In *The Coptic Encyclopedia*, edited by Aziz A. Atiya, 1395. New York: Macmillan Publishing Company, 1991.

—. "The Pilgrimage Center of Abu Mina." In *Pilgrimage and Holy Space in Late Antique Egypt*, edited by David Frankfurter, 281–302. Leiden: Brill, 1998.

—. "Faw Qibli – 1986 Excavation Report." *Annales du Service des Antiquités de l'Égypte* 76 (2000): 143–148.

—. *Christliche Architektur in Ägypten*. Leiden, Boston & Köln: Brill, 2002.

—. "Zum Grab des Schenute." *Journal of Coptic Studies* 6 (2004): 83–103.

—. "Badeeinrichtungen in Ägyptischen Frühchristlichen Klöstern." In *Le Bain Collectif en Égypte*, edited by Marie-Françoise Boussa, Thibaud Fournet and Bérangère Redon, 287–296. Cairo: Institut Français d'Archéologie Orientale, 2009.

Grossmann, Peter, Darlene L. Brooks Hedstrom, Mohamed Abdal-Rassul, and Elizabeth S. Bolman. "The Excavation in the Monastery of Apa Shenute (Dayr Anba Shinuda) at Suhag, with an Appendix on Documentary Photography at the Monasteries of Anba Shinuda and Anba Bishoi." *Dumbarton Oaks Papers* 58 (2004): 371–382.

Grossmann, Peter, Darlene L Brooks Hedstrom, Saad M.M.Osman, Hans-Christoph Noeske, Mohamad A.A Al-Rahim, Tarik S.A. Al-Fatah, Mahmud A. Al-Mugdi, Johann Wolfgang. "Second Report of the Excavation in the Monastery of Apa Shenute (Dayr Anba Shinuda) at Suhag." *Dumbarton Oaks Papers* 63 (2009): 167–219.

Harlow, Mary, and Wendy Smith. "Between Fasting and Feasting: The Literary and Archaeobotanical Evidence for Monastic Diet in Late Antique Egypt." *Antiquity* 75 (2001): 758–768.

Harmless, William S.J. *Desert Christians. An Introduction to the Literature of Early Monasticism.* Oxford: Oxford University Press, 2004.

Den Heijer, Johannes. "History of the Patriarchs of Alexandria." In *The Coptic Encyclopedia*, edited by Aziz S. Atiya, 1238–1242. New York: Macmillan Publishing Company, 1991.

—. "The Composition of the History of the Churches and Monasteries of Egypt: Some Preliminary Remarks." In *Acts of the Fifth International Congress of Coptic Studies*, edited by David Johnson, 209–219. Rome: C.I.M., 1993.

Hillier, Bill, and Julienne Hanson. *The Social Logic of Space.* Cambridge: Cambridge University Press, 1984.

Hirschfeld, Yizhar. *The Judean Desert Monasteries in the Byzantine Period.* New Haven & London: Yale University Press, 1992.

Hobson, Barry. *Latrinae et Foricae: Toilets in the Roman World.* London: Duckworth, 2009.

Hodge, Trevor. "Collection of Water." In *Handbook of Ancient Water Technology*, edited by Örjan Wikander, 21–28. Leiden, Boston, Köln: Brill, 2000.

—. "Wells." In *Handbook of Ancient Water Technology*, edited by Örjan Wikander, 29–34. Leiden, Boston, Köln: Brill, 2000.

Hopkins, Heather J. "Using Experimental Archaeology to Answer the Unanswerable: A Case Study Using Roman Dyeing." In *Experiments with Past Materials*, edited by George Children and Dragos Gheorghiu, 81–92. BAR International Series 2302. Oxford: Archaeopress, 2011.

Hoss, Stephanie. *Baths and Bathing: The Culture of Bathing and the Baths and Thermae in Palestine from the Hasmoneans to the Moslem Conquest; with an Appendix on Jewish Ritual Baths (Miqva'ot).* Oxford: Archaeopress, 2005.

Howard-Johnston, James. *Witnesses to a World Crisis: Historians and History of the Middle East in the Seventh Century.* Oxford: Oxford University Press, 2010.

Hunter-Crawley, Heather. "Pilgrimage Made Portable: A Sensory Archaeology of the Monza-Bobbio Ampullae." *HEROM. Journal on Hellenistic and Roman Material Culture* 1 (2012): 135–156.

Innemée, Karel C. "The Word and the Flesh." In *Christianity and Monasticism in Aswan and Nubia*, edited by Gawdat Gabra and Hany N. Takla, 187–199. Cairo & New York: The American University in Cairo Press, 2013.

Jansen, Gemma C.M. "Urban Water Transport and Distribution." In *Handbook of Ancient Water Technology*, edited by Örjan Wikander Leiden, Boston, Köln: Brill, 2000.

Jansen, Gemma C.M., Ann Olga Koloski-Ostrow, and Eric M. Moormann. *Roman Toilets: Their Archaeology and Cultural History*. BABesch Supplementa 19. Leuven: Peeters, 2011.

Jensen, Robin M. "Archaeology of Christian Initiation." In *A Companion to the Archaeology of Religion in the Ancient World*, edited by Rubina Raja and Jörg Rüpke, 253–267. Oxford: Wiley Blackwell, 2015.

Jeffreys, David G., and Harry S. Smith. *The Survey of Memphis*. London: Egypt Exploration Society, 1985.

Johnson, Allan C., and Louis C. West. *Byzantine Egypt: Economic Studies*. Amsterdam: Adolf M. Hakkert, 1967.

Johnson, David W. "Nestorius." In *The Coptic Encyclopedia*, edited by Aziz S. Atiya, 1786–1787. New York: Macmillan Publishing Company, 1991.

Jones, Michael. "The Early Christian Sites at Tell El-Amarna and Sheikh Said." *Journal of Egyptian Archaeology* 77 (1991): 129–144.

Jomard, Edme F., and Charles L.F. Panckoucke. *Description de l'Égypte: ou, Recueil des observations et des recherches qui ont été faites en Égypte pendant l'expédition de l'Armée française*. Paris: Impr. C.L.F. Panckoucke, 1821.

Judge, Edwin A. "The Earliest Use of Monachos for Monk (P. Coll. Youtie 77) and the Origins of Monasticism." *Jahrbuch für Antike und Christentum* 20 (1977): 72–89.

Kahle, Paul E. *Bala'izah. Coptic texts from Deir el-Bala'izah in Upper Egypt*. London: Oxford University Press, 1954.

Kamash, Zena. "An Exploration of the Relationship between Shifting Power, Changing Behaviour and New Water Technologies in the Roman Near East." *Water History* 4 (2011): 79–93.

Kanawati, Naguib. *The Rock Tombs of EL-Hawawish. The Cemetery of Akhmim I–X*. Sydney, Australia: Macquarie Ancient History Association, 1980-.

—. *Sohag in Upper Egypt. A Glorious History*. Cairo: Ministry of Culture, Egypt, 1990.

Kasser, Rodolphe. *Survey Archéologique des Kellia (Basse-Égypte): Rapport de la Campagne 1981*. Leuven: Peeters, 1983.

—. *Le Site Monastique des Kellia (Basse-Égypte): Recherches des Annèes 1981–1983*. Leuven: Peeters, 1984.

Keenan, James G. "Aurelius Phoibammon, Son of Tridelphus: A Byzantine Egyptian Land Entrepreneur." *Bulletin of the American Society of Papyrologists* 17.3–4 (1980): 145–154.

Kees, Hermann. "Kulttopographische und Mythologische Beiträge." *Zeitschrift für ägyptische Sprache und Altertumskunde* 63–64 (1929): 266–282.

Kemp, Barry. "Amarna's other Period." *Egyptian Archaeology* 3 (1993a): 13–14.

—. "Kom el-Nana." *Journal of Egyptian Archaeology* 79 (1993b): vi–vii.

—. "Kom el-Nana." *Journal of Egyptian Archaeology* 80 (1994): vii–ix.

—. "Soil (Including Mud-brick Architecture)." In *Ancient Egyptian Materials and Technology*, edited by Paul T. Nicholson and Ian Shaw, 78–104. Cambridge: Cambridge University Press, 2000a.

—. "Tell el-Amarna, 2000." *Journal of Egyptian Archaeology* 86 (2000b): 12–14.

Kemp, Barry J., and Gillian Vogelsang-Eastwood. *The Ancient Textile Industry at Amarna*. London: Egypt Exploration Society, 2001.

Kennedy, Hugh. “Egypt as a Province in the Islamic Caliphate, 641–868.” In *The Cambridge History of Egypt*, edited by Carl F. Petry, 62–85. Cambridge: Cambridge University Press, 1998.

King, Geoffrey R. D. “Islam, Iconoclasm, and the Declaration of Doctrine.” *Bulletin of the School of Oriental and African Studies* 48.2 (1985): 267–277.

Klotz, David. “Triphis in the White Monastery: Reused Temple Blocks from Sohag.” *Ancient Society* 40 (2010): 197–213.

—. “A Naos of Nectanebo I from the White Monastery Church (Sohag).” *Göttinger Miszellen* 229 (2011): 37–52.

Kotsifou, Chrysi. “Books and Book Production in the Monastic Communities of Byzantine Egypt.” In *The Early Christian Book*, edited by William E. Klingshirn and Linda Safran, 48–68. Washington, D.C.: The Catholic University of America Press, 2007.

—. “Bookbinding and Manuscript Illumination in Late Antique and Early Medieval Monastic Circles in Egypt.” In *Eastern Christians and their Written Heritage: Manuscripts, Scribes and Context*, edited by Juan P. Monferrer-Sala, Herman G.B. Teule and Sofia Torallas Tovar, 213–244. Leuven, Paris & Walpole, MA: Peeters, 2012.

Krause, Martin. “Libraries.” In *The Coptic Encyclopedia*, edited by Aziz S. Atiya, 1447–1450. New York: Macmillan Publishing, 1991.

—. “Die koptischen Kaufurkunden von Klosterzellen des Apollo-Klosters von Bawit aus abbasidischer Zeit.” In *Monastic Estates in Late Antique and Early Islamic Egypt. Ostraca, Papyri, and Essays in Memory of Sarah Clackson*, edited by Anne Boud’hors, James Clackson, Catherine Louis, and Petra M. Sijpesteijn, 159–169. Cincinnati, Ohio: The American Society of Papyrologists, 2009.

Krawiec, Rebecca. “Space, Distance and Gender: Authority and the Separation of Communities in the White Monastery.” *Bulletin of the American Society of Papyrologists* 35 (1998): 45–63.

—. *Shenoute and the Women of the White Monastery: Egyptian Monasticism in Late Antiquity*. Oxford & New York: Oxford University Press, 2002.

—. “The Role of the Female Elder in Shenoute’s White Monastery.” In *Christianity and Monasticism in Upper Egypt*, edited by Gawdat Gabra and Hany N. Takla, 59–71. Cairo & New York: The American University in Cairo Press, 2008.

Kuhlmann, Klaus P. *Materialien zur Archäologie und Geschichte des Raumes von Achmim*. Mainz am Rhein: Verlag Philipp von Zabern, 1983.

Kuhn, Karl H. *The Works of Besa, from a MS in the British Museum*. PhD. diss., University of Durham, 1952.

—. “A Fifth Century Egyptian Abbot. I. Besa and his Background.” *Journal of Theological Studies* (1954): 36–48.

—. “A Fifth Century Egyptian Abbot. II. Monastic Life in Besa’s Day.” *Journal of Theological Studies* (1954): 174–187.

—. “A Fifth Century Egyptian Abbot. III. Besa’s Christianity.” *Journal of Theological Studies* (1955): 35–48.

—. *Letters and Sermons of Besa*, 2 vols. Corpus Scruptorum Christianorum Orientalium. Leuven: Imprimerie Orientaliste, 1956.

—. “Besa.” In *The Coptic Encyclopedia*, edited by Aziz S. Atiya, 378–379. New York: Macmillan Publishing, 1991.

Kuhn, Karl H., and William J. Tait. *Thirteen Coptic Acrostic Hymns from Manuscripts M574 of the Pierpont Morgan Library*. Oxford: Griffith Institute, Ashmolean Museum, 1996.

Kupelian, Mary. “The Ascension Scene in the Apse of the Church at Dayr Qubbat al-Hawa. A Comparative Study.” In *Christianity and Monasticism in Aswan and Nubia*, edited by Gawdat Gabra and Hany N. Takla, 201–212. Cairo & New York: The American University in Cairo Press, 2013.

Van Lantschoot, Arnold. *Recueil des colophons des manuscrits chrétiens d'Égypte*, 2 vols. Leuven: J.B. Istas, 1929.

Layton, Bentley. "Social Structure and Food Consumption at an Early Christian Monastery." *Le Muséon* 115 (2002): 25–55.

—. "Rules, Patterns, and the Exercise of Power in Shenoute's Monastery: The Problem of World Replacement and Identity Maintenance." *Journal of Early Christian Studies* 15.1 (2007): 45–73.

—. "The Ancient Rules of Shenoute's Monastic Federation." In *Christianity and Monasticism in Upper Egypt*, edited by Gawdat Gabra and Hany N. Takla, 73–82. Cairo & New York: The American University in Cairo Press, 2008.

—. "The Monastic Rules of Shenoute." In *Monastic Estates in Late Antique and Early Islamic Egypt. Ostraca, Papyri, and Essays in Memory of Sarah Clackson*, edited by Anne Boud'hors, James Clackson, Catherine Louis, and Petra M. Sijpesteijn, 170–177. Cincinnati, Ohio: The American Society of Papyrologists, 2009.

—. *The Canons of Our Fathers. Monastic Rules of Shenoute*. Oxford: Oxford University Press, 2014.

Lefebvre, Gustave. "Deir el-Abiad." In *Dictionnaire d'Archéologie Chrétienne et de Liturgie*, edited by Fernand R.D. Cabrol and Henri R.P.D. Leclercq, 459–502. Paris: Librairie Letouzey et Ané, 1916.

Lefort, Louis T. "Les Premiers Monastères Pachômiens: Exploration Topographique." *Le Muséon* 52 (1939): 379–407.

—. Œuvres de S. Pachôme et de ses Disciples. Leuven: Imprimerie Orientaliste, 1956.

Lehner, Mark. "Fractal House of Pharaoh: Ancient Egypt as a Complex Adaptive System, a Trial Formulation." In *Dynamics in Human and Primate Societies. Agent-Based Modeling of Social and Spatial Processes*, edited by Timothy Kohler and George Gumerman, 275–354. Oxford: Oxford University Press, 2000.

Leipoldt, Johannes. *Schenute von Atripe und die Entstehung des national ägyptischen Christentums*. Leipzig: J.C. Hinrichs, 1903.

—. *Shenithii Archimandritae Vita et Opera Omnia*, 3 vols. Corpus Scriptorum Christianorum Orientalium 41, 42, 73. Paris: Imprimerie Nationale, 1906–1913.

Lopez, Ariel G. *Shenoute of Atripe and the Uses of Poverty: Rural Patronage, Religious Conflict and Monasticism in Late Antique Egypt*. Berkeley, CA: University of California Press, 2013.

Louis, Catherine. "The Fate of the White Monastery Library." In *Christianity and Monasticism in Upper Egypt*, edited by Gawdat Gabra and Hany N. Takla, 83–91. Cairo & New York: The American University in Cairo Press, 2008.

Lubomierski, Nina. *Die Vita Sinuthii: Form- und Überlieferungsgeschichte der hagiographischen Texte über Schenute den Archimandriten*. Studien und Texte zu Antike und Christentum 45. Tübingen: Mohr Siebeck, 2007.

—. "The Coptic Life of Shenoute." In *Christianity and Monasticism in Upper Egypt*, edited by Gawdat Gabra and Hany N. Takla, 91–98. Cairo & New York: The American University in Cairo Press, 2008.

Lucas, Alfred, and John R. Harris. *Ancient Egyptian Materials and Industries*. London: E. Arnold, 1962.

Lundhaug, Hugo. "Baptism in the Monasteries of Upper Egypt. The Pachomian Corpus and the Writings of Shenoute." In *Ablution, Initiation, and Baptism: Late Antiquity, Early Judaism, and Early Christianity*, edited by David Hellholm, Tor Vegge, Øyvind Norderval, Christer Hellholm, 1347–1380. Berlin: Walter de Gruyter, 2011.

McNally, Sheila. "Dayr Al-Adhra." In *The Coptic Encyclopedia*, edited by Aziz S. Atiya, 713–714. New York: Macmillan Publishing Company, 1991.

—. "Dayr Mar Tumas." In *The Coptic Encyclopedia*, edited by Aziz S. Atiya, 835–836. New York: Macmillan Publishing Company, 1991.

—. "Transformations of Ecclesiastical Space: Churches in the Area of Akhmim." *Bulletin of the American Society of Papyrologists* 35 (1998): 79–95.

—. "Syncretism in Panopolis? The Evidence of the 'Mary Silk' in the Abegg Stiftung." In *Perspectives on Panopolis. An Egyptian Town from Alexander the Great to the Arab Conquest*, edited by A. Egberts, Brian Paul Muhs, Joep Van der Vliet, 145–164. Leiden, Boston & Köln: Brill, 2002.

McNally, Sheila, and Ivancica D Schrunk. *Excavations in Akhmim, Egypt: Continuity and Change in City Life from Late Antiquity to the Present*. British Archaeological Reports International Series 590. Oxford: Tempus Reparatum, 1993.

McQuitty, Alison. "An Ethnographic and Archaeological Study of Clay Ovens in Jordan." *Annual of the Department of Antiquities of Jordan* 28 (1984): 259–267.

MacCoull, Leslie S.B. "Chant in Coptic Pilgrimage." In *Pilgrimage and Holy Space in Late Antique Egypt*, edited by David Frankfurter, 403–415. Brill: Leiden, Boston, Köln, 1998.

Malouta, Myrto, and Andrew Wilson. "Mechanical Irrigation: Water-Lifting Devices in the Archaeological Evidence and in the Egyptian Papyri." In *The Roman Agricultural Economy: Organisation, Investment and Production*, edited by Alan Bowman and Andrew Wilson, 273–305. Oxford: Oxford University Press, 2013.

El-Masry, Yahia. "Seven Seasons of Excavations in Akhmim." In *Proceedings of the Seventh International Congress of Egyptologists, Cambridge 3–9 September 1995*, edited by Christopher Eyre, 759–765. Leuven: Peeters, 1998.

—. "More Recent Excavations at Athribis in Upper Egypt." *Mitteilungen des Deutschen Archäologischen Instituts Abteilung Kairo* 57 (2001): 205–218.

—. "Recent Explorations in the Ninth Nome of Upper Egypt." In *Egyptology at the Dawn of the Twenty-First Century. Proceedings of the Eight International Congress of Egyptologists, Cairo 2000*, edited by Zahi Hawass and Lyla Pinch Brock, 331–338. Cairo: The American University in Cairo Press, 2002.

Mattingly, David J. "Megalithic Madness and Measurement. Or How Many Olives Could an Olive Press Press?" *Oxford Journal of Archaeology* 7.2 (1988): 177–195.

—. "Oil for Export? A Comparison of Libyan, Spanish and Tunisian Olive Oil Production in the Roman Empire." *Journal of Roman Archaeology* 1 (1988): 33–56.

—. "Olea Mediterranea?" *Journal of Roman Archaeology* 1 (1988): 153–161.

Mays, Larry W. "Water Technology in Ancient Egypt." In *Ancient Water Technologies*, edited by Larry W. Mays, 53–65. London & New York: Springer, 2010.

Meinardus, Otto F.A. *Christian Egypt. Ancient and Modern*. Cairo: Cahiers d'Histoire Égyptienne, 1965.

—. *Monks and Monasteries of the Egyptian Deserts*. Cairo: American University in Cairo Press, 1989.

—. *Two Thousand Years of Coptic Christianity*. Cairo: American University in Cairo Press, 2002.

Ménassa, Laïla, and Laferrière, Pierre-Henry. *La Sāqia. Technique et vocabulaire de la roue à eau Égyptienne*. Cairo: Institut Français d'Archéologie Orientale, 1974.

Meurice, Cédric. "L'intervention du Comité de conservation des monuments de l'art arabe au Couvent Blanc de Sohag." In *Études coptes XI, Treizième journée d'études (Marseille, 7–9 juin 2007)*, edited by Anne Boud'hors and Catherine Louis, 277–288. Cahiers de la Bibliothèque copte 17. Paris: De Boccard, 2009.

—. *Jean Clédat en Égypte et en Nubie (1900–1914)*. Cairo: Institut Français d'Archéologie Orientale, 2014.

Middleton-Jones, Howard. "The Digital 3D Virtual Reconstruction of the Monastic Church, Qubbat al-Hawa." In *Christianity and Monasticism in Aswan and Nubia*, edited by Gawdat Gabra and Hany N. Takla, 221–229. Cairo & New York: The American University in Cairo Press, 2013.

Mikhail, Maged S.A., and Mark Moussa, *Christianity and Monasticism in Wadi al-Natrun: Essays from the 2002 International Symposium of the Saint Mark Foundation and the Saint Shenouda the Archimandrite Coptic Society.* Cairo: The American University in Cairo Press, 2009.

Minnen, Peter van. "The Letter (and other Papers) of Ammon: Panopolis in the Fourth Century A.D." In *Perspectives on Panopolis. An Egyptian Town from Alexander the Great to the Arab Conquest*, edited by A. Egberts, Brian Paul Muhs, Joep Van der Vliet, 177–199. Leiden, Boston & Köln: Brill, 2002.

Moawad, Samuel. "The Relationship of St. Shenoute of Atripe with his Contemporary Patriarchs of Alexandria." In *Christianity and Monasticism in Aswan and Nubia*, edited by Gawdat Gabra and Hany N. Takla, 107–120. Cairo & New York: The American University in Cairo Press, 2008.

Mohammed, Mahmoud A., and Peter Grossmann. "On the Recently Excavated Monastic Buildings in Dayr Anba Shinuda: Archaeological Report." *Bulletin de la Sociéte d'Archéologie Copte* 30 (1991): 53–63.

Monneret de Villard, Ugo. *Les Couvents près de Sohag*, 2 vols. Milan: Tipografia Pontificia e Arcivescovile S. Giuseppe, 1925–1927.

—. *Il Monastero di S. Simeone presso Aswan*. Milano: Tipografie e Libreria Pontificia Arcivescovile S. Giuseppe, 1927.

Montserrat, Dominic. "Pilgrimage to the Shrine of SS Cyrus and John at Menouthis in Late Antiquity." In *Pilgrimage and Holy Space in Late Antique Egypt*, edited by David Frankfurter, 257–280. Leiden: Brill, 1998.

Moreland, John. *Archaeology and Text*. London: Duckworth, 2001.

Morrisson, Cécile. "No Title." *International Numismatic Newsletter* 17 (1990): 15–16.

Moschos, John. *The Spiritual Meadow (Pratum Spirituale)*. Kalamazoo, Michigan: Cistercian Publications, 1994.

Nau, François N. "Une version syriaque inédite de la Vie de Schenoudi." *Revue sémitique d'épigraphie et d'histoire ancienne* 7 (1899): 357–363.

—. "Une version syriaque inédite de la Vie de Schenoudi." *Revue sémitique d'épigraphie et d'histoire ancienne* 8 (1900): 153–167, 252–265.

Van Neer, Wim, and David D.E. Depraetere. "Pickled Fish from the Egyptian Nile: Osteological Evidence from a Byzantine (Coptic) context at Shanhur." *Revue de Paléobiologie* 10 (2005): 159–170.

Van Neer, Wim, Sheila Hamilton-Dyer, René Cappers, Konjev Desender, and Anton Ervynck. "The Roman Trade in Salted Nilotic Fish Products: Some Examples from Egypt." *Documenta Archaeobiologiae* 4 (2006): 173–188.

Van Neer, Wim, Wim Wouters, Marie-Hélène Rutschowscaya, Alain Delattre, Delphine Dixneuf, Konjev Desender, and Jeroen Poblome. "Salted Fish Products from the Coptic Monastery at Bawit, Egypt: Evidence from the Bones and Text." In *The Role of Fish in Ancient Time*, edited by Heidemarie Hüster Plogmann, 147–159. Rahden: Verlag Marie Leidorf, 2007.

Nielsen, Inge. *Thermae et Balnea: The Architecture and Cultural History of Roman Public Baths*. Aarhus: Aarhus University Press, 1993.

Noeske, Hans-Christoph. *Münzfunde aus Ägypten I. Die Münzfunde des ägyptischen Pilgerzentrums Abu Mina und die Vergleichsfunde aus den Dioecesen Aegyptus und Oriens vom 4–8. Jh. n. Chr. Prolegomena zu einer Geschichte des spätrömischen Münzumlaufs in Ägypten und Syrien*, 3 vols. Berlin: Gebr. Mann Verlag, 2000.

Norden, Frederik L. *Voyage d'Égypte et de Nubie*, 3 vols, edited by L. Langlès. Paris: P. Didot, 1795–1798.

O'Connell, Elisabeth R. "Transforming Monumental Landscapes in Late Antique Egypt." *Journal of Early Christian Studies* 15 (2007): 239–274.

—. "The Discovery of Christian Egypt. From Manuscript Hunters towards an Archaeology of Late Antique Egypt." In *Coptic Civilization: Two Thousand Years of Christianity in Egypt*, edited by Gawdat Gabra, 163–176. Cairo: The American University in Cairo Press, 2014.

Oleson, John P. *Greek and Roman Mechanical Water-Lifting Devices: The History of a Technology.* Toronto, Buffalo, London: University of Toronto Press, 1984.

—. "Water-Lifting." In *Handbook of Ancient Water Technology*, edited by Örjan Wikander, 217–302. Leiden, Boston, Köln: Brill, 2000.

Orlandi, Tito. "The Library of the Monastery of Saint Shenoute at Atribe." In *Perspectives on Panopolis. An Egyptian Town from Alexander the Great to the Arab Conquest*, edited by A. Egberts, Brian Paul Muhs, Joep Van der Vliet, 211–231. Leiden, Boston, Köln: Brill, 2002.

Papaconstantinou, Arietta. "The Cult of the Saints: A Haven of Continuity in a Changing World?" In *Egypt in the Byzantine World 300–700*, edited by Roger S. Bagnall, 350–367. Cambridge: Cambridge University Press, 2007.

Peers, Charles R. "The White Monastery near Sohag, Upper Egypt." *The Archaeological Journal* LXI, 242 (1904): 131–153.

Perry, Charles. *A View of the Levant: Particularly of Constantinople, Syria, Egypt, and Greece. In Which Their Antiquities, Government, Politics, Maxims, Manners, and Customs, (with Many Other Circumstances and Contingencies) Are Attempted to be Described and Treated on.* London: T. Woodward, C. Davis, and J. Shuckburgh, 1743.

Petrie, William M.F. *Athribis*. London: School of Archaeology in Egypt, 1908.

Pococke, Richard. *A Description of the East and Some Other Countries*. London: printed for the author by W. Bowyer, 1743.

Popovic, Svetlana. *The Architectural Iconography of the Late Byzantine Monastery*. Toronto: Canadian Institute of Balkan Studies, 1997.

—. "The 'Trapeza' in Cenobitic Monasteries: Architectural and Spiritual Contexts." *Dumbarton Oaks Papers* 52 (1998): 281–303.

—. "The Byzantine Monastery: Its Spatial Iconography and the Question of Sacredness." In *Hierotopy. Creation of Sacred Spaces in Byzantium and Medieval Russia*, edited by Alexei Lidov, 150–185. Moscow: Progress-tradition, 2006.

—. "Dividing the Indivisible: The Monastery Space – Secular and Sacred." *Recueil des travaux de l'Institut d'études byzantines* XLIV (2007): 47–65.

Pyke, Gillian. "Survey of the Christian church and later remains in the tomb of Panehsy (no. 6)." In "Tell el-Amarna, 2006-7," edited by Barry Kemp, 35–49. *Journal of Egyptian Archaeology* 93 (2007).

—. "A Christian Conversion: The Tomb of Panehsy at Amarna." *Egyptian Archaeology* 32 (2008): 8–10.

—. “Panehsy Church Project 2009: Settlement Survey.” In “Tell el-Amarna, 2008–9,” edited by Barry Kemp, 27–30. *Journal of Egyptian Archaeology* 95 (2009).

Pyke, Gillian, Louise Blanke, and Mary Ownby. “Panehsy Church Project 2009–10: Settlement Survey.” In “Tell el-Amarna, 2010,” edited by Barry Kemp, 1–30. *Journal of Egyptian Archaeology* 96 (2010).

Pyke, Gillian, and Darlene L. Brooks Hedstrom. “The Afterlife of Sherds: Architectural Reuse Strategies at the Monastery of John the Little, Wadi Natrun.” In *Functional Aspects of Egyptian Ceramics within their Archaeological Context*, edited by Bettina Bader and Mary Ownby, 307–326. Leuven: Peeters, 2012.

Pyke, Gillian, Anna Stevens, and Johanna Sigl. “Panehsy Church Project 2008: Settlement Survey.” In “Tell el-Amarna, 2007–8,” edited by Barry Kemp, 44–54. *Journal of Egyptian Archaeology* 94 (2008).

Quirke, Stephen. *Lahun Studies*. Reigate: SIA publishing, 1998.

Ramzi, Muhammad. *Al-Qamus al-Jughrafi lil-Bilad al Misriyyah*, 3 vols. Cairo: Matba'at Dār al-Kutub al-Misrīyah, 1953–1968.

Rapp, Claudia. “Desert, City and Countryside in the Early Christian Imagination.” In *The Encroaching Desert: Egyptian Hagiography and the Medieval West*, edited by Jitse Dijkstra and Mathilde van Dijck, 93–112. Leiden: Brill, 2006.

Richter, Sigfried G. “The Coptic Manichaean Library from Madinat Madi in the Fayoum.” In *Christianity and Monasticism in the Fayoum Oasis*, edited by Gawdat Gabra, 71–78. Cairo & New York: The American University in Cairo Press, 2005.

Richter, Tonio S. “The Cultivation of Monastic Estates in Late Antique and Early Islamic Egypt. Some Evidence from Coptic Land Leases and Related Documents.” In *Monastic Estates in Late Antique and Early Islamic Egypt. Ostraca, Papyri, and Essays in Memory of Sarah Clackson*, edited by Anne Boud'hors, James Clackson, Catherine Louis, and Petra M. Sijpesteijn, 205–215. Cincinnati, Ohio: The American Society of Papyrologists, 2009.

Rickman, Geoffrey. *Roman Granaries and Store Buildings*. Cambridge: Cambridge University Press, 1971.

Roberts, Colin H. *Manuscripts, Society and Belief in Early Christian Egypt*. London: Oxford University Press, 1979.

Rousseau, Philip. *Pachomius. The Making of a Community in Fourth-Century Egypt*. Berkeley, Los Angeles & London: University of California Press, 1985.

Ruffini, Giovanni. *Medieval Nubia. A Social and Economic History*. Oxford & New York: Oxford University Press, 2012.

Sandy, Brent D. *The Production and Use of Vegetable Oils in Ptolemaic Egypt*. Bulletin of the American Society of Papyrologists, Supplement 6. Atlanta, Georgia: Scholars Press, 1989.

Samuel, Delwen. “Their Staff of Life: Initial Investigations on Ancient Egyptian Bread Baking.” In *Amarna Reports V*, edited by Barry Kemp, 253–290. London: Egypt Exploration Society, 1989.

Sauneron, Serge, Jean Jacquet, and Helen Jacquet-Gordon. *Les Ermitages Chrétiens du Désert d'Esna*. Cairo: Institut Français d'Archéologie Orientale du Caire, 1972.

El-Sayed, Rafed. “Schenute und die Tempel von Atripe. Zur Umnutzung des Triphisbezirks in der Spätantike.” In *Honi soit qui mal y pense. Studium zum Pharaonischen, Griechisch-Römischen und Spätantiken Ägypten zu Ehren von Heinz-Josef Thissen*, edited by Hermann Knuf, Christian Leitz and Daniel von Recklinghausen, 519–539. Leuven & Walpole, MA: Peeters, 2010.

El-Sayed, Rafed, Yahia El-Masry, and Victoria Altmann. *Athribis. I, General Site Survey, 2003–2007, Archaeological and Conservation Studies: The Gate of Ptolemy IX: Architecture and Inscriptions.* Cairo: Institut Français d'Archéologie Orientale, 2012.

Schachner, Lukas A. *Economic Production in the Monasteries of Egypt and Oriens, AD 320–800.* PhD diss., University of Oxford, 2005.

Schaten, Sofia, and Jacques Van der Vliet. "Monks and Scholars in the Panopolite Nome: The Epigraphic Evidence." In *Christianity and Monasticism in Upper Egypt: Akhmim and Sohag*, edited by Gawdat Gabra and Hany N. Takla, 131–142. Cairo & New York: The American University in Cairo Press, 2008.

Schroeder, Caroline T. "Prophecy and Porneia in Shenoute's Letters: The Rhetoric of Sexuality in a Late Antique Egyptian Monastery." *Journal of Near Eastern Studies* 65.2 (2006): 81–97.

—. *Monastic Bodies: Discipline and Salvation in Shenoute of Atribe.* Philadelphia: University of Pennsylvania Press, 2007.

Serpico, Margaret, and Raymond White. "Oil, Fat and Wax." In *Ancient Egyptian Materials and Technology*, edited by Paul T. Nicholson and Ian Shaw, 390-429. Cambridge: Cambridge University Press, 2009.

Severin, Hans-Georg. "On the Architectural Decoration and Dating of the Church of Dayr Anba Bishuy ("Red Monastery") near Suhag in Upper Egypt." *Dumbarton Oaks Papers* 62 (2008): 75–112.

Seybold, Christian F. *Alexandrinische Patriarchengeschichte von S. Marcus bis Michael I., 61–767: Nach der ältesten 1266 geschriebenen Hamburger Handschrift.* Hamburg: Lucas Gräfe, 1912.

Shore, Arthur F. "Extracts of Besa's Life of Shenoute in Sahidic." *Journal of Egyptian Archaeology* 65 (1979): 134–139.

Sidarus, Adel Y. "The Copto-Arabic Renaissance in the Middle Ages: Characteristics and Socio-Political Context." *Coptica* 1 (2002): 141–160.

Sigl, Joanna. "Pits with Cross-Bars – Investigations on Loom Remains from Coptic Egypt." In *Studia Aegyptiaca XVIII. Proceedings of the Fourth Central European Conference of Young Egyptologists*, edited by Kata Endreffy and András Gulyás, 357–372. Budapest: NKTH, 2007.

—. "Weaving Copts in Amarna. Further Studies on Coptic Loompits in the Northern Tombs of Tell el-Amarna." *Studien zur Altägyptischen Kultur* 40 (2011): 357–386.

Smith, Wendy. *Archaeobotanical Investigations of Agriculture at Late Antique Kom el-Nana (Tell el-Amarna).* London: Egypt Exploration Society, 2003.

Spencer, A. Jeffrey. *Brick Architecture in Ancient Egypt.* Warminster: Aris & Phillips, 1979.

Stevenson, Alice. "Artefacts of Excavation. The British Collection and Distribution of Egyptian Finds to Museums, 1808–1915." *Journal of the History of Collections.* Advance Access (August 23, 2013): 1–14.

Strzygowski, Josef. *Die Baukunst der Armenier und Europa: Ergebnisse einer vom Kunsthistorischen Institute der Universität Wien 1913 durchgeführten Forschungsreise*, 2 vols. Vienna: A. Schroll & Co, 1918.

Swanson, Mark N. *The Coptic Papacy in Islamic Egypt 641–1517.* Cairo & New York: The American University in Cairo Press, 2010.

—. "An Eclipsed History. Towards a Framework for the Medieval History of the Red Monastery." In *The Red Monastery Church. Beauty and Asceticism in Upper Egypt*, edited by Elisabeth S. Bolman, 193–201. New Haven and London: Yale University Press, 2016.

Takla, Hany N. "The Library of the Monastery of St. Shenouda the Archimandrite." *Coptica* 4 (2005): 43–51.

—. "Biblical Manuscripts of the Monastery of St. Shenoute the Archimandrite." In *Christianity and Monasticism in Upper Egypt*, edited by Gawdat Gabra and Hany N. Takla, 155–168. Cairo & New York: The American University in Cairo Press, 2008.

Talmon-Heller, Daniella, and Katia Cytryn-Silverman. *Material Evidence and Narative Sources. Interdisciplinary Studies of the History of the Muslim Middle East*. Leiden & Boston: Brill, 2015.

Timbie, Janet. "A Liturgical Procession in the Desert of Apa Shenoute." In *Pilgrimage and Holy Space in Late Antique Egypt*, edited by David Frankfurter, 415–444. Leiden, Boston, Köln: Brill, 1998.

—. "Once More into the Desert of Apa Shenoute: Further Thoughts on BN 68." In *Christianity and Monasticism in Upper Egypt*, edited by Gawdat Gabra and Hany N. Takla, 169–178. Cairo & New York: The American University in Cairo Press, 2008.

Timm, Stefan. *Das Christlich-Koptische Ägypten in Arabischer Zeit: Eine Sammlung Christlicher Stätten in Ägypten in Arabischer Zeit, unter Ausschluss von Alexandria, Kairo, des Apa-Mena-Klosters (Der Abu Mina), der Sketis (Wadi n-Natrun) und der Sinai-Region*. Wiesbaden: Reichert, 1984–2007.

Vansleb, Johann M. *The Present State of Egypt or A New Relation of a Late Voyage into that Kingdom, Performed in the Years 1672 and 1673*. Farnborough: Gregg International Publishers, 1972 (first published in 1678).

Veilleux, Armand. *Pachomian Koinonia*. Kalamazoo, Michigan: Cistercian Studies, 1980–1982.

Viaud, Gérard. *Les Pèlerinages Coptes en Égypte*. Cairo: Institut Français d'Archéologie Orientale, 1979.

Vivian, Tim. *Histories of the Monks of Upper Egypt and the Life of Onnophrius*. Kalamazoo, Michigan: Cistercian Publications, 1993.

Walters, Clifford C. *Monastic Archaeology in Egypt*. Warminster: Aris & Phillips, 1974.

Ward, S. Benedicta. *The Sayings of the Desert Fathers*. Kalamazoo, Michigan: Cistercian Publications, 1975.

Warner, Nicholas. "An Architect Abroad. The Life and Work of Somers Clarke in Egypt." *Mitteilungen des Deutschen Archäologischen Instituts Abteilung Kairo* 68 (2012): 237–261.

—. "Architectural Survey." In *The Red Monastery Church: Beauty and Asceticism in Upper Egypt*, edited by Elizabeth S. Bolman, 49–77. New Haven: Yale University Press, 2016.

Warner, Nicholas, and Cédric Meurice. ""A Strange Jumble of Roman Detail." Western Explorers and Antiquarians at the Red Monastery: 1673–1926." In *The Red Monastery Church: Beauty and Asceticism in Upper Egypt*, edited by Elizabeth S. Bolman, 231–241. New Haven: Yale University Press, 2016.

—. "The Comité. Conserving the Red Monastery Church in the Early Twentieth Century." In *The Red Monastery Church: Beauty and Asceticism in Upper Egypt*, edited by Elizabeth S. Bolman, 243–259. New Haven: Yale University Press, 2016.

Von Wartburg, Marie-Louise. "Design and Technology of the Medieval Refineries of the Sugar Cane in Cyprus. A Case Study in Industrial Archaeology." In *Paisajes del Azúcar. Actas del Quinto Seminario Internacional Sobre la Cana de Azúcar*, edited by Antonio Malpica, 81–116. Granada: Disputaciòn Provincial de Granada, 1995.

Wellard, James. *Desert Pilgrimage*. London: Hutchinson & Co, 1970.

Wilcocks, William. *Egyptian Irrigation*. London: Spon, 1889.

Wilfong, Terry G. "The non-Muslim Communities: Christian Communities." In *The Cambridge History of Egypt*, edited by Carl F. Petry, 175–197. Cambridge: Cambridge University Press, 1998.

Wilkinson, Gardner. *A Handbook for Travellers in (Lower and Upper) Egypt. Handbook for Egypt and the Sudan. Being a new ed. of 'Modern Egypt and Thebes'*, 2 vols. London: John Murray, 1847.

Wilkinson, John. *Jerusalem Pilgrimage*. London: Hakluyt Society, 1988.

Wilson, Andrew. "Industrial Use of Water." In *Handbook of Ancient Water Technology*, edited by Örjan Wikander, 127–150. Leiden, Boston, Köln: Brill, 2000.

—. "Drainage and Sanitation." In *Handbook of Ancient Water Technology*, edited by Örjan Wikander, 151–178. Leiden, Boston, Köln: Brill, 2000.

Wimbush, Vincent L., and Richard Valantasis. *Asceticism*. Oxford: Oxford University Press, 1998.

Winlock, Herbert E., Walter E. Crum, and Hugh G. Evelyn-White. *The Monastery of Epiphanius at Thebes*. New York: Metropolitan Museum of Art, Egyptian Expedition, 1926.

Wipszycka, Ewa. *Les Ressources et les Activités Économiques des Églises en Égypte du IVe au VIIIe Siècle*. Bruxelles: Foundation Égyptologique Reine Élisabeth, 1972.

—. "Le Monachisme Égyptien et les Villes." *Travaux et Mémoires* 12 (1994): 1–44.

—. *Moines et Communautés Monastiques en Égypte*. The Journal of Juristic Papyrology, Supplement XI. Warsaw: The Raphael Taubenschlag Foundation, 2009.

—. "Monks and Monastic Dwellings: P. Dubl. 32–34, P.KRU 105, and BL MS.Or 6201–6206 Revisited." In *Monastic Estates in Late Antique and Early Islamic Egypt. Ostraca, Papyri, and Essays in Memory of Sarah Clackson*, edited by Anne Boud'hors, James Clackson, Catherine Louis, and Petra M. Sijpesteijn, 236–243. Cincinnati, Ohio: The American Society of Papyrologists, 2009.

—. "Resources and Economic Activities of the Egyptian Monastic Communities (4th–8th century)." *The Journal of Juristic Papyrology* XLI (2011): 159–263.

—. "A Look at the Origins of Monasticism in Egypt from a Geographical Point of View." *Przegląd Humanistyczny* 2 (2013): 109–126.

Wüstenfeld, Ferdinand. *Macrizi's Geschichte der Copten*. Göttingen: Dieterichsche Buchhandlung, 1847.

Yakut ibn 'Abd Allah al-Hamawi. *Geographisches Wörterbuch*, 6 vols, edited by Ferdinand Wüstenfeld. Leipzig: In Comission bei F.A: Brockhaus, 1866–1873.

Yasin, Ann. M. *Saints and Church Spaces in the Late Antique Mediterranean. Architecture, Cult and Community*. Cambridge: Cambridge University Press, 2009.

Yegül, Fikret. *Baths and Bathing in Classical Antiquity*. New York: Architectural History Foundation, 1992.

—. *Bathing in the Roman World*. Cambridge: Cambridge University Press, 2010.

Zanetti, Ugo. "Un Index Liturgique du Monastère Blanc." In *Christianisme d'Égypte: Hommages à René-Georges Coquin*, edited by Jean-Marc Rosenstiehl, 55–75. Paris: Peeters, 1994.

Zanetti, Ugo, and Stephen J. Davis, "Liturgy and Ritual Practice in the Shenoutean Federation." In *The Red Monastery Church. Beauty and Asceticism in Upper Egypt*, edited by Elizabeth S. Bolman, 27–35. New Have: Yale University Press, 2016.

Zereteli, Grigoriĭ F., and Peter Jernstedt. *Papyri russischer und georgischer Sammlungen*, 5 vols. Tiflis: Universitätslithographie, 1925–1935.

Zoega, Georg. *Catalogus Codicum Copticorum Manu Scriptorum Qui in Museo Bordiano Velitris Adservantur*. Repr. ed. Hildesheim & New York: Georg Olms Verlag (1973), 1810.

WEBPAGES

"Food and Agriculture Organization of the United Nations." Acessed on 20.01.2018. http://www.fao.org/docrep/010/ah810e/AH810E05.htm

"InspectApedia on Water recovery rate." Acessed on 20.01.2018. https://inspectapedia.com/water/Well_Flow_Rate.php

"Islamic Art Network (Comité bulletin)." Acessed on 20.01.2018. http://www.islamic-art.org/comitte/BArchMain.asp

"Islamic Art Network (Comité overview)." Acessed on 20.01.2018. http://www.islamic-art.org/comitte/Comite.asp

"Living for Eternity. The White Monastery and its Neighbourhood." Acessed on 20.01.2018. http://egypt.umn.edu

"The White Monastery Project (Yale Monastic Archaeological Project (South))." Acessed on 20.01.2018. https://egyptology.yale.edu/expeditions/current-expeditions/yale-monastic-archaeology-project-south-sohag

"World Health Organisation. How much water does one person need per day?" Acessed on 20.01.2018. http://www.who.int/water_sanitation_health/emergencies/qa/emergencies_qa5/en/

UNPUBLISHED ARCHAEOLOGICAL REPORTS
(marked with * in footnotes)

Blanke, Louise. "Square Summary. Area 1, square B & C, Area 3, square E & F." White Monastery Project interim report, 2005.

—. "Square Summary. Area 2, square G." White Monastery Project interim report, 2006.

—. "Final Report of Area 3 Unit M. December 2006 – January 2007." White Monastery Project interim report, 2007.

—. "White Monastery Federation Project 2008. Area 3 Unit P. Report of Preliminary Work." Yale Monastic Archaeology Project (South) interim report, 2008.

—. "White Monastery Federation Project 2008. Area 1 Unit N. Triconch Funerary Chapel, Excavation of Unit N3 and N4. Excavations and further Observations in the Triconch Funerary Chapel." Yale Monastic Archaeology Project (South) interim report, 2008.

—. "White Monastery Project 2009. Archaeological Recording and Observations at Area 3 Unit P." Yale Monastic Archaeology Project (South) interim report, 2009.

—. "White Monastery Project 2009. Area 1 Unit N. Excavation of Unit N6, N7, N8 & N9. Micro Excavation and Observation in the Triconch Funerary Chapel." Yale Monastic Archaeology Project (South) interim report, 2009.

—. "White Monastery Federation Project 2010. Area 3 Unit P." Yale Monastic Archaeology Project (South) interim report, 2010.

—. "Red Monastery Survey. Preliminary Report on the Mapping of the Archaeological Remains, Spring 2011." Red Monastery Project interim report, 2011.

—. "White Monastery Project 2011. Area Q." Yale Monastic Archaeology Project (South) interim report, 2011.

—. "White Monastery Project 2012. Area Q." Yale Monastic Archaeology Project (South) interim report, 2012.

Brooks Hedstrom, Darlene L. "White Monastery Federation Project Excavation Report: Season 1 & 2, 2005–2007." White Monastery Project interim report, 2007.

Davis, Stephen J., and Gillian Pyke. "Preliminary Report on the Yale Monastic Archaeology Project Excavations at Atripe, Sohag. February–March 2016." Athribis interim report, 2016.

Dolling, Wendy. "White Monastery Sohag. Tri-conch Funerary Chapel & South Hall. Archaeological Excavations Trench N1 – October 2008. Brief Report." Yale Monastic Archaeology Project (South) interim report, 2008.

—. "White Monastery Sohag. Archaeological Excavations Trench N5, Nov/Dec 2009. Preliminary Report." Yale Monastic Archaeology Project (South) interim report, 2009.

Ownby, Mary F. "Preliminary Petrographic Analysis of Plasters and Mortars from the Triconch Church Project, White Monastery, Sohag." Yale Monastic Archaeology Project (South) interim report, 2012.

Petrie, William Matthew Flinders. 3 Notebooks. Located in the Petrie Museum, UCL, London, 1907.

Pyke, Gillian. "White Monastery Project 2005 Preliminary Report." White Monastery Project interim report, 2005.

—. "White Monastery Project 2006. Preliminary Plaster Report." White Monastery Project interim report, 2006.

—. "White Monastery Pottery Report 2006." White Monastery Project interim report, 2006.

—. "White Monastery Pottery Report 2007." White Monastery Project interim report, 2007.

—. "White Monastery Project: Pottery Report. Autumn 2008." Yale Monastic Archaeology Project (South) interim report, 2008.

—. "White Monastery Triconch Funerary Chapel: Painted Plaster Report. October 2008." Yale Monastic Archaeology Project (South) interim report, 2008.

—. "White Monastery 2009: Pottery Report." Yale Monastic Archaeology Project (South) interim report, 2009.

—. "White Monastery 2010: Pottery Report." Yale Monastic Archaeology Project (South) interim report, 2010.

—. "Red Monastery 2011: Architectural Observations and Pottery Report." Red Monastery Project interim report, 2011.

—. "The Work of the Supreme Council of Antiquities at the White Monastery." Yale Monastic Archaeology Project (South) interim report, 2011.

—. "White Monastery 2011: Pottery Report." Yale Monastic Archaeology Project (South) interim report, 2011.

Pyke, Gillian, Stephen J. Davis, Gaber Ahmed Hafez, Rashed Mohammed Badary, Sayed Mohammed Mahmoud. "White Monastery 2011: Window Inscriptions." Yale Monastic Archaeology Project (South), 2011.

Sheehan, Peter. "White Monastery Project. Unit D." White Monastery Project interim report, 2006.

—. "Dayr Anba Shenouda/ The White Monastery, Sohag. Archaeological Observations at the Tri-conch Funerary Chapel, January 2007." White Monastery Project interim report, 2007.

Stevens, Anna. "White Monastery Project 2008. Report on Excavations North of the Triconch Funerary Chapel, Area 1, Unit 2 (Trench 2). 30th September–15th October 2008." Yale Monastic Archaeology Project (South) interim report, 2008.

INDEX

Abbasid Civil War 32, 40, 182
Abbasid Period 3, 111–112, 143, 182
abbot 10, 12–14, 22, 31–38, 59, 183
Abd Allah ibn 'Abd al-Malik, Caliph 111, 142
Abraham of Farshut 15, 16
abstinence 16
Abu al-Hasan Ali ibn al-Husayn ibn Ali al-Masudi, *see* Masudi
Abu al-Makarim 18, 20, 32, 39, 41, 44, 118, 131, 153, 180
Abu Mena (Egypt), Site of 144, 148, 149
Abu Sayfayn (Egypt), Monastery of 18, 20
Abydos (Egypt) 33, 174, 175, 185
accommodation 60, 129, 149
administration, monastic 16, 26, 91, 117, 168, 178, 184, *see also diakonia*
Adribah (Egypt), Mountain of 39
agriculture 1–2, 43, 47, 59, 119, 132, 138, 140, 178, *see also* cultivation
Ahmed al-Yaqubi, *see* Yaqubi
Akhmim (Egypt) 7, 14, 15, 17, 19–20, 31, 33, 34, 38, 57, 133, 142, 143, 170
  monasteries 6, 9, 14, 18, 20–21, 112
al-Asbagh 111, 182
al-Hafiz, Caliph 41
al-Hawawish (Egypt), Village of 18, 20
al-Mara'igh (Egypt) 38
al-Mustain, *see* Abbasid Civil War
al-Mutazz, *see* Abbasid Civil War
al-Nasir Muhammad Ibn Qalawun, Sultan 118
al-Qasim ibn Ubaydallah 32, 39, 45, 69, 111
Alexander II, Patriarch of Alexandria 39
Alexandria (Egypt) 1, 9, 11, 14, 15, 23, 34, 38, 39, 55, 144
altar 41, 146–147
Amarna (Egypt) 12, 23, 26, 28, 139, 176, 184
Ammon, Archive of 20
anchorite 16, 24
angels 12, 145
animals 16, 18, 57, 64, 69, 103, 113, 122, 123, 128, 130, 133, 134, 166
anointment, oil for 134, 147, 148
Ansina (Egypt) 25, 174
Antinoopolis (Egypt) 11, *see also* Ansina
antiquities trade (antiquities market) 2, 3, 44, 48
Apa Ioustos, Leader of the White Monastery 32, 41
Apa Seth, *Archimandrite* of the White Monastery 32, 39
Aphrodito (Egypt) 32, 39
Apollo (Bawit, Egypt), Monastery of 16, 17, 23, 68, 119, 184
apotactic 11
Arab conquest of Egypt 7, 142
archaeobotany 29, 63, 133, 139
archimandrite 15, 32, 36, 38, 39, 40, 42, 183
archives 16, 17, 20, 39, 54, 94
Armenian 32, 41–42, 153, 168
Asad ad-Din Shirkuh, *see* Shirkuh
asceticism 9–12, 13, 16, 26, 34, 39, 151, 152, 181, 184
Aswan (Egypt) 12, 25, 26, 50, 64, 69, 102, 119, 130, 160, 180
Aswan High Dam (Egypt) 118
Athanasius, Patriarch of Alexandria 11–12
Athribis (Egypt), *see* Atripe
Atripe (Egypt) 1, 4, 6, 7, 25, 33, 34, 38, 51–54, 92, 100, 117, 129, 131, 140, 148, 151–178, 180–181, 183, 185
Aurelius Phoibammon 119
authorities, Muslim 39
Ayyubid Incursion 32, 41, 182
Ayyubid Period 3
Bahram the Armenian 32, 41, 153
bakeries 18, 117, 118
baptism 1, 2, 23, 134, 148–149, 152, 184
baptistery 147–148
barter, *see* trade
Bartholomew, Apostle 32, 40, 148, 184
Basil, Steward of the White Monastery 32, 40
basilica, architecture 14–15, 50, 160
Basilius al-Bishoi, Father 50–51
basketry 130, 131, 139, 168, 178, 183
bathhouse 20, 22, 26, 38, 53, 100, 102, 118, 149
baths, bathing, *see* bathhouse
Bawit (Egypt) 16, 17, 23, 68, 119, 130, 181, 184
benches, refectory 25, 172–173, 180
Benjamin I, Patriarch of Alexandria 57, 137, 142
Besa, Fourth Leader of the White Monastery 32, 33–34, 36, 37–38, 57, 139, 168, 169, 171
Bet Shean (Israel), *see* Scythopolis
Bisadah the Bishop (Egypt), Monastery of 18, 20, 21
bishop 1, 11, 20, 42, 140
Black Death 7, 112, 183
Blemmyes 37, 129
Blessed Virgin at Nahaya (Egypt), Monastery of 39
blessing 1, 145, 147, 184
body-care 133
Bohairic 13, 36, 42
boilers, water 76, 78–79, 81
books, production of 27–28, 139–140, 183–184
Borgia, Cardinal Stefano 32, 48
bread 25, 37, 166, 178
  production of 37, 78, 91, 133, 137–138, 151, 165, 168, 180, 184
  store 37, 118

British Museum 48
British School of Archaeology in Egypt 54
bucket chain, *see* pot garland
burials 2, 6, 70, 71, 103, 104–105, 111, 162, 169, 184
Caesarius, Son of Candidianus 17, 183
Cairo (Egypt) 47, 48, 50, 55, 56, 112, 141, 142
camels 122, 162
Candle Room 139
Canopos 14
caravan, Ethiopian 32, 44
catchment pits 74–76, 90
catechumens, *see* novices
celibacy 14
cells 12, 17, 18, 22, 24–25, 26, 27, 28, 60, 117, 137, 173, 184
cemeteries 1, 6, 18, 19, 20, 60, 63, 66, 71, 103, 119, 152, 170, 174
cesspits 27
Chael, *Archimandrite* of the White Monastery 32, 40
Chalcedon 15, 142, 147
chamber pots 117
chickens 2, 47, 60
children 1, 37, 131, 149, 178
Church, Red Monastery 42, 50, 152–155, 160–161, 163, 166, 169, 170, 178, 183
  decoration 154, 162, 166, 178
  long hall 160
  sanctuary 160–161, 162, 166
  well 160, 164, 165
Church, White Monastery 1, 2, 17, 33, 37, 39, 40, 42–51, 55, 57, 117–118, 122, 139, 146–149, 178, 181, 182, 183
  decoration 32, 41, 42, 71, 112, 148
  dome 32, 41
  galleries 46
  paintings 32, 41–42, 61
  restoration 33, 41–42, 50–51, 71, 112, 137
  sanctuary 40, 41, 45, 146–147
  St Michael, painting of 42
  triconch 41, 68–69, 146, 148
  well 40, 127–130, 140, 180
churches 8, 12, 14, 15, 17, 20, 21, 22, 23, 41, 112, 143–144, 147, 182
ciborium 43
cisterns, *see* water supply: cisterns
Clarke, George Somers 33, 48–50, 51, 154, 163
Clédat, Jean 50
clerestory 50
clergy 148
coenobiticism 13–16, 20–22, 24, 25–26, 34, 52, 61, 91, 151, 171
coins 71, 105, 141–143
  copper 55, 57, 69, 141–143, 185
  gold 56–57, 141–143, 184
  hoards 55–57, 73, 76, 91, 93, 110, 111, 141–143, 182, 184–185
Comité de Conservation des Monuments de l'Art Arabe 33, 50–51, 71, 154
conflagration of the White Monastery 64, 66, 107, 108, 110–111
Constans II, Emperor 56, 141
Constantine I, Emperor 52, 53
Constantine IV, Emperor 142
Constantinople (Turkey) 26, 34, 55
cooking 78, 125, 133–134, *see also* kitchens
Coptic Museum, Cairo (Egypt) 55, 141
Coptic Orthodox Church 1, 8, 15, 51
craft production 14, 117, 122, 130–131, 132, 139–141, 149, 165, 168, 177, 183
criminals 14
Crocodilopolis (Egypt) 45
crops 113, 124, 130, 133, 135, 137, 178, *see also* agriculture
cross 46, 84, 142–143, 145
crushing basin 55, 82–84, 85, 89, 94, 98, 100–101, 102, 134–136, 140, 156–157, 165–166, 184
crypt 147
cultivation 1–2, 28, 37, 37, 48, 52, 118, 140, 152, 169, 170, *see also* agriculture
Curzon, Robert 32, 47, 49, 57, 110
Cyril I, Patriarch of Alexandria 15, 34
Cyril II, Patriarch of Alexandria 40, 41
Cyril III Ibn Laqlaq, Patriarch of Alexandria 42
De Bock, Vladimir G. 33, 44, 48, 51, 154
death 2, 26, 37, 39, 112, 181
  Pachomius 14, 17
  Shenoute 3, 4, 7, 32, 35, 179, 184
Deir al-Bachit (Egypt) 25, 176
Deir al-Bahari, *see* Phoibammon (Egypt), Monastery of
Deir al-Bala'izah (Egypt) 16, 23, 25, 27, 28, 119, 149, 182
Deir al-Fakhuri (Egypt) 174
Deir Anba Bishoi in the Desert of Abu Makar (Egypt) 44
Deir Anba Hadra (Egypt) 23, 25, 26, 50, 119, 173, 180
Deir el-Muharraq (Egypt) 23
Delta (Egypt), River Nile 7, 11, 12, 39, 144
demography, monastic 178
  brother 37
  children 37, 131, 133, 149, 178
  elderly 117, 133, 173, 178, 180
  father 34, 50, 51, 151
  men 91, 171, 179, 185
  monks 1–2, 8, 11, 14, 16–17, 22, 27, 28, 35, 41, 45, 46, 51, 91, 117, 129, 162, 180–181
  mother 151
  nuns 35, 129, 172, 178, 180
  sick 16, 27, 117, 133, 148, 173, 180
  women 34, 35, 37, 40, 151, 169, 171, 176, 178, 185
demons 11, 144
Dendera 185
Denon, Dominique-Vivant 32, 46, 47, 110, 154
desert 1, 8, 10–13, 27, 28, 34, 44, 63, 118, 123, 129, 131, 144, 152, 169
  myth of 11–12
devil 11
diakonia 16, 26, 91, 117, 121, 131, 142, 143, 151, 168, 184
diet, ascetic 26, 37, 133, 137
dinars 39, 143, 182
Diocletian, Emperor 100
Dioscorus, Patriarch of Alexandria 34
dipinti 41
disciples 10, 13, 24, 34, 36
diseases 147
dodekanummi 142
donations 2, 47, 149, 166, 182, 183, 184
donkeys 45, 47, 123, 162
donors 149, 182, 183
dormitories 22, 24–25, 26, 78, 121, 174
dovecote 177
drains for waste water, *see* water supply, drainage
drinking, water for 22, 129, 175
drought 37, 38
dump, *see* garbage
dung 69
dwellings 10, 22, 24–25, 26, 46, 53
dying, *see* death
Early Medieval Period 1, 3, 4, 8, 55, 71, 108, 111, 143, 144, 170, 178, 182
earthquake 32, 42, 112, 161, 166, 177, 183
Easter 148
Eastern Mediterranean 130
Ebonh, Leader of the White Monastery 34
Egypt Exploration Fund 54

- Egyptian Antiquities Organisation, *see* Supreme Council of Antiquities
- Elijah, Biblical prophet 11
- enclosure wall 14, 22–23, 39–40, 41, 49, 52–53, 59, 61, 63, 103, 104, 107, 118, 122, 132, 146, 149, 163, 169, 174
- Ephesus, Council of 15, 34
- Epiphanius, Monastery of 13, 26, 111, 176
- Esna 14, 24, 25, 174
- Ethiopic language 32, 36, 43
- *Etrigamou* (White Monastery), Church of the 146
- Eucharist 138, 152, 169
- Europe 42, 102, 164, 184
- exchange, *see* trade
- famine 37, 113
- Farshut (Egypt), Monastery of 15
- Fatimid Period 3, 21
- Faw Qibli (Egypt), *see* Pbow
- Fayoum (Egypt) 11, 28, 39
- feast day 1, 39, 71, 145–146, 149, 152
- *fellaheen* 48
- fertiliser 57, 162
- festival, *see* feast day
- fields 37, 118, 122, 132, 133, 137, 180
- fire 46, 80, 87, 101, 107, 108, 110–111, 137, 182
- fireplace 55, 75
- fish sauce, *see garum*
- flax 131, 132, 139, 168, 178
- floods, *see* inundation of the Nile
- food
  - forbidden, according to Shenoute's rules
    - cheese 133
    - eggs 133
    - fish 133
    - meat 133
    - milk 133
    - wine 16, 133, 138, 153, 162
  - permitted, according to Shenoute's rules
    - beans 133
    - bread 133, *see also* bread
    - cucumbers 133
    - gourd family 133
    - herbaceous vegetables 133
    - lentils 133
    - olives 133
    - pickles 133
    - pumpkins 133
    - sweet fruit 133
    - vinegar 133, 152, 162
  - produced at the White Monastery
    - barley 133
    - flour 37, 133, 137–138, 165–166, 181
    - olive oil, *see* oil, production of
    - salted food 133
    - vegetables 37, 118, 133, 180
- Frange (Western Thebes, Egypt), Hermitage of 13, 16
- French Government 44
- fruit 131, 133, *see also* orchards
- fuel 131, 133, 138, 141
- fulling 132–133, 139
- funeral, *see* burials
- Funerary Chapel (White Monastery), *see* Triconch Funerary Chapel
- funerary material 2, 19
- furniture 24
- garbage 49, 57, 63, 64, 70–71, 94, 103, 104, 109, 110, 119, 158, 177
- gardens 22, 24, 28–29, 37, 41, 118, 133, 180
- *garum* 85, 138
- gate 23, 40, 45, 53, 117, 122, 169, 177
  - gatehouse 22, 27, 39, 131, 145, 168, 171
  - gate-keeper 22, 117, 171, 177
- Gaza 69
- geophysics 61, 70, 118, 119
- geriatric wards 117, 174
- Ghazali (Sudan), Monastery of 27
- gifts 17, 28, 166
- goats 47
- Gournet Murrai (Western Thebes, Egypt) 176
- graffiti 18, 42, 50
- grain 137–138, 139, 164, 166, 178, 181, 183, 184
  - granaries 91, 164
  - mill 37, 118, 136, 137, 140, 165–166, 177, 178, 180, 181
- Granger, Claude 32, 45, 118
- graveyard, *see* cemeteries
- Great Basilica at Abu Mena (Egypt) 144, 148, 149
- Greco-Roman Period 19
- Greece 134
- Gregory, Bishop of the Armenian Colony in Egypt 42
- Ground Penetrating Radar (GPR) 61
- guard 14, 22, 26, 169, 171, 177, *see also* gate: gate-keeper
  - guardhouse, *see* gate: gatehouse
- guesthouses 22, 27, 149, 152
- gymnasium 20
- hagiographies 2, 11, 13, 28, 34, 36, 118, 144, 145, 179, 180, 181, 183
- harvest 124, 131, 136
- healing 144, 147, 148
- heaven 12, 145
- Helena, Empress 45
- Hellenistic Period 3, 130
- Heraclius, Emperor 55, 57, 141
- heresy 26
- hermitages 10, 13, 119
- hermits 10, 12, 34
- Hermopolis Magna 11, 129
- Hisham, Caliph 111
- Holy Family 144
- Holy Virgin (Egypt), Monastery of the 20
- horses 39
- Horus 33
- hospital, *see* infirmaries
- humility 39
- hydraulics, *see* water supply
- hygiene, *see* sanitation
- hypocaust 164
- Ibn Fadl Allah al-Umari 118
- icon 146
- immersion tank 148
- infirmaries 22, 27, 117, 131, 174
- infrastructure 6, 7, 22–29, 40, 59, 113, 119–127, 130, 137, 149
- inscriptions 17, 19, 28, 31, 32, 38, 41–44, 50, 68, 153, 160, 161, 178, 179, 181, 183
- inundation of the Nile 113, 118, 129, 131–132, 163, 180, 181
- irrigation 113, 118, 124, 131–132
- Isaac the Monk 11
- Islam 111–112
- Islamic Museum, Cairo (Egypt) 56, 142
- Islamic Period 3, 149, 168, 182
- Jerome 10, 12
- Jerusalem (Israel) 145
- Jesus 11, 145
- *jizyah*, *see* tax
- John Cassian 9
- John Moschos 26
- John the Little (Wadi Natrun, Egypt), Monastery of 24
- Joseph, Biblical character 144
- Judean Desert (Israel/Palestine) 27, 149
- Justinian I, Emperor (r. 527–565) 15, 56, 141, 142
- Karnak (Egypt) 185
- keep 22, 23–24, 41, 118, 153, 161, 169
- Kellia (Egypt) 6, 12, 23, 24, 26

Kesun (Turkey) 42
Kha'il, Patriarch of Alexandria (r. 744–767) 39
kharaj, *see* tax
Kharga Oasis (Egypt) 26
kiln, pottery 55, 65, 132, 139, 184
kitchens 14, 22, 24, 25–26, 60, 72, 73, 76–81, 93, 117, 121, 126, 131, 133, 152, 164, 166, 174
koinobion 13–14, 27, 53
koinonia 13–15, 16, 27, 148
Kom al-Nana (Amarna, Egypt), Monastery of 23, 28, 139
Koursios, son of Joseph, Administrator at the White Monastery 32, 38
labour 22, 96, 110, 113, 130, 131, 140–141, 152, 162, 166, 168, 177, 178
lamps 55, 78, 91, 107, 111
  oil for 134
landholdings, monastic 1, 35, 59, 110, 112, 118–119, 133, 136, 138, 149, 180, 181, 183, 184, 185
Late Antiquity 1, 3, 10, 20, 27, 102, 119, 122, 139, 143, 147, 168, 179
Latopolis (Egypt), *see* Esna
latrines 22, 23, 24, 26–27, 96–97, 117
laundry 118
laura 12–13
leadership, monastic 17, 34, 53, 139, 145, 151, 168, 171, 180
Lefebvre, Georges 50
Levant 184–185
library 2, 3, 15, 27–28, 31, 35, 36, 40, 42, 44, 47, 48, 117, 139, 145, 169, 182, 183–184
Limestone Massif (Syria) 147
linen 139, 168, 183
liturgy 22, 36, 45
livestock 16, 49, 60, 89, 94, 131, 165, 182, 183
Lycopolis (Egypt), *see* Asyut
Macarius 145
magnetometry 61, 70, 118
Mamluk Period 3, 21
Manicheans 9
manuscripts 2, 28, 38, 40–44, 46–48, 131, 139–140, 151, 152, 178, 182
Maqrizi 1, 18, 20, 42–44, 112, 153, 180, 183
market, *see* trade
Martyrius 145
Martyrius (Egypt), Monastery of 27, 149
martyrs 20, 21, 144, 147
Martyrs (Egypt), Monastery of the 20, 21
Maspero, Gaston C.C. 33, 48
mass 145
Masudi 19
Mawhub ibn Mansur ibn Mufarrij 39
meals 10, 12, 13, 14, 22, 25–26, 117, 133, 137, 171, 172–175, 177, 180
medicine 37
Medieval Period 3, 21, 32, 36, 44, 55, 130, 179
Menouthis 144
Mercurius 42, 44, 152
Meschie (Egypt), *see* Sohag
Michael the Archangel (Egypt), Monastery of 20
middens, *see* garbage
mills, *see* grain: mills
miracles 36, 37, 183
monastic rules 2, 13–14, 15, 16, 20–22, 24, 27, 34, 133, 151, 162, 169, 174, 178, 180, 184
Monneret de Villard, Ugo 33, 50, 154
mortuary landscape, Pharaonic 12–13
Moses 11, 144, 146
moulid, *see* feast day
mountains 1, 8, 39, 41, 122, 140, 145, 151, 166, 169
Muqtadir, Caliph 143
Muslims 31, 39, 47
Nag al-Deir (Egypt), Village of 50, 59, 70, 103
Nag al-Mesheyeki (Egypt) 33
Nag Hammadi (Egypt) 28
Napoleon 46
Naqlun (Egypt), Monastery of 143, 180
narthex 39–40, 49, 55, 68, 160
National Museum of Scotland 54
nave 39–40, 43, 44, 45, 47, 49, 50, 55, 57, 67, 68, 71, 110, 148, 154, 160, 162, 165, 166, 177
necropolis, *see* cemeteries
Neolithic Period 3, 31
neophytes, *see* novices
Nestorius, Archbishop of Constantinople 26, 34
New Testament 42
Niceae, Second Council of 147
niches 24–25, 41, 53, 78, 85, 91, 108, 143, 147, 164–165, 174
Nile 8, 9, 11, 14, 15, 19, 20, 31, 34, 44, 118, 124, 127, 140, 144, 180
Nile Valley 1–2, 47, 144
nipterion 117
Nitria 12
Norden, Frederik L. 32, 45
North Tombs, Amarna (Egypt) 26, 176, 184
novices 1, 14, 16, 50, 51, 148–149, 182
Nubia 132
oil, production of 28, 76, 82–83, 102, 122, 133–137, 165, 177, 178, 184
Onnophrius 12
oratory 24, 25
orchards 22, 28–29, 37, 118, 131–132, 133, 136, 180
ostraca 2, 63, 111, 179
Ottoman Period 3, 21, 101, 102
oven, bread 37, 76, 78, 80–81, 91, 137–138, 164, 165–166, 177, 181
ox 123
Oxyrhynchus (Egypt) 11, 132
Pachomian Federation 6, 13–15
Pachomius, Saint 10, 13–15, 17, 20, 26, 27, 34
Palestine 47, 149
Palladius 11
panegyrics 15
Panopolis (Egypt), *see* Akhmim
Paphnutius 12
passageways, *see* streets
pastophorium 147
patriarchate, Coptic 39
patronage, *see* donations
Patronios, Second Leader of the Pachomian Federation 17
Paul the Hermit 10
Paul, *Archimandrite* of the White Monastery 42
Pbow (Egypt) 14, 15, 22, 148, 173, 180
Pcol, founder of the White Monastery 15, 32, 34, 151, 152
Peers, Charles R. 51
perfume 133
Perry, Charles 32, 46
Persian occupation of Egypt 7, 66, 110, 111, 142, 182
Petrie Museum 54
Petrie, William Matthew Flinders 4, 7, 33, 49, 51–54, 61, 103, 104, 107–109, 118, 122, 170, 171, 176
Pharaonic Period 3, 7, 12, 19–20, 31, 45, 53, 132, 170, 174, 184, 185
Philae (Egypt) 185
philosophy 20, 133
Phocas, Emperor 55, 57, 141, 142
Phoibammon (Egypt), Monastery of 13, 28
Phoibammon, *Archimandrite* of the White Monastery 42

physicians 37, 38, 45
piety 39, 181
pilae, *see* hypocaust
pilgrimage 6, 21, 23, 35, 40, 117, 137, 143–149, 168–169, 180, 182, 184
pilgrims 1–2, 27, 51, 60, 144–146, 184
  Ethiopian 44
pipes
  tobacco 55, 102
  water, *see* water supply: conduits
plague, *see* Black Death
plumbing, *see* water supply
Pococke, Richard 32, 45, 118, 154
poetry 20
possession, *see* demons
pot-garland, *see* water supply: pot-garland
pottery, production of 28, 122, 125, 130. 132, *see also* kiln, pottery
poverty 35, 45, 141, 183, 184
  voluntary 14, 16, 151, 168
prayers 1, 10, 12, 14, 22, 41, 145, 177, 184
priest 38, 39, 45, 46, 48, 57, 131, 148
privy, *see* latrines
prophet 146–146
psalms 44
Pshoi, Founder of the Red Monastery 151, 152–153, 162, 168, 169
Ptolemaic Period 3, 33, 87, 124, 169
Ptolemais 33
pulpit 43, 44
Qal'at Sim'an (Syria) 149
Qubbat al Hawa (Egypt) 12
QUICKBIRD, *see* satellite images
railway 19, 33, 48
Red Monastery Conservation Project 154, 160
refectories 14, 22, 25–26, 27, 60, 71, 73, 76, 82, 93, 117, 121, 122, 131, 142, 149, 152, 169, 170–174, 175, 178, 180
refuge 23, 37–38, 129, 181, 184
relics 21, 32, 40, 144, 146–148, 184
reliquaries 147
Repyt (Atrip, Egypt), Temple of 33, 100, 169
residences 12, 71, *see also* dwellings
resistivity 61, 63
revenue 7, 21, 111, 136, 137, 138, 139, 168, 182, 184
rituals 146, 148
roads, *see* streets
robbers 45
rodents 74, 164
Roman Period 3, 33, 136–137
rope making 130, 131, 139, 168, 183
Roufail, Nazeer Gayed, *see* Shenoute III
Royal Scottish Museum 51
rubbish, *see* garbage
Rufinus 11
rules, *see* monastic rules
Sahidic 13, 36
saint, patron 1, 38, 144, 145, 184
saints, cult of 143–144, 169
sanitation 22, 26, 122, 129, 149
saqiya, *see* water supply: *saqiya*
Saqqara 23, 68, 119, 130, 184
satellite images 60, 119
scriptoria 22, 27–28, 44, 139, 178
Scythopolis (Israel) 142
semisses 56, 141
servant 10, 24, 112, 180
Seven Mountains (Egypt), Monastery of 20, 21
sewage, *see* water supply: drainage
shahada 69
Shandawil (Egypt) 34
sheep 45
Sheikh Hamad (Egypt), *see* Atripe
Sheikh Said (Egypt) 12
Shenoute I, Patriarch of Alexandria 23
Shenoute III, Patriarch of Alexandria 1, 33, 51
Shenoute, Saint, Third Leader of the White Monastery 1–4, 7, 15, 16, 21, 23–27, 31–38, 41, 47, 51, 53, 57, 60–61, 66, 68, 71, 93, 117–118, 121, 129, 131, 133, 134, 137–139, 144–146, 147, 148, 162, 168 169, 171 174, 176–184
Sheykh Aboo Shenóodeh, *see* Shenoute, Saint
Shirkuh 41
sick, care of the, *see* infirmaries
Simon the Zealot, Apostle 32, 40, 148, 184
sin, redemption from 144
Sinai (Egypt) 119, 144
Sitt Dimyanah (Egypt), Monastery of 18, 20
Sketis (Egypt), *see* Wadi Natrun
slaves 14
sleeping quarters, *see* dormitories
Sohag (Egypt) 4, 19, 33, 45, 47, 50, 51, 54, 55, 60, 129, 154, 170, 174
solidi 37, 55–57, 129–130, 140–143, 182
Space Syntax Analysis 120
spoil heaps, modern 63, 64, 66, 69, 141
SS Cyrus and John (Egypt), Shrine of 144
St Anthony (Egypt), Monastery of 23–26
St Catherine (Egypt), Monastery of 119
St George 146–148
St George (Egypt), Monastery of 18, 20
St Hilarion (Israel/Palestine), Monastery of 149
St Jeremias (Egypt), Monastery of 25, 119, 130, 184
St Macarius (Egypt), Monastery of 28, 36, 39
St Martyrius (Israel/Palestine), Monastery of 149
St Michael at Pantoou (Egypt), Monastery of 28
St Moses (Egypt), Monastery of 174–175
St Paul (Egypt), Monastery of 18, 23, 25
St Pshoi (Egypt), Monastery of 152–153
stables 14, 69
steward 14, 32, 40
storerooms 14, 22, 24, 25–26, 74–75, 78–79, 106–107, 171
  cold 74–75
streets 22, 52, 70, 71, 72–73, 77–78, 85, 94–97, 100, 101, 102, 117, 118, 119–121, 122, 125, 126, 136, 163, 164, 174
Sudan 27
superior 14, 151
Supreme Council of Antiquities (SCA) 4, 7, 19, 51, 54–57, 59, 60, 61, 63, 64, 65, 66, 70, 71, 87, 91, 94, 102, 104, 109, 118, 132, 137, 139, 141, 142, 154, 156, 159, 160, 170, 185
survey, archaeological 61, 92, 94, 118, 130, 154, 158
Syene (Egypt) 130
Syria 47, 147, 149
Syriac 36
Tabennese (Egypt) 13, 22
Tahta (Egypt) 45
tanneries 133, 172
Taqi al-Din al-Maqrizi, *see* Maqrizi
tax, taxation 39, 43, 111–112, 149, 182
Tbew (Egypt) 17
teachings, monastic 13, 39, 169
Technical Institute of Darmstadt 33, 50
temples 4, 11, 12, 20, 33, 34, 51, 53, 100, 169–171, 174, 176, 177, 184, 185
textile production 19, 20, 28, 102, 122, 132–133, 139, 176, 178
  dyeing 102, 133, 168, 170–171, 174–178, 183
theatres 20
Theban Tombs (Egypt) 13, 176
Thebes (Egypt) 13, 16, 47, 111, 176

Theodore the Artist 42
Theodosius, Emperor 53
theophany 11
Theophilus, Patriarch of Alexandria 34
Therapeutae 9
thoroughfares, *see* streets
Timothy I, Patriarch of Alexandria 34
toilets, *see* latrines
tombs 18, 20, 21, 66–68, 70, 71, 93, 103, 146
  rock-cut 12, 31, 170
tower of refuge, *see* keep
trade 1–2, 21, 110, 130, 131, 133–134, 137, 139–141, 143, 145, 177–179, 183, 184, 185
transport 22, 69, 98, 99, 108, 126, 130, 131, 132, 134, 135, 136, 140, 160, 175
travellers 38, 118, 144, 149, 180, 181
  European 3, 32, 38, 44–47, 94, 154, 170, 183
trees 28, 41
  olive 131–132
Triconch Funerary Chapel (White Monastery) 66–70, 119, 146
Tse (Egypt) 14, 18, 20
Tsemine (Egypt) 15, 20
Tunisia 64, 69, 102
Umar, Caliph 111–112
Umayyad Period 3, 8, 39, 69, 111–112, 141, 182
urine 133
Vansleb, Johann M. 32, 44–45, 127, 154
Vatican library 48
vermin 74, 164
Victor, *Archimandrite* of the Pachomian Federation 15
vineyards 137
Virgin (Egypt), Monastery of the 18, 28, 41
Virgin Mary 146–147, 148
visitation, *see* pilgrimage
Wadi Bir al-Ayn (Egypt) 20
Wadi Natrun (Egypt) 12, 23–24, 28, 36, 39
Wadi Sarga (Egypt) 16, 130
wall, enclosure, *see* enclosure wall
Wansleben, Johann M., *see* Vansleb, Johann M.
Ward, Edwin 51
warehouses, *see* storerooms
water supply
  channel 87–88, 92, 96, 100, 124, 126–127, 164
  cisterns 18, 53, 76, 80–81, 82–84, 91, 93, 98, 99, 124, 126, 128–130, 155, 156, 158, 164–165, 175, 176
  conduits 27, 52, 55, 65–66, 77, 80, 81, 84, 87, 88, 89, 91, 92–93, 96, 98–100, 101, 102, 121, 124–127, 130, 131, 132, 156, 160, 164–165, 175, 176, 177
    lead 85, 124
  distribution 6, 81, 122–127, 130, 164, 168
    distribution boxes 125–126, 168, 175
  drainage 6, 26–27, 88, 98, 124, 126, 127, 130, 132, 139, 176
  inspection boxes 100, 124, 126, 175
  irrigation, *see* irrigation
  mineral encrustration 124
  pipelines, pipes, *see* water supply: conduits
  pot-garland 123–24, 128, 164
  saqiya 91, 122–124, 127–130, 132, 164, 174, 175
  saqiya pots 64, 124, 128
  sedimentation tanks 92–93, 124, 125, 164, 176
  sluice gates 127, 164–165, 168
  soak-aways 85, 96, 99, 101, 124, 126
  vats 53, 98–99, 125, 131–133, 156, 164, 176
  waste water 27, 99, 100, 126
  wells 37, 45, 55, 64, 72, 89, 90, 91–92, 93, 98, 122–132, 140, 153, 155–156, 160, 164–165, 170, 174–175, 180
wealth 14, 15, 16, 23, 69, 111, 140, 143, 149, 182, 183, 184
weaving 130, 131, 176, 183
Wellard, James 50
Western Desert (Egypt) 1
Western Thebes (Egypt) 16, 176
wheat 133, 180
White Monastery Church, *see* Church, White Monastery
White Monastery, jobs at
  baker 131
  bell ringer 131
  catechizer 131
  chanter 131
  construction worker 131, 169
  cook 131
  copyist of manuscripts 131
  craft worker 131
  deacon 131
  diakonia worker 131
  diakonia cleaner 131
  doctor 131
  field hand 131
  food server 131
  fruit picker 131
  fuel gatherer 131
  gatehouse server 131
  grinder and miller 131
  guardian of keys and locked objects 131
  harvester 131
  infirmary cleaner 131
  kitchen cleaner 131
  livestock herder 131
  nurse 131
  pall bearer 131
  priest 131
  refectory cleaner 131
  rope maker 131
  supervisor of children 131
  transportation worker 131
  waiter 131
widows 10
Wilcocks, William 118
Wilkinson, Gardner 33, 47, 154
windows 45, 96, 107
wine 16, 37, 69, 130, 133, 138, 152, 162
  production of 1–2, 28, 122, 130
women 34, 35, 37, 39–40, 47, 57, 144, 151, 169, 171, 176, 177, 178, 179, 185
wool 131, 132, 139, 168, 178, 183
workmen 47, 54
workshops 2, 14, 16, 22, 28, 60, 117, 132, 176
World Health Organisation (WHO) 129
worship 13, 22, 144, 145, 169
Yakut ibn ʿAbd Allah Al-Hamawi 42
Yaqubi 19
Yusab, Patriarch of Alexandria 137, 144, 182
Zenobios, Fifth Leader of the White Monastery 32, 38

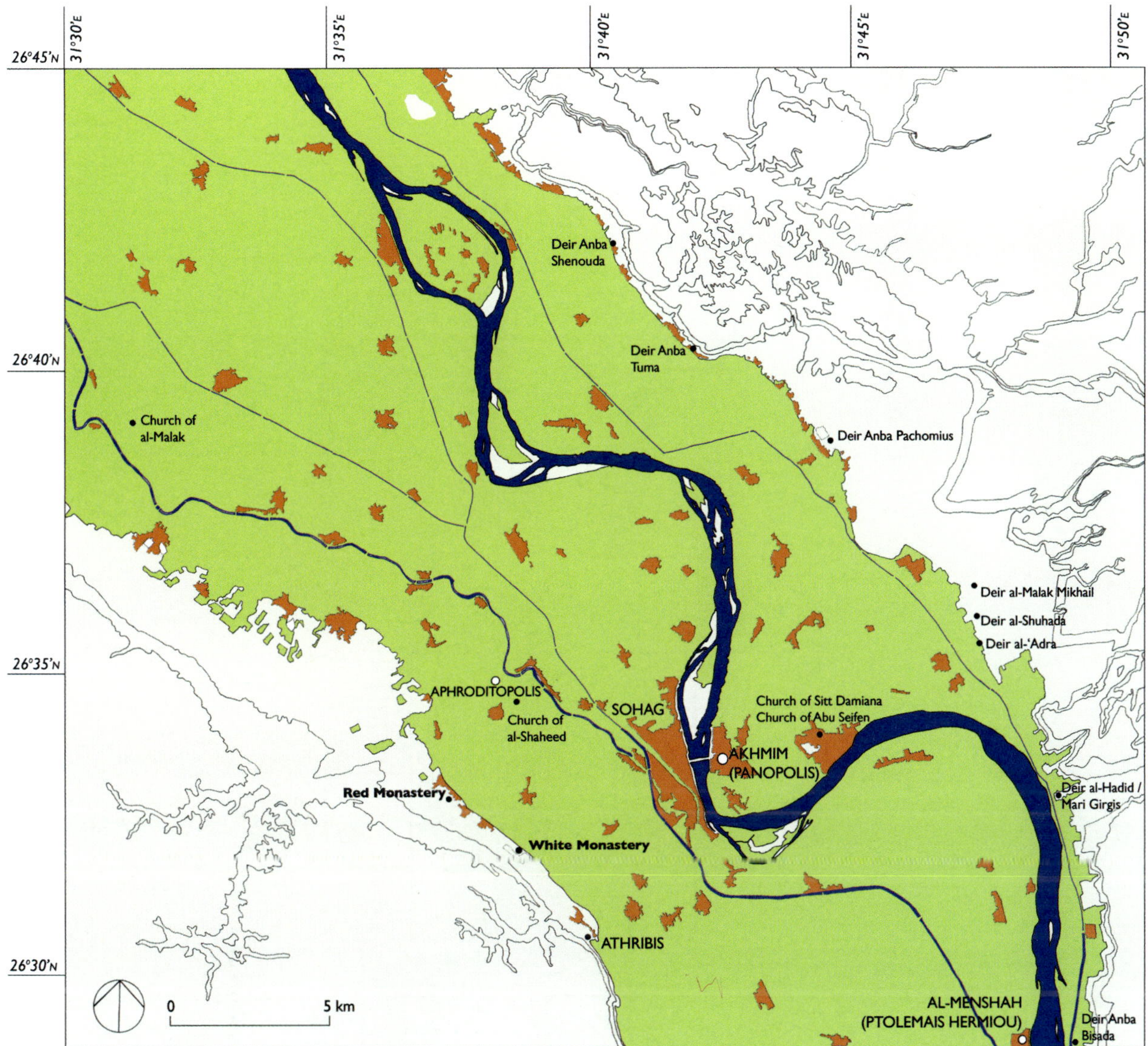

Pl. 1. Map showing the location of the White Monastery federation in relation to Sohag and Akmim. Drawing by Nicholas Warner. Bolman, "Introduction," fig. 13. © ARCE.

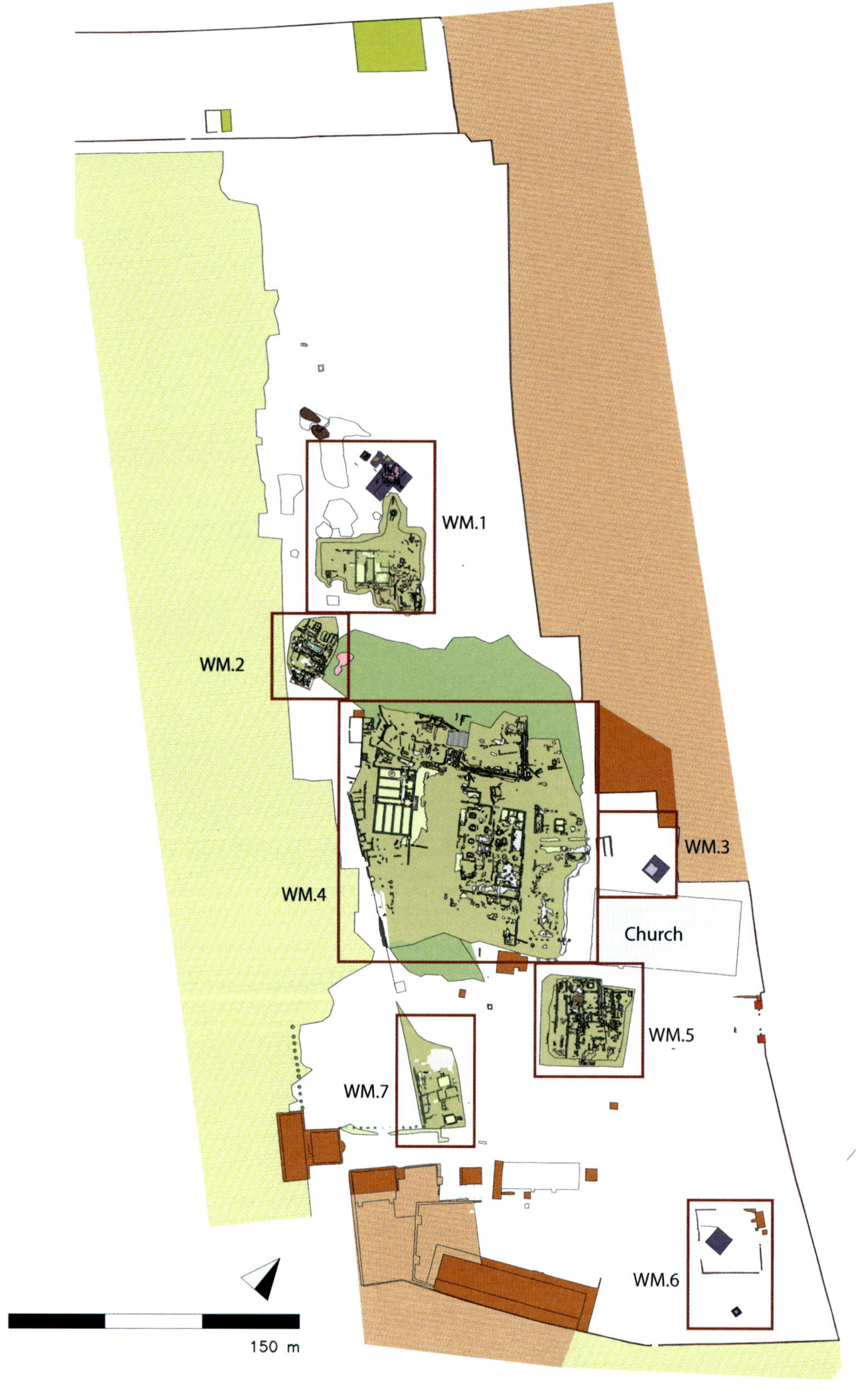

Pl. 2. Overview of the seven excavated areas within the White Monastery. Map by Dawn McCormack and the author. © YMAP.

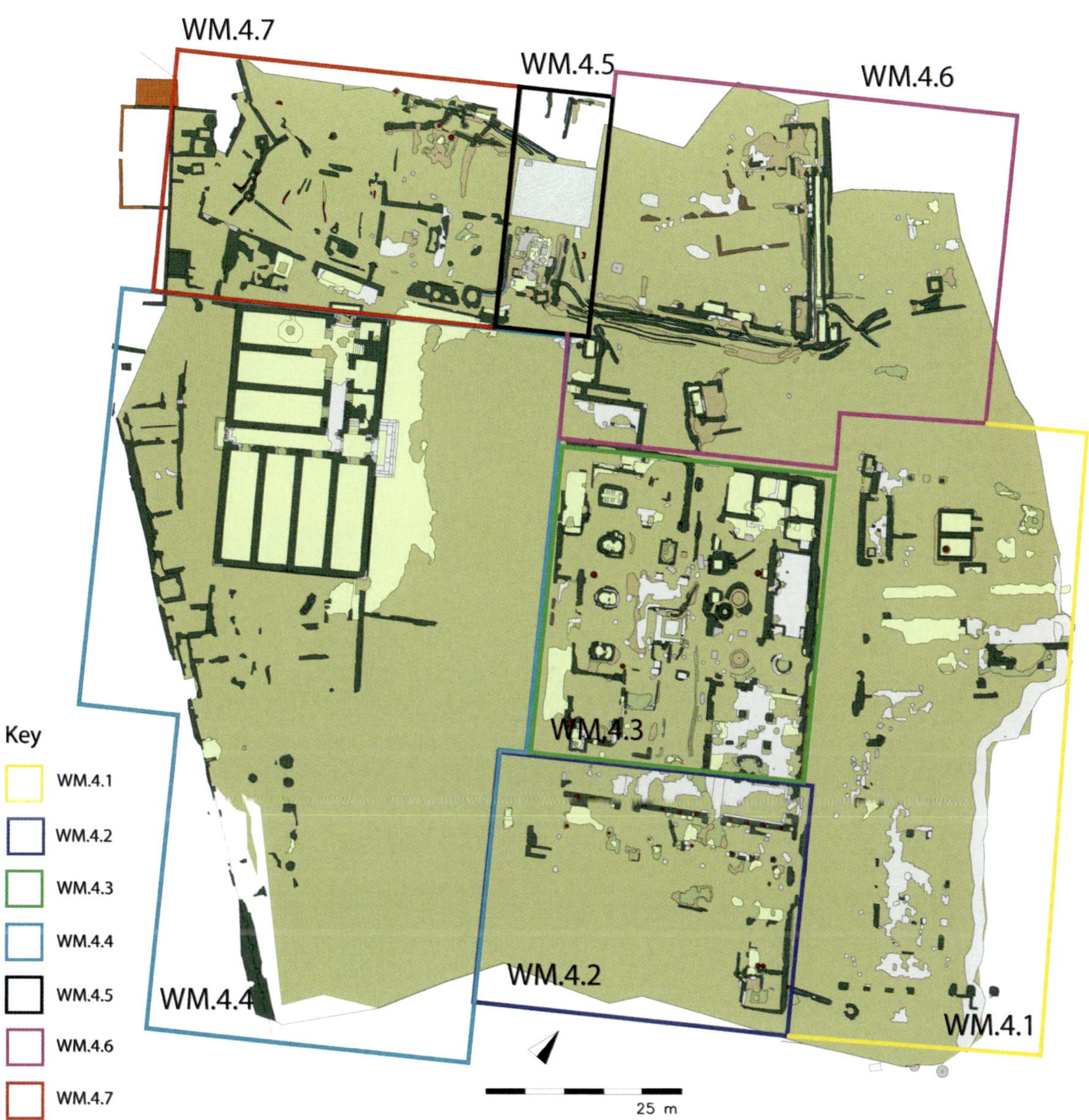

Pl. 3. WM.4 showing zones. Map by Dawn McCormack and the author. © YMAP.

Pl. 4. WM.4 showing sections. Map by Dawn McCormack and the author. © YMAP.

Pl. 5. Map details from the geophysical magnetic survey of the White Monastery. Geophysical map by Tomasz Herbich. Brooks Hedstrom & Bolman, "White Monastery," fig. 2. Image used with permission from Darlene L. Brooks Hedstrom and Elizabeth S. Bolman.

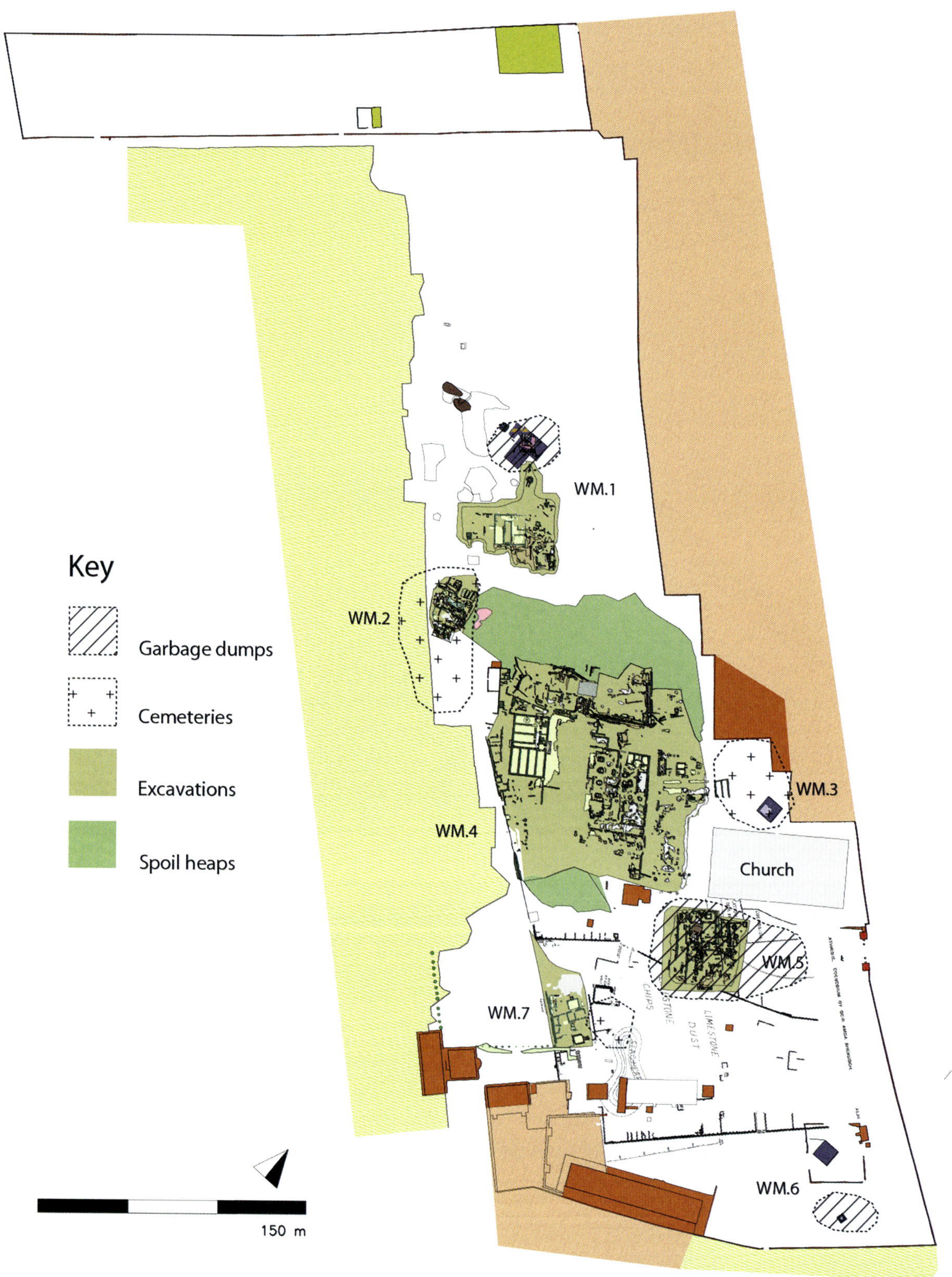

Pl. 6. Map showing changing locations of garbage dumps and cemeteries as the monastery decrease in size over time. Map by Dawn McCormack and the author. © YMAP.

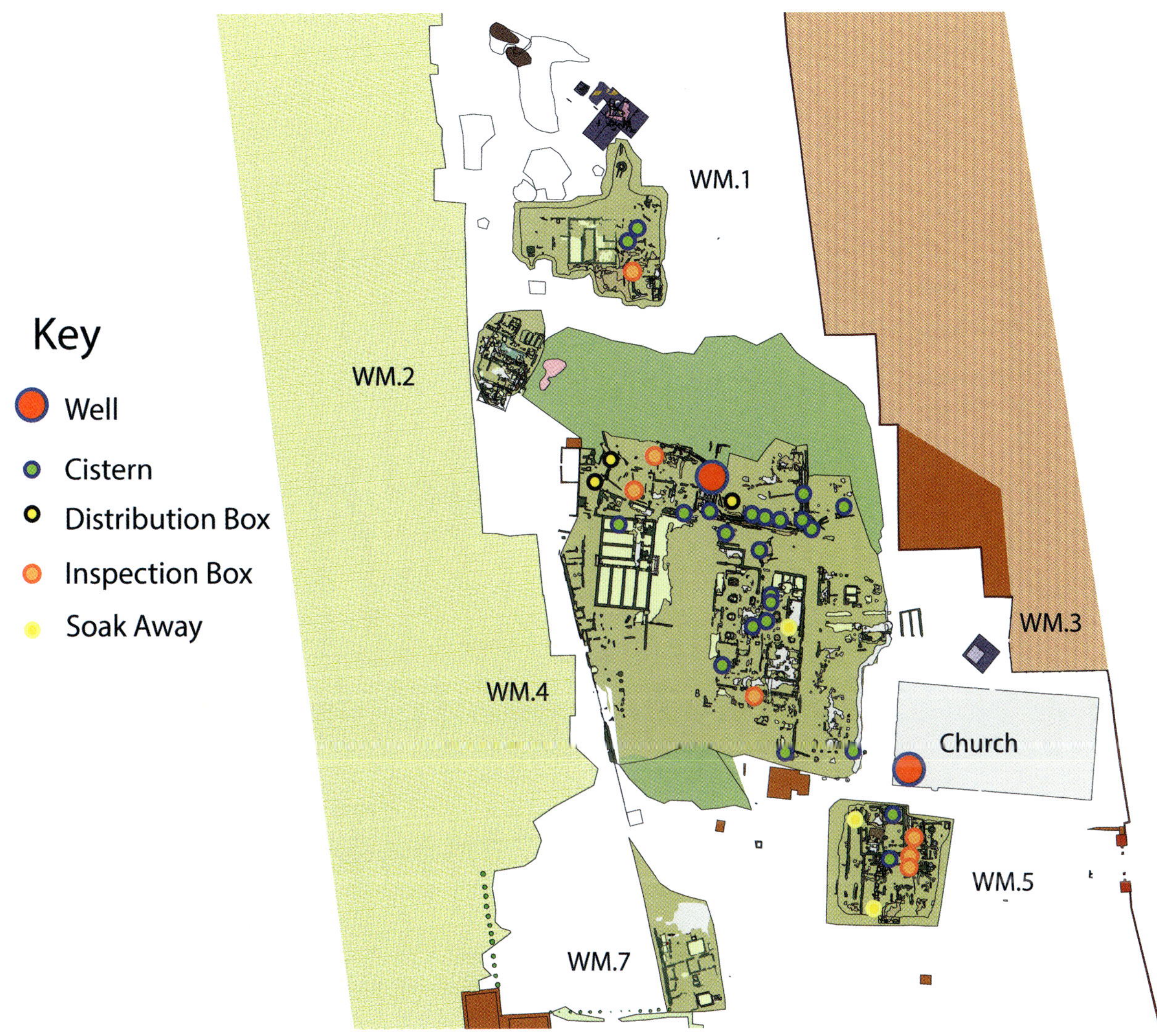

Pl. 7. Map of archaeological remains at White Monastery, showing location of wells (blue circle with red core); cisterns and sedimentation tanks (blue circle with green core); distribution boxes (black circle with yellow core); inspection boxes (orange); and soak-aways (yellow). Map by Dawn McCormack and the author. © YMAP.

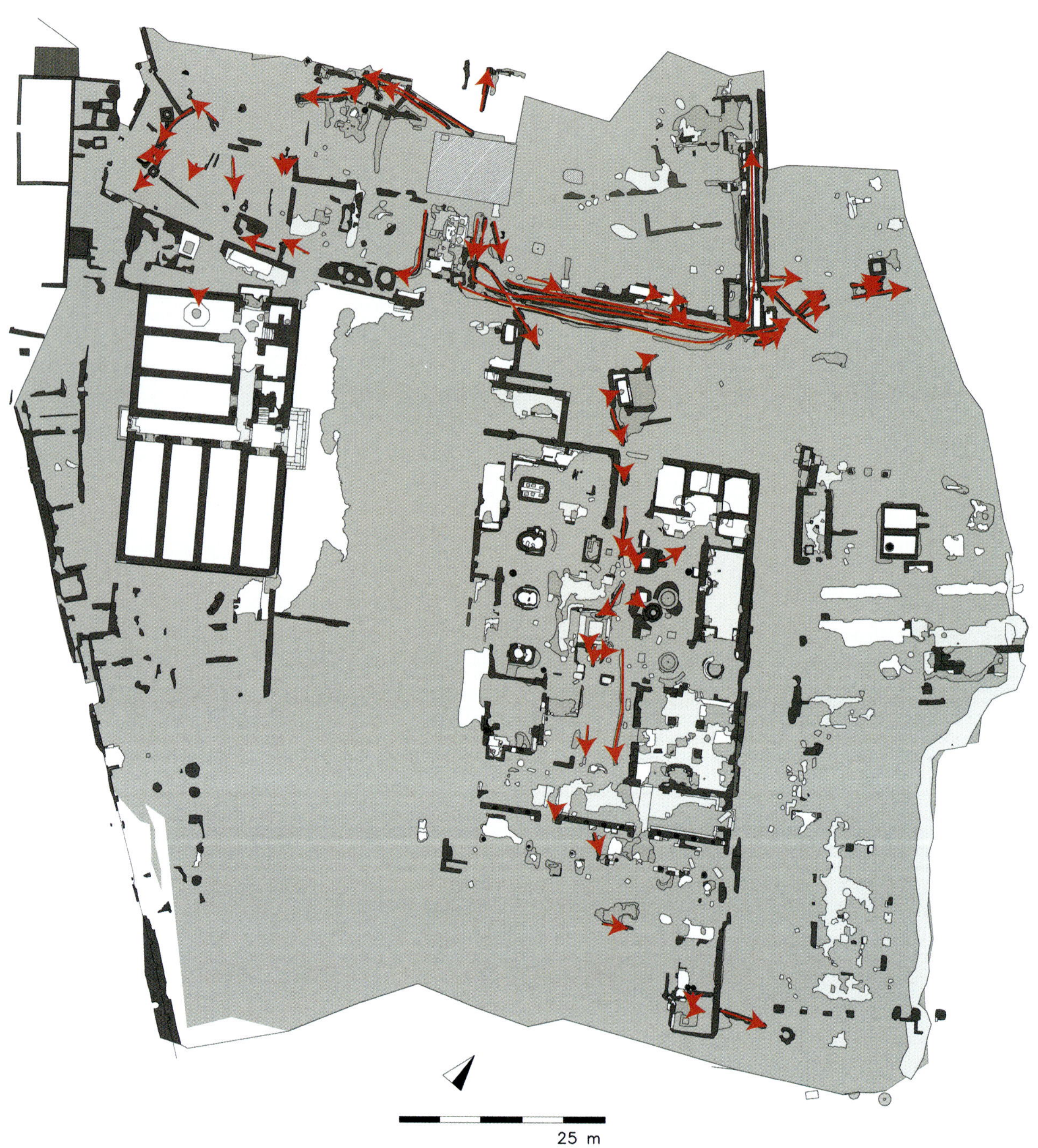

Pl. 8. Map showing distribution of pipelines in WM.4. Note concentration of east-west running pipes east of well in WM.4.6.32. Map by Dawn McCormack and the author. © YMAP.

RED MONASTERY 2011

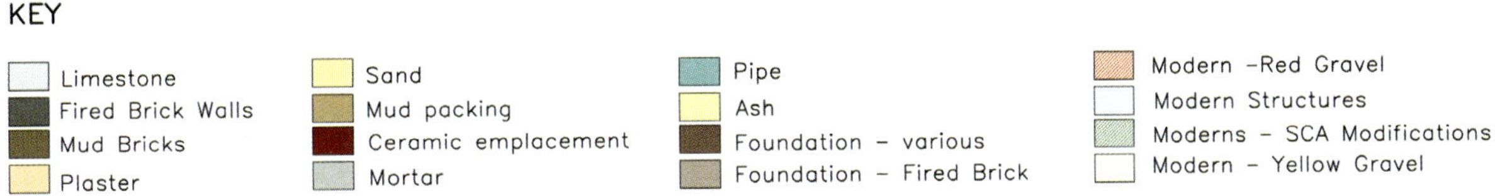

3.2
3.1
2.3
2.2
2.1
1.1
1.2
1.3
50 m

Pl. 9. Red Monastery archaeological site with area division. Map by the author.

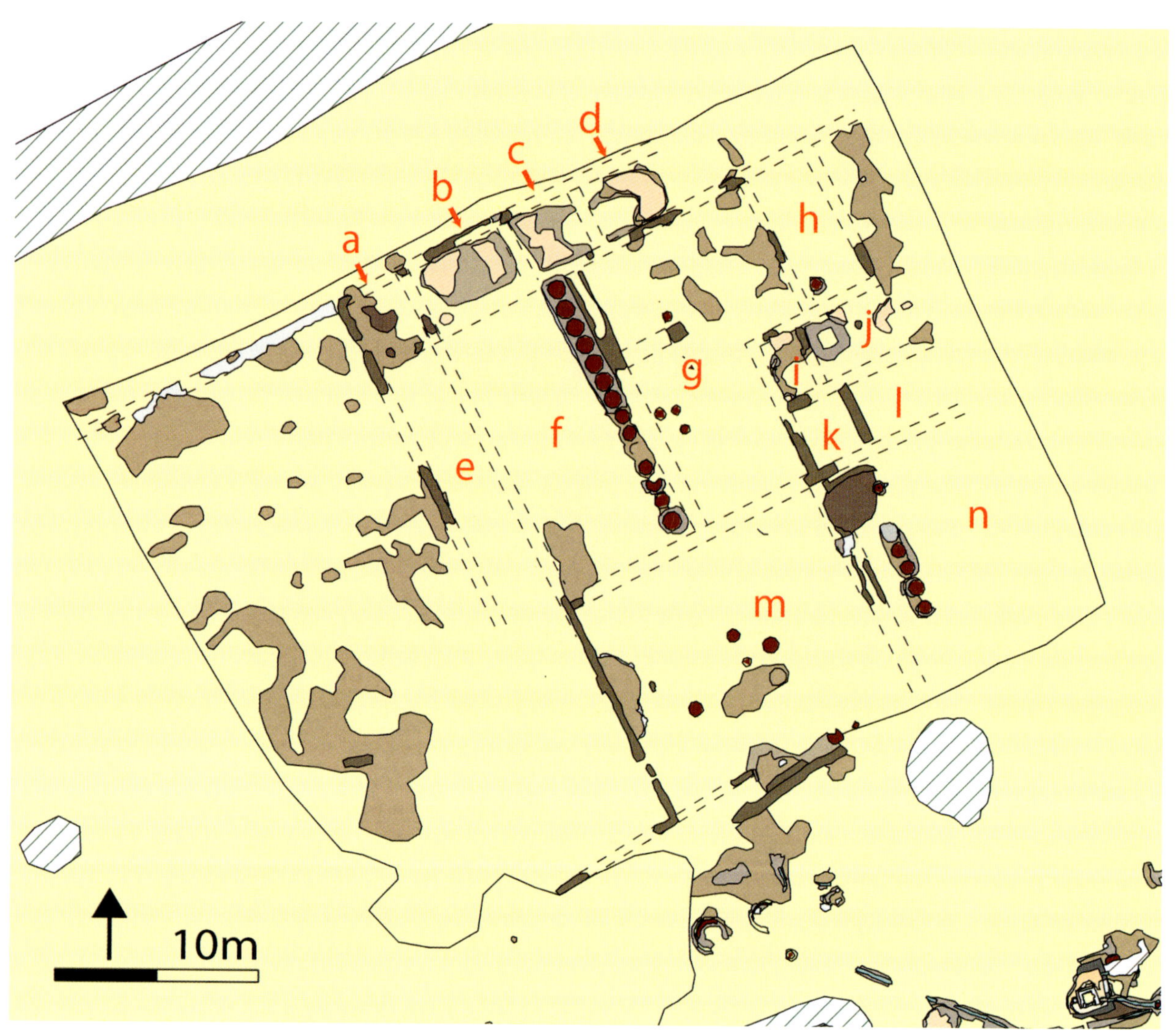

Pl. 10. Map detail of RM.3. showing extension of walls with dotted lines. Letters suggest location of rooms. Map by the author.

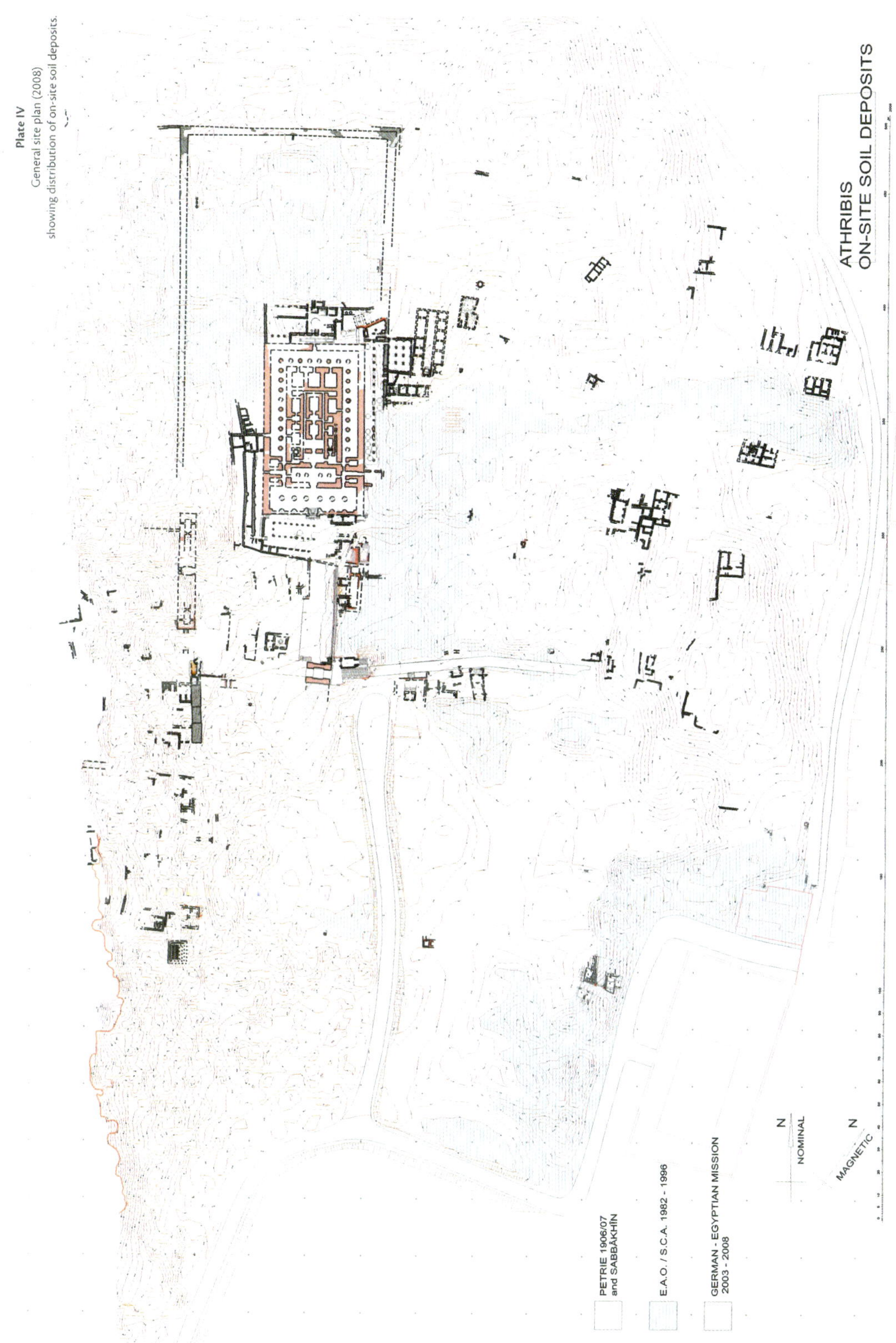

Pl. 11. Map of Atripe archaeological site. El-Sayed and EL-Masry, Athribis, plate IV. Reproduced with permission from Christian Leitz and Universität Tübingen.